To admit the action of literature on men — this is perhaps the wisdom in which the people of the Book will be recognized.

EMMANUEL LEVINAS

The Bible has a literary influence upon English literature not because it has been considered literature, but because it has been considered the report of the Word of God.

T. S. ELIOT

ALSO BY DAVID LYLE JEFFREY

The Early English Lyric and Franciscan Spirituality (1975)

By Things Seen: Reference and Recognition in Medieval Thought (1979)

Chaucer and Scriptural Tradition (1984)

Toward a Perfect Love: The Spiritual Counsel of Walter Hilton (1986)

English Spirituality in the Age of Wesley (1987)

The Law of Love: English Spirituality in the Age of Wyclif (1988)

The Anglo-Norman Lyric (with B. J. Levy) (1990)

A Dictionary of Biblical Tradition in English Literature (1992)

People of the Book

Christian Identity and Literary Culture

DAVID LYLE JEFFREY

WILLIAM B. EERDMANS PUBLISHING COMPANY
GRAND RAPIDS, MICHIGAN / CAMBRIDGE, U.K.
WITH
THE INSTITUTE FOR ADVANCED CHRISTIAN STUDIES

© 1996 Wm. B. Eerdmans Publishing Co.
255 Jefferson Ave. S.E., Grand Rapids, Michigan 49503 /
P.O. Box 163, Cambridge CB3 9PU U.K.
Published in cooperation with
The Institute for Advanced Christian Studies

Printed in the United States of America

01 00 99 98 97 96   7 6 5 4 3 2 1

Library of Congress Cataloging-in-Publication Data

Jeffrey, David L., 1941-
    People of the Book: Christian identity and literary culture /
  David Lyle Jeffrey.
        p.   cm.
    Includes bibliographical references.
    ISBN 0-8028-4177-5 (pbk.: alk. paper)
    ISBN 0-8028-3817-0 (cloth: alk. paper)
    1. Bible — Criticism, interpretation, etc. 2. Bible — Influence —
Western civilization. 3. Bible as literature. 4. Christianity and literature.
5. Identification (Religion) I. Title.
BS511.2.J44   1996
220'.09 — dc20   96-6419
                                                   CIP

The author and publisher gratefully acknowledge permission to include excerpts (on
pp. 329-331 herein) from the poem "Boom" by Howard Nemerov, published in *The
Collected Poems of Howard Nemerov* (Chicago: University of Chicago Press, 1977).

For Katherine

Os suum aperuit sapientiae,
et lex clementiae in lingua ejus.

Contents

List of Illustrations

Preface

IT APPEARS THAT THE FAMILIAR PHRASE "PEOPLE OF THE BOOK" MAY have been coined by Muhammed, the Prophet of Islam. In the Quran the term is used self-consciously to distinguish a religious culture in which revelation is handed down orally (Islam) and the two religions in which it is both handed down and authoritatively transmitted in writing (Judaism and Christianity). The Quran attaches the phrase primarily to the Jews as a term of opprobrium: "The People of the Book," we are to understand, are those who "demand that thou cause a Book to descend upon them from heaven," for the Quran a blasphemous importunity exceeded only by "an even more preposterous demand from Moses: they demanded, 'Show us Allah visibly.' "[1] The Quran implicates Christians in the opprobrium both by association:

> There is none among the People of the Book but will continue to believe till his death that Jesus died on the cross, and on the Day of Judgment Jesus shall bear witness against them.[2]

and directly:

> People of the Book! . . . Indeed, the Messiah, Jesus son of Mary, was but a Messenger of Allah and the fulfillment of glad tidings

1. Al-Nisa 4.6.154; cf. Al-'Imran 3.3.60, 65-116.
2. Al-Nisa 4.6.160-61.

which He conveyed to Mary and a mercy from him. So . . . say not:
there are three gods. Desist, it will be better for you.[3]

As a development from Judaism, Christianity clearly also stressed
from the beginning the importance for faith of written revelation,
namely the Jewish Scriptures. Soon enough there were, of course, additional writings, the books and epistles of the New Testament, which
augmented the scrolls of the Law, the Prophets, and the writings of the
Jewish canon. The first Epistle of Clement (A.D. 95) cites "the Scriptures"
in the familiar Jewish way (cap. 28), while the ancient Christian sermon
known as Clement II (A.D. 100) affords the first known citation of the
words of Jesus as "Scripture" (cap. 3). With respect to the central place
of "Scripture," therefore, in the early days of Christianity there would
have been little by which an outsider might have distinguished the new
sectaries of the crucified rabbi from others in the tradition of Jewish
reverence for the "Book of Books."

We should perhaps note that this last phrase is not, as sometimes
thought, comparative: it refers to the fact that the Bible is after all an
anthology, a book composed of many books. Our word "Bible" has its
origins in the Septuagint Greek of Daniel 9:2, where tā biblia, "the
books," apparently refers to the general body of Jewish "Scriptures"
available to the prophet from which Daniel is consulting the book of
Jeremiah. Its common synonym in New Testament Greek is the word
grapho(s), a collective noun meaning "writings," as when Jesus is quoted
by John as saying, "Search the scriptures, because you think that in them
you have eternal life, and it is they that testify on my behalf" (John
5:39). This is the term employed also by St. Paul when he writes to
Timothy that "all scripture is inspired by God, and is useful for teaching;
for reproof, for correction, and for training in righteousness" (2 Tim.
3:16; cf. 1 Cor. 1:7) and by St. Peter when he writes his caution that "no
prophecy of scripture is a matter of one's own interpretation" (2 Peter
1:20). The sense of a deposit of "writings," a book which contains all
"the holy books," is preserved in St. Jerome's term for his fourth-century
translation of the Bible into Latin, the language of the Roman Empire:
biblioteca divina means literally the "divine library." Our somewhat nar-
rower notion of the Bible as a single book comes much later, with a

3. Al-Nisa 4.6.172.

shift in Latin usage in the thirteenth century, by which the neuter plural *(biblia)* came to be regarded as a feminine singular *(biblia)*, an almost unnoticed shift from "the books" to "the Book" in the textual tradition of western Europe. *Biblia Sacra,* "the Holy Book," is what by the time of Aquinas *tā biblia* had become; "The Bible," the English equivalent in this singular sense, first appears a century later in the English writings ascribed to John Wyclif, as well as, almost simultaneously, in the poetry of Geoffrey Chaucer and William Langland. For all of these writers, the Bible was preeminently "the Book," or, as Chaucer has it, "oure Book," the foundation text which gives rise to a whole world of books.

Though first intended pejoratively, "People of the Book" in Jewish tradition came to be accepted with pride as a legitimate reference to a cultural and religious identity rooted fundamentally in Torah, the originary book of the Law. The rabbi in Howard Nemerov's poem "Debate with the Rabbi" expresses this traditional affirmation against a skeptical American modernist:

> We are the people of the Book, the Rabbi said.
>   Not of the phone book, said I.
> Ours is a great tradition, said he,
> And a wonderful history.
>   But history's over, I said.[4]

The denigrating voice in Nemerov's poem might easily be that of a "postmodern" literary theorist. But that a negatively intended characterization should be transposed into a badge of honor among the denigrated is not, in the history of religion at least, unusual. Nor is it unusual that the badge should be worn proudly as one means of resisting further denigration: one need only think of Puritans, Methodists, Quakers, and Shakers. In fact, the first of these groups are foremost among those in the Christian tradition who claim the term in question, proud themselves to be in their own way identified as "a People of the Book."

In early Christian experience the New Testament was added to the whole Jewish "Tanakh" (an acronym from Torah, the Law, Nebi'im, the prophets, and Kethubim, the other canonical writings). This larger an-

---

4. Howard Nemerov, "Debate with the Rabbi," in *The Collected Poems of Howard Nemerov* (Chicago: University of Chicago Press, 1977), 270.

thology, which after St. Jerome's translation tended more and more to be bound up as a single volume, had for those to whom the Christian missionaries came bearing it all the import of a unified *locus* of authority: "*the* Book." "People of the Book" unsurprisingly translates many an early vernacular name for Christian missionaries among African, Asian, and Native American peoples of both hemispheres. The fact that these missionaries regularly put enormous effort into reducing the language of these people to writing so as to provide a written translation of the Bible — an activity which, under such organizations as the Wycliffe Bible Translators and the United Bible Societies, has resulted in at least part of the Christian Bible now being available in 2,100 languages — has lent an identification with the phrase among evangelical Christians in particular almost as strong as pertains among Jews. This identity comprises the Christian converts among evangelized cultures, the more recently evangelized the more naturally so, since for many of them, just as for the English-speaking peoples, the first written texts ever produced in their language have been a portion of the Bible. For all such cultures, the Bible becomes the founding text in their own subsequent national literature.

In Western Christian tradition, especially in the modern evangelical lineage which finds its exemplar in the early Puritans, this sense of the Bible's uniqueness and centrality for Christian identity can have at times the force of exclusionary singularity. John Bunyan's credo is an early representation of this emphasis: "that the holy scriptures, of themselves, without the addition of human inventions, are able to make the man of God perfect in all things."[5] The strength of Bunyan's preference for the Bible leads him to eschew other books: "Had I all their aid and assistance at command, I durst not make use of ought thereof, and that for fear lest that Grace, and those Gifts that the LORD hath given me, should be attributed to their Wits, rather than the Light of the Word and Spirit of God."[6] To see oneself as part of "the People of the Book" in Bunyan's tradition (for example in a Baptist or Brethren context) can accordingly involve construing those not of one's own persuasion in this matter as spiritually "pagan," or, in a sense ironically obverse to that which it acquires

5. John Bunyan, *A Confession of My Faith,* in *The Whole Works of John Bunyan,* ed. G. Offor (London, 1862), 2.593.

6. John Bunyan, *Miscellaneous Works,* ed. R. Sharrock (Oxford: Oxford University Press, 1978), 3.71.

in humanistic tradition after Matthew Arnold, "philistine." That is, such a person might regard the indebtedness of some Christians to many books rather than to just the one Book as evidence of their departure from the "true Israel" of "biblical Christianity." At the most extreme reach of this impulse is the instinct to sacralize one particular translation. In America one can find chapters of a "King James Bible Church," advertising itself as "independent, literal, fundamental, and premillennial." One thinks of the tale of the midwestern preacher who is reported to have said, "If the King James Bible was good enough for the apostle Paul, it is good enough for me." Perhaps the tale is not apocryphal.

My principal concern in this book is not with theological or ecclesiastical matters, but with the cultural and literary identity among Western Christians which the centrality of "the Book" has helped to create. While deeply indebted to its roots in Jewish identity as a "People of the Book," Christian use of the phrase signals wide-ranging and nuanced differences of understanding. Some of these differences in Christian usage emerge as a result of historical change, others as a function of the rhetorical advertisement of doctrinal differences. In general, however, being able to distinguish between what the term means for Jewish identity and literary culture and what it suggests to Christian identity and literary culture can be of great value in understanding the place and role of the Book in the evolution of Western literary tradition.

This interfaith difference resists succinct summary. The main points at issue, however, can be clarified in general terms. For most Christians, at least until the time of the Reformation, the Bible was not so much itself the *locus* as the recording *witness* to God's authority. Its purpose as text was thought to assist in the reestablishment of right relationship between God, the ultimate Author, and his fallen, alienated readers. When this relationship between God and the believer was taken to be essentially sound, a fullness of experience of theological virtues would be axiomatically lived out by the individual Christian. Since this "Christ-life" seemed after all the goal of reading the Bible, there was a sense in which the unlettered believer already living this life — one might think of peasant converts in modern China as readily as in the largely oral culture of Europe or Africa during the first Christian centuries — would not for himself need the actual Book. St. Augustine concludes the first book of his *On Christian Doctrine* by saying:

Thus a man supported by faith, hope, and charity, with an un-
shaken hold upon them, does not need the Scriptures except for
the instruction of others. And many live by these three things in
solitude without books.[7]

In her superb study, *Slayers of Moses: The Emergence of Rabbinic
Tradition in Modern Literary Theory,* Susan Handelman points out that
"such a statement would be unthinkable in Rabbinic tradition."[8] The
reason for this is Augustine's emphasis on the mere instrumentality of
biblical language. As we shall come to see in chapter 3, below, in his
precedent-setting work the sign is always inferior to that which it signifies; speech is inferior to the silence which attends perfect communion. For Augustine the deficiency in Jewish reading practice is its
persistence in taking things in the Bible at a literal level, rather than
seeing them typologically or as allegorical signs referring beyond themselves to the new life of the spirit. After all, the letter kills; it is the spirit
that gives life (2 Cor. 3:6). But in Handelman's distinction, "it is precisely
this reification of signs that is idolatry to the Jews"; the apparently
mutual exclusivity of word and thing is rejected in Judaism, not because,
as Augustine thought, Jews take the sign for the thing,

> but because there is no primal division between word and thing
> in Jewish thought, and no conception of reality in terms of Greek
> metaphysics, or of truth as a totally self-identical present being.
> Jews adhere to signs because reality innately is consituted as lin-
> guistic for them. For the Jew it is precisely the cancellation of the
> sign or word for thing that is idolatrous.[9]

Idolatry for the Augustinian Christian is to become fixated on the word
or sign; idolatry for the Jews is to separate the word (or sign) from the
reality it purports to signify in the first place. While it is conceivable for
a serious Jew to say, as does Emmanuel Levinas in his *Difficile Liberté:
Essais sur Judaism,* that "to love the Torah more than God [is] protection

7. St. Augustine, *On Christian Doctrine,* trans. D. W. Robertson, Jr. (New York:
Bobbs Merrill, 1963), 1.39.43.
8. Susan Handelman, *Slayers of Moses: The Emergence of Rabbinic Tradition in
Modern Literary Theory* (Albany: SUNY Press, 1982), 115.
9. Ibid., 117.

against the madness of a direct contact with the sacred"[10] (Derrida quotes this dictum approvingly in an essay on Levinas), for Christians from Augustine to Kierkegaard this would represent a most serious confusion concerning the purpose of "Torah," or Scripture.

Handelman instances Jacques Derrida and Harold Bloom as exemplary postmodern Jewish "heretics" whose disposition to misdirect rabbinic views of language has come to characterize their theories of literature. The disposition has also, it seems to me, characterized their misrepresentations of Christian literary tradition, for which reason Derrida and Bloom both figure in this book as well, not so much for the intrinsic merits of their own praxis as for the clarifying challenge they propose to Christian literary tradition.

Among other things, such theories of language and poetry as Bloom's and Derrida's strive to effect a misconstruction of the historical role of the Bible among Christian writers and readers. In this misconstruction, residual respect for the Bible's continual witness in the form of a metaphysical "grand narrative" (the term is Lyotard's but the concept readily allies itself with Derrida's "logocentrism"), or for its place as the perceived foundation of literary tradition in the once-Christian West, is to be erased. This erasure is to be effected by the tactics of subversion, by reading and writing which overthrows the "precursor," the previously respected text. Such programmatic "overthrowing," whether by "perversity of the spirit" in a calculated "misprision" or misreading of classic texts, as in Bloom, or by a refusal of logic and normative lexical and grammatical conventions, as in Derrida, has become not merely a kind of fantasy or playful miscreance on the part of such theorists but, on their own attestation and that of many others, an attack on the central values embodied in the Christian biblical tradition as most have understood it. Yet, as may be suggested by even the title of Bloom's *jeu d'esprit* novel — *The Flight to Lucifer: A Gnostic Fantasy* (1979) — the fantasies of rhetorically gifted and influential writers can lead in a direction many might wish to be chary of following. One need not be confessionally Christian or Jewish, I think, to take this point.

No more than Jewish tradition, however, is Christian tradition conveniently reducible to accountable representation by one foundational

---

10. Emmanuel Levinas, *Difficile liberté: Essais sur le Judaisme* (Paris: Editions Albin Michel, 1963).

thinker — not even when the thinker is as influential as Augustine. Notably, not all faithful Christians after the late Middle Ages followed Augustine in viewing the Bible instrumentally. The Puritans offer examples of a tendency among post-Reformation and evangelical Protestants to elevate the Bible to the status of a shibboleth, seeing it in effect as *autopistos* — drawing its authority from itself. Some such believers came to grant to the Bible an almost talismanic power, a tendency their opponents would call "bibliolatry," which in some important respects is scarcely to be distinguished from that loving of "the Torah more than God" which Derrida was so happy to take from Levinas and secularize. In Christianity this worship of the Book was also secularized; one form of the secularization, as structuralist and poststructuralist theorists have been quick to point out, is the New Criticism of Cleanth Brooks, Allen Tate, and Robert Penn Warren. There are, of course, others.

The chapters which follow may be taken to comprise, in the sense of the term intended by Jean-François Lyotard (*The Postmodern Condition* [1979, trans. 1984]) and Anthony Giddens (*The Consequences of Modernity* [1970]), a book about the character and meaning of the Christian "grand narrative." I do not mean to suggest that this is a book about "the canon" — the generally accepted repertoire of formative authors in the Western tradition whose general neglect now even Harold Bloom has come to lament (*The Western Canon* [1995]). The reader will see clearly enough that Dante, Chaucer, Marlowe, Goethe, Bunyan, Coleridge, Arnold, Hawthorne, Melville, and Dostoevski among others figure in the long list of authors whose texts have seemed to me metonymic for something of the main character and persistent questions for Christian identity and literary culture. Yet there are no chapters on the works of Shakespeare, Milton, Pope, Blake, Wordsworth, Browning, Tolstoy, Hopkins, Eliot, and scores of others whose writings would make almost anyone's charter list of "great books." (There are, of course, many excellent studies of all these writers which consider them in their biblical and Christian perspective, and almost any of them will prove far more useful to their own purposes than anything I could hope to offer, especially in so short a space.) My purpose here is overview; a general historical sketch of the embracing tradition which might serve to clarify its authentically Christian features — and indeed its inauthentically Christian features. One ought not to accept uncritically the characterization of Christian literary culture by those who declare themselves

opposed to it, any more than one accedes to any other denigration of
religious tradition which is prejudiced or unfair. On the other hand,
one ought to try to look at one's tradition, as much as is possible, from
a perspective unself-flattering enough to countenance embarrassments.

In the ten chapters of this study which follow I try to let Bloom and
Derrida prompt the agenda, but not determine it. The questions which
I have asked will, I hope, reflect this effort. The most obvious of these
questions are as follows: Is there such a thing as a Christian literary
theory? If so, where and with whom does its articulation begin? How
does a literary theory formulated to deal with Revelation — sacred
Scripture — develop in such a way as to deal with products of the
writerly imagination — "secular scripture"? What is the connection between Christian convictions about the primacy of the Book and the
literacy of peoples? In what way has the ideal of "the Book" been realized
as a broad, culturally formative trope? What about the continuing status
of the book, the practical problem of its maintaining authority — or,
to put it in another way — the readers' resistance to the text? In what
way does the perceived authenticity of biblical narrative become a criterion for authenticating secular narrative? Does this transference, among
Christians, undermine secular narrative, or, as may seem more likely,
does it in the end undermine biblical narrative? Can there be, in Christian practice, a veneration of the Bible so opaque as to render the
allegiance indeed idolatrous? And in the final analysis, does commitment to preeminence of the Book (or books) permit sufficient distance
on the self to beware misprision of a personal and spiritual as well as
critical nature? That is, have we taken our task seriously enough to
countenance the cost — to ourselves and to others — of getting things
wrong?

There are, of course, other questions. This book is as introductory
as it is interrogative for the tradition it explores. But it is my hope that
readers will find it a helpful point of departure for interrogations of
their own.

*   *   *

Portions of chapters 1, 2, 5, and 6 appeared in an earlier form elsewhere.
In respect to chapter 1, I want to acknowledge the editors of *Religion
and Literature,* who published "Mistakenly Logocentric: Poetics in a

Scriptural Tradition" in vol. 22, no. 1 (1990). An early version of part
of chapter 2 appeared as "How to Read the Hebrew Prophets," in *Mapping the Biblical Terrain,* ed. Vincent Tollers and John Maeir (Bucknell
University Press, 1989). In chapter 5, I return to ideas first explored in
my introduction to *By Things Seen: Reference and Recognition in Medieval Thought* (University of Ottawa Press, 1979); and an article entitled
"John Wyclif and the Hermeneutics of Reader-Response," *Interpretation*
29, no. 3 (1985): 272-87, is reflected in chapter 6.

I am deeply grateful for a release-time fellowship from the Institute
for Advanced Christian Studies, which assisted materially in my research
and writing.

My list of obligation to friends and colleagues is long, and cannot
here be inclusive. I want especially, however, to thank David Shore,
Graeme Hunter, Nicholas von Maltzhan, Dominic Manganiello, David
Staines, Ina Ferris, Camille La Bossière, Leo Damrosch, Seymour Mayne,
Susan Handelman, George Steiner, Michael Edwards, Grant Wacker,
Arthur Holmes, and Carl F. H. Henry for invaluable comments and
suggestions. Among my graduate students in several lively seminars at
the University of Ottawa, as well as in two critical theory workshops at
Princeton University (one for IFACS and one for InterVarsity Graduate
Ministries), I have been particularly indebted for vigorous interlocution
to Alan Jacobs, Stephen Dunning, Michael Treschow, Anne LeDressay,
Paul Contino, Curtis Gruenler, Martin Kevorkian, Gregory Maillet,
Michael Price, Patricia Sunderland, Sidney Stoyan, and Tim Wilson. My
greatest obligation, however, is to Katherine Beth Jeffrey, in this as in all
things my dearest friend and collaborator.

DAVID LYLE JEFFREY
UNIVERSITY OF OTTAWA

Chapter One

Logocentrism and Scriptural Tradition

For he, whose is the Word and image, is neither image nor Word.

ANSELM OF CANTERBURY

MORE THAN A DECADE AGO, IN HIS PROVOCATIVE MANIFESTO essay, "The Breaking of Form," Harold Bloom asserted that "theory of poetry" invites one of two extreme views of language as the precondition for its praxis. The first of these he called "a magical theory of all language," in which language is credited with "plenitude" of meaning, and is, in his characterization, "totally overdetermined." This view he identified with gnosticism, the Kabbalists of old, and with Jewish and Christian "logocentrists" such as Samuel Coleridge (with a view "founded on the Johannine Logos"), and, more recently, with such diverse practitioners as Walter Benjamin, Owen Barfield, and Walter Ong. Its alternative he called "a thoroughgoing linguistic nihilism, which in its most refined form is the mode now called Deconstruction," a theory which sees in language a "dearth of meaning" and "*absolute* randomness." In the volume in which his essay appeared, *Deconstruction and Criticism,* he readily identified this theory with his colleagues Jacques Derrida, Paul de Man, Geoffrey

1

Hartman, and J. Hillis Miller.[1] Typically of his own work, what he wished to stress in the fruitful opposition of language theories is their pertinence to the "agonistic" element in "good poems"; the agonistic, by extension, makes for good theory on similar grounds:

> All I ask is that the theory of language be extreme and uncompromising enough. Theory of poetry, as I pursue it, is reconcilable with either extreme view of poetic language, though not with any views in between. Either the new poet fights to win freedom from death, or from plenitude, but if the antagonist be moderate, then the agon will not take place, and no fresh sublimity will be won. Only the agon is of the essence.[2]

From such a viewpoint, the *via media* instincts of "British academic journalists and their American counterparts" can only be met with the disdain fashion reserves for the painfully unfashionable.[3]

As a credal manifestation of post-Romantic hermeneutics, complete with due acknowledgments of Nietzsche, Bloom's paradigmatic "either / or" is designed to establish a tactical symmetry: an authorial antagonist is more or less custom-constructed to focus the critic-protagonist's deconstructive creativity. In a reiteration of Blake, the resulting "system" created to avoid "enslavement by that of another" thus explicitly depends upon the system it would overthrow, validating the desired "agon" at the incidental expense of artificializing — and protracting — the tactical conflict. This general postulate of a necessary condition for theory of poetry leads Bloom's collaborator J. Hillis Miller to describe a modified relation between the extremes in language theory as a reciprocity in which "nihilism is the latent ghost encrypted within any expression of a logocentric system," so that:

> the two . . . are related to one another in a way which is not antithesis and which may not be synthesized in any dialectical

---

1. *Deconstruction and Criticism* (New York: Seabury, 1979). Geoffrey Hartman, in his preface to the collaborative effort, wished to distance himself and Bloom a little, saying they should be understood as "barely deconstructionists" (ix).

2. Ibid., 4.

3. Ibid., 5.

Aufhebung. Each defines and is hospitable to the other, host to it as parasite.[4]

This symbiosis unto death (*parasitos,* "beside the grain") prompts Miller further to image the unnamed Poem in terms analogous to the Host in the Eucharist, "host in the sense of victim, sacrifice . . . broken, divided, passed around, consumed by the critics canny and uncanny who are in that odd relation one to another of host and parasite," a relation in which both nihilistic and logocentric (or "univocal") readings are "fellow guests 'beside the grain', host and guest, host and host, host and parasite, parasite and parasite. The relation is a triangle, not a polar opposition."[5]

Notable in both Bloom's and Miller's structurations is the felt need to avoid resolution of the projected conflict, or indeed a synthesis; theory of poetry on their reckoning can only be animated by the extremes in conflict. Reconciliation or mediation, they seem to say, would prove fatal. Also striking is their familiar recursion in each case to a vocabulary which pits transcendence against immanence, the immutable *Wahrheit* against transparent *mutabilitie,* eternal against time-locked sense. Their self-conscious religious vocabulary (whether *Kabbalah* or *mysterium*) is here coupled with the deconstructionist's scrupulous resistance to a precipitated middle way, be it *tertium quid* or temperate measure.[6] The very terms of Bloom and Miller's dicta, however, inevitably invite a measure of historical reflection on the contribution of religious — especially biblical — criticism to the occidental history of literary theory. This inevitability is dictated, at least in part, by the origin in modernist biblical criticism of the polarities upon which both *agon* and frustrated *Aufhebung* depend. For the sake of formulating certain initial questions about the necessary conditions for literary theory asserted by these post-structural paradigms we may confine ourselves to a few well-known and representative Christian texts from late antiquity and the Middle Ages.

No single "Christian" literary theory, alas for Bloom's paradigm, can

4. Ibid., 228.

5. Ibid., 225, 224.

6. Cf. George Steiner, *Real Presences* (Chicago: University of Chicago Press, 1989), 164-65; John M. Ellis, *Against Deconstruction* (Princeton: Princeton University Press, 1989), 45-51.

be conveniently identified. From Origen's Neoplatonic allegorism through its severe modification in Augustine's referentialism to the neo-Aristotelian postulations concerning relations of language and form in the work of Hugh of St. Victor or Bonaventure, or in Dante's elaborated polysemeity, on to Sidney's "Protestant poetics," Milton's recension of it, the pragmatic formalism of Pope, the Scotian poetics of neorealist Gerard Manley Hopkins, the neo-Dantism of Eliot, Auden's postconversion ethical poetic, and the latter day montanism of the New Critics, there have been any number of "literary theories" which might lay reasonable claim to the adjective "Christian." One may doubt that any of these various theorists would have been content to be described as "logocentrist."[7] Rather, they might well have thought the term to involve a serious misconstruction, imagining with Augustine that the function of language is preeminently to be a means of expressing intention,[8] and that meaning resides thus not in the word but in the person.[9] They might well have thought, too, that the common element in their positions which could seem polar to nihilism was not an apotheosis of the verbal construct but a primary affirmation of Being. George Steiner accurately apprehends the general content of such a view when he says, for example, that "a Logos-order entails . . . a central supposition of 'real presence.'"[10]

Being in opposition to nonbeing composes indeed a plausible altercation; the evident contraries here are actually theism and nihilism. The intense antagonism in Derrida and some of his adherents (e.g., Culler) to what they call the "logocentric" tradition, a conflict which has "necessarily to take the form of a struggle to the death, a confrontation that straighta-

---

7. I ought to confess that I have myself been guilty of having acquiesced in the misconstrual, observing that "logocentrism is about as good a name as any other for the tradition of literary theory in which Christians, I believe, have usually found themselves . . ." in D. L. Jeffrey, "*Caveat Lector:* Structuralism, Deconstruction and Ideology," *Christian Scholars Review* 17, no. 4 (1988): 442. I was responding to a paper by Patricia Ward (in the same issue of *CSR*) on Barthes and Derrida, and accepted the nomenclature as describing my own territory, though adding ". . . we ought . . . to be extremely prudential about how we continue to define it [logocentrism]." This chapter attempts a more nuanced clarification.

8. St. Augustine, *On Christian Doctrine*, trans. D. W. Robertson, Jr. (New York: Bobbs Merrill, 1963), 1.35.39.

9. Ibid., 1.13.12; 2.2.3. Hence, the centrality of the ethical in Augustine's theory of meaning.

10. Steiner, *Real Presences*, 96.

way excludes any possibility of reconciliation or mediation,"[11] clearly counterpoises things other than a "dearth" of verbal meaning and unbounded "plenitude," its "mystical" opposite. Otherwise, the case could hardly be argued in the way Bloom, for example, suggests. Like Derrida, he characterizes the logocentric tradition as roughly inclusive of the whole Western traditional hierarchy of values which gives intellectual privilege to concern for truth and rationality and then, elsewhere, he narrowly defines its theory of language of poetry in terms of Kabbalah, gnosticism, Coleridge, and theosophy. However conventional this reductivism may be in a postmodernist Romanticism, it nonetheless patently distorts the complex history of Western literary theory,[12] and in such a way as to beg the question raised by the opposition: nihilism / logocentrism.

Experimentally, let us appeal again to a foundational voice from late antiquity to help clarify a more or less characteristically Christian theory of verbal signification.

All instruction concerns either things or signs, but things are learned by signs. Strictly speaking, I have here called a "thing" that

11. The words are Derrida's, cited in J. Greisch, K. Neufeld, and C. Theobald, *La Crise contemporaine. Du modernisme à la crise des herméneutiques* (Paris: Editions de Seuil, 1973), 157; cf. Jonathan Culler, "Beyond Interpretation," in *The Pursuit of Signs: Semiotics, Literature, Deconstruction* (Ithaca, N.Y.: Cornell University Press, 1981), 6. An indispensable discussion of Derrida apropos his opposition to Christian theories of language is that by Susan Handelman, *Slayers of Moses: The Emergence of Rabbinic Tradition in Modern Literary Theory* (Albany: SUNY Press, 1982), esp. 163-78.

12. Cf. Roger Lundin, "Emerson and the Spirit of Theory," *Religion and Literature* 21, no. 2 (1989): 17-42. Bloom's notion of "strong reading" precludes his being concerned, of course, with any charge of misrepresentation. For Bloom, for example, meritorious poets such as Dante, Milton, or Blake must "ruin the sacred truths to fable and old story" (the phrase is borrowed from Andrew Marvell's poem "On *Paradise Lost*") because in his view virtue in poetry necessarily attaches to originality: "the essential condition for poetic strength," he writes, "is that the new song, one's own, always must be a song of one's self." Bloom's allusion to Whitman here properly Americanizes his Romanticism — and gnosticism — in ways which align his subversion of Judaism with parallel developments among post-Christian Romantics. The result is, as much in Bloom as in Blake or Whitman, a "triumphant" infernal reading of sacred texts in particular. For Bloom, much as for Northrop Frye, therefore, Blake is especially heroic because he "rewrites Milton and the Bible to make them commentaries upon his own Bible of Hell." See his *Ruin the Sacred Truths: Poetry and Belief from the Bible to the Present* (Cambridge, Mass.: Harvard University Press, 1989), esp. chap. 5.

which is not used to signify something else, like wood, stone, cattle, and so on; but not that wood concerning which we read that Moses cast it into bitter waters that their bitterness might be dispelled, nor that stone which Jacob placed at his head, nor that beast which Abraham sacrificed in place of his son. For these are things in such a way that they are also signs of other things. There are other signs whose whole use is in signifying, like words. For no one uses words except for the purpose of signifying something. From this may be understood what we call "signs"; they are things used to signify something. Thus every sign is also a thing, for that which is not a thing is nothing at all; but not every thing is also a sign.[13]

Augustine's pre-Saussure distinction here is designed to establish a hierarchy in which signs of any kind, including words, are clearly subservient to that which they signify, e.g., created things. Signs, then, are merely conventional. The only "use" of words is signification; they are a means rather than an end;[14] meaning inheres finally in that which is signified, ultimately in the fact of Creation and its postulate, the Creator, "that thing which they place above all other things."[15] Confusion of sign and thing of any kind is taken by Augustine (and most later Christian theorists) to be a species of idolatry; since meaning resides not in the word abstracted, but in those entities and actions which words can serve, retreat to questions of language for their own sake is a form of intellectual debilitation: "he who sees the truth and flees has weakened the acuteness of his mind through the habit of carnal shadows."[16] Only one "Word" transcends the mere convention-

13. Augustine, *On Christian Doctrine*, 1.2.

14. Ibid., 1.4.4.

15. Ibid., 1.7.7.

16. Ibid., 1.9.9. These points are usefully discussed by Handelman, for whom Derrida and Bloom, while Jewish heretics, are nonetheless representatively Jewish in opposing Augustine's notion of semiological idolatry. She correctly imagines that "Augustine doubtless would view Derrida more than anyone else a slave of the sign, a stubborn adherent of word play who refuses to recognize any proper referents whatever" (*Slayers of Moses*, 118). Contrastively, the Christian reification of a few signs (e.g., baptism and the eucharist) as sacraments is "idolatry to the Jews" (117). Her whole discussion (108-20) is useful for grasping clearly how one might understand the phrase "People of the Book" in Jewish as distinct from Christian tradition. The differences loom at least as large as the continuity.

ality and asymptotic liability of all other words, and that word is manifestly not of human utterance. The "word made flesh" we grasp, indeed, only by imperfect analogy:

> It is as when we speak. In order that what we are thinking may reach the mind of the listener through the fleshly ears, that which we have in mind is expressed in words and is called speech. But our thought is not transformed into sounds; it remains entire in itself and assumes the form of words by means of which it may reach the ears without suffering any deterioration in itself. In the same way the Word of God was made flesh without change that He might dwell among us.[17]

God's Word and the words of men and women are certainly not identical: whereas we speak with words, God speaks with things, persons, and events, preeminently so in the event of the Incarnation. For the Christian theorist at least, this primal Word-event may charge our words with extra and even transformational meaning, but it does not make of our language acts, even in poetry, events (or significations) of the same stature. For the Christian theorist (*pace* Blake) human speech can never in this sense aspire to rise above "second level" discourse. In Bahktin's terms, it remains normatively "dialogic"; humans do not authorize any "absolute word."[18]

The categorical distinction that Augustine and others are at pains to maintain, even as they draw the Johannine analogy, is precisely what the construct of Bloom, Derrida, and others of their ilk most readily confounds. For the typical Christian "theorist" from St. John the Divine and the writer of the Epistle to the Hebrews to T. S. Eliot, its mediation between presence and absence, time and eternity, makes the word aptly suggestive of the relationship of God to the world, Being to being. But, as John Freccero puts it (speaking of Augustine and Dante):

> Christian reality was neither the Platonic dream of a disembodied logos, an intellectual reality totally divorced from the world, nor

17. Augustine, *On Christian Doctrine*, 1.13; cf. *De Trinitate* 15.9.16ff.
18. Mikhail Bahktin, "Epos i roman," *Voprosy literatury i estetiki: Issledovanija raznyx let* (Moscow: Xudoz, 1975), 447-83.

an unintelligible nightmare irredeemably lost *in* the world: it was rather, like syntax, time pressed into the service of eternity.[19]

Accordingly, for the Christian, theory of poetry cannot responsibly be formulated from either polar view about the nature and properties of language, since such an absolute dichotomization misrepresents reality, either idolizing language (logocentrism) or repudiating it as useful means to understanding (nihilism).

Still more disturbing is the way any such misprision as Bloom's masks the nature of the actual *agon* in which men and women struggle to communicate and commune, to know and be known, to love and seek truth. Neither Dante nor Eliot, for example, could say with Bloom that whichever theory of language one chooses is immaterial for theorizing about poetry as long as it is "extreme enough and uncompromising"; for the Christian theorist the choice does not lie between sense and nonsense, a surplus of meaning and no certain meaning at all.[20] Rather, it lies more profoundly between life and death (Deut. 30:19), truth and denial of truth (Rom. 1:25). In the imperfect area of human signification, where we see now "as in a mirror enigmatically," the asymptotic character of fallen language is a source of endless frustration as well as momentary joy.

Michael Edwards reminds us that even when aspiring to true *grandeur*, the poet's language is forever falling tragically into *misère*,[21] though failed locution can be as meet as "successful" utterance for our insight. After all, as Richard Wilbur muses in his poem "Event":

It is by words and the defeat of words,
Down sudden vistas of the vain attempt,
That for a flying moment one may see
By what cross-purposes the world is dreamt.[22]

19. John Freccero, "Dante's Medusa: Allegory and Autobiography," in *By Things Seen: Reference and Recognition in Medieval Thought,* ed. D. L. Jeffrey (Ottawa: University of Ottawa Press, 1979), 33.

20. See, e.g., Dominic Manganiello, *T. S. Eliot and Dante* (London: Macmillan, 1989), 84-121.

21. Michael Edwards, *Toward a Christian Poetics* (London: Macmillan; Grand Rapids: Eerdmans, 1984), 107-8.

22. *The Poems of Richard Wilbur* (New York: Harcourt, Brace, 1963), 106.

Or, as Steiner reiterates in what might well seem a prose translation of Wilbur's poem: "The falling short is a guarantor of the experienced 'otherness' — the freedom to be or not to be, to enter into or abstain from a commerce of spirit with us — in the poem."[23] But such locutions hardly imply assent to an apotheosis of language — logocentrism as deconstructionists characterize it. Rather, they admit to a struggle in *and out* of language for communion and identification with the Person in whom ultimate meaning resides. All language is born crippled by the desire it lives to express; what actually is yearned for, as Dante makes explicit, is silence — but the silence of Being, not of nothingness.[24] Our language is like the language of lovers; even when most circular and redundant, not entirely vacuous. In Augustine's formulation, our expression stretches its feeble lineaments toward a day of transforming investiture, the "reading out" by Another such as will let our words be put at last to rest, a day when "justi et sancti," the redeemed soul may be at last "fruuntur Verbo Dei sine lectione, sine litteris."[25]

The first (and relatively modest) point I wish to make here will by now be fairly clear. The tradition which the deconstructionists have dubbed for our time as "logocentric" is subtly but seriously misrepresented by the term. At its least damaging, it attributes to Christian literary theory an idealism concerning language which by and large it certainly does not possess. Christian literary theories are generally affirmative of an ultimate Truth or Logos, but also firm in their insistence on the limitations of human language more than dimly to refract that Logos. It may be that the "Word from the beginning" teaches us considerably more about the properties of "word" than theoretical discussions about language afford insight into the Logos. This much is suggested, for example, in the late medieval hermeneutics of John Wyclif; the function of words even in Scripture is merely to lead us into conversation — a relationship with the Logos as personal knowledge. Encountering the Word-event reminds us, in turn, that "Christ and many of the saints did not even write except in the sense of [inscribing] the tablets of the heart, where alone [the communication] may be per-

23. Steiner, *Real Presences*, 175.

24. Cf. E. D. Blodgett and H. G. Coward, *Science, the Word, and the Sacred* (Waterloo: Wilfred Laurier University Press, 1989), 207-20.

25. Maurice Pontet, *L'Exégèse de S. Augustin predicateur* (Paris: Aubier, 1954), 96.

fected."[26] Wyclif's point is the same as Augustine's: what centers Christian discourse is not either extreme view of language, but a profoundly mediated theory of the "meaning of persons" to which language is functionally subordinate, merely tropic, merely indicative.[27] Christian theory may be Logos-centered, but it is not logocentrism.

Polysemeity, therefore, is not on these grounds a limitless and endlessly mutating reduction of the principle of reference to sublime absurdity. If this were true it would indeed, as Bloom says, cause polysemeity to join full circle with the nihilistic dearth-of-meaning view. Language is polysemous simply as the human imagination is various at the practical level — yet polysemeity functions in relation to an intermediate *totum integrum,* either to the constructs of a text as a whole, or to the known community of interpreters. Limit is of the essence of such a relationship. "Meaning," Augustine says, is finally "dependent upon truth,"[28] and perception of "truth" is at once enhanced by the diversity of individual "readings" and yet entirely limited by the *concensus gentium* of such readings.[29] The reading of any text by such a community is not then univocal, but, as Wyclif is at pains to say is true of Jesus' use of language in parable, it is "equivocal," alternatively spoken, even "poly-vocal."[30] What gets voiced, always partially even when truly, presumably continues to deserve diverse voicing because it is repeatedly found, in multiplied encounters, to be incomplete in itself, yet in some proper sense of the term meaning-full.

This point explains also the catholicity of taste in poetry exhibited by even the most stringently orthodox of historic Christian theorists: "every

26. John Wyclif, *De Veritate Sacrae Scripturae,* 3 vols., ed. R. Buddenseig (London: Wyclif Society; Trubner, 1905-7), 3.44.

27. See the discussion of Wyclif's theory in chapter 6, below.

28. Augustine, *On Christian Doctrine,* 3.27.38; see chap. 3 following.

29. A contemporary approach, more strictly from the linguistic point of view, is represented by J. M. Moravcsik, in *Language* 48 (1972): 446-47: "In order to understand problems of semantic theory it is crucial to understand why most philosophers think of the notion of reference as the key element in such theories. Reference is the relation between singular term and bearer, as well as between general predicate and the entities of which the predicate is true. With the notion of reference go the notions of naming, describing, and — therefore — truth. Thus the ability to express thought in language is one of the fundamental abilities that a semantic theory must help account for; and crucial to this ability is the ability to refer, to describe and to judge what is true or false."

30. Wyclif, *De Veritate,* 1.167-82.

good and true Christian should understand that wherever he may find truth, it is his Lord's," says Augustine,[31] echoing his teacher Ambrose. All good poetry, however superficially alien, is troped (especially tropologized) as "Egyptian gold," vessels refitted to a "nobler" ethical use.[32] Referentiality implies responsibility. Since meaning resides finally in the person and is not intrinsically a property of mere words, reading responsibly is regarded as an ethical activity. As Dante suggests in his discussion of the polysemous language of his *Commedia* in the accessus for Can Grande della Scala, practicality is of the essence in such a theory of poetry. The "branch of philosophy" to which his own work is subject, he emphasizes, "in the whole as in the part, is morals or ethics."[33]

Here, and this is my second point, we come to the most unfortunate loss in deconstruction's misrepresentation of literary theory in Western scriptural tradition — the latter's traditional foregrounding of the ethical in questions of interpretation and literary theory. Typically, it need hardly be said, ethical compunction tends to be as often a *lapsus* in gnostic as in nihilist theoreticians.[34] Literary theory in the mainstream of Western scriptural tradition has by contrast always found ethical contingency more or less inescapable. Augustine's test of charity, Dante's test of civic morality, Wyclif's scrutiny of intention in the reader, Sidney's insistence — and Pope's and Fielding's and even Arnold's — on the distillation of poetry as moral action, all reiterate the basic premises: what valorizes literary and linguistic heurism is an ultimate unity of truth; what conditions recovery and use of any part of "truth" is not merely the frailty of words but the primacy in inquiry of intention, of the human will. Literary theory in the scriptural tradition has usually tried to face this problem squarely, if not always successfully. From Augustine's confessional acknowledgment that as with the theory of anyone else, his too is autobiographical, through Chaucer's extended examination of the ethical burden of conflicting "entente" in readers and authors in *The Canterbury Tales*, to Søren Kierke-

31. Augustine, *On Christian Doctrine*, 2.18.28.

32. Ibid., 20.40.60.

33. Dante Alighieri, *Letter to Can Grande della Scala*, in *Literary Criticism of Dante Alighieri*, trans. Robert S. Haller (Lincoln: University of Nebraska Press, 1981).

34. Steiner observes, for instance, that "the Kabbalist would translate understanding not into action but into final illumination. . . . Such knowing is self-contained" (*Real Presences*, 42). It hardly need be added that self-containment is of the essence of nihilistic formulations as well.

gaard's excursus into the ways in which life imitates art in *Fear and Trembling,* the primary question has never been one of dearth or plenitude of meaning. Rather, assuming *ab initio* sufficient meaning for the choice to be made, the issue has been one of responsible reading and of ethical praxis. Here, I think, despite all the vagaries and inconsistencies that inevitably attend upon some of the personal histories, is an area of contribution from the scriptural tradition which we would impoverish ourselves to overlook or misrepresent.

In the modular antithesis of nihilism / logocentrism, distortion occurs chiefly by associated depersonalization in the right-hand term. While the impetus to abstract in this way is basic to gnostic or mystic Neoplatonism and deconstructive nihilism alike, it is always, as is well known, being resisted by the tradition currently identified as "logocentric." A comparison of two modern formulations will perhaps clarify the true nature of the *agon,* or antagonism between these views. The first may be represented by a familiar passage from Roland Barthes:

> Once the Author is removed, the claim to decipher a text becomes quite futile. To give a text an Author is to impose a limit on that text. . . . Literature . . . by refusing to assign a 'secret', an ultimate meaning, to the text (and to the word as text) liberates what may be called an antitheological activity, an activity that is truly revolutionary since to refuse to fix meaning is, in the end, to refuse God and his hypostases — reason, science, law.[35]

This type of strategem for theory of poetry rightly identifies the privilege accorded to textual authority and the place of meaning with the Judaeo-Christian world view. Barthes's position then defines itself in part by rejecting the moral authority associated with this world view. The perspective is not unknown in the field of biblical criticism itself, where indeed it predates its secular counterparts.[36]

35. Roland Barthes, *S/Z,* trans. Richard Miller (New York: Hill and Wang, 1974), intro.

36. Two studies offer a valuable historical perspective on this matter: Henning Graf Reventlow, *The Authority of the Bible and the Rise of the Modern World,* trans. John Bowden (London: SCM, 1984); and Hans W. Frei, *The Eclipse of Biblical Narrative: A Study in Eighteenth- and Nineteenth-Century Hermeneutics* (New Haven: Yale University Press, 1974).

More than a century ago Kierkegaard employed an Augustinian rhetorical strategy to query the ethical implications of a type of criticism which spends most of its energy evading the moral suasion of its foundational texts. His parable poses the question "What is the difference between criticism of a text and radical accountability to it?" It is worth our consideration in its entirety:

Imagine a country. A royal command is issued to all the office-bearers and subjects, in short, to the whole population. A remarkable change comes over them all: they all become interpreters, the office-bearers become authors, every blessed day there comes out an interpretation more learned than the last, more acute, more elegant, more profound, more ingenious, more wonderful, more charming, and more wonderfully charming. Criticism which ought to survey the whole can hardly attain survey of this prodigious literature, indeed criticism itself has become a literature so prolix that it is impossible to attain a survey of criticism. Everything became interpretation — but no one reads the royal command with a view to acting in accordance with it. And it was not only that everything became interpretation, but at the same time the point of view for determining what seriousness is was altered, and to be busy about interpretation became real seriousness. Suppose that this king was not a human king — for though a human king would understand well enough that they were making a fool of him by giving the affair this turn, yet as a human king he is dependent, especially when he encounters the united front of office-bearers and subjects, and so would be compelled to put the best face on a bad game, to let it seem as if all this were a matter of course, so that the most elegant interpreter would be rewarded by elevation to the peerage, the most acute would be knighted, &c. — Suppose that this king was almighty, one therefore who is not put to embarrassment though all the office-bearers and all the subjects play him false. What do you suppose this almighty king would think about such a thing? Surely he would say, "The fact that they do not comply with the commandment, even that I might forgive; moreover, if they united in a petition that I might have patience with them, or perhaps relieve them entirely of this commandment which seemed to them too hard — that I could forgive

them. But this I cannot forgive, that they entirely alter the point
of view for determining what seriousness is."[37]

Here, surely, no further commentary is required: the words of the parable convey a caution few readers will fail to identify, however diverse their reactions.

Some readers may feel that I have thus far anchored my reconstitutive characterization of literary theory in the biblical tradition too exclusively in Christian texts. But the evidence could readily be deepened and extended. Although it is Western literary theory which has been principally at issue in recent debate, the Christian sources here referred to have in fact learned to formulate both language theory and the nature of the poet's agon in a characteristically Hebraic way. So much is this the case that Western theistic theories of poetry (or, if one insists, Logos-grounded theory), might almost as well be instanced by a single poem from the Hebrew Scriptures: Psalm 19 (Vulg. Ps. 18), a psalm ascribed to David, is poignantly expressive of a poet's discovery of both the power and the limitations of such language as poets may use.[38] Once again, let us put the whole text before us:

> The heavens declare the glory of God; and the firmament
>   sheweth his handywork.
> Day unto day uttereth speech, and night unto night
>   sheweth knowledge.
> There is no speech nor language, where their voice is not heard.
> Their line is gone out through all the earth, and their words
>   to the end of the world. In them hath he set a tabernacle
>   for the sun.
> Which is as a bridegroom coming out of his chamber,
>   and rejoiceth as a strong man to run a race.
> His going forth is from the end of the heaven, and his circuit
>   unto the ends of it; and there is nothing hid from the

37. Søren Kierkegaard, *For Self-Examination* . . . , trans. Walter Lowrie (Princeton: Princeton University Press, 1944), 58-59.

38. I am aware that an older argument, represented in *The Interpreters Bible,* emphasizes the two halves of the poem as distinct entities. I side, however, with the multitude of those biblical critics who see the psalm as a skillfully composed unit in its present redaction.

heat thereof.
The law of the Lord is perfect, converting the soul:
the testimony of the Lord is sure, making wise the simple.
The statutes of the Lord are right, rejoicing the heart;
the commandment of the Lord is pure, enlightening the eyes.
The fear of the Lord is clean, enduring for ever: the judgments
of the Lord are true and righteous altogether.
More to be desired are they than gold, yea, than much fine gold:
sweeter also than honey and the honeycomb.
Moreover by them is thy servant warned: and in keeping
of them there is great reward.
Who can understand his errors? cleanse thou me from secret faults.
Keep back thy servant also from presumptuous sins;
let them not have dominion over me: then shall I be upright,
and I shall be innocent from the great transgression.
Let the words of my mouth, and the meditations of my heart,
be acceptable in thy sight, O Lord, my strength,
and my redeemer.[39]

The poem begins by heralding the nonverbal signal: nature, or Creation, "declares" the glory of God. The heavens proclaim, the cosmos displays, the very calendar pours forth knowledge which is universal, known in every tongue and nation (vv. 1-3). The spindrift of this knowledge takes on language: these words too are found on every shore and constitute there a habitation for human creativity, for poetry (v. 4). This language vivifies the imagination — as in other mediterranean myths of the sun-god (in the Babylonian version Shamash, in the Greek Helios, in the Roman Phoebus) the poet's bridegroom springs forth like a virile athlete from the east and runs across the heavens his diurnal course, questing after Aurora (v. 5). Yet en route his searching light unmasks each Asir and Ashteroth, Ares and Aphrodite, Mars and Venus, exposing their deeds done in darkness (v. 6).

If creation is a language, speaking forth the divine *chabod* (glory), poetry is another — incomplete to be sure, but *bona fide* in its attempt at declaration, or translation, and a clearer language because it can integrate the personal voice. Yet what speaks even more fulsomely, says

39. I am here quoting the Authorized (KJV) Version.

the poet, is "the law of the Lord," his Torah, "perfect because it is the articulation from above, *parfait, par-fecit,* the word He makes to set beside us: *para-situ,* or, perhaps, *parasitos,* to go against our grain. Not only does Torah transpose the soul, but, in another register of understanding, the "testimony" (the [νωμος] *nōmos,* or instruction, as in the Decalogue) of the Lord secures the soul because it is dependable, granting wisdom to the simple of an order they could never of themselves hope to attain (v. 7). To put it another way, the "statutes" of the Lord are just, rejoicing the heart"; his "commandments" are "pure," therefore "enlightening the eyes";[40] the "fear of the Lord" — literally observance of his *religio* or ordinance — is "clean." Like refined and burnished gold,[41] it is perdurable good. Finally, his "judgments" are "truth" in every respect. For the Hebrew poet no single human word can begin to capture what is suggested by these many attempts to speak about the revealed Word; all human language, even that by which Torah is translated, is asymptotic, earnestly reaching toward its goal of perfect signification, but repeatedly falling short of its object. The perennial generation of words, *dor le dor,* is not a function of either the dearth or the plenitude of their meaning. It is a function rather of our getting it at best about half-right, because language, even when communicating the divine Word, is simultaneously both revelatory and distorting.

Clearly the view of the psalmist is not nihilistic. Nor, evidently, is it a species of gnostic or mystical idealism. For the Hebrew poet the various expressions of God's language are more desirable than the security of gold, more satisfying than the rarest honey. They have supremely practical value for an ethically responsible (and rewarding) life (v. 11). Yet it ought not be imagined that even those most perfect temporal reflections of God's glory can be "mastered" — there is always the limit of skewed intention in the mind of the hearer or reader (v. 12). Who can even understand his own errors, prejudices, self-deceived subversions, self-justifying interpretations? The presumptuous sin from which the poet would be delivered (v. 13) is like the "great transgression," whether of Eden or of Babel, because he too is tempted to play God, imagining to "create a new word," and withal an alternative moral — or amoral — order.

40. Cf. Ps. 119:105.
41. Cf. Ps. 28:19.

Hence the coda of the poem is an *envoi* to the ultimate Reader. Or Author. What it seeks, in view of the poem's acknowledgment of the insufficiency of any human "reading" (the failure even of "sublimity"), is for the poet (not just the poem) to be most charitably, mercifully read by One who, beyond the poet's failings and the limits of language, can redeem intention in the human heart. That is, the poet does not presume to ask that he be made a perfect translator or interpreter of divine glory but rather that he himself be translated by the One whose participation in the reading he has come to see as a necessary condition for his poem to "be" at all.

For the biblical poet there is indeed an *agon*. This *agon* in its more restrained expression is the contest between self and God, partiality and plenitude, self will and divine will. At its most extravagant reach, it is figured as the struggle between God and primal chaos — *inana et vacua* ("inanity and vacuousness") as the Vulgate pertinently translates it (Gen. 1:2; KJV "without form and void") — Being and nothing. Humanity struggles from the middle, in this view, to choose life rather than death, meaning rather than madness — or mindlessness. Forced to acknowledge the probability of both semantic and moral error, the poetic inscribed in this psalm implicates itself much more intimately than some obvious alternatives in respect of the matter of ethical compunction. In this sense Psalm 19 anticipates quite well the mainstream preoccupations of Western literary theory.

Theory of poetry in the biblical tradition transvalues above all else the personal, in the threefold sense of the personhood of God, other, and of course self. What poetic language can do, and ought to do, as Gerard Manley Hopkins suggests (e.g., in his untitled sonnet, "As kingfishers catch fire"), is metaphorically to "incarnate," give verbal flesh to personal realities, for it is there always that ". . . Christ plays in ten thousand places, / Lovely in limbs, and lovely in eyes not his / To the Father, through the features of men's faces."[42] In both ancient Jewish and modern Christian poets what remains at the center is not the word but the person; words are but a *means* of centering, philology but a love of words transcended by a higher love. To conclude where we began, with Augustine:

---

42. *The Poems of Gerard Manley Hopkins*, ed. W. H. Gardiner and N. H. Mackenzie (London: Oxford University Press, 1967), no. 57.

The sum of all we have said since we began to speak of things thus comes to this: it is to be understood that the plenitude and the end of the Law and of all the sacred Scriptures is the love of a Being which is to be enjoyed and of a being that can share that enjoyment with us, since there is no need for a precept that anyone should love himself. That we might know this and have the means to implement it, the whole temporal dispensation was made by divine Providence for our salvation. We should use it, not with an abiding but with a transitory love and delight like that in a road or in vehicles or in other instruments, or, if it may be expressed more accurately, so that we love those things by which we are carried along for the sake of that toward which we are carried.[43]

The tradition of scripturally grounded poetics often mischaracterized as "logocentric" is not, it should already be clear, the straw idol (or hollow man) it has recently been represented to be. Indeed, a good deal of the "chaff" (as Augustine might have put it) may lie to the other side of the threshing floor. One thing that seems to be needed, then, especially if we would contemplate a serious return to pursuit of an ethical poetic, is to thresh out more thoroughly — and with greater candor — the rich harvest of "theoretical" texts already gathered for us in the library of Western scriptural tradition.

---

43. Augustine, *On Christian Doctrine*, 1.25.39.

Chapter Two

Scripture upon Scripture

Secret things belong to the Lord our God, but the revealed things belong to us and to our children forever, to observe all the words of this law.

DEUTERONOMY 29:29

These things happened to them to serve as an example, and they were written down to instruct us, on whom the ends of the ages have come.

1 CORINTHIANS 10:11

CHRISTIAN IDENTITY, IT MAY FAIRLY BE SAID, IS STILL DERIVATIVELY Jewish. As such, it is inextricably bound up with book culture. The formative elements in Judaism are well known: the giving of the Law to Moses at Sinai, God's repeated commandments to Moses his *nabi'* and to successive generations of prophets to speak or write (Deut. 1:1-5; Isa. 8:1ff.; Ezek. 2:9–3:4; Amos 7:14-15; cf. Rev. 1:10-11, etc.) and the subsequent creation of book-inscribed rather than exclusively oral traditions of law, history, and poetry. Even by themselves these features have been sufficient to guarantee the central authority of the Book in Jewish cultural identity.

When the prophets were sent to call Israel back to repentance and faithfulness, they did so by repeated reference to the authority of the Scriptures. In the annals of the four evangelists Jesus does the same, even intensifying the relationship of righteousness to "right reading" of Scripture. He does this by proposing a way of reading Scripture that surpasses the merely literal observance of the text with an insistence upon "fulfillment" of the Scripture, real conformity to the spirit or intent of the text, an ultimate holiness of thought as well as deed before God and the world. In the four evangelists, but especially in the prologue to John's Gospel, Jesus himself is the perfected fulfillment of all that the law and the prophets have spoken, the promised full expression of God's divine Authorial intent for the world, the Word from the Beginning now made flesh in his Incarnation — effectively the Living Book of God. All written Scripture, past and present, the evangelists suggest, testifies to him.

Paul in his letters and the early church generally echo and advance this dramatic escalation of the place of "the Book" in Christian identity to the point where in the minds of some outsiders it can finally seem, as it did to Muhammed, that Christians had become, perhaps most self-consciously, the "People of the Book."[1]

The Prophets

For both the Jews and early Christians, of course, the first textual content called up by the metaphor of the book is Torah, or the Pentateuch. The five books of the Law associated with Moses have always been central to Jewish worship: Genesis, Exodus, Leviticus, Numbers, Deuteronomy. Torah, in a real as well as metaphoric sense, is the foundation upon which all subsequent Scripture is built. So much is this so that precisely at that point in the Hebrew Scriptures where an inexperienced reader might expect the text to offer striking novelties — in the books of the

1. See preface, p. ix. In Orthodox Judaism, it should be noted, the term has particular association with the old European practice of *Lernen,* lifelong dedication to study and spiritual meditation upon biblical texts, mystical tracts, and especially Talmud. This tradition, and its continuance in American Jewish Orthodoxy, is the subject of a book by Samuel C. Heilman, *People of the Book: Drama, Fellowship and Religion* (Chicago: University of Chicago Press, 1983).

prophets, for example — the dominantly intertextual relationship of later biblical writing to Torah is most evidently maintained. Consciousness of this indebtedness remains pervasive in Christian art. Thus, when Michelangelo represents Isaiah on the Sistine Chapel ceiling (ca. 1510) the prophet is holding a large volume in which his inserted fingers mark the place in the scriptural text to which he wishes to return; the iconography had long been established [Fig. 1]. As with his precedessors, the Christian artist of the sixteenth century is entirely faithful to the evidence of the text of Isaiah itself — as well as to traditional iconography employed also for that faithful reader among the apostles, St. James [cf. Fig. 2] — in representing the prophet in this way. The book in his hand, as Christian viewers still recognize, is figuratively the literary testament of Moses.

"The Lord is One, and his divine inspiration is always the same," writes Ibn Ezra (1092-1167); "the prophecies vary only according to the receptive faculty of the prophet, which is not always the same."[2] However paradoxical it might seem from a late twentieth-century perspective, the biblical prophet in his own context — and for two millennia afterwards — was thought of as so textually derivative, so subordinate in authority to his own ultimate Author, that for practical purposes he might more accurately be perceived as a "non-author." In the literary discourse of our own time, by contrast, indeed any time after those Romantic poets whom Harold Bloom quite aptly styled a "visionary company"[3] — a "prophet" or someone to whom we are likely to attach that name is very much an "author," presenting himself above all as an author of novelties. Indeed, the claim to novelty has become the most compelling self-advertisement of modern and calculatedly forward-looking writers.

The most sensational representations of this post-Romantic notion of a "prophetic" literature unsurprisingly tend to color the preconceptions some modern students bring to the biblical text. In the discourse of our time, a prophet is often a kind of forecaster. He or she may be a student of politics or economics, a popular journalist or a political or

2. The most influential Jewish commentary on Isaiah, translated by M. Friedlander, is *The Commentary of Ibn Ezra on Isaiah*, 2 vols. (London and New York: Philipp Feldheim, 1873), 1.1.

3. Harold Bloom, *The Visionary Company: A Reading of English Romantic Poetry* (Garden City, N.Y.: Doubleday, 1961).

Figure 1. *"Prophet." Cloister of Burgos Cathedral, Spain, ca. 1225. Courtesy: Francke Verlag.*

economic advisor who consults the right polls and collects the right samples so as to be able to "call" an election, predict a coup, anticipate a fall from political favor or rise in the stockmarket. Such nomenclature might attach itself as easily to a gossip columnist clairvoyant, a popular entertainer with an eye and ear for Hollywood careers and the *National Enquirer* — or even to an individualistic minister of the electronic gospel, with his eye in a fine frenzy rolling. From the point of view of the Hebrew Scriptures, however, all of these might more properly be characterized as subspecies of the "false prophet."

In ancient Israel, a true prophet could have nothing in common with such televisable commodities. Instead of being defined in terms of political sensitivity or entertainment value, the vocational worth of a prophet twenty-six hundred years ago stood directly in proportion to his or her detachment from politics, obtuseness to what was popular, and separation from formal institutions of religion. That is to say, a prophet was "a voice crying in the wilderness" by definition, not by some accident of bad career management.[4]

To begin with, it is essential to the character of a true Hebrew prophet that he himself has never sought the role. He is a *nabi'* (נָבִיא) — "one who is called" (Deut. 18:15ff; 34:10). Often, in fact, as in the case of Moses, Jonah, and Ezekiel, the prophet is not at all sure he wants the job. Moses pleads inadequacy, Jonah is revolted by his itinerary, and the astonished Ezekiel is forced to swallow his marching orders whole like medicine. And when appointed, or "called," the prophet is required to submit his own skills and conscious imagination utterly, permitting himself to be seized by the Spirit of God and given directly whatever words he has to speak — or indeed, as in the case of Ezekiel (3:25–5:5) and Hosea (1:2-9; 3:1-3), ordered whatever alarming symbolic acts to perform.

The prophet has no prophetic training because none is necessary, and none is available. He is not a sorcerer, because he deals not so much with "secrets" or hidden things as with that which has been revealed (cf. Deut. 29:28–30:3). He is not a shaman. He is simply and wondrously a

---

4. See Sheldon Banks, " 'Of a Truth the Lord Hath Sent Me': An Inquiry into the Source of the Prophet's Authority," in *Interpreting the Prophetic Tradition*, ed. Harry M. Orlinsky (New York: Ktav, 1969), 1-20; also Geza Vermes, *Scripture and Tradition in Judaism* (Leiden: Brill, 1961) for general context.

Figure 2. *"Apostle James" by Hans Leinberger, ca. 1520.*

mouthpiece, an amanuensis, a voice. His own previous vocation is, to this purpose, irrelevant. He may have been a shepherd, a householder, a civil servant, a priest. He may even stay in his initial line of work for his daily bread. But he must be ready always for the divine imperative to burst upon him without so much as a moment's notice. The call of Jeremiah provides a useful illustration:

Now the word of the Lord came to me, saying,

"Before I formed you in the womb I knew you;
before you were born I consecrated you;
I appointed you a prophet to the nations."

Then I said, "Ah, Lord God! Truly I do not know how to speak, for I am only a boy."

But the Lord said to me,
"Do not say, 'I am only a boy';
for you shall go to all to whom I send you
and you shall speak whatever I command you.
Do not be afraid of them,
for I am with you to deliver you,
says the Lord."

Then the Lord put out his hand and touched my mouth; and the Lord said to me:

"Now I have put my words in your mouth."

(Jer. 1:4-9)[5]

5. The New Revised Standard Version is used for the prophets, unless otherwise specified. The sense of the Hebrew in v. 9 is somewhat more emphatic than captured by the NRSV, however; the Jerusalem translation (Garden City, N.Y.: Doubleday, 1966) renders it better: "See! I am putting words into your mouth." Cf. Harold Bloom, who acknowledges that by *nebi'im* "we ought to speak of 'the proclaimers' rather than 'the prophets' [though] no one among us will choose to do so, since we are deeply invested in the overtones of 'the prophets' and 'prophecy'. " See his *Ruin the Sacred Truths: Poetry and Belief from the Bible to the Present* (Cambridge, Mass.: Harvard University Press, 1989), 12.

The first thing which must strike the reader of this passage is the fidelity with which it mimes the calling of Moses, first fully to assume the task of the *nebi'im,* in Exodus (3 and 4, esp. 4:10-12). The authors of Hebrew prophetic literature consistently represent the prophet himself as a non-author, one who has words put in his mouth.[6] God will be always *the* Author, and to his authority the prophet will be as an actor on the stage is to his playwright / producer. For that is just the point these texts make about the genesis of prophecy — it is an authorial intervention into the unfolding script of history, editorial, critical, and invariably pedagogical. The prophet is one forced to stand at the flashpoint, where the current is grounding and the sparks fly, as the divine Author comments definitively on his people's performance. The prophet, like other men, belongs to his time, yet he stands for a terrible moment also outside of temporal order: one foot in the *kronos,* the other in *kairos,* his ear to eternity and mouth toward the city, he speaks as he is directed. And the proclamation is, alas, usually a judgment, bad news for the hearers.

It is a notoriously unpopular thing to be the bearer of bad tidings, and it usually incurs considerable risk for the messenger.[7] But there is not much the prophet can do about this. Consider the case of the prophet Micaiah in 1 Kings 22, when he is brought against his will to confront the unregenerate despot, King Ahab. Ahab's four hundred flattering court prognosticators, led in their raving dance by a chief shaman called Zedekiah dressed up in a mask with iron horns (22:11), have already been entertaining the king with what they perceive he wants to hear:

> The messenger who had gone to summon Micaiah said to him,
> "Look, the words of the prophets with one accord are favorable to
> the king; let your word be like the word of one of them, and speak
> favorably." But Micaiah said, "As the Lord lives, *whatever the Lord
> says to me, that will I speak.*"

6. A case can be made that Jeremiah is atypical. He adds considerably to God's utterances with his own complaint: he is aggrieved with the insensitivity of his hearers, and takes their rejection of God personally. In his case, as Joel Rosenberg has put it, to some degree "the lavishness of prophetic pathos flows more from the breakdown of missionary purpose than from an enactment of it" (in *The Literary Guide to the Bible,* ed. Frank Kermode and Robert Alter [Cambridge, Mass.: Belknap Press, 1987], 187).

7. See Orlinsky, "The So-Called "Suffering Servant" in Isaiah 53," 225-76, in his *Interpreting the Prophetic Tradition,* esp. pp. 248ff.

When he had come to the king, the king said to him, "Micaiah, shall we go to Ramoth-gilead to battle, or shall we refrain?" He answered them, "Go up and triumph; the Lord will give it into the hand of the king." But the king said to him, "How many times must I make you swear to tell me nothing but the truth in the name of the Lord?" Then Micaiah said, "I saw all Israel scattered on the mountains like sheep that have no shepherd; and the Lord said, 'These have no master; let each one go home in peace.'" The king of Israel said to Jehoshaphat, "Did I not tell you that he would not prophesy anything favorable about me, but only disaster?"

Then Micaiah said, "Therefore hear the word of the Lord: I saw the Lord sitting on his throne, with all the host of heaven standing beside him to the right and to the left of him. And the Lord said, 'Who will entice Ahab, so that he may go up and fall at Ramoth-gilead?' Then one said one thing, and another said another, until a spirit came forward and stood before the Lord, saying, 'I will entice him.' 'How?' the Lord asked him. He replied, 'I will go out and be a lying spirit in the mouth of all his prophets.' Then the Lord said, 'You are to entice him, and you shall succeed; go out and do it.' So you see, the Lord has put a lying spirit in the mouth of all these your prophets; the Lord has decreed disaster for you."

Then Zedekiah son of Chenaanah came up to Micaiah, slapped him on the cheek, and said, "Which way did the spirit of the Lord pass from me to speak to you?" Micaiah replied, "You will find out on that day when you go in to hide in an inner chamber." The king of Israel then ordered, "Take Micaiah, and return him to Amon the governor of the city and to Joash the king's son, and say, 'Thus says the king: Put this fellow in prison, and feed him on reduced rations of bread and water until I come in peace.'" Micaiah said, "If you return in peace, the Lord has not spoken by me." And he said, "Hear, you peoples, all of you!"

So the king of Israel and King Jehoshaphat of Judah went up to Ramoth-gilead. The king of Israel said to Jehoshaphat, "I will disguise myself and go into battle, but you wear your robes." So the king of Israel disguised himself and went into battle. Now the king of Aram had commanded the thirty-two captains of his chariots, "Fight with no one small or great, but only with the king of

Israel." When the captains of the chariots saw Jehoshaphat, they
said, "It is surely the king of Israel." So they turned to fight against
him; and Jehoshaphat cried out. When the captains of the chariots
saw that it was not the king of Israel, they turned back from
pursuing him. But a certain man drew his bow and unknowingly
struck the king of Israel between the scale armor and the breastplate; so he said to the driver of his chariot, "Turn around, and
carry me out of the battle, for I am wounded." The battle grew hot
that day, and the king was propped up in his chariot facing the
Arameans, until at evening he died; the blood from the wound had
flowed into the bottom of the chariot. Then about sunset a shout
went through the army, "Every man to his city, and every man to
his country!"

So the king died, and was brought to Samaria; they buried the
king in Samaria. They washed the chariot by the pool of Samaria;
the dogs licked up his blood, and the prostitutes washed themselves
in it, according to the word of the Lord that he had spoken.

(1 Kgs. 22:13-38, my emphasis)

Back in the court, the false prophets are nowhere to be seen. The
throne is empty. In the stark, swift contours of this powerful narrative, the
reader is made to see the main point: Ahab's court has been judged by
another court, tried and found wanting. Heaven and earth have both
witnessed against the tyrant. Judgment has been pronounced, and executed. Of the bearer of the summons we hear nothing more; Micaiah
may be rotting somewhere in a dungeon, left to the rats. Or freed. But from
the writer's point of view the role of the prophet has been played out
consummately: the word from out of time has been proclaimed in time,
giving an agenda for true justice and integrity by which Ahab's greed and
false balances are swept from the stage and his regal pomp reduced to dog
food and gutter wash. The announcer of justice is as apparently unlooked
for as its instrument: a nameless archer who, "drawing his bow at random,
hit the king of Israel between the corslet and the scale-armour of his
breastplate" (Jerusalem trans. — a place about the size of a good coin).
Not self-intended, perhaps, but not unbidden either. And so the shaft, like
the rhetoric, plunges deep into its intended target.

The raving four hundred, Ahab's shamanistic vizers, are among those called *ro'eh* (רֹאֶה); from the active participle form of the verb "to see" (Isa. 30:10; 1 Chron. 29:29) or *hozeh* (הֹזֶה) (2 Chron. 19:2; cf. Ezek. 13:8, 16). Persons called by these names could be merely diviners or clairvoyants of an unexalted sort; their role can be loftier only if the character of a true *nabi'* has first been established, that is, if the "call" has already been authenticated.

The term *nabi'* (or plural, *nebi'im*) is not restricted to the "authors" of the major and minor prophetic books, or even their chief protagonists.[8] In fact, the first to receive this denomination was Abraham (Gen. 20:7), even though prophetism as such only takes on its characteristic form with Moses (Deut. 18:15; 34:10). The prophetic vocation has thus a long tradition in Hebrew history and literature, and the nature of the divine transmission to which the prophets are prompted is pre-textual; it may appear as symbolic act (a mime, a sacrifice, a life journey), as proclamation of divine judgment (bad news about impending desolation or a sentence of death), or as prediction of the future (the promise of Canaan, the fall of Jerusalem). The pattern of prophetic activity is already well established in Israel's history and chief literature by the time of the major prophets and it reflects — in the Torah as in the time of the divided kingdoms — God's insistence on maintaining a conversation with his people Israel. When they will not incline their ear to hear what he is saying in a soft voice, or when they have forgotten the character of his conversation with their parents, or lost the book which records it, then he calls out a chosen *nabi'* to shout in their ears and get their attention. For that is the whole end of Hebrew prophetic texts — to restore conversation with the original and ultimate Author.

Torah Rhetoric in Isaiah's Prologue

In some of the situations in which the prophets find themselves it seems almost as though God's people have forgotten the very language of that conversation. That is to say, they have forgotten the Torah, the five books of Moses, and the other scriptures. Hence the basic drive of prophets

8. For a helpful discussion of this term see W. F. Albright, "Samuel and the Beginnings of the Prophetic Movement," 149-76 in Orlinsky, *Interpreting the Prophetic Tradition.*

like Isaiah, Jeremiah, Amos, and Ezekiel is to carry the fragmenting memory of Israel back to its roots in that source. And for this very reason, both in the object and in the rhetorical form of their discourse, the prophetic books require most of all for our understanding that we know and refer them to the Torah, to the history of the conversation. We see this quite readily, I think, in the prologue to Isaiah:

> The vision of Isaiah son of Amoz which he saw concerning Judah and Jerusalem in the days of Uzziah, Jotham, Ahaz and Hezekiah, kings of Judah.

> Hear, O heavens; and listen, O earth;
> for the Lord has spoken:
> I reared children and brought them up,
> but they have rebelled against me.
> The ox knows its owner
> and the donkey its master's crib;
> but Israel does not know,
> my people do not understand.

> Ah, sinful nation,
> people laden with iniquity,
> offspring who do evil,
> children who deal corruptly,
> who have forsaken the Lord,
> who have despised the Holy
> One of Israel,
> who are utterly estranged!

> Why do you seek further beatings?
> Why do you continue to rebel?
> The whole head is sick,
> and the whole heart faint.
> From the sole of the foot even to the head,
> there is no soundness in it,
> but bruises and sores
> and bleeding wounds;
> they have not been drained, or bound up,
> or softened with oil.

Your country lies desolate,
your cities are burned with fire;
in your very presence
aliens devour your land;
it is desolate, as overthrown
by foreigners.

And daughter Zion is left
like a booth in a vineyard,
like a shelter in a cucumber field,
like a besieged city.
If the Lord of hosts
had not left us a few survivors,
we would have been like Sodom,
and become like Gomorrah.

Hear the word of the Lord,
you rulers of Sodom!
Listen to the teaching of our God,
you people of Gomorrah!
What to me is the multitude of your sacrifices?
says the Lord;
I have had enough of burnt
offerings of rams
and the fat of fed beasts;
I do not delight in the blood of bulls,
or of lambs, or of goats.

When you come to appear before me,
who asked this from your hand?
Trample my courts no more;
bringing offerings is futile;
incense is an abomination to me.
New moon and sabbath and
calling of convocation —
I cannot endure solemn
assemblies with iniquity.
Your new moons and your
appointed festivals

my soul hates;
they have become a burden to me,
I am weary of bearing them.
When you stretch out your hands,
I will hide my eyes from you;
even though you make many prayers;
I will not listen;
your hands are full of blood.
Wash yourselves; make
yourselves clean;
remove the evil of your doings
from before my eyes;
cease to do evil,
learn to do good;
seek justice,
rescue the oppressed,
defend the orphan,
plead for the widow.

Come now, let us argue it out,
says the Lord:
though your sins are like scarlet,
they shall be like snow;
though they are red like crimson,
they shall become like wool.
If you are willing and obedient,
you shall eat the good of the land;
but if you refuse and rebel,
you shall be devoured by the sword;
for the mouth of the Lord has spoken.

(Isa. 1:1-20)

We may readily divide this prologue into three rhetorical movements, each having a binary construction.

I. Presentation of the problem:
   a) Rebellion against the fatherhood (authority)
       of God the Creator (1:2-4)

    b) Result: sickness in the body — creature and creation (5-9)

II. Disparate analysis:
    a) Human response: more rebellion or meaningless
       sacrifices (10-15)
    b) The Author's prescription: ethical obedience (16-17)

III. Presentation of Options:
    a) To see history and the book as a conversation to set things
       in perspective (18) — or reject it
    b) To choose enactment of the Word — or to deny it (19-20)

The predominance in Hebrew of the short phrase lends itself naturally to parallelism, a feature much noted in the discussion of Hebrew poetry.[9] Here, in its basic dyadic form, it suits perfectly the larger ethical oppositions which the argument of Isaiah is concerned to elaborate. When reinforced by the rhetorical ordering of argument observed here, the effect of the alternating elements is to force the reader almost relentlessly toward a personal engagement of the ethical imperative. As Luis Alonso Schökel has aptly observed, here in verses 16 and 17, "two alliterative verbs and nouns say it all: *limdu heytev, dirshu mishpat*, "cease to do evil, learn to do good."[10] Such parallelism echoes the movement of the main argument throughout the text; patterns of metaphorical elaboration, cryptic judgments, and gentle encouragement all formally anticipate a stark either / or ethical moment toward which they draw. Thus, in powerful contrasts such as those between desert and garden,

9. Robert Lowth's Oxford Poetry Lectures for 1741 were published as the epoch-making *Lectures on the Sacred Poetry of the Hebrews* (1753), and especially after their translation in 1787 had a wide influence. Subsequent scholarship has largely confirmed Lowth's characterization of Hebrew poetry; see especially Adele Berlin, *The Dynamics of Biblical Parallelism* (Bloomington: Indiana University Press, 1983); and Robert Alter, *The Art of Biblical Poetry* (New York: Basic Books, 1985); for insight into the resonance of Hebrew parallelism in English poetry and poetics see Stephen Prickett, *Words and the Word: Language, Poetics and Biblical Interpretation* (Cambridge: Cambridge University Press, 1986), 41-43; 105-17, and Françoise Deconinck-Brossard, "England and France in the Eighteenth Century," in *Reading the Text: Biblical Criticism and Literary Theory*, ed. Stephen Prickett (Oxford: Blackwell, 1991), 136-81.

10. In Kermode and Alter, *Literary Guide*, 169.

Babylon and Jerusalem, harlot and bride, the element of suggestion or suasion can be as pointed as the imperative itself:

> Though your sins are like scarlet,
> they shall be like snow;
> though they are red like crimson,
> they shall become like wool.

Though many of Isaiah's tropes are broadly referential to a moral ecology in which the whole of creation is implicated, the force of the rhetoric is always to present implications for the ethical responsibility of each reader / hearer of the text:

> If you are willing and obedient,
> you shall eat the good of the land;
> but if you refuse and rebel,
> you shall be devoured by the sword;
> for the mouth of the Lord has spoken.

As a whole, the book of Isaiah is evidently an anthology, an orchestration through several genres on many aspects of a plurality of themes. There are tone poems, songs, dirges, oracles, recitations of judgment, even a section of historical narrative. Yet throughout this whole anthology, whose sixty-six chapters have sometimes been seen as a synechdoche for the shape and movement of the whole scriptural anthology,[11] runs a unifying pattern of discourse — problem / analysis / options — an implied rhetorical argument repeating itself over and over again as in a motet or canon, or a majestic fugue (chapters 1–5; 6–12; 13–24; 24–27; 28–35; [36–39]; 40–55; 56–66). In Isaiah we see a book concluded, some would argue, over two generations, possibly by several hands, as Isaiah's faithful successors finished the task after his untimely execution.[12] But the overall

---

11. One of the more interesting discussions is afforded by John Wyclif: see D. L. Jeffrey, "John Wyclif and the Hermeneutics of Reader Response," *Interpretation* 39 (1985): 272-87.

12. Manasseh is said by some sources (Babylonian Talmud Ye bamoth 49b; Tal. Jerushalmi, Sanhedrin 10.2) to have been Isaiah's executioner because the prophet claimed to have seen the Lord (6:5) in contradistinction to Exod. 33:20, "There shall no man see me and live." Ibn Ezra thinks on textual grounds it more likely that he died in

result is beautifully symphonic, a text, as generations of critics have observed, of astonishing literary unity. How, given such a complex of features and circumstances, does it achieve this apparent unity? The simple answer is that Isaiah, as a book of prophecy, is itself a powerful "reading" of another book, the Torah, and that its unity comes from the established shape of the canonical transmission of Hebrew Scripture and history — the implied as well as explicit rhetorical patterning of its foundational texts. And this, then, is essential perspective for reading Hebrew prophetic literature: one is required to read it with one eye on the first five books of the Bible. This remains true — even most particularly true — when one is reading prophets such as Daniel and Ezekiel who seem to be speaking of the far future, of events that have not yet come to pass.[13]

Time in Prophetic Discourse

It is of the essence of the predictive as well as of the proclamatory character of these books that one reads God's judgments on the future in terms of what he has already said and done in the past. Or, to put it another way: we are to understand that "future" and "past" are going to be like each other in significant content, even as the content of the divine Author's character is eternal and unchanging — his justice and integrity, his jealous love, his insistence on the conversation. In fact, the Hebrew language of the text makes this point clear to the reader in its normative distinction, effectively, between only two orders of time or tenses with respect to our ephemeral prospect as mortal readers.

As readers, of course, or as hearers, we stand circumscribed by our limit in time present, what the text calls *hayyōm hazzeh* (הַיּוֹםהַזֶּה). But this limitation is qualified by the fact that what we read is either of the

---

the days of Hezekiah, perhaps after chap. 39, upon which Ibn Ezra makes no comment. See *The Commentary of Ibn Ezra on Isaiah*, p. 3.

13. Although undeveloped in his argument in *The Great Code: The Bible and Literature* (Toronto: Academic Press, 1982), Northrop Frye's observation that "Deuteronomy was the germ out of which the whole canon eventually developed" (201) seems to me, at least figuratively speaking, correct and pertinent to the matter of this entire chapter.

past, *bayyōm hahû* (ביומההוא) or the future, also *bayyōm hahû*.[14] That is, "this day," the "today" of our reading, is distinguished categorically from the "that day" of the text. But the phrase "in that day" is the same whether the prophetic text is speaking of God's actions in the past or of what he says he will do in the future. (This phrase is used largely in the prophetic books, especially Isaiah, but see also Exod. 8:22; Deut. 31:17ff.; 1 Sam. 3:12). References to the future are signified by context rather than by verb, since the Hebrew verb does not make our distinction of future tense. Thus, in Isaiah 2:11, 17:

> The haughty eyes of people shall be brought low,
> and the pride of everyone shall be humbled;
> and the Lord·alone will be exalted in that day [*bayyōm hahû*].

References to time past, "in that day" *(bayyōm hahû),* are to moments of revelatory confirmation, as of God's eternal character, of the character of his promise, the covenant with his people. In Exodus 14, after the crossing of the Red Sea, the text reads: "Thus the Lord saved Israel that day [*bayyōm hahû*] out of the hands of the Egyptians" (v. 30; cf. Josh. 24:25; Gen. 15:18; 1 Sam. 7:10; 2 Sam. 23:10). In this "past" context, the phrase "in that day" is often used as an epitome, a summarizing characterization concerning a particular day in which Israel's God was in some way seen to be active in a crucial confrontation with his people.

"That day," the recurrent prophetic reference, is then a reference to the larger divine conversation, a conversation with the reader, which has its present aspect as we read. *Bayyōm hahû,* past or future as we should normatively think it, is really all one in God's perspective of eternity, and it is indeed all one for us too — at least in the sense that both past and future are beyond our immediate experience. *Bayyōm hahû* is book time; *hayyōm hazzeh* is reader time, or hearer time. But *hayyōm hazzeh* is of crucial importance for the response we make as readers to our text; indeed, the dramatic conscriptions of prophets like Jeremiah, Isaiah, and Ezekiel are put in the text partly to model this point. "This day,"

---

14. General students will find helpful the discussion by Simon John DeVries, *Yesterday, Today, and Tomorrow: Time and History in the Old Testament* (Grand Rapids: Eerdmans, 1975).

"today" is the day which is really always being appealed to by the prophetic books, because it is only in "this day" that the reader's response can be relevant. *Hayyōm hazzeh* is, in effect, the moment of ethical decision, such as is captured in the challenge of Joshua: "Choose *this day* whom you will serve . . . but as for me and my household, we will serve the Lord" (Josh. 24:15; cf. Exod. 12:14). The culminating point of prophetic rhetoric is thus an imperative insistence on the reader's option, as well as a reminder of what is at stake in the choosing.

The framework of prophetic discourse — the interspersed relation of vision and prophetic dream to the flow of historical events — is a simulacrum of this "grammar" of the text, point-counterpoint. It is indeed as though one is confronted in a prophetic book with two texts, or a text within a text. The first or "surface" text is the one with which we have least difficulty. It presents the general narrative, the historical context into which the prophetic utterance suddenly comes as an interruption. The syntax of this narrative is predictable, topical, and characterized by causal relationships. In the decline and fall of an empire, the logic of cause and effect is apparent enough even to the chronicler: the syntax of history is the normative, conscious syntax of our language of observation and critique. The encroachments of Babylon, the dissipation of Ahab's kingdom, the aggrandizements of Nebuchadnezzar, all these are the stuff of narrative order as we expect to find it on the reader's side of the page.

But there is in the prophetic books another text, the text within the text. This other text is not, in any wooden way, the literal codex of the Torah, but its incorporated substance as ethical vision. It is the psychological commentary, the story within that comments upon and interprets the story without. It is not simply the record of unfolding historical events but rather the reading community's shared transcript of sacred memory and dream. And this other text, superimposed upon the surface narrative of events in such a way as to confound and redirect their expected flow, exhibits another syntax all its own. For the syntax of memory and dream does not abide by causal logic, nor does it follow strict temporal governance. Here the temporal, the *kronos,* is confounded by a continuum of accessible past and future, a *kairos* which startles and overflows the temporal imagination. The prophet is one who is called repeatedly into this second flow of syntax, and whose speaking is thus according to the grammar and logic of eternity, admonishing the finitude of the temporal, causal perspective. The visions and interpretation of dreams in Daniel (interspersed with his patient stewardship as a high bureaucrat in the governments of two empires); Isaiah's divine ambassadorship, interpreting fateful signs to the kingdom of Hezekiah: these are the stuff of visionary order, and they wash across and reinterpret the surface or historical text (and context) of the prophetic books in which they occur. In the case of the parallel courts in the confrontation of Micaiah and Ahab, for example, it is in the prophet's access to the syntax of memory and dream that we see the special advantage of his "book." For it is in this extraordinary syntax that the Author's side of the divine conversation is clearly heard.

Tone in Prophetic Discourse

Many different kinds of style are exhibited by the prophets. The haranguing style of Amos is close to popular stereotype; Jeremiah's style is verbally volatile, ranging from euphoric and ecstatic reverie to wailing complaint to sarcastic, even vitriolic taunting (he is the Mercutio of the prophets); the style of Daniel (part 1) is as balanced, measured, and temperate as that of a seasoned scholar; Hosea's is passionate, lyrical, and, appropriately enough to his situation, dramatic. Ezekiel and Isaiah, like Micaiah, are masters of irony. And all of them use devices of patterning and rhythm, repetition and refrain, to build up a sense of interrelatedness and emphasis in their message.

Beyond these differences, however, there is a stylistic feature more or less common to the prophets which is so much part and parcel of the character of Hebrew prophecy that it deserves our careful attention. What I am referring to is really a matter of tone and mood. As even the character of the few examples given here will illustrate, most readers are inclined to think first of the accusatory voice in prophetic literature, and to think of the style of the prophets as being largely in the line of Jeremiah's and Amos's condemnations and predictions of doom. This is natural and, to a point, entirely appropriate. For it is the prophet's *vocation* after all to announce God's judgment of his people for their sins and to proclaim his Law and obedience to it as the only remedy against sin's consequences.

The tone and mood of such proclamations are thus not to be

imagined as reflecting high dudgeon on the part of the prophet himself; rather, the tone and mood are attributed to God in his character as an offended Lord, a betrayed lover, a slandered judge: the voice is that of an offended party to a covenant, and it expresses anger toward those who have breached and turned away from the covenant relationship. Since the offended party is God, the aggrievement is not an idle matter. The prophets spend much of their time denouncing offenses and predicting judgment.

But this is far from a complete picture. Indeed, if it were, readers over the centuries would almost surely have found these books too much to bear. In fact, the style of prophetic books has also two sides, two moods — even in the grammatical sense — to match the dualistic nature of the conversation to which they are enjoined by their Author. This is well illustrated in Isaiah. An early example comes at the beginning of chapter 11, where after several chapters of condemnation in which God's judgment is seen always in its condemnatory character, there comes a refreshing wind (*ruāh,* v. 2) of transformation. Suddenly, the prophet's testimony to God's judgment is presented in a compassionate, hopeful tone. Until chapter 11, the concept of this witness of judgment against the people has been expressed only in the imperative and indicative mood *(ādāh).* It is a "testimony of accusation." In this context, the reader or hearer is driven to despair at the coming of such bad news. Now, there is a new breath; that other side of the Spirit of the Lord speaks, and the expectation of judgment is transformed into a hope of remission, release, and comfort. The announcement of judgment is now not *ādāh* (imperative and indicative) but *teudah* (subjunctive and optative).[15] Not only God's justice, but also his integrity (vv. 4, 5) is to be expressed, and in this word, the tyranny of that purely causal syntax of history is subverted by a radically compensatory promise of future redemption. In such a vision of life, "the wolf lives with the lamb . . . the calf and the lion cub feed together, with a little boy to lead them." The mood is one of play, in a world where all things are possible — a harkening back to that

15. This break in the mood of the text has been observed by George Steiner in his *After Babel: Aspects of Language and Translation* (Oxford: Oxford University Press, 1975), 146-47. His observations here are more useful to the reader's sense of the rhetorical power of the text than are conventional efforts to account for the shift of mood in chap. 11 by appeal to another author for the second half of the chapter.

very first conversation, between Adam and Eve and God in the garden. The shift from imperative and indicative directive to subjunctive and optative possibility is a movement from a world of things given, whose consequences we must simply accept, to a new world in which "we may" become something other, and in which "we can" rejoin the divine conversation. That is, the dramatic shift of tone and mood which so characterizes a book like Isaiah mirrors the shift from one order of meaning, or syntax, to another — from the determinism of the surface text to the open world of the text within, "reading" as it "writes" the syntax of memory and dream. The shift is a reminder, as Martin Buber puts it, that in prophetic biblical texts behind every proclamation of disaster a message of consolation lies hidden.[16]

It is this feature then, at every level — rhetorical, grammatical, logical and stylistic — which is the irreducible contribution of the prophets to Hebrew literature, the central content of the unfolding "conversation" in which they participate. For it is not their proclamation of warning alone which privileges their place in the canon of Scripture and in the great tradition of Western literature, but also conveyance of a promise of consolation. This promise signals both their faithful relationship to the Book, and their commitment to the reader's need for an avenue of hope, hope beyond the despair we feel and peace beyond the tyranny of marching history.

After the rhetoric of the divine conversation has been played out for thirty-five chapters over the pattern of a crumbling kingdom's refusal to learn from history, Isaiah includes a three-chapter narrative from the regency of Hezekiah which illustrates, in précis, the whole sad course of forgetfulness which the divine Author, through the mouths of his prophets, is lamenting. At the end of it, well begun though he was, Hezekiah has become so preoccupied with himself and so obtuse to the hearing he has had of the Lord that it is sufficient consolation for him merely that destruction will fall on his children and not upon himself. "Oh good," he says, when hearing Isaiah's prophecy of the destruction soon to come, "at least peace and security will last through my own lifetime" (39:8). In Hezekiah's very response we see why it is that doom is falling. Despair lies heavily over the text.

But then comes that other mood, that shift in the tone of the

16. Martin Buber, *The Prophetic Faith* (New York: Harper & Row, 1949), 103.

Author's voice. It is a reiteration of the prophet's call, his call to be a *nabi'*. And what it says is heard gladly the world over whenever People of the Book are overwhelmed with any kind of imperative, indicative reading of our sorrowful world:

> Comfort ye, comfort ye my people, saith your God. Speak ye comfortably to Jerusalem, and cry unto her, that her warfare is accomplished, that her iniquity is pardoned: for she hath received of the Lord's hand double for all her sins.
>
> (Isa. 40:1-2, KJV)

When we read the Hebrew prophets we are reading in the ebb and flow, the give and take, of a conversation between earth and heaven. If we are to read well, the writers suggest, we must apprentice ourselves to the larger conversation as we find it in the scriptural canon. For their point is everywhere the same: though men and women forget, though they lose the language or stop their hearing, the divine Author does not forget. His Word remains forever, and even in the midst of the ruins of Babylon, his voice is speaking still: "Did you not know?" "Had you not heard?" (Isaiah projects God's voice as both a plea and a taunt.) "Was it not told you from the beginning?" (Isa. 40:21).

Accordingly, the message of the prophets remains the message of the Torah:

> The secret things belong to the Lord our God, but the revealed things belong to us and to our children forever, to observe all the words of this law. When all these things have happened to you, the blessings and the curses that I have set before you, if you call them to mind among all the nations where the Lord your God has driven you, and return to the Lord your God . . . then the Lord your God will restore your fortunes and have compassion on you, gathering you again. . . .
>
> (Deut. 29:29–30:3)

> I call heaven and earth to witness against you today that I have set before you life and death, blessings and curses. Choose life so that you and your descendants may live.
>
> (Deut. 30:19)

So ends the reading of the Torah, and so also concludes the prophets. The collection of the twelve minor prophets summarizes the concern of all Hebrew prophetic literature in a characteristic appeal for ethical praxis, and for seeing that praxis as having its roots in the Law:

> Remember the Law of my servant Moses to whom at Horeb I prescribed laws and customs for the whole of Israel. Know that I am going to send you Elijah the prophet before my day comes, that great and terrible day. He shall turn the hearts of fathers towards their children and the hearts of children towards their fathers, lest I come and strike the land with a curse.
>
> (Mal. 3:22-24, Jerusalem)[17]

Jesus

Over the page from the last words of Malachi in the Old Testament, the Christian New Testament begins with "An account of the genealogy of Jesus the Messiah, the son of David, the son of Abraham" (Matt. 1:1). To understand the impact of Jesus Christ upon the literary consciousness of his world — indeed the subsequent Christian world — one must understand him not only as the embodiment of a universal principle or eternal utterance, but as indeed a living, breathing Jewish workman, a man with a Jewish family tree and Jewish textual tradition; the carpenter's son, Jesus of Nazareth. It is this mundane and very specific historicity, in one dimension, coupled with his extraordinary history in another, that grounds for all Christendom the meaning of his life and his words, as well as his death and resurrection.

17. It is the rhetorical coherence of the Bible which, despite the parsing of modern form criticism, has continued to characterize its literary appreciation. In the principles of reiteration and envelope structure, illustrated here, we see why it is that a literary critic such as Northrop Frye can rightly claim, for his purposes, that the Bible "has influenced Western imagination as a unity" and that "Wherever we stop, the unity of the Bible as a whole is an assumption underlying any part of it" (*The Great Code*, xiii; 62). Frye attributes this to what he calls "implicit metaphor"; I have here characterized the ground of unity as explicit and rhetorical, the result of a reiterated ethical vision.

If this ordinariness of a mundane historical existence is hard for modern intellectuals to square with the idea of God, it was apparently not less difficult for many among Jesus' contemporaries, most of whom were not in our sense of the term intellectuals. Nowhere is their experience of dissonance between the proclamation of Jesus — the way in which he presents his claim upon his hearers — and the physical person of Jesus, more apparent than in the sabbath scene of his reading a passage from the *nebi'im*, the prophets, as it is recorded by Luke (4:16ff):

> When he came to Nazareth, where he had been brought up, he went to the synagogue on the sabbath day, as was his custom. He stood up to read, and the scroll of the prophet Isaiah was given to him. He unrolled the scroll and found the place where it was written:
>
> > "The Spirit of the Lord is upon me,
> > because he has anointed me to bring good news to the poor.
> > He has sent me to proclaim release
> > to the captives and recovery of sight
> > to the blind,
> > to let the oppressed go free,
> > to proclaim the year of the Lord's favor."
>
> And he rolled up the scroll, gave it back to the attendant, and sat down. The eyes of all in the synagogue were fixed on him. Then he began to say to them, "Today this scripture has been fulfilled in your hearing." All spoke well of him and were amazed at the gracious words that came from his mouth.

The gracious words of Jesus, added to those of Isaiah, are not recorded for us by Luke except in the initial and perhaps summarizing phrase: "Today this Scripture has been fulfilled in your hearing." The précis, however, is more than sufficient to explain what follows, as the congregation begins to shift its focus from the gracious words of Jesus to what they can only regard as the oddity, even impropriety, that such words should proceed from the mouth of a man who is, after all, but a fellow villager. Then, in dawning recognition of the messianic character of the Isaiah passage he has applied to himself, they begin to feel doubly scandalized:

They said, "Is not this Joseph's son?" He said to them, "Doubtless you will quote to me this proverb, 'Doctor, cure yourself!' And you will say, 'Do here also in your hometown the things that we have heard you did at Capernaum.'" And he said, "Truly I tell you, no prophet is accepted in the prophet's hometown. But the truth is, there were many widows in Israel in the time of Elijah, when the heaven was shut up three years and six months, and there was a severe famine over all the land; yet Elijah was sent to none of them except to a widow at Zarephath in Sidon. There were also many lepers in Israel in the time of the prophet Elisha, and none of them was cleansed except Naaman the Syrian." When they heard this, all in the synagogue were filled with rage. They got up, drove him out of the town, and led him to the brow of the hill on which their town was built, so that they might hurl him off the cliff. (vv. 22-29)

From hospitable acceptance to dismissal with murderous intent in a few minutes, the reaction of Jesus' hometown neighbors to a perceived incommensurability between his evidently spirit-filled words and his just as evidently homespun humanity is, in both its poles of feeling and course of action, metonymic for Jesus' prophetic reception and fate at the hands of his countrymen more generally. But the means by which Jesus declares himself to them is similarly a metonym, for what is absolutely characterisitic about Jesus' ministry and message is that from first to last he situates himself temporally in the world by reference to the enduring Word of God. He, who wrote no book, is above all to be understood as a "man of the book" — explicable and not indefinitely mysterious, predictable even if unprecedented, in terms of the Scriptures by which all of his Jewish hearers would have claimed at some level to order their own lives.

Fulfilling the Law and the Prophets

The teaching of Jesus is therefore not, in the measure an untutored reader might expect, fundamentally novel. In fact, his use of Hebrew Scriptures in numerous places is such as to make him appear to his hearers as emphatically conservative with respect to the text:

Do not think that I have come to abolish the law or the prophets; I have come not to abolish but to fulfill. For truly I tell you, until heaven and earth pass away, not one letter, not one stroke of a letter, will pass from the law until all is accomplished. Therefore, whoever breaks one of the least of these commandments, and teaches others to do the same, will be called least in the kingdom of heaven; but whoever does them and teaches them will be called great in the kingdom of heaven. For I tell you, unless your righteousness exceeds that of the scribes and Pharisees, you will never enter the kingdom of heaven.

(Matt. 5:17-20)

The words of Jesus, however filled with grace, are not by him construed as thereby novel with respect to the Law. In fact, so far is this from being the case that, like the prophets, he continually recurs to the Law to characterize such fundamental distinctions as that between true and false righteousness.[18] In this his method as well as his language is transparently evocative of the prophets.

It is understandable therefore that many among his hearers thought either that Jesus was a prophet (Mark 8:27; Matt. 21:11) or that in him "John the Baptist, Elijah, or one of the prophets had returned" (Matt. 16:14). His disciples particularly saw him in this way (e.g., John 1:45). In the narrative of the transfiguration (Mark 9:2-8) in which "upon a high mountain apart" Jesus is seen by Peter, James, and John transfigured, clothed in dazzling white, conversing with Moses and Elijah, Jesus' full conversation with the Law (Moses) and the prophets (Elijah) is dramatized; when Moses and Elijah at last disappear and the voice from the cloud (v. 7) says "This is my Son, the Beloved; listen to him!" an order of transferred authority confirming Jesus' claim to have come to fulfill the Law and the

18. A repeated rebuke of the Pharisees and Sadducees is that in the intensity of their concern for fine points (most at issue, perhaps, in their disputes with one another), they fail to apply the plain moral sense of the law where that seems most called for (e.g., Matt. 12:5; 23:23; John 7:19-23). But cf. here the discussions by D. Daube, *The New Testament and Rabbinic Judaism* (London: Athlone, 1965); Jacob Neusner, *Rabbinic Traditions about the Pharisees* (Leiden: Brill, 1971); E. P. Sanders, *Jesus and Judaism* (Philadelphia: Fortress, 1985), and his *Jewish Law from Jesus to the Mishnah* (Philadelphia: Trinity Press, 1990).

prophets is divinely verbalized. For the disciples, the writers of the New
Testament, and the early church, there was no question but that the claims
of Jesus were comprehensible in terms of the Hebrew Scriptures and that
they could be tested against those Scriptures. Indeed, Jesus regularly encourages this confidence (e.g., Luke 16:16-17; Matt. 26:56; 5:12). Conversely, reluctance to believe in him, even in the evidence of his resurrected
body before their very eyes, causes Jesus to say to the disciples on the road
to Emmaus: "Oh, how foolish you are, and how slow of heart to believe all
that the prophets have declared!

> Was it not necessary that the Messiah should suffer these things
> and then enter into his glory?" Then beginning with Moses and
> all the prophets, he interpreted to them the things about himself
> in all the scriptures.
>
> (Luke 24:25-27)

For Jesus, the witness of the Scriptures is sufficient to explain him, and
to validate his message. Further, in the case of those who reject the
Scriptures, not even his resurrection will be likely to persuade. In Jesus'
parable of Lazarus and the rich man, Abraham refuses the rich man's
cry out of Hades for comfort and special persuasion for his kinsmen,
saying, "If they do not listen to Moses and the prophets, neither will
they be convinced even if someone rises from the dead" (Luke 16:31).

This does not mean that Jesus intended to be seen as yet another
in the succession of the prophets, or simply as a second Moses. The
force of the textual comparisons by which he illuminates his own life
and sayings — that distinctive feature of New Testament writing we
have come to call typology — is similar in method to the way in which
the prophets read Torah, but it is not identical. For example, when Jesus
gives his Sermon on the Mount (Matt. 5–7), the analogy with Moses
receiving the Law upon Sinai is certainly present in Matthew's mind as
he recounts the sermon — he stresses the location (5:1; 8:1) and identifies Jesus in his teaching "as one having authority, and not as [the]
scribes" (7:29). The parallels are most obviously invited by Jesus himself,
to begin with by his assurance that he purports not to abolish but fulfill
the Law and the prophets (5:17-18), but then emphatically by his *intensification* of notable provisions of the Law delivered upon Sinai: "You
have heard that it was said, 'You shall not commit adultery.' But I say to

you that everyone who looks at a woman with lust has already committed adultery with her in his heart" (5:27-28). Following the Beatitudes (5:2-12) with the exception of brief passages such as his model prayer ("Our Father" [6:9ff]), almost everything else in the sermon expounds or comments upon central passages from the Mosaic Law, and the so-called "Golden Rule" (7:12) makes an explicit reference for understanding and validation back to traditional scriptural sources: "In everything do to others as you would have them do to you; for this is the law and the prophets." Yet whereas Moses, like other *nebi'im,* reports what "God the Lord has commanded," expressing the divine Law, so to speak, in quotation marks, Jesus utters each instance of intensification or escalation of a principle in the Law by referring the authority directly to himself: "But I say to you . . ." (5:22, 28, 32, 34, 39, 44, etc.). As Goppelt and others have pointed out, no one scripturally literate in Jesus' audience could fail to appreciate the significance of this simultaneous referral and transference in Jesus' claims to be the fulfillment of "all that the law and the prophets have declared."[19]

It is his connection to the prophets which perhaps most vividly situates Jesus in this textually inscribed *modus vivendi.* We see this centrally in Jesus' preaching, which, so much in the fashion of the prophets, is directed toward repentance. Even in his dramatic cleansing of the Temple (Mark 11:15-19) his expulsion of the money changers recalls both the tone and the actions of the prophets. In this episode Jesus seems, as Goppelt has shown clearly, to have had Jeremiah in mind (Jer. 7:1ff; 26:1ff), borrowing the phrase "den of robbers" from the prophet's great sermon on repentance (Jer. 7:11; Mark 11:17).[20] Yet what the prophets promised was restoration of a purified temple worship in the messianic age, and Jesus demonstrates his accord with this expectation by immediately quoting Isaiah 56:7: "My house shall be called a house of prayer for all peoples" (cf. Mark 11:17). Jesus hurls Isaiah's word about hypocritical lip service (Isa. 29:13) at his own contemporar-

19. Mark 3:6. Leonhard Goppelt's *Typos: The Typological Interpretation of the Old Testament in the New* was first published in Germany in 1939. Goppelt's emphasis on the rootedness of the New Testament in the Hebrew Scriptures was unpopular in pre-war Germany for obvious reasons; since then, however, his book has come to be regarded as seminal. The English translation is by Donald H. Madvig (Grand Rapids: Eerdmans, 1982). See here 68ff.

20. Goppelt, *Typos,* 66.

ies as if it were written with them in mind (Mark 7:6);[21] he repudiates
the legalism of the Pharisees by quoting Hosea (6:6; cf. Matt. 12:7; 9:13).
Here again, Jesus speaks not only as one who is immersed in what the
prophets have written by way of judgment, but also as the voice of the
prophet's wounded Lover, the God of Israel himself:

> Therefore I have hewn them by the prophets,
> I have killed them by the words of my mouth,
> and my judgment goes forth as the light.
> For I desire steadfast love and not sacrifice,
> the knowledge of God rather than burnt offerings.
>
> (Hos. 6:5-6)

Yet as the one who in his person — his physical human presence
— bears the Word, Jesus appreciates from the beginning the axiomatic
character of the prophet's own fate. Of the eight passages in Mark which
explicitly refer to the Old Testament prophets, six — all spoken by Jesus
— refer to the suffering and death of the Messiah.[22] Moreover, the
prophets' repeated experience that the people have "eyes to see and see
not," "ears to hear and hear not" (Ps. 115:5-6; 135:16-17; Jer. 5:21; Ezek.
12:2; cf. Mark 8:18) is not only reiterated in the ministry of Jesus, but
typologically brought to final fulfillment in his rejection and execution.
The "hardening of the heart" exemplified not only by Pharaoh but by
the people of God who remain disobedient to his Word (Isa. 6:9-10) is
the subject of many of his own parables, especially those directed against
the scribes and Pharisees — those whose institutional control of the
"law and the prophets" seems to mean that their own texts no longer
speak to them, as we now say, in ways they can hear.

Jesus quotes the famous Isaiah passage (6:9ff) in responding to his
disciples' question about why he so often speaks in figurative or indirect
discourse (parables) when asked a question which seems to require a
propositional answer (or dogma). According to the version in Mark
(4:11ff; cf. Luke 8:10), his use of figurative discourse is to ensure that
those who are unwilling to hear his call of repentance may confirm their

---

21. Ibid.

22. Ibid., 77. See here the valuable study by Patrick Grant, *Reading the New Testament* (Grand Rapids: Eerdmans, 1987).

wish; according to Matthew (13:13) the people are indeed already hardened, just as Isaiah had prophesied.[23] In either case, Jesus' contextualizing of his own call to repentance, and his association of those comfortable in their possession of the Law with a general rejection of repentance, clearly finds its precedent and reference for understanding in the previous writings of the prophets. The parable of the wicked tenants of the vineyard (Matt. 21:33-45; cf. Mark 12:1-12) links the fate of the prophets (the servants of the absent Lord who come to ask for the rent which is due) with his own, precipitating the ultimate form of rejection by those of hardened heart: "This is the heir; come, let us kill him and get his inheritance" (Matt. 21:38). The chief priests and Pharisees understand their own connection with the wicked tenants — those who have always abused prophets who call sinners to repentance (v. 45) — but despite their rage they are unable to arrest Jesus because the crowds also recognize Jesus' mode of repentance discourse, and so have "regarded him as a prophet" (v. 46).

When later Jesus rebukes the scribes and Pharisees at length, he encourages the people to do whatever is actually taught them by these religious leaders out of the Law itself (23:2-3) while at the same time avoiding at all costs an imitation of the Pharisees' own actual mode of life. That is, he refers them to the text of the Law rather than to its present mode of religious representation. Unsparingly, he calls the Pharisees and scribes themselves "blind guides" (v. 16) and "hypocrites" (vv. 15, 23, 27, etc.). Apparent devotées to religious tradition, they are willing to honor the tombs of the prophets, but not the prophets' words — their call to repentance:

> Woe to you, scribes and Pharisees, hypocrites! For you build the tombs of the prophets and decorate the graves of the righteous, and you say, "If we had lived in the days of our ancestors, we would not have taken part with them in shedding the blood of the proph-

23. Goppelt observes: "Matthew places the word of Isaiah in the mouth of Jesus as a kind of fulfillment citation so that he designates the hardening of the people as the fulfillment of that prediction. Mark, however, has preserved what is clearly the more original form of the introduction. In it Jesus simply alludes — although unmistakably — to the word of the prophet indicating that what was said in that passage, as well as in many other places in the prophets (cf. Jer. 5:21; Ezek. 12:2; Deut. 29:3), is now fulfilled typologically. The original is not important" (*Typos*, 78).

ets." Thus you testify against yourselves that you are descendants
of those who murdered the prophets. Fill up, then, the measure of
your ancestors. You snakes, you brood of vipers! How can you
escape being sentenced to hell?

(Matt. 23:29-34)

Jesus challenges even the scribes' and Pharisees' sense of genre by
repeatedly treating the Psalms of David as though they were part of the
prophetic tradition formally.[24] When, in a culminating moment in his
own reiteration of the rhetorical argument of the prophets, Jesus asks
the Pharisees at last, "What do you think of the Messiah? Whose son is
he?" (Matt. 22:41-42), they reply with self-assured accuracy, "the Son of
David." Jesus' riposte does not discount the literal probity of their answer: as the genealogies in Matthew (1:1-17) and Luke (3:23-38) attest,
the son of Mary and, "as was thought" of her kinsman husband Joseph,
traces his line of human ancestry directly back to David, as for the
Messiah it was to be. (To the Pharisees' dismay, hundreds — perhaps
thousands — of Palestinian Jews had already begun to voice the question: "Is this not the Son of David?" [Matt. 12:23; cf. Matt. 9:27; 15:22;
20:30-31; cf. Mark 10:47-48; Luke 18:38-39]). Rather, he calls into question their merely naturalistic, merely historic sense of the derivation to
whomever they imagine it might be applied:

He said to them, "How is it then that David by the Spirit calls him
Lord, saying 'The Lord said to my Lord, "Sit at my right hand until
I put your enemies under your feet" '? If David calls him Lord, how
can he be his son?"

(Matt. 22:43-45)

24. The usual genre division in the Hebrew canon was threefold — Torah (Pentateuch), Nebi'im (prophets), and Kethubim (writings), of which the Psalms were in the
last group, first among the Hagiographa. While the strong sense that David should be
regarded as a prophet in Christian tradition — especially of the late Middle Ages and
among Calvinists at the time of the Reformation — relates directly to Matt. 22:41-42,
the Babylonian Talmud in arguing for the inspiration of all Scripture by the Spirit of
God extends the designation of "prophet" to all canonical writers of Scripture (Baba
Bathra 14b). Still, the 2nd century B.C. baraitha (unauthorized gloss) to Baba Bathra
lists the Psalms among the Kethubim, not among the prophets. See G. A. Marx and
G. Dalman, Traditio Rabbinorum Veterrimi (1884), trans. in H. E. Ryle, The Canon of
the Old Testament (London: MacMillan, 1892; 1899), 284ff.

At this the Pharisees are dumbfounded. Of the distinction between *kronos* and *kairos,* temporalities and the genuinely prophetic sense, they know nothing: "No one was able to give him an answer, nor from that day did anyone dare to ask him questions" (v. 46).

Each aspect of Jesus' prediction of his passion — his suffering, death and resurrection — has its scriptural basis in the typology of the prophets.[25] The day of his atonement appears as the *bayyōm hahû* of which they spoke. But of all his messianic quotations from the Old Testament, more than half come from the Psalms, the bedrock text of Jewish liturgy. Jesus begins his ministry with Psalm 2:7, and dies on the cross with Psalm 22 on his lips. If the genealogy of Jesus with which the New Testament begins (Matt. 1:2-17) traces the human ancestry of Jesus back to David the psalmist in such a way as to suggest, before introducing the doctrine of the Virgin birth, that Jesus is to be recognized as of "David's royal line" — a key messianic qualification — Jesus' complete immersion in the words of the Psalmist make him seem a "true" son of David, almost a David *redivivus* re-presenting his words as a living Word. As Luke records the final commissioning of the disciples by Jesus at his ascension, the notion of fulfillment explicitly extends to the Psalms as well:

> Then he said to them, "These are my words that I spoke to you while I was still with you — that everything written about me in the law of Moses, the prophets, and the psalms must be fulfilled." Then he opened their minds to understand the scriptures. . . .
>
> (Luke 24:44-45)

Yet the Matthean genealogy also reaches back beyond David to Abraham, linking the entire lineage with the call to Abraham and the original tradition of covenant faithfulness. Jesus is the descendant also of Abraham; he is the one in whom the original covenant promises made to Abraham are at last fulfilled.[26] This is to be a point of abiding significance for Christian notions of fulfillment of the old covenant. It is developed later in the writings of Paul and the Epistle to the Hebrews, and remains central in the reading of the Old Testament narratives by

25. Goppelt, *Typos,* 91-92.
26. See Goppelt, *Typos,* 84, n. 103 for a useful list of parallel passages.

the major patristic exponents of Christianity, including notably Ambrose, Augustine, and Jerome. If the cryptic warning note in the last words of the prophet Malachi (4:5, quoted above) concerning the prophetic preaching of repentance — figured there as a return of Elijah "before the great and terrible day of the Lord" — could be seen by Jesus' contemporaries as fulfilled in John the Baptist's preparing the way for Christ (Matt. 11:9ff; Mark 9:13; Luke 1:16-17), so too the redemptive healing of the breach between the "generations" this repentance was to effect, reestablishing the covenant continuity, could be seen as the coming at last of the fruit of the tree of Jesse, David's "royal son." It is no accident that in later Christian ordering of the books of the Bible Malachi was printed last in the Old Testament, immediately preceding the genealogy of Jesus in the first chapter of Matthew.[27]

The "Word from the Beginning" in John's Prologue

The opening of the first chapter of John signals the special character of this Gospel as distinct from the synoptic Gospels with which we have thus far been concerned, Matthew, Mark, and Luke. Whereas the burden of demonstration in those texts was placed upon Jesus as fulfillment of the Law and the prophets, and quotation from Jesus' own typological reading of the Old Testament carried the bulk of the burden, in John's Gospel the prologue sets out in a strikingly different way the character of Jesus' historic person as fulfillment of the providential grand design for human salvation. If Matthew goes back as far as Abraham, Mark (1:1-3) to Isaiah (40:1-3), and Luke only to the birth of John the Baptist and the annunciation to Mary, John's prologue will carry the scripturally literate reader back in the text as far as the very opening words of Genesis: "In the beginning God created the heavens and the earth. . . ."

Writing self-consciously for more hellenized readers, perhaps, than the synoptic writers, John makes every effort to stress that that which

27. In traditional (tannaitic) ordering of Tanakh, Malachi (a title which means "my messenger"; cf. radical in *shaliach*, "sent one") is last of the prophets and thus precedes all of the *Kethubim* or "writings" which begin with the Psalms and end with 2 Chronicles. The order reflected in early Christian Bibles reverses the order of the *Nebi'im* and *Kethubim* precisely so that the closing words of Malachi concerning Elijah become transitional to the New Testament.

can only be seen as historical event — not just the covenant and broken history of Israel but also the physical life, ministry, death, and resurrection of Jesus — is nevertheless the ultimate demonstration of the *archē* (origin, principle), *dikē* (justice), and *sophia* (wisdom) of the universe, so long the objects of philosophical reflection in the hellenized world. Yet, though he writes for a Jewish audience in which many were inclined to hellenistic and ultimately proto-gnostic forms of abstraction of truth from history, the form of his Gospel address to them is emphatically a typical Jewish insistence on the concrete historicity of truth, and the conformity therefore of the actual life (words and work) of Jesus with the very origin of the universe, and with the principle, "wisdom," which sustains it.

John's prologue is probably not, as has sometimes been supposed, directly influenced by gnosticism.[28] More demonstrably, it might be construed by early readers as a corrective to gnostic impulses which had begun to manifest themselves in hellenized Judaism, particularly after the time of Philo. Unpacking the intricacies of recent scholarship in this area is not an appropriate task for the present chapter,[29] but some account of the relation of John's prologue to the climate of later hellenistic and particularly Neoplatonic theorizing is necessary.

28. It was, on the other hand, very appealing to gnostics. In fact, the first commentary on John's Gospel was by the gnostic Heracleon, leading Irenaeus to demonstrate at length its essential nongnostic character. See W. Von Loewenich, *Das Johannes verstandnis in zweiten Jahrhundert* (Wittenburg: Luther-Verlag, 1932); also Elaine H. Pagels, *The Johanine Gospel in Gnostic Exegesis: Heracleon's Commentary on John* (Nashville: Abingdon, 1973).

29. R. H. Strachan's view in *The Fourth Gospel* (London: Student Christian Movement Press, 1941), 44ff, that the Gospel was intended as a polemic against gnosticism, specifically Docetism, is now regarded as somewhat extreme, while the views of F. C. Grant, in *The Gospels, Their Origin and Their Growth* (New York: Harper, 1957), 163ff, like those of E. F. Scott, *The Fourth Gospel, Its Purpose and Theology* (Edinburgh: T & T Clark, 1908), 86-103, and Heinz Becker, *Die Reden des Johannes evangeliums und der Stil der gnostischen Offenbarungs reden* (Gottingen: Vandenhoek and Ruprecht, 1956), and of course his teacher Bultmann, *Das Evangelium Johannes* (Berlin: Töpelmann, 1953) that the author himself was part of a group of early Christian gnostic-mystics, has been discredited. See also C. F. D. Moule, *The Birth of the New Testament* (London: Blackwell, 1962); also E. R. Goodenough, "John: A Primitive Gospel," *Journal of Biblical Literature* 64 (1945): 145-82, esp. 164-65; and the articles of C. K. Barrett and J. Munck in W. Klassen and G. F. Snyder, *Current Issues in New Testament Interpretation* (New York: Harper, 1962), 210-33; 234-38.

By far the most influential figure in hellenized Judaism was Philo of Alexandria. Philo's commentary on the Hebrew Scriptures is heavily freighted with Greek philosophical concepts and terminology. Scholars have often noted in connection with John's language in his prologue striking similarities to Philo's language.[30] John says, "In the beginning [archē] was the Word [logos]"; Philo calls God's "first-born" the "Word [logos] . . . who is called 'the beginning' [archē]." Philo identifies the principal Word of God with the name God (theon; theos) and Lord (kyrios); the instrument or agency of creation in Philo is the "word of God"; the light is said to be a source of life (cf. John 1:4); God's Word is the "human being [anthropos] after his image" (cf. John 1:14); and the divine Word is the "image of God."[31] Some of Philo's language is only apparently hellenistic: the Wisdom of Solomon begins with praise of sophia (Wisdom 1:4; 9:4) but concludes with the agency of wisdom, logos (Wisdom 18:15). Most persuasively pertinent is the personified Wisdom (Heb. chōkma; Gk. sophia) of Proverbs 7–9, especially as she speaks in Proverbs 8:22-36:

> The Lord created me at the beginning [archē, LXX] of his work,
> the first of his acts of long ago.
> Ages ago I was set up,
> at the first, before the beginning of the earth.
> When there were no depths I was brought forth,
> when there were no springs abounding with water.
> Before the mountains had been shaped,
> before the hills, I was brought forth —
> when he had not yet made earth and fields,
> or the world's first bits of soil.
> When he established the heavens, I was there,
> when he drew a circle on the face of the deep,

30. For an up-to-date survey of the scholarship on Philo in relationship to the New Testament, and an excellent study in its own right, see Craig A. Evans, Word and Glory: On the Exegetical and Theological Background of John's Prologue (Sheffield: JSOT Press, supp. series no. 89, 1993), 100-145.

31. Texts with translations given in Evans, 101; a reliable translation of all cited passages in The Works of Philo, trans. C. D. Yonge (Peabody, Mass.: Hendrikson, 1993) — a revised and updated version of Yonge's classic but not entirely dependable 1854 translation.

when he made firm the skies above,
when he established the fountains of the deep,
when he assigned to the sea its limit,
so that the waters might not transgress his command,
when he marked out the foundations of the earth,
then was I beside him, like a master worker;
and I was daily his delight,
rejoicing before him always,
rejoicing in his inhabited world
and delighting in the human race.
And now, my children, listen to me:
happy are those who keep my ways.
Hear instruction and be wise,
and do not neglect it.
Happy is the one who listens to me,
watching daily at my gates,
waiting beside my doors.
For whoever finds me finds life
and obtains favor from the Lord;
but those who miss me injure themselves;
all who hate me love death.

It is clear enough that in John's "logos from the beginning" we are to understand a relationship between God's initial word in creation (Heb. *dab'ar*) and his final word in recreation, so to speak, the work of redemption effected in Christ. But the resonance of this notion of the "Word from the beginning" is greatly deepened and enriched by the "word of Wisdom" as it enters Jewish thought through the writing associated with Solomon. That the Greek word *logos* is in Philo a rendering of the supreme articulation of divine Wisdom as creative agency drawing on both Genesis and the wisdom texts seems fairly clear; that this synthesis could also have been latent in the minds of literate readers of John's Gospel seems equally likely.[32]

The kind of agency suggested in Proverbs 8 has, of course, parallels in Platonic discourse; one need only reflect upon Plato's *Timaeus* and the cosmology there traced. In Plato the realm of Being, the ideal

32. Evans, 112-13.

("divine") order of perfect knowledge (Form, Idea), transmits itself to the transient and ephemeral world of becoming (images, shadowy tangible realities) through the (not very clearly defined) agency of the demiurge. That is, for Plato the inferior ·visible world is postulated as a kind of "object" predicated upon the invisible "world" of pure ideas as Subject; the demiurge mediates between the two in what remains, for Plato, a largely mysterious fashion.[33] Similarly with Philo's *logos:* "The incorporeal world is set off and separated from the visible one by the mediating Logos as by a veil."[34]

Here we can most clearly see, however, that the crucial element for John is unparalleled in Philo — or Plato either, for that matter. For John the logos does not as idea or as agency remain abstract, but in fact becomes a concrete, living historical being.[35] Indeed, identification of the Word from the beginning, the *logon archē*, with a living person is nowhere anticipated in the Wisdom books of the Hebrew Bible. And perhaps almost as tellingly for John's hellenized readers, the implication of the Word incarnate in Jesus for human salvation, for knowledge of the truth, stands in radical contradistinction to the epistemological assumptions of hellenistic philosophy. For Plato, as a relevant comparison, knowledge of the truth was to be had by a diligent ascent from the "cave" of mere shadowy appearances (this world's physical reality), of which we can have mere "opinion" or "belief," through a process of careful and tutored dialectic which will eventually lead us up out of the cave into the light of *gnosis* and *dianoia* — definitive intelligible truth. But in the prologue to John's Gospel the suggestion is not that a privileged and intellectually gifted few may, by their private efforts of mental struggle, rise up out of the cave of mortal darkness into the realm of eternal light, but rather that "the true light, which enlightens *everyone,* [is] coming into the world" (1:9). The "life which is the light of *all people*" (v. 4) descends into the metaphorical cave — not just the cave of the Bethlehem stable (though that historical event must have

33. Trans. F. M. Cornford for the Library of Liberal Arts series (Indianapolis and New York: Bobbs-Merrill, 1959).

34. *Quaestiones in Exodum* 2.68 (sup. Exod. 25:21); cf. *Op. Mund.* 5.20.

35. See Evans, 104-5; also R. H. Tobin, "The Prologue to John and Hellenistic Jewish Speculation," *Catholic Biblical Quarterly* 52 (1990): 252-69; René Girard, "The Logos of Heraclitus and the Logos of John," in *Things Hidden Since the Foundations of the World* (London: Athlone Press, 1978), 263-82.

helped make the point transparent for many) but into all of the clouded unknowing which might be symbolized for a hellenized world by Plato's cave.[36] For historic Christianity the light of truth is obtained not by great and perseverant intellects abstracting *from* the world but by the gift of God's redemptive grace in sending Jesus *into* our common world.

The Incarnation is accordingly for John not really an abstract idea. Nor is it, in the popular sense of the word, a "mystical" or ethereal notion — an emanation of the divine, an angelic visitation or a kind of beatific vision or "illumination." Rather it is the advent of a concrete personal presence, Jesus of Nazareth, Mary's son, the boy who grew up in the carpenter shop of Joseph (his father, "as was thought") in (of all places) lowly Nazareth. Completely unprecedented in any order of hellenic thought is the ordinariness, in this sense, of the "medium" by which the "message" comes — the humble family, the lowly birth, the hidden village life. Yet the message so incarnated is claimed by John to be not less than the very Word of God, from the beginning with him, indeed identical with God (1:1-2) in his eternal glory. To the psalmist's lyrical questions (Ps. 19) about how it is we are to "read" God's declaration of his eternal glory, John answers effectively, "In this man who was our friend, who lived with us our daily life, even such as we are." Like the Law which was given through Moses (1:17), the glory of which the psalmist sang, the restoration of God's glory and truth was entirely a matter of God's doing, not of human effort: "And the Word became flesh and lived among us, and we have seen his glory, the glory as of a father's only son, full of grace and truth" (1:14). Nevertheless, it is still by the most common humane things of this corporeal world — flesh, ordinary life, a father's love for his only child — that we are to see, hear, and come to understand this eternal truth and glory of God.

What the synoptic writers accomplish primarily through the force of historic confirmation in Jesus of "all that the prophets have spoken" — their extended testimony recording in his deeds as well as words

36. G. K. Chesterton in his work of Christian apologetics, *The Everlasting Man* (Garden City, N.Y.: Doubleday, 1955), 171-88, entitles his chapter on the Incarnation, in particular the birth of Jesus in a Bethlehem hillside stable, "The God in the Cave," a figure of speech by which he intends to suggest a Christian response to Plato's allegory.

Jesus' claim to "fulfill the law of the prophets" — John here reinforces by a dramatic identification of Jesus' person with the awesome divine utterance in creation itself. Jesus is not merely known to be the *shaliach* ("sent one") of God through the confirming force of the words of Moses and the prophets in his words, he is also to be seen as the preexistent Word of God which informs all such words and works. The Word from the beginning has heretofore found expression in creation, in the words of men and most articulately in the Law and the prophets (Ps. 19). Now in its ultimate fullness of expression it is revealed as a Person, Jesus of Nazareth. Jesus is like a prophet in speaking what he has been sent to speak (John 12:49-51), but he is unlike the prophets in that the source of the words, the Word from the beginning, actually dwells within him "fully": "the words that I say to you I do not speak on my own but the Father who dwells in me does his works" (John 14:10). Hence, for the disciples to know Jesus is for them "to know [the] Father also" (14:7). Whereas the prophets were mouthpieces for the Word of God by whom "long ago God spoke to our ancestors in many and various ways,"

> . . . in these last days he has spoken to us by a Son, whom he appointed heir of all things, through whom he also created the world. He is the reflection of God's glory and the exact imprint of God's very being, and he sustains all things by his powerful word.
>
> (Heb. 1:1-3)

In emphasizing Jesus' connections to the prophets so strongly, the synoptic writers present him as *ne plus ultra* the "Man of the Book," the "one of whom the prophets have spoken." In emphasizing Jesus' connections to the original utterance of God and to the word of Wisdom by which he sustains the world, John and the author of Hebrews present him as the very Word of God which the book of Scripture has been at pains to "translate," to express and prepare for. "I am the way, and the truth and the life," Jesus says, declaring to his disciples that to have seen him is to have seen the Father (John 14:6-7). In the synoptic Gospels, we see Jesus as the perfect man of God, the suffering servant inscribed from the outset in the text; in John we see him as the Author of the Book itself.

In either case, he is kept before the reader of the New Testament as

Jesus of Nazareth. In all of Jesus' preaching of repentance, word and action are inextricably bound to his person. Repeatedly the decision that he urges upon us concerns his person: "Who do you say that I am?" (Matt. 16:15-16; Mark 8:29; Luke 9:20). And the raison d'être of the texts of the Gospels themselves is accordingly bound to his person: "these are written," John says at last, "so that you may come to believe that Jesus is the Messiah, the Son of God, and that through believing you may have life in his name" (John 20:31).

Each of the Gospels as intertextual argument is thus not merely a reiteration of the prophet's rhetoric, it is an intensification of it, pressed even to the point of a shocking reversal of its expected conclusion. The personal Jesus of the Gospels also speaks to the facts of human rebellion and its consequences and the historical dialectic of human and divine analysis concerning them. And he does so by inviting his present hearers too into a conversation, humanly, reasonably, to set things into perspective (cf. Isa. 1:18). But as with Isaiah's prologue, so with the Gospels — the force of the conversation is to move the interlocutor to a choice. "I have set before you this day life and death; therefore choose life . . ." (Deut. 30:19); as we have seen, the familiar words of Torah are echoed in Isaiah (1:20). But in Jesus' formulation the choice for life is paradoxically to be the choice of death, death to the self: "Except a grain of wheat falls into the ground and dies it remains just a single grain; but if it dies, it bears much fruit. Those who love their life lose it, and those who hate their life in this world will keep it for eternal life" (John 12:24-25). The invitation of Jesus is not, as a hellenized reader might expect, to some pacific state of enlightened self-consciousness, but rather to self-denying, self-sacrificing imitation of his own so starkly mortal praxis: "Take up your cross and follow me" (Matt. 16:24; Mark 8:34; Luke 9:23; cf. Matt. 10:38). Small wonder that there have been so many attempts to theorize away into the harmlessness of a platitude the persistently disturbing presence in the text of the carpenter's son, Jesus of Nazareth.

Saint Paul

For later writers of the New Testament and the whole of subsequent Christendom the gospel which told of Christ's coming was not, like much of what the prophets told their hearers, to such a striking degree "bad news." Rather, the call of Jesus to repentance, so like that of the prophets in many respects, was joined by virtue of the resurrection to an unprecedented emphasis on the *teudah,* the optative word of comfort. For Christians therefore — those to whom Paul could write "If Christ be not resurrected . . . then is your faith in vain" (1 Cor. 15:12-14) — Christ's coming permitted a new order of hope: the Gospel accounts, like the many verbal accounts which ran around the Mediterranean world, were truly to their hearers "good news" (Gk. *euangelion;* Lat. *evangelium*).

Not that this "good news" was unthreatening to established patterns of religious thinking. At its very least, what we might call the "literary theory of Jesus" involved a radical proposal for re-reading the entire Hebrew Scriptures. In this reading, which effectively does become the theory or hermeneutic of St. Paul and the early church, the whole of the Hebrew Scriptures suddenly becomes a *prolepsis,* a text preliminary to another text, dependent for closure and full meaning upon that which is now to come. At one level of imaginative integration — the prophetic anticipation of the messianic Son of David and Israel's final redemption — it might be argued that this re-reading had been inscribed from the beginning in Scripture's text. However, another heuristic reading of Scripture could be racked with frustration and offense. Plainly, by Jesus' death upon the cross, his resurrection, and his ascension, the long anticipated "last days" were seen by his followers as having now only begun, with hope for final closure projected into an indefinite future. At the very least, this dimmed the hope that in Jesus there was for their present oppression any political or social "solution" available.

Yet there is more: for those within the Jewish community who came to see Jesus as the promised Messiah, that the Scriptures could now be seen as the historic and textual preparation for the final and perfect work of God in history made of the Hebrew Scriptures the literary record of their "Old Covenant," or "Old Testament" as it came to be called. For the followers of Jesus — unlike most of their fellow Jews — this designation was not pejorative, for they saw the Old Testament, on the authority of Jesus, as necessarily foundational to the "New Testament in his blood" (Matt. 26:28; Mark 14:24; Luke 22:20; 1 Cor. 11:25). Jesus' own reading of the "Old Testament" thus became the pivot upon which all subsequent Christian reading of the Bible would turn: it provided a single coherent scheme for understanding history and the text, with himself as the focus. As R. T. France observes:

> Such a use of the Old Testament was not only original; it was revolutionary. It was such that a Jew who did not accept it must violently oppose it. It is not surprising that a community founded on this teaching soon found itself irreconcilably divided from those Jews who still looked forward to a Messiah.[37]

New Testament writers after the evangelists — Paul, John, Peter, James, Jude, and the unknown author of the Epistle to the Hebrews — exhibit no significant dependence upon contemporary Jewish ways of reading the Old Testament. They are rather — and emphatically — dependent upon the literary theory of Jesus.[38] This remains true for the early church and, with modifications, for the Western church generally.[39]

The basis of this "literary theory of Jesus" is what has come to be called *typology*, from Paul's original use of the Greek word *typos* "as a term for the prefiguring of the future in prior history."[40] Paul's novel employment of the word seems to derive from its normative use in referring to a "blow" by a hammer or molding instrument; *typos* could signify a struck image such as is produced by the imprint of a mold or seal — the obverse, so to speak, being the finished coinage for which the mold was designed.[41] For Paul, God's actions in the shaping of Israel's history are such *typoi*, the molds or seals from which the life of Jesus and of the church is pressed out in the fabric of the world: in his first letter to the Corinthians Paul writes,

> I do not want you to be unaware, brothers and sisters, that our ancestors were all under the cloud, and all passed through the sea, and all were baptized into Moses in the cloud and in the sea, and

37. *Jesus and the Old Testament* (London: Tyndale Press, 1971), 224. A useful further study is A. T. Hanson's *Jesus Christ in the Old Testament* (London: SPCK, 1965).

38. France echoes Goppelt: "The school in which the writers of the early church learned to use the Old Testament was that of Jesus" (225).

39. See E. E. Ellis, *Prophecy and Hermeneutic in Early Christianity* (Grand Rapids: Eerdmans, 1978).

40. Goppelt, *Typos,* 4-5.

41. Ibid., 5, n. 14.

> all ate the same spiritual food, and all drank the same spiritual
> drink. For they drank from the spiritual rock that followed them,
> and the rock was Christ.
>
> (1 Cor. 10:1-4)

Paul goes on to say that "these things occurred as examples for us" (v. 6),
and as such *typoi* "they were written down to instruct us, on whom the
ends of the ages have come" (v. 11).

This notion of the *typos* as example is further reaching than the
English translation here suggests. In Romans Paul will describe Adam,
the prototype of all fallen humanity, as the *typos*, the "figure" or "type
of the one who was to come" (5:14) — that is, Christ. Christ is the
obverse of Adam, so to speak:

> For since death came through a human being, the resurrection of
> the dead has also come through a human being; for as all die in
> Adam, so all will be made alive in Christ.
>
> (1 Cor. 15:21-22)

The resurrection of Jesus reverses the imprint of death (v. 26), and "in
Christ," bearing now his "image" rather than the image of fallen humanity, the Christian has a hope which transcends that mortal stamp: "Just
as we have borne the image of the man of dust, we will also bear the
image of the man of heaven" (v. 49).

Most of these "hammer-blows" or drop-molds which leave their
redoubtable impression upon the New Testament text derive, as Jean
Daniélou among others has shown,[42] from the book of Exodus. Exodus
is the narrative concerned with Israel's liberation from bondage, exile,

---

42. Jean Daniélou, *From Shadow to Reality: Studies in the Biblical Typology of the
Fathers,* trans. W. Hibberd (Westminster, Md.: Newman, 1961). Cf. Michael Walzer's
Exodus and Revolution (New York: Basic Books, 1985) which argues for the character
of Exodus as a historic template for revolutionary politics — precisely the application
which Jesus and the writers of the New Testament rejected. Walzer's reading is, however,
very instructive for Jewish history, especially in respect of messianism (including Marx),
and it is a key to the difference between Walzer's subject and New Testament typology
on this point that he can say of the Jewish tradition: "It is the prophet Moses, not David
the king, who hovers in the background of this messianic vision and suggests the nature
of the deeds to come" (137).

and pilgrimage toward the Promised Land, and the role in that narrative of "law" and "promise" is reciprocal. When members of the community at Corinth read Paul's words about Christ being "our passover," they would be unable to miss the connections: the crucifixion of Jesus is not only "like" the slaying of the sacrificial lamb in Egypt, a substitutionary atonement which protects the "chosen" from the wrath of God; they are led to see the slain paschal lamb as but the "sign" or "type" whose fulfillment is the finally redemptive messianic coinage for the whole world. Analogy becomes the relation of type and antitype, mold and coin, old and new:

> Your boasting is not a good thing. Do you not know that a little yeast leavens the whole batch of dough? Clean out the old yeast so that you may be a new batch, as you really are unleavened. For our paschal lamb, Christ, has been sacrificed. Therefore, let us celebrate the festival, not with the old yeast, the yeast of malice and evil, but with the unleavened bread of sincerity and truth.

> (1 Cor. 5:6-8)

This typological reading leads to a revision of the central notion of the *berith*, the covenant itself. Whereas in the Old Testament it was unmistakably the assurance of God's election of his chosen people Israel, the descendents of Abraham, Isaac and Jacob, now the covenant promise is seen — because of Jesus' reading of the Old Testament in reference to himself — as having not only the messianic hope as its context but the person of the promised Christ as its ultimate recipient or, as in a "last will and testament," its intended beneficiary: "Now the promises were made to Abraham and to his offspring; it does not say 'And to offsprings' as of many, but it says 'And to your offspring', who is Christ" (Gal. 3:16). By this revolutionary redirection of the text of the old covenant so that its final intention is seen to be not the many but the One, or as envisioning not the whole narrative of God's unfolding authorship in history but its metonym in his Word fulfilled in Jesus, the whole fabric of Old Testament narrative becomes open to a charged or layered potential in interpretation: semeity opens to polysemeity, albeit in an order of focus which centers all the more intensively upon Jesus. When patristic and medieval commentators make Isaac a type of Christ, they are thinking not only about the almost sacrifice and the substition-ary lamb on Mt. Moriah, they are thinking about God's astonishing covenant promise to barren Sarah and to aged Abraham, and to "his seed after him," Christ.[43]

The basic pattern in all of the "reading" of the old Testament by Jesus, then, is that afforded by what Paul came to call the *typoi*, typology. Paul's own ready extension of this typological impulse takes on, how-ever, a somewhat expansive form. In his epistle to the Galatians just quoted he moves on from the *typos* of the promise to Abraham to discuss the two offspring of Abraham. The first of these was the natural son whom, as a result of Sarah's despair and his own impatience, he had by Sarah's Egyptian handmaiden Hagar. To Abraham's own mind (Gen. 17:18), Ishmael was God's promised heir, and he was surprised as well as overjoyed when the promised covenantal or "spiritual" son, Isaac, was conceived and born to Sarah. Ultimately Hagar and her son were, at Sarah's request, sent away, and in the first Old Testament record of a covenant promise of the deity to a woman, Hagar is promised that Ishmael will be the father of many nations — most of whom, ironically enough for Jewish readers of the Genesis text, were understood to be their now not very friendly neighbors (Gen. 21:17-18; cf. 16:10-13).

When Paul "reads" this story for his friends in Galatia (4:21) he describes these things not as *typoi* but as *allegoria*, an allegory.[44] Here

43. See, e.g., Augustine, *Sermone* 130.3; *De Consensu Evangelistarum* 25.39; also J. Daniélou, "La typologie d'Isaac dans le Christianisme primitif," *Biblia* 28 (1947): 363-93.

44. The Antiochine fathers, committed to typology and the literal sense and re-sistant to the allegorical methods of the Alexandrian school, are echoed in the opinion of some modern scholars who incline to the view that Gal. 4:22-27 is still technically not allegory. This view has, however, been rejected by the majority of modern scholars, who find the passage to embody a truly allegorical method — one of two such New Testament passages to do so, the other being 1 Cor. 9:9ff. See here the useful summary and discussion of Richard Longenecker, *Biblical Exegesis in the Apostolic Period* (Grand Rapids: Eerdmans, 1975). See also E. E. Ellis, *Paul's Use of the Old Testament* (Edinburgh: Oliver and Boyd, 1956), and R. P. C. Hanson, *Allegory and Event* (London: SPCK, 1959). Looking forward to chap. 3, it is interesting that St. Jerome translates Paul's Greek directly as "sunt per allegoriam dicta" and, by contrast, is discriminating about *typos*. When it refers to persons or events of the historical past Jerome has *figura* (e.g., 1 Cor. 10:6); where *typos* clearly means a prefiguration of Christ (e.g., 5:14), Jerome translates *forma*, and where the model is more impersonal (as with respect to the plan of the tabernacle in Hebrews 8:5) he uses *exemplar* (cf. Vulg. Titus 2:7; 1 Tim. 4:12).

his reading clearly follows the typological impulse, but the reach of the analogy is both wider than the usual singular focus on Christ, and in respect of the Old Testament — here Torah — subversive of the normative expectation one might have even of a moralized reading of the passage:

> Tell me, you who desire to be subject to the law, will you not listen to the law? For it is written that Abraham had two sons, one by a slave woman and the other by a free woman. One, the child of the slave, was born according to the flesh; the other, the child of the free woman, was born through the promise. Now this is an allegory: these women are two covenants. One woman, in fact, is Hagar from Mount Sinai, bearing children for slavery. Now Hagar is Mount Sinai in Arabia and corresponds to the present Jerusalem, for she is in slavery with her children. But the other woman corresponds to the Jerusalem above; she is free, and she is our mother. For it is written,
>
> > "Rejoice you childless one, you who bear no children,
> > burst into song and shout, you who endure no birth pangs;
> > for the children of the desolate woman are more numerous
> > than the children of the one who is married."
>
> Now you, my friends, are children of the promise, like Isaac. But just as at that time the child who was born according to the flesh persecuted the child who was born according to the Spirit, so it is now also.
>
> (Gal. 4:21-29)

Two things are notable here. First, in what for the Jewish Christians to whom Paul was writing must have been a shocking novelty, the Law is associated by the apostle not with Isaac, the son of the covenant promise, but with the father of the Arab nations. Paul's explanatory analogy extends to link the Law with carnality and the "natural son" who is a "slave"; it therefore connects the spiritual son, born in "freedom," with the state of grace, the enriched existence of those who by believing in the One who has fulfilled the Law now live according to his spirit in perfect freedom (4:31–5:1, 13-14). Second, the redirection of the usual typological flow (which depends upon the historical fulfillment of the Law and the prophets in Jesus) effects a subversion of the sacrosanct place of Torah (the Law) as the singular source of type; implicitly, Jesus himself is now the spiritual Isaac, the freeborn son according to the promise, and the Christians to whom Paul writes are *his* heirs, even as he was Abraham's in the previous chapter (3:16). This subtle shift from normative typology to what Paul calls here allegory is, in effect, the exchanging of one hammer for another, or of the original seal for its imprint. The typos imprint is now the seal, the mold, for some subsequent kinds of reading. When Paul wants to talk about the life of the Christian in the church, he invites his readers to see that life as molded according to the stamp of Christ, *imitatio Christi,* not the stamp of the Law either in its functional sense of legal proscription or even in its broader sense as the pattern of patriarchal history:

> There is therefore now no condemnation for those who are in Christ Jesus. For the law of the Spirit of life in Christ Jesus has set you free from the law of sin and of death. For God has done what the law, weakened by the flesh, could not do: by sending his own Son in the likeness of sinful flesh, and to deal with sin, he condemned sin in the flesh, so that the just requirement of the law might be fulfilled in us, who walk not according to the flesh but according to the Spirit. For those who live according to the flesh set their minds on the things of the flesh, but those who live according to the Spirit set their minds on the things of the Spirit. To set the mind on the flesh is death, but to set the mind on the Spirit is life and peace.
>
> (Rom. 8:1-6)

Here we see, of course, that the "law" which the Christian ought to eschew is the "law of sin and death" (v. 2) — not the Law or Torah which Christ came to fulfill. For Paul the "law of sin and death" nonetheless problematizes our relationship to Torah. The scriptural Law proves to be, by virtue of mere human flesh, too "weak" (v. 3) to bring about its own purpose ("that the just requirement of the Law might be fulfilled in us") — that is, in mere human flesh the Law could not come to fulfillment because human nature is too much subject to the lower law of our fallen nature, the "law of sin and death." Christ, however, in our place has actually *fulfilled* already the scriptural Law, bodied forth at last its Word in total obedience, freeing us to live no longer tyrannized by the law of our flesh (fallen nature) or by the impossibility of our mortal and fallen nature ever fulfilling the written Law of God.

By living in his "Spirit" we experience life anew as though it were now for us stamped out in his image. Ironically again, only the mind which turns away from the flesh and its "law of sin and death" can ever hope to "submit to God's law" (v. 7) as it is found in Torah, and "imitate" in this way the life of Christ. This "imitation" or mimesis, as submission to God's gift to us of a perfect fulfillment of the law in Jesus, is the highest order of freedom, in that by it we are "conformed to the image of his Son" (v. 29), the fullest revelation of our human potential. This submission (bearing Christ's image) is for a Christian the New Law, or the Law renewed in Christ, what St. James calls elsewhere "the perfect law of liberty," because what is done is done not through fear or constraint but through love, the love that imitates the beloved.[45]

"In Christ," Paul says to the Romans, we are no longer living "in a spirit of slavery" (v. 15) but in the spirit of those who have, by "adoption," been made full legal members of the covenant and accordingly joint heirs of its promise made to Abraham. Here too, Paul's Gentile readers can find their place in the text. The narrative of the old covenant is not their genetic lineage, the promise to Abraham not their family promise. Yet even though they are not in any racial sense "heirs" (Jesus was above all the "heir" of the *berith* for Paul), by understanding that Isaac is a type of Jesus and that the promise made to Abraham that all the world (not just Jews) would be blessed in him has been extended to the Gentiles through Jesus (Gen. 12:3), the Gentile believers in Jesus also suddenly have access to God as Father.

For [God] says to Moses,

> "I will have mercy on whom I have mercy,
> and I will have compassion on whom I have compassion."

So it depends not on human will or exertion, but on God who shows mercy.

(Rom. 8:15-16)

---

45. James 1:25; 2:12; cf. John 13:34-35; 2 Cor. 3:17; Gal. 5:1. The "law of liberty" is opposed to what Paul calls "the law of sin and death."

Typology focuses the light of Scripture forward from the Old Testament onto Christ; allegory typically refracts the intensified light back upon the Scriptures from the prospect of the experience or life of the church. If *typology* in the early church continues to be, as it was in the Gospels, the interpretation of the scriptural text in terms of the life of a Person — the person of Jesus of Nazareth — *allegory,* much as it is elsewhere in the hellenized world, becomes in this light the interpretation of one text in terms of another text. In Paul specifically nonetheless, allegorical interpretation is still a function of the modeling of life upon a text. Now, however, the life is his own and that of all Christian believers, and the "text" is not only the Old Testament but also the life of Jesus. The "Suffering Servant" of Isaiah (53), a prophetic poem seen by the early church as fulfilled and made historically concrete in the New Testament life of Jesus (Rom. 10:15-16; Acts 8:32-35; 1 Peter 2:22-25; cf. Matt. 8:17; John 12:38), is by the Christian's "life in the Spirit" also rendered *imitatio Christi,* a full pattern for authentic life for those who follow Jesus at any time. This application or "imitation" opens the door to a view of history (whether personal or general) in which one can read concrete events as though they were written down in a book, and ordinary books as though they could best be understood in reference to "the Book," the Scriptures Old and New. Pivotal for Christian allegory is thus a schema which, unlike typology, is not extensively developed in the Bible itself. Here the New Testament is unambiguously the central text, and the Word made flesh in Jesus has become as the message to humanity to which all of the Old Testament was merely proleptic, while that which comes after the New Testament is necessarily a kind of exposition.

On such a view the New Testament becomes a generative or foundational text, much as the Old Testament had been, and capable of replacing it in relation to subsequent Christian writing. In this way, pretty much all Christian literature until well after the Middle Ages was regarded as " 'literary' application of the New Testament to life."[46] Accordingly, the literary theory of early Christian culture itself becomes an imprint, a mirror image as well as an elaboration of the literary

---

46. The apt phrase is John Freccero's, in "Dante's Medusa: Allegory and Autobiography," in *By Things Seen: Reference and Recognition in Medieval Thought,* ed. D. L. Jeffrey (Ottawa: University of Ottawa Press, 1979).

theory of Jesus, and that literary theory becomes in turn a fundamental source of identity in the Christian community. When Paul writes his second letter to the Corinthian community he says to them:

> Surely we do not need, as some do, letters of recommendation to you or from you, do we? You yourselves are our letter, written on our hearts, to be known and read by all; and you show that you are a letter of Christ, prepared by us, written not with ink but with the Spirit of the living God, not on tablets of stone but on tablets of human hearts. Such is the confidence that we have through Christ toward God. Not that we are competent of ourselves to claim anything as coming from us; our competence is from God, who has made us competent to be ministers of a new covenant, not of letter but of spirit; for the letter kills, but the Spirit gives life.
>
> (2 Cor. 3:1-6)

Reading in quest of the spirit rather than the letter privileges the trope; it also suggests that the letter, the sign, is the impermanent and fragile element, whereas the Spirit, that to which the sign points, is enduring — indeed will last forever (Matt. 24:35). The Christian view of language and its implied principles of literary theory are hardly then, *pace* Bloom and Derrida, bound to the mere semeity of texts. Human words are creatures of the moment, even as are the bodies of those who speak the words; fleetingly they are present and then they pass away. For Paul the writer, this very human fragility teaches us the fundamental virtue of God's Word, its enduring and hence extraordinary power. In a metaphor which for our own time unavoidably calls up images of Bedouin shepherds peering at long lost scrolls wrapped up in clay jars in the caves of Q'mran, Paul writes:

> But we have this treasure in clay jars, so that it may be made clear that this extraordinary power belongs to God and does not come from us. We are afflicted in every way, but not crushed; perplexed, but not driven to despair; persecuted, but not forsaken; struck down, but not destroyed; always carrying in the body the death of Jesus, so that the life of Jesus may also be made visible in our bodies. For while we live, we are always being given up to death

for Jesus' sake, so that the life of Jesus may be made visible in our
mortal flesh.

(2 Cor. 4:7-11)

The scroll in the jar is a worthy treasure, because it conveys through
its words the Word of God. For Paul and the early church, however, the
better text is the life of Jesus, and the only time this text can be "read"
and handed on is when, through death to the obtrusive self, the imprint
of Jesus becomes legible in the "mortal flesh," the "earthen vessel" (KJV),
of an ordinary life. Ironically, the most necessary "text" is thus the most
vulnerable; yet *imitatio Christi* becomes hereafter the only mode of
authentic "reading" for Christian People of the Book.

Chapter Three

Secular Scripture:
The "Beautiful Captive"

What has Horace to do with the Psalter? Or Virgil with the Gospel? Or Cicero with the Apostle?

ST. JEROME

Every good and true Christian should understand that wherever he may find truth it is his Lord's.

ST. AUGUSTINE

We take every thought captive to obey Christ.

2 CORINTHIANS 10:5

IF TYPOLOGY IS THE DISTINCTIVE HISTORICAL METHOD BY WHICH Jesus taught the early (Jewish) church to read the Old Testament, allegory became the excursus upon that method which most appealed to the hellenized Gentiles who had become children of the covenant by "adoption." The teaching at Antioch, the preaching of the Apostolic Fathers, the exegesis of Irenaeus, and even the pictures in the catacombs all illustrate how normative the typological strategy came to be.[1] But Mediterranean Gentiles were also habituated to the allegorical reading of Greek and Roman poetry, and especially among Alexandrian Jews and Christians, though typology persisted, allegory came to be, as it was for Philo, the predominant interpretive strategy.[2] Alexandria, the city of Philo, was an important agent in this shift. Through the Alexandrian convert Origen and others, the allegorical method by which hellenized readers customarily interpreted classical poetry came to be adapted systematically to the exegesis of Scripture among the Gentile converts. Chief among those who adapted this allegorical method to literary theory were St. Augustine, the North African bishop (A.D. 354-430), and St. Jerome, the Dalmatian scholar and translator of the first great vernacular Latin Bible (A.D. 342-420). For these dominant figures in Christian literary history, allegory served not only as a way of getting beneath the "letter" of the scriptural text to the living "spirit" of which it was the medium, but also as a way of extending the principle of "adoption" or conversion of the Gentiles more pervasively through the redemption of Gentile culture by the gospel. St. Paul's notion of adoption (e.g., Eph. 1:4-5) came thus to be a mode of relation to non-Christian literary texts, whose incorporation into Christian literary identity became possible only through allegorical readings referring them to the Bible. What allegorical method in both spheres — the reading of Scripture and the reading of pagan texts — accordingly produced was a theoretical bias which eschewed formalism in favor of an unabashedly ideological appropriation of the text.

1. See André Grabar, *Christian Iconography: A Study of Its Origins,* Bollingen Series 35.10 (Princeton: Princeton University Press, 1968); also E. Earle Ellis, foreword to *Typos: The Typological Interpretation of the Old Testament in the New,* by Leonhard Goppelt, trans. D. H. Madvig (Grand Rapids: Eerdmans, 1982).

2. See Jean Pépin, *Mythe et allegorie: les origines grecques et les contestations judaeo-chrétiennes* (Paris: Editions Montaigne, 1958), and Philip Rollinson, *Classical Theories of Allegory and Christian Culture* (Pittsburgh: Dusquesne University Press, 1981).

Figure 3. *"St. Augustine in his Cell" by Botticelli, ca. 1480. Courtesy: Alinari/Art Resource, NY.*

St. Jerome and the Redemption of Profane Literature

St. Jerome, who has in modern times been seen as one of the most puritanical of church fathers, may seem an odd spokesman for the Christian use of secular literature [Fig. 4]. Though rhetorically skillful, he was hardly a belletriste in his own writing. Most of his intellectual energy went into the learning of biblical languages (Greek, Hebrew, Chaldean [Aramaic], Syriac) so that he could with competence translate the Bible into Latin. His celebrated translation, the basis for the Latin Vulgate text, remained the vernacular Bible of Western Christianity for more than a millenium, until Latin was in fact no longer a vernacular. His reflections on reading, and especially on the reading of secular literature, are understandably less well known than this monumental achievement but, in that they faithfully represent central tenets of historical Christian thinking about the place of literature, they deserve to be restored to memory.

Jerome is in fact typical of Christian apologists in the latter stages of Roman culture in his condemnation of mere belletrism. As a Roman, Jerome was revolted by the appetite for degrading "entertainment" in his time, whether as represented notoriously in the Coliseum, or as found in the violent pornographic predations of contemporary theater.[3] Though a minimal knowledge of the practices of the Roman stage is likely to obtain sympathy for his revulsion from all but the most addicted pornophile, Jerome is usually remembered for his negative utterances about what we would now characterize as classical literature, comments which have often been used unfairly to characterize him as a philistine. The most notorious of these remarks appear in his letter of spiritual counsel to a Roman matron, Eustochium (*Epist.* 22).[4] Endeavoring to persuade her to abandon the worldly pleasures of her

3. Vivid description of the lurid fare is afforded by Martial, in chapter 7 of his *De Spectaculis* — also by Suetonius's *Nero* (chap. 12) and the *Historia Augusta, Vita Heliogabali* (chap. 25), all of which state plainly that "similitude" of sexual acts and sexual violence could be the actual thing, with slaves or prisoners made victims for the sake of performance. Sometimes this called for the actual murder or execution of the "actor." Tertullian criticizes such practices with virulence in his *De Spectaculis*, especially in chapters 4, 26, and 30.

4. Jerome's letters are conveniently translated in P. Schaff, *The Nicene and Post-Nicene Fathers*, Second Series (Grand Rapids: Eerdmans, 1954), vol. 6.

Figure 4. *"St. Jerome in his Study" by Albrecht Dürer, 1511. Courtesy: Foto Marburg/Art Resource, NY.*

privileged and affluent peers for the sake of the kingdom of God, he urges that she eschew aesthetic display and such fashionable literary pretensions as desiring to "seem . . . witty in making lyric songs in meter." He continues:

> Do not imitate the enervated and delicate affectation which has arisen among matrons, who now with teeth clenched, now with lips wide, now with a stuttering tongue, cut their words in half, regarding anything else as the speech of bumpkins, to such a degree does adultery, even of the tongue, give them pleasure. For "what fellowship has light with darkness? And what concord has Christ with Belial?" (2 Cor. 6:14-15). What has Horace to do with the Psalter? or Virgil with the Gospel? or Cicero with the Apostle? . . . Although "all things are clean to the clean" (Tit. 1:15) and "nothing is to be rejected that is received with thanksgiving" (1 Tim. 4:4), nevertheless we should not drink at the same time from the cup of Christ and the cup of demons. (29)

Jerome then makes clear that his concern is with priorities, with the ordering of Christian life in such a way that extrinsic interests remain secondary. He recalls how in his own case it had been much easier to give up the considerable comforts of home and a wealthy family than to put his devotion to Christ ahead of the library which he "had gathered with the greatest diligence and labor at Rome." He found himself all too readily absorbed in Cicero and Plautus, neglecting the Scriptures because of their "rude [i.e, plain or unadorned] style." This neglect led to a spiritual crisis in which his intellectual pride came into direct confrontation with the gospel imperative to humble Christian servanthood. The tension between intellectual pride and spiritual responsibility eventually produced an almost complete physical and mental breakdown, during which he experienced a dream or vision in which, he says, he was required before the "Judge of all" to declare his *status,* his identity. His answer, that he was a Christian, obtained a swift dismissal: " 'You lie. You are a Ciceronian, not a Christian; for where your treasure is, there will your heart be also' (Matt. 6:21)" (30). Jerome's point in this confession is simply that his former obsession with eloquence or literariness, figured conventionally here as "Cicero," had usurped the primacy of his commitment to the wisdom and love of Christ, his "apostolate." *Corruptio optima pessima.* He fears the same conflict for his correspondent, and so offers a classic Pauline defense against potential idolatry, reminding her that many things which are valuable as long as they are subordinated to their function as means, become spiritually destructive when allowed, however subtly, to become the actual end in view, the dominating animus of one's primary energies.

But it is this same prioritizing of means and end which allows Jerome in a letter to another correspondent, the Roman orator and convert Magnus (*Epist.* 70), to *defend* the considerable use of non-Christian classical authors in his own writing. The concern Magnus had expressed over Jerome's many literary citations, the old scholar suggests, belies in the first instance an understandably guilt-tinged preoccupation with Cicero (i.e., the eloquence of classical authors) on the part of Magnus. Jerome himself, he implies, knows all about such guilt. But in its extremism, the complaint of Magnus creates a false dichotomy. Jerome's reply, a kind of "apology for poetry," accordingly makes several arguments in defense of a Christian use of secular literature — which use is presented as not at all the same thing as an idolatrous passion for literature *per se.* Jerome's "defense of poetry" in Epistle 70 provides an outline, as it turns out, for numerous subsequent defenses in Christian tradition, all of which make the distinction between means and end basic to their affirmation of putatively "pagan" eloquence in the pursuit of Christian wisdom.

Jerome's argument runs as follows: (1) the Hebrew Scriptures themselves make abundant use of gentile literature. Following Josephus, he ascribes such borrowings to the books of Moses, the prophets, and to "Solomon" (the Wisdom books in general) — an identification of incorporated material which has been confirmed in detail by modern biblical scholars. He reads the injunction of Dame Wisdom in the book of Proverbs to "understand prudent maxims and shrewd adages, parables, and obscure discourse, the words of the wise and their dark sayings" (Prov. 1:1-6), as exemplified by the wisdom discourse in the book of Proverbs itself, and sees their study as the province of "the dialectician and the philosopher" (70.2). That is, Old Testament biblical texts engage textual skills and textual sympathies of the secular disciplines. (2) Further, the New Testament continues the practice begun in the Old. For example, the apostle Paul quotes from Epimenides in his letter to Titus (1:12); from Menander in 1 Cor. 15:33; from Aratus in Acts 17:28.

(3) The principle for this type of appropriation of pagan wisdom to the cause of Christ is exemplified in the Scriptures tropically, as, for example, when David uses Goliath's own sword to hack off the giant's head, or when, in the book of Deuteronomy (21:10-13), the Lord commanded that in the aftermath of war a captive woman might be ritually purified and, having "her head shaved, her eyebrows and all her hair cut off and her nails pared, she might then be taken to wife." Developing his second text as allegory, Jerome continues:

> What wonder is it if I also, admiring the fairness of her from the grace of her eloquence, desire to make that secular wisdom which is my captive and my handmaid a rightful matron of the true Israel? Or that shaving off and cutting away in her all that is dead, whether this be idolatry, pleasure, error or lust, I take her to myself clean and pure, and beget by her servants for the Lord of Hosts? In my efforts to promote the advantages of Christ's family, this putative "defilement" with an alien actually increases the number of my fellow servants. Hosea took a whore for a wife [at God's command] . . . and this harlot bore him a son called Jezreel, or the seed of God [Hosea 1:2-4]. (70.2)

Through a patently allegorical procedure, already thoroughly conventionalized among readers of classical literature since Homer and Hesiod, Jerome thus instances and grounds his policy toward pagan literature in an extrinsic paradigm.[5] And this colorful example is but a prolegomenon. Elsewhere, in defending the preparatory use of profane literature as an accessus to Christian wisdom he cites Theophras-

---

5. The argument is borrowed from Origen and becomes a medieval commonplace. See Henri de Lubac, *Exégèse Médievale: Les Quatre sens de l'Écriture* (Paris: Aubier, 1954), vol. 1. Allegorical interpretation in the Fathers is a development of classical practice, and actually a disciplined mode of criticism — not nearly so arbitrary as it might appear from a modern distance. A very high view of the poetry is involved, since allegorical interpretation depends upon the belief that poets such as Virgil and Ovid really do express truth in their allegories — a truth that is expressed in different terms by philosophers, scientists, and theologians. The poets thus become in the full medieval sense "authorities," and much as was the case for hellenic readers in the Heraclitian allegorical tradition, the ethical responsibility of the reader is to "look for the truth hidden in the fable." See also Pépin, chapters 1-2.

tus, Plato, Isocrates, Pythagoras, Democritus, Xenocrates, Zeno, Cleanthes, Homer, Hesiod, Simonides, Stestichorus, Sophocles' *Oedipus*, and Cato. He also finds an analogy in the crucial role in the *historia humana salvationis* played by Rahab, the prostitute of Jericho (Josh. 2:18), who enters even into the lineage of the Messiah (Matt. 1:5). His ostensible point is that while not every member of Christ's body has need of literary learning, certainly some members do if the whole body is to be well served. That is, he argues not for a final idealization of profane literature for itself, but its appropriation for a higher purpose — proportionate fittedness of each member of the whole body of Christ for service: "The rude and simple brother must not suppose himself a saint just because he knows nothing, even as he who is educated and eloquent must not measure his degree of sanctity merely by his fluency."[6]

Finally, Jerome points to the magnificent contribution of classical literary influence to the apologetic, catechetical and theological writings of the church between the time of St. Paul and his own day (70.3-5). Here he sets forth a rich bibliography of patristic writers, Christian and Jewish philosophers, bishops, and apologists who have drawn heavily on secular literature (e.g., Plato, Aristotle, Cicero, Virgil, Quintillian) to explain, defend, and extend the reach of the gospel. Jerome's argument is now complete: the eloquence and wisdom of secular literature, when made captive to the service of Christ and his kingdom, is of great value. Indeed, on the witness of the Old Testament, New Testament, and Christian tradition alike, it is of invaluable assistance in the propagation of understanding and truth.

Augustine and the Development of Christian Literary Theory

Only in the sense that he incorporates normative early Christian hermeneutics, especially a tropic reading of the Old Testament as justification for his use of secular literature, is Jerome's *apologia*, properly speaking, theoretical. His contemporary, however, the rhetorician and former

6. *Epist.* 52.2-4, 9.

teacher of classical literature, St. Augustine, was to go much further. While Augustine clearly contributed to the apologetic aspect of Jerome's argument, it was in the larger context of developing a theoretical basis for the understanding of the language and text of Scripture that his writings were to become the foundation for more general literary theory in the Middle Ages. The most important discourse in Augustine's extensive reflection on the way texts work is his *De Doctrina Christiana* (A.D. 427).[7] Properly speaking, then, this is a book about hermeneutics — the "rules," Augustine suggests, which as properties of language and genre should inform careful reading of Scripture — rather than a theological treatise or body of given scriptural exposition. In this sense, *On Christian Doctrine* is an explicitly theoretical document.

Why, Augustine asks, should a literary theory pertinent to Scripture be formulated? Evidently some in his audience expected that the univocal true meaning of scriptural texts would always, as in certain miraculous instances, be revealed by the Holy Spirit independently of human effort at understanding. To this kind of intemperate enthusiasm Augustine replies that it is not appropriate to cite the miracle of Pentecost (or any analogous extraordinary prophetic moment of revelation) as an excuse for refusing to teach Scripture and the hermeneutic skills necessary to read it.

Rather, those things which can be learned from

> men should be learned without pride. And let anyone teaching another communicate what he has received without pride or envy. We should not tempt Him in whom we have believed, lest, deceived by the wiles and perversity of the Enemy, we should be unwilling to go to church to hear and learn the Gospels, or to read a book, or to hear a man reading or teaching, expecting instead to be "caught up to the third heaven," as the Apostle says. . . .[8]

---

7. The best modern English translation is by D. W. Robertson, Jr., in the Library of Liberal Arts Series (New York: Bobbs-Merrill, 1958), and is used for all quotations. Valuable recent studies of *De doctrina* include Duane W. H. Arnold and Pamela Bright, eds., *De doctrina christiana: A Classic of Western Culture*, vol. 9 in the series Christianity and Judaism in Antiquity (Notre Dame: University of Notre Dame Press, 1995), and Edward D. English, *Reading and Wisdom: The De doctrina christiana of Augustine in the Middle Ages* (Notre Dame: University of Notre Dame Press, 1995).

8. *On Christian Doctrine* (hereafter referred to as *OCD*), Prol. 5.

That is to say, there is a normative and accessible "science" of interpretation just as there is a "science" of reading at the most basic level, and those who would profit from what God has made available in Scripture and the writings of holy authors should apprentice themselves humbly to their deeper understanding, in order that Christian obedience in the stewardship of love might not be hindered.

On Christian Doctrine is divided into four books. Book 1 takes up the subject of "semiotics," the basic principles of linguistic signification. Augustine's theory of signification codes is not labeled *semeia*, Ferdinand de Saussure's term (from the Gk. *semeion*, "sign"), but his intent is clearly to deal with some obvious implications of what Saussure (who was in fact indebted to Augustine even as he opposed him) was later to call a "science that studies the life of signs within society."[9] Augustine's explicit concern is strictly with language as means, as a vehicle for teaching (doctrine), and, as we have seen in chapter 1, his presupposition in this regard is that of a commonsense realist:

> no one uses words except for the purpose of signifying something. From this may be understood what we call "signs"; they are things used to signify something. Thus every sign is also a thing, for that which is not a thing is nothing at all; but not every thing is also a sign. (*OCD* 1.2.2)

Communication of every sort evidently depends upon a theory of signs by which interpretation is ordered. But crucial to Augustine's observation concerning signification is that, though as derived from and dependent upon convention the form of signs may appear arbitrary, the *use* of signification itself is not. Signs are a vehicle, capable of variable direction, and also of being themselves mistaken for the destination toward which they are designed to move the mind. Hence Augustine lays down an elementary distinction upon which his theory will depend again and again, that between use and enjoyment:

9. Introduction to his *Cours de Linguistique Génerale* (Paris: Gallimard, 1916; reprint, Wiesbaden: Harrasowitz, 1967).

> To enjoy something is to cling to it with love for its own sake. To
> use something, however, is to employ it in obtaining that which
> you love, provided that it is worthy of love. (*OCD* 1.4)

"Enjoyment" here means not the mere pleasure we might take in any
aspect of language or learning but an idolatrous elevation of means over
end, a confusion about the *terminus ad quem* of our intellectual and
spiritual endeavor. For the Christian the only objects worthy of "enjoyment" in Augustine's sense are "the Father, the Son, and the Holy Spirit":
the Godhead is the ultimate "thing" signified by the universe and indeed
its actual "cause."[10] The supreme glory of the human person is that "in
the dignity of a rational soul" it is made "in the image of God." But this
does not imply that a human person is to be loved "for its own sake"
as ultimate value, any more than any other image, graven in whatever
manner (cf. Exod. 20:4), is to be loved as ultimate value. Augustine
thinks that the human person, as *imago Dei*, is also a sign, and hence
to be "loved for the sake of something else" — obviously that divine
Person whose image each human person bears (*OCD* 1.22.20). Accordingly, Augustine says,

> no one ought to love himself either, if you observe the matter
> closely, because he should not love himself on account of himself
> but on account of Him who is to be enjoyed.

Augustine then quotes the Great Commandment to clarify his point:
"Thou shalt love the Lord thy God, with all thy heart, with all thy soul
and with all thy mind, and thy neighbour as thyself" (Deut. 6:5; Matt.
22:37-39). The *caveat* to intellectual enterprise, including perhaps especially any theory of signs, is the basic question of priority and purpose:

> Whatever else appeals to the mind as being loveable should be
> directed into that channel into which the whole current of love
> flows. (1.22.21)

10. Hence, "it is not easy to find a name [sign] proper to such excellence, unless it
is better to say that this Trinity is one God, and that 'of him, and by him, and in him
are all things'" [cf. Col. 1:17; 2 Cor. 5:6] (*OCD* 1.5.5).

For Augustine even a theory of signs is therefore ultimately based on considerations of intention and the ordering of value. That is, he does not believe it is possible to elaborate a theory of signs without first taking into account the sphere of the ethical. A self-centered or self-serving (let alone self-referential) use of signs cannot maintain an ordered relationship of means to end. It is bound rather to pervert and distort, and in so doing hinder the development of love, since, for Augustine, love necessarily involves a proper understanding of the relationship of signs to things, an understanding which serves the Other (community) as it makes communication possible.[11] Accordingly, even the text of Scripture is finally a means, not an end. Hence the semiotic and theoretical disciplines pertinent to reading Scripture, the sphere of philology, describe a closely contextualized affection:

> . . . it is to be understood that the plenitude and the fulfillment of the Law and of all the sacred Scriptures is the love of a Being which is to be enjoyed and of a being that can share that enjoyment with us, since there is no need for a precept that anyone should love himself. That we might know this and have the means to implement it, the whole temporal dispensation was made by divine Providence for our salvation. We should use it, not with an abiding but with a transitory love and delight like that which we have in a road or in vehicles or in other instruments, or, if it may be expressed more accurately, so that we love those things by which we are carried along for the sake of that toward which we are carried. (*OCD* 1.35.39)

I have returned here deliberately to a passage from *On Christian Doctrine* introduced in the first chapter because now we are able to see to what degree Augustine's theory of language mirrors the Christocentric typology of the New Testament and the early church. As the significance of all that the Law and the prophets have spoken is realized fully only when Jesus is seen as their actual signified "end term," so the means by which language signifies only achieves its full comprehension in the *datum* of the Incarnation, the Word-made-flesh. It is not so much that

---

11. For thorough development of this Augustinian tradition from the fifth to twelfth centuries see de Lubac, vols. 1-2.

the way language works helps us to understand the theology of the Incarnation, but rather that the theology of the Incarnation helps us profoundly to understand the way in which language works.[12]

Augustine's strategic reason for stressing the means / end distinction at such length in book 1 is to prepare for his observation in book 2 that signification is not merely socially arbitrary or fixed as numbers in the *ratio* of creation, but also inescapably in some measure volitional. Semiotics, mathematics, music, iconography: the conventions of rhetoric are fundamentally intertwined and interactive. A text is a web *(textus)* of established conventions and varying intentions. Though both verbal signs and rhetorical figures become intelligible through an understanding of their normative conventions, referentiality is never simply or narrowly a conventional matter. Signs can lie. They can also point faithfully, but in a complex (or circuitous) rather than straightforward fashion. For example, writers may make fruitful use of obscurity, or of ambiguous reference. This may well deceive the casual reader, but can considerably enrich a serious reader, the intensity of whose pleasure in the disciplines of discovery imprints the memory more firmly: "No one," Augustine says, "doubts that things are perceived more readily through similitudes [tropic, metaphoric, or nuanced language] and that what is sought with difficulty is discovered with more pleasure" (2.6.8). The serious reader is able to confirm his or her reading of a "dark passage," moreover, by testing it for agreement with what is said more discursively elsewhere. Obscurity is not in Scripture purposeless, but grounded in demonstrable sense and definable textual relations. Texts are not only to be read with a view to their most apparent object of reference but tested and qualified in the light of other readings.

Augustine reflects the consensus of early Christian thought about interpretation in his belief that no single fallen human perspective can be assured of complete understanding, and therefore that the conversation of readers, the witness of the body of Christ both in the here and now and also of generations past, must constitute an important control on any single effort. Reading, like writing, is unavoidably a contextualized activity, both synchronically and diachronically (2.8.12-14). We read *now*, others have read previously, and every text we read is a creature

---

12. See Augustine's extensive bipolar exploration of the analogy in his *De Trinitate* 15.9.15–15.16.26.

of the past — even if of a relatively recent past. Moreover, we can hardly do without the readings of our predecessors any more than those of our contemporaries. Knowledge of the relevant languages is imperative (2.10.15–2.11.16), and comparison of various translations is almost invariably useful (2.12.17–2.13.20). Figurative language almost always requires some knowledge of the pertinent culture, as is particularly evident in the special figurative properties of Hebrew names in the Old Testament (2.16.23-26), which cannot be understood without reference to Hebrew wordplay. While secular poetic conventions (such as the supposition of the "nine Muses") may well arise from historical accident more than rational design, these and other conventions, once established (such as those more pertinently of meter and music), are certainly not to be shunned "because of superstition of the profane":

> . . . if we can find anything useful therein for understanding the Holy Scriptures. . . . We should not think that we ought not to learn literature because Mercury is said to be its inventor, nor that because the pagans dedicated temples to Justice and Virtue and adored in stones what should be performed in the heart, we should therefore avoid justice and virtue. Rather, every good and true Christian should understand that wherever he may find truth, it is his Lord's. (2.18.28)

Consistent with his principles, Augustine does not hesitate to use and give credit to the literary theory of a scholar he takes to be tainted with heresy, the sometime Donatist Tyconius (3.30-37), and pagan classical authors of reputation are clearly among the principal sources of his theory.

Augustine's sense of the utility of those disciplines most closely related to the literary vehicle of divine truth does not, he says, extend to "theatrical frivolities" and superstitious practices (2.22.33), but is limited to rational "agreements" which have become already institutionalized. It goes without saying for him that such conventions are not self-explanatory: one needs to know something of their historical context and inner logic to make use of them. This is particularly evident in the realm of symbol, whether of action or of image, as in the conventional iconography of the plastic arts. Conventions, systems of verbal and visual signs, have to be taught and learned according to their own

inherent systems. Aesthetic reflection is accordingly a species of anthro-
pological reflection. For example,

> if those signs which the actors make in their dances had a natural
> meaning and not a meaning dependent on the institution and
> consent of men, the public crier in early times would not have had
> to explain to the Carthaginian populace what the dancer wished
> to convey during the pantomime. Many old men still remember
> the custom, as we have heard them say. And they are to be believed,
> for even now if anyone unacquainted with such trifles goes to the
> theater and no one else explains to him what these motions signify,
> he watches the performance in vain. (2.25.38)

Even the science of numbers, yet another convention, is part of what is
required in a reader, and certainly the science of logic, notably "the truth
of valid inference," is essential to good reading. These examples from
mathematics and logic show that not all conventions are a product of
human invention; some are a result rather of human observation of
systematization preexistent in the creation itself, "perpetually instituted
by God in the reasonable order of things. Thus, the person who narrates
the order of events in time does not compose that *ordo* himself"
(2.32.50).

Augustine can think of no discipline of thought or inquiry which
does not deserve to be studied and systematized, and to have a theory
of its conventions elaborated — in order that the greatest clarification
of signs and sign theory might be achieved. Accordingly, pagan writings,
especially where they are "found to be true and well accommodated to
our faith, should not be feared." Rather they should be "converted" to
Christian use.

> Just as the Egyptians had not only idols and grave burdens which
> the people of Israel detested and avoided, so also they had vases
> and ornaments of gold and silver and clothing which the Israelites
> took with them secretly when they fled, as if to put them to a better
> use. . . . In the same way all the teachings of the pagans contain
> not only simulated and superstitious imaginings and grave burdens
> of unnecessary labor, which each one of us leaving the society of
> pagans under the leadership of Christ ought to abominate and

avoid, but also liberal disciplines more suited to the uses of truth, and some most useful precepts concerning morals. (2.40.60)

What Augustine advocates is not a syncretism but a discriminating borrowing according to fixed and ordinate principles laid down in Scripture itself.[13]

In Augustine's view the incentive for so much learning is not then by any means mere mastery of knowledge for its own sake; such ambition "puffs up" the mind and makes it an object of idolatrous worship. What prompts earnest and excellent scholarship in the Christian is "fear of the Lord" (cf. Prov. 1:7): the motivation for a better reading of Scripture is a desire for conformity of the will of the scholar with the will of God. The true reader wants to know principally what is to be done — his or her concern for understanding is not merely a matter of aesthetics or even epistemology, but is incipiently ethical. Book 3 of *On Christian Doctrine* is therefore dedicated to the issue of scholarly motivation. For Augustine the Christian student is one whose efforts always begin in a desire to obey the Great Commandment: progressing in a process of patient and laborious refinement of insight, they end in obedience as well. In his most concise summary, anyone "fearing God diligently seeks His will in the Holy Scriptures" (3.1.1). Distraction or misdirection on the intellectual pilgrimage is just what it will be to

13. Not all the Western fathers can be credited with an equally vigorous attempt to avoid syncretism. Clement of Alexandria (late second century A.D.), for example, illustrates how the allegorically inclined exegete could readily open the door to syncretism rather than mere borrowing. In his *Stromata* especially he deliberately syncretizes myth, religion, and philosophy of Egyptian, Greek, ancient Hebrew, and Christian origin in such a way as to suggest that the symbolism and "allegories" of the Old Testament are more or less identical in purpose to those of Plato, Orpheus, or Euripides. Only a kind of gnostic overview can effect a reduction of these texts, as well as the New Testament, to a fully integrated truth. This position, as Jaroslav Pelikan suggests, came very close to heresy. See Pelikan, *The Emergence of the Catholic Tradition*, in *The Christian Tradition: A History of the Development of Doctrine* (Chicago: University of Chicago Press, 1971), 1.81-97. As Jean Seznec has shown, however, there grew up a widespread tendency to imitate the very pagan allegorizings Augustine had eschewed in favor of their subordination to Scripture. See his *Survival of the Pagan Gods,* trans. Barbara Sessions (Paris, 1953; reprint, New York: Harper, 1961), and Don Cameron Allen, *Mysteriously Meant* (Baltimore: Johns Hopkins University Press, 1970) for accounts of the later European tradition of pagan allegoresis.

Bunyan's pilgrims on their spiritual journey — a form of derailment and bondage, a "miserable servitude of the spirit in this habit of taking signs for things, so that one is not able to raise the eye of the mind above things that are corporal and created to drink in eternal light" (3.5.9). Moreover, "just as it is a servile infirmity to follow the letter and to take signs for the things they signify, in the same way it is an evil of wandering error to interpret signs in a useless way" (3.9.13).

What prompts a *useful* reading is (consistently) "charity, the motion of the soul toward the enjoyment of God for his own sake and the enjoyment of one's self and one's neighbor for the sake of God." *Useless* reading is a product rather of cupidity, "a motion of the soul toward the enjoyment of one's self, one's neighbor, or any corporal thing for the sake of something other than God." A self-serving, narcissistic attitude toward the text is bound to be ultimately sterile, however clever, while a "charitable" reading has the power to strengthen virtue and understanding together. Uncontrolled, cupidity corrupts the soul. For Augustine, any manifestation of this self-justifying preoccupation is properly called a "vice." And, he observes, "when vices have emptied the soul and led it to a kind of extreme hunger, it leaps to more flagrant miscreance *(facinora)* by means of which impediments to the vices may be removed and the vices themselves sustained" (3.10.16).

There is always an assumption in Augustine's discussion that useful reading is reading whose import can be shared. Book 4 turns, accordingly, to the second aspect of Augustine's study, the matter of teaching, or the employment of rules and strategies of eloquence *(eloquentia)* by which wisdom *(sapientia)* is communicated. Here, as a skilled rhetorician, Augustine is aware of the potential for misuse of eloquence by the rhetorician himself, the tendency of powerful teaching to corrupt and pervert as much as uphold and convey wisdom faithfully. Part of his purpose therefore is to protect the Christian reader against the skilled rhetorician's powers by arming him with a competence in rhetorical analysis (4.2.3) as well as a capacity for skilled (and charitable) use of the discursive arts. His goals, even in this area, remain focused on clear and truthful speech and writing rather than aureate eloquence (4.5.7-8; 4.6.9; 4.9.23). Eloquence is to serve wisdom, and not the reverse, "for it is a work of good and distinguished minds to love the truth within words and not the words" (4.11.26). That is, the purpose of eloquence in teaching or in writing is to "move minds," "not that they may know what is to be done, but that they may *do* what they already know should be done" (4.12.27). And for this (as indeed the whole history of humane letters and experience attests), "the life of the speaker has greater weight in determining whether he is obediently heard than any grandness of eloquence" (4.27.59). *Ecce homo.*

No work of literary theory for more than a millennium carried the weight and authority of Augustine's *On Christian Doctrine,* and though his literary theorizing is also to be found in others of his works (e.g., *On the Letter and the Spirit*) this remained the work most read and reflected upon by subsequent theorists, theological and secular, until after the Reformation. It is therefore proper to an inquiry into Christian thinking about texts and their study to grasp firmly its central thesis and principles. When we do so we see that above all Augustine's theory is teleological: the distinction and ordering of means and end, enjoyment and use, cupiditous and charitable motivation, eloquence and sapience, letter and spirit, sign and thing, are such as to carry the energies of textual study outward into the whole realm of human inquiry, the *universitas* of humane wisdom, but only to draw their comprehension back again into concrete enactment of the word and will of God as summarized in the Great Commandment. When Augustine and medieval writers after him speak of "ordinate" thinking, this is the ordination, the order of priorities they imply. Anything less would be idolatry.

Latter-Day Idolatry of the Text

With many in our time it has been otherwise. Professors and critics of literature have tended, especially in the middle third of the twentieth century, to believe that the high ground in textual study should be occupied by rigorously formalist and "objective" or "scientific" approaches. Some of these practitioners have accordingly endeavored to eschew ideology as a species of adulteration which could only taint and compromise the professionalism of their work. In the last third of this century such astringent views, often associated, interestingly enough, with Christianity, have come increasingly under attack as disingenuous. Every literary theory, like every interpretive practice, it is now argued, is unavoidably ideological. Hence, any notion of a "pure" formalism must be regarded as a phantasm.

In fact we have seen that Christian literary theory in late antiquity and the early Middle Ages was itself explicitly, not merely tacitly, ideological. Indeed, its own bias was entirely against formalism. To be fair, this owes in part simply to the fact that it was developed in relationship to a foundational religious text, the Bible. It also derives, however, from the Christian conviction that no reading takes place in an ethical vacuum, and that even the most technical elaborations of linguistic and genre conventions will have at their foundation the question of function, of action. When approaching secular literary texts, early Christian theorists were anxious to understand them in terms of their own conventions, and to remain conscious of their sometimes alien purpose, but their motivation for study of such texts was to subvert what they regarded as those alien purposes. In effect, though learning from pagan authors required of them respect for the conditions and conventions within which those texts were produced — a respect which resulted in the preservation of these texts in Christian monasteries following the destruction of the Roman Empire — the Christian theorists were entirely unapologetic about taking their pagan beauty captive for the sake of propagating quite different ultimate values. Formalist or belletristic considerations ultimately played little part in justification for the preservation or for the study of classical authors either in late antiquity or through much of the Middle Ages.

By contrast, a great deal of modern literary criticism has tended to draw heavily on various formalist methods and approaches to the text. The contrast is instructive. These formalisms used to be defended (in part) for the technical virtue they bear in *explication de texte;* they imply aesthetic criteria, practical method, and even a sort of scientific or at least quasi-empirical analysis. Indeed, such elements have often been seen as important to disciplinary defense of literary study against the disdainful encroachments of science and social science. Notably, when rigorously applied, formalist approaches to the text can seem to have about them a certain inbred elegance of praxis *(dulce)* and a considerable claim to undergird the development of real literacy *(ultile)*. For these reasons at least, literary criticism among Christian writers from the third quarter of the nineteenth century until the 1960s tended to differ very little in practical method from their more avowedly secular contemporaries. The pursuit of literacy in the common reader, and the desire to respect, comprehend, and give appreciative credit to the intellectual and imaginative integrity of a work of art were common goals. Finally, the formalist methods were themselves typically derived from the practicum of biblical studies, in which sphere many Christian critics had first become habituated to the methodology.[14] Accordingly, a comparable decorum of gratitude for the unique "gift" of a literary text came to be tacit in critical engagement.

New Criticism, the American formalism associated with distinguished critics such as Cleanth Brooks, I. A. Richards, René Welleck, Austin Warren, and Allen Tate in the past generation, is still perhaps the best known among the formalist schools.[15] New Criticism, it might still be said, offers much to the serious reader, not least in its focus on the disciplines and skills of attentive reading. It has been the kind of formalism, moreoever, to which an ethically sensitive critic might still attach considerable value. For example, one aspect of the implicit theorizing undergirding formalist and especially New Critical approaches naturally attractive to traditional Christian thinking about texts is the supposition of the legitimate "otherness" of the text. Having its own integrity, the text has "something to say," and read carefully and in a disciplined fashion it might declare itself to a reader with the will and the skill to

14. This reciprocating influence of post-Enlightenment literary and biblical theory has been admirably studied by Hans Frei, *The Eclipse of Biblical Narrative: A Study of Eighteenth and Nineteenth Century Hermeneutics* (New Haven: Yale, 1974) and Stephen Prickett, *Words and the Word: Language, Poetics and Biblical Interpretation* (Cambridge: Cambridge University Press, 1986).

15. See for example René Wellek and Austin Warren, *Theory of Literature* (New York: Harcourt, Brace, 1942; 2nd ed. 1955). Stanley Hyman, *The Armed Vision: A Study of the Methods of Modern Literary Criticism* (New York: Knopf, 1948); William K. Wimsatt and Cleanth Brooks, *Literary Criticism: A Short History* (New York: Knopf, 1957; 1969); and the call for "ontological criticism" as a corrective to New Criticism in John Crowe Ransom's *The New Criticism* (New York: New Directions, 1941). There are, of course, other kinds of formalisms, including the neo-Aristotelian rhetorical criticism of the Chicago school, including especially Elder Olsen, R. S. Crane, and Wayne Booth. Most luminously, the classical formalism of T. S. Eliot, represented in his essay "Tradition and the Individual Talent" is a synthesis of other elements. Eliot's formalist bias, as we shall see in a later chapter, has nonetheless been criticized by subsequent critics for ethical blindness as well as formal self-contradiction. See, e.g., George Steiner's *In Bluebeard's Castle* (London: Faber and Faber, 1971).

read.[16] It will be readily apparent that such a formulation has characteristic Protestant resonances, and indeed the New Criticism's central impulse can be traced back to the Reformation and Luther's hermeneutics of the independent Bible reader.

However, an important but problematic corollary of this New Critical principle, derived from its own self-conscious secularity, was the desire to keep itself formally aloof from the explicit theological and metaphysical presuppositions from which its predecessors in biblical interpretation had operated.[17] Summarily, these involved the sacrosanct place of the text as revelation in Christian theology, the peculiar quality attributed to the Bible as a uniquely privileged and transcending document. In fact, New Criticism typically elevated secular texts to a similar or parallel order of unique creation, a kind of secular scripture in place of sacred Scripture: all reflection on the text became therefore, by analogy, a second-order discourse; "criticism" became not so much interpretation or mediation as a kind of intelligent homiletical homage, especially to the text's formal or aesthetic properties — its special development of literary conventions such as genre, tropic language, or meter. The secular text, in short, held much the same place of reverence as the text in biblical criticism. It was a distinguished "other"; what critics might say about the text did not finally compromise the integrity

16. In an essay entitled "The 'Literal Reading' of Biblical Narrative in the Christian Tradition: Does It Stretch or Will It Break?" Hans Frei illustrates the powerful connection between primacy of the literal sense in Christian hermeneutics and its secular version: "The older tradition . . . in one of its shapes . . . ended up in this century as Anglo-American 'New Criticism,' denying all creative status to the second-order activity which was now called 'criticism' rather than 'interpretation,' and banishing (usually, but not consistently) the notion of textual reference to a contextualized world, together with intentional and affective fallacies. The literary text itself had an unchangeable, almost sacred, status conferred upon it and became a self-enclosed imagistic world, structured by such devices as paradox and irony, which the second-order commentator must, above all, leave as they are and not translate into some didactic 'meaning' by way of prose paraphrase. For all its difference from hermeneutical theory, this outlook shares with it a belief in the possibility of valid, if not invariant, reading and (despite itself) a sense of the common, humanistic world shared by the 'literary' work and the reader." In *The Bible and the Narrative Tradition*, ed. Frank MacConnell (New York: Oxford University Press, 1986), 44.

17. Ransom's awareness of the loss of a theological basis for Western literary theorizing and the evident need for something to replace it functionally motivates his analysis and critique of I. A. Richards, William Empson, T. S. Eliot, and Ivor Winters.

of that otherness, and lack of decorum on this point was regarded as critical bad manners, even vulgar presumption. Criticism, at least in this sense, was thought to be most honorable if conducted in a formally disinterested fashion.

Many kinds of readers found something to admire in a critical method that sought to protect a text — whether by T. S. Eliot or by D. H. Lawrence — from the imposition of "alien ideology." It is not difficult to see why many modern literary critics who were Christians found even this *regula* of the New Critics epistemologically, ethically, and even theologically a comfortable framework in which to operate, despite its potential impediments to the moral or theological heurism which regularly enough intruded in any case into some Christian critical writing.[18]

The force of postmodern poststructuralist theorizing has been brought directly to bear on these formalist values and assumptions. As is well known, the notion of objective "otherness" of the text has been ridiculed as naive by proponents of front-line theories of "suspicion" (not only deconstructionists but also the structuralists, neo-Freudians, Marxists, and some feminists). The groundwork for their dismissal is not only to be found in the comparatively recent assertion by phenomenologists that the observer unavoidably projects self onto whatever is observed (so distorting any projected "otherness"). It is also and more influentially supported by the general post-Romantic subjectivism which has characterized celebrated literary self-reflection at least since Rousseau. The anti-historical bias of secularized modern thought, the erasure in modern institutions (home life, curriculum, and religion) of what Hannah Arendt has called the "authority of the past," palpably undergirds the unapologetic narcissism and ego-preoccupation asserted in elegant and vulgar modern writing alike. That is, the obsessive predilections of those whom Paul Ricoeur has called "masters of suspicion" are as much a product of our recent moral and psychological history as

18. Exemplary here are Cleanth Brooks and Robert Penn Warren in *Understanding Poetry* (New York: Holt, Rinehart and Winston, 1960) and *Understanding Fiction*, 2nd ed. (New York: Appleton-Century-Crofts, 1959), and later, much more explicitly, in Brooks's *Tragic Themes in Western Literature* (New Haven: Yale University Press, 1955) and *Hidden God: Studies in Hemingway, Faulkner, Yeats, Eliot, and Warren* (New Haven: Yale University Press, 1963). See also Brooks's "Christianity, Myth, and the Symbolism of Poetry," in *Christian Faith and the Contemporary Arts*, ed. Finley Eversole (New York: Abingdon Press, 1962); Prickett, *Words and The Word*.

any consequence of the theorist's logic, everywhere reflexively confirming (without irony) the earlier phenomenologist's dour observations. "Advocacy" takes little pleasure in anything outside itself.

The enshrining of such a consensual subjectivism means, of course, that the usual *animus* in poststructuralist theory against the "otherness" of the text, and against any ideal of disinterestedness in formalist criticism, is often doubly freighted. Interestedness is the very *raison d'être* of every contemporary theory, and it is essential to a defense of theory as advocacy or propaganda that pretensions of any "objectifying" interpretation in alternative views — especially formalist theory — be unmasked as self-deceived apologetics for an outmoded ideology. Perceiving this, Christian critics have sometimes felt called upon to uphold a pristine formalist approach to the text in ethical or even theological terms, seeing New Criticism's defense of the autonomy and integrity of the text in particular as a sort of moral high ground from which to defend against the attacks of ideology hostile to biblical tradition.[19] There has been, we shall see, more than a little unintended self-disclosure in the special pleading on both sides, but the antipathy of overtly ideological theory to defenses of the "integrity" of the text has certainly contributed to the marginalization of New Critical formalism in particular, and its alienation from what had been perceived as a virtuous critical task shared by critics of many divergent "metaphysical" persuasions. This alienation has been particularly intensified where defenders of integrity of the text were indebted to Judaeo-Christian vocabulary and formulation.

19. The bias here is, of course, ultimately Arnoldean — a commitment "to see the art object as it really is." The value in this perspective is not by any means negligible, and it has stimulated a considerable body of useful Christian reflection on literature (see, e.g., the essays collected by Leland Ryken in *The Christian Imagination: Essays on Literature and the Arts* [Grand Rapids: Baker, 1981] and Roland M. Frye's *Perspective on Man: Literature and the Christian Tradition* [Philadelphia: Westminster, 1961]). A fundamental desire to represent another's point of view faithfully is itself ethically Christian, and without it historical scholarship, or indeed the sort of comparative analysis being undertaken here, is without value. My point here is that as a singular means of defense, even when articulate, this strategem is intrinsically vulnerable to the poststructuralist's denigration to the degree that it remains historically unselfconscious. See also Patricia Ward, "Ethics and Recent Literary Theory: The Reader as Moral Agent," *Religion and Literature* 22, nos. 2-3 (1990): 21-32; and the helpful essays collected in David Barrett, Roger Pooley, and Leland Ryken, eds., *The Discerning Reader: Christian Perspectives on Literature and Theory* (Grand Rapids: Baker, 1995).

From a historical perspective then, what must seem odd about many "Christian" defenses of formalism is their apparent forgetfulness that the inaugural commitment of Christianity to literature was itself hardly of a formalist character.[20] Relationship with the ultimate Author of the sacred Text was always the end in view for the fathers of the church, and the better understanding of sacred Scripture their only justification for a profitable study of secular texts, including major works of classical poetry. The very notion of a "secular Scripture" composed of these texts would to them, as we have seen, been charged with the opprobrium of incipient idolatry. Ironically, idolatry of the secular text is pretty much the charge leveled by poststructuralist critics of the late twentieth century against the New Critics generally.[21]

By the third quarter of the twentieth century the teleology of formalist criticism in the Judaeo-Christian tradition had largely lost sight of the motivating spiritual values so evident to Jerome, Augustine and their successors. Perhaps as a result, the self-transcending capacity of even those with professed formalist "disinterestedness" had become seriously compromised. When a new generation of critics and theorists, for a variety of personal and political reasons unsympathetic to critical vestiges of the Christian tradition and having other ideologies to serve, accused the formalists of cynical or self-deceived ideological practice — including idolatry of the text — they were not unjustified. This blind practice, as deconstructionists were to claim, was a naive "logocentrism," a belief in the fundamental capacity of conventional signs to refer to meaning that had no warrant in terms of the knowledge of modern

20. In addition to Brooks and Warren, see here Eliseo Vivas's confession of this *lapsus* in *The Moral Life and the Ethical Life* (Chicago: University of Chicago Press, 1950); the point is stressed both by T. S. Eliot in his famous essay "The Frontiers of Criticism" (1956) and J. Maritain in *Art and Scholasticism*, trans. J. F. Scanlan, 2nd ed. (New York: Scribner, 1949).

21. Northrop Frye's notion, in *Secular Scripture: A Study of the Structure of Romance* (Cambridge, Mass.: Harvard University Press, 1976), derives in his own case from "a sense of a double tradition, one biblical and the other romantic, growing out of an interest in Blake which seemed to have contained them both" (6). Frye's sense that the construal of secular literature as a "Scripture" owes to Blake, and as he later makes clear, Arnold, is unsurprisingly general among twentieth-century literary theorists and critics. See my review of Frye's *Creation and Recreation* in *Canadian Literature* 91 (1981): 111-17; also chapter 8 below.

phenomenology.[22] In the view of structuralists such as Roland Barthes, for New Critics to claim "disinterestedness" and "tolerant" analysis of texts as their purpose is to be culpable of intellectual dishonesty: structuralism at least could openly acknowledge its "interested" pursuit of the "functional" in interpretation.[23] And Marxist critics since Marx and Engels have been citing Western formalists' *lack* of an explicit and socially directed critical ideology as evidence of the ethical bankruptcy of Western intellectuals.[24] To some considerable degree, it must be admitted, twentieth-century criticism in the Anglo-American tradition has proven vulnerable to the charge. Moreover, confessionally Christian practitioners among these formalists may even be more radically "guilty" than their detractors indicate, in the sense that they often seem to operate without the benefit of a rich tradition of specifically Christian literary theory from which Marxists and poststructuralists have learned so much. Meanwhile, if we may speak in patristic analogies, much dearly purchased gold and captive beauty has been carried back into "Egypt."

22. The argument is developed in Derrida's *Of Grammatology* (Baltimore: Johns Hopkins, 1976) and *Speech and Phenomenon,* trans. D. B. Allison (Evanston: Northwestern, 1973).

23. Barthes, *Degré zero l'écriture et Elements de sémiologie* (Paris: Editions de Seuil, 1964).

24. See Karl Marx and Frederick Engels, *Literature and Art* (New York: International, 1947); Christopher Caudwell, *Illusion and Reality* (New York: International Publications, 1937); Granville Hicks, *The Great Tradition* (Chicago: Quadrangle Books, 1933; reprint, 1969); and more recently, Terry Eagleton, *Literary Theory, An Introduction* (Minneapolis: University of Minnesota Press, 1983).

Chapter Four

Evangelization and Literacy

Go therefore and make disciples of all nations, baptizing them in the name of the Father and of the Son and of the Holy Spirit, and teaching them to obey everything I have commanded you. And remember, I am with you always, to the end of the age.

MATTHEW 28:19-20

Think what punishment shall come upon us on account of this world, when we have not ourselves loved [the gift of literacy] in the least degree, or enabled others to do so.

KING ALFRED

WHAT WAS EUROPEAN PAGANISM REALLY LIKE — BEFORE THE ADvent of Christianity? This question is worth reflecting upon, even if necessarily here only briefly, not merely for an historical perspective on the impact of the Christian missionaries upon European tribal society, but also because a romanticized neopaganism has in our own era sometimes been proclaimed as an attractive alternative to our residually Christian society.

Life among the Germanic Pagans

The historical record clearly shows that pre-Christian culture in Britain, as elsewhere in Europe, requires a great deal of creative anachronism to romanticize. The conditions of life were almost unbelievably elemental and cruel; the character of life, as Thomas Hobbes would later put it, "nasty, brutish and short." Only the strong survived: the disabled, weak or infirm were exposed to die or (more often) directly put to death, as were the elderly and unwanted, especially female, children. In Nordic culture, medicinal knowledge was negligible. Physically less powerful males, like weaker dogs in a pack, were made to live in abject servitude to strong men with superior athletic prowess or battle cunning. The life of women in such a culture was fearful slavery. Intertribal conflict was a chief preoccupation, and the only social status worth having was that to be won by conquest and survival in perennial raids, battles, looting, and pillage — the "sword-play," as they called it, of Germanic manhood.

The Germanic tribes who made conquest of England and settled it area by area after the fifth century came from northwestern Europe — Saxons, Friesans, Angles, Jutes, and later other Danes, Baltic Scandinavians, Norsemen and Swedes. These northmen invaded not only England but also France, Spain, and Sicily. The Eruli, inhabitants of the Baltic coast and Danish islands, were from the same area as the Angles who invaded England, but on their viking raids traveled as far as the Black Sea. The way of life of all these wayfaring, warfaring Germanic people was much the same — piratical, predatory, and ferocious to a degree that campaign-hardened Roman commentators such as Tacitus and Julius Caesar found seriously disquieting. Even the barbarian Gauls, Caesar said, showed some susceptibility of civilization, but the Germanic tribes were intractably *feri* — utter savages.

In battle they were decidedly unconventional and highly effective. They fought partly or wholly naked — especially the opportunistic *berserkir,* who could fight for either side in intertribal conflicts and change sides on a moment's notice. More conventional warriors dressed in the short capes seen in Roman representations and on some peat-bog corpses of sacrificial victims, which covered no more than the shoulders and breast, the rest of the body being left bare.[1] They disdained armor.

1. Malcolm Todd, *Everyday Life of the Barbarians: Goths, Franks and Vandals* (New

In land battle their chief instruments were spears and wooden shields, and their martial strategies were strictly offensive. Battles against them would often last barely ten minutes; in the opinion of Caesar, if they could be prevented from annihilating their opponents for much longer than that the fortunes of the other side might well improve steadily.

The Germanic tribesmen, Saxons included, were big people; all the commentators marvel at their size. A warlord mentioned in *Beowulf*, Hygelac, or Huigelaucus, king of the Geats, was apparently so huge that at the age of twelve no horse could be found strong enough to carry him; his skeleton was preserved for many years as a curiosity and totem by a tribe at the mouth of the Rhine.[2] Graves in Iceland and Greenland have yielded significant numbers of well-preserved remains of men in the 6'6" to 6'8" range of height, whose heavy bone structure suggests fighting weights of two hundred and fifty to perhaps almost three hundred pounds. Even slightly less massive Saxons would have seemed huge to the fine-boned Celtic Britons (whose contemporary skeletal remains suggest an average male height of 5'2" to 5'4"), especially in hand-to-hand combat.

How did the invaders become so much larger of body than other Europeans? Part of the answer, at least, may be as simple — and as chilling — as eugenics. The pagan northmen killed off not only unwanted infants, aged parents, and the weak or infirm; they also sacrificed to the gods Tiw and Oðinn (Odin or Woden) the weakest and poorest men.[3] Moreover, while, as Tacitus notes, they typically permitted ordinary warriors but one wife, it is now known that men of more exalted rank — whose status was determined almost exclusively by battle prowess — might add slave girls or concubines, with important chieftains or "kings" having many of these.[4] Survival of the fittest — and

York: Dorset, 1988) is a readable general history (see here pp. 85-86); also Francis Owen, *The Germanic People* (New York: Bookman, 1960), who remarks sardonically: "It is evident that the equipment of the Germanic warrior was intended to emphasize attack rather than defence" (131), and suggests that the lack of encumbering vestments would permit "greater freedom of movement during battle."

2. Gwynn Jones, *A History of the Vikings* (London: Oxford University Press, 1968), 30.

3. E. O. G. Turville-Petre, *Myth and Religion of the North* (London: Weidenfeld and Nicolson, 1964), 253; a graphic example is recorded in the *Kristni Saga*, 12.

4. Todd, *Everyday Life*, 29ff.

murder of those considered inferior stock — must have over time contributed, through selective breeding, to the physical size and strength of
the Germanic warriors.

The rule of greatest strength, the effectively unquestioned assumption
that might is right, is a simple but far-reaching law. Nowhere does it show
to less flattering advantage than in the treatment accorded women. As
Malcolm Todd notes, "Wives were no more than chattel. They were
bought like slaves and not even suffered to sit at the same tables as their
lords."[5] The slave girl's lot was still less enviable. For reasons that will
become apparent on reflection, women took a strong interest in the
outcome of battles — on the sidelines often "cheering on" their side, and
sometimes, with creditable ferocity, joining in. They had much to lose:
women on the defeated side often committed suicide to avoid their sordid
fate.[6] A cruel subjugation of women was general, the prevalence of
"goddess" religions notwithstanding. The mystic aura of the special priestesses, remarked upon by the Romans, had no tempering effect upon
Germanic barbarity. Tacitus observes that the priestesses were in fact
deeply implicated in it. When prisoners of war were sacrificed to Odin, it
was the priestesses who cut their throats one by one, foretelling the future
from the way the blood of each victim gushed into the receiving cauldron.
Unchristianized Swedish pagans were still sacrificing their own children,
women presiding, as late as A.D. 1000.[7] And the funerary customs of *suttee*,
of which evidence begins in the fourth century and which are found
continuously to the early twelfth century in the far Scandinavian north
(last Christianized), are graphic witness to the real value of goddess
fertility religion for women. When one of the more powerful overlords
died, he was cremated along with several possessions. Animals — often
horses, but also dogs and roosters — were killed, and one or more of his
wives or slave girls also "accompanied him on his journey." Here too the
pagan priestess played an expedient role. One of the extended accounts is
that of the Arab Ibn Fadlan, recorded while he was among the Scandi-

5. Todd, *Everyday Life,* 30. A notable exception, although in its modesty indicating
conventional restraint, is afforded in the evidently Christian era poem *Beowulf.* Hrothgar's queen Wealtheow makes a gracious appearance in the hall, "bestowing gifts of
mead" upon the warriors — refilling the cups — then exits.

6. Tacitus, *Germaniae,* 8; cf. Plutarch, *Marius,* 27, are among the earliest sources to
note these practices.

7. Tacitus, *Germaniae,* 9; Turville-Petre, *Myth and Religion,* 252-53.

navian tribes near the Baltic (A.D. 920-922). The following brief excerpt of Fadlan's account will more than suffice to indicate the nature of the practice, though it concerns only the final portion of the ceremony, after the slave girl has been taken onto the cremation "ship" with the corpse of her master and the sacrificial animals:

> Then men came with shields and sticks. She was given a cup of *nabid;* she sang at taking it and drank. The interpreter told me that she in this fashion bade farewell to all her girl companions. Then she was given another cup; she took it and sang for a long time while the old woman incited her to drink up and go into the pavilion where her master lay. I saw that she was distracted; she wanted to enter the pavilion, but put her head between it and the boat [sic]. Then the old woman seized her head and made her enter the pavilion and entered with her. Thereupon the men began to strike with the sticks on the shields so that her cries could not be heard and the other slave-girls would not be frightened and seek to escape death with their masters. Then six men went into the pavilion and each had intercourse with the girl. Then they laid her at the side of her master; two held her feet and two her hands; the old woman known as the Angel of Death re-entered and looped a cord around her neck and gave the crossed ends to the two men for them to pull. Then she approached her with a broad-bladed dagger, which she plunged between her ribs repeatedly, and the men strangled her with the cord until she was dead.[8]

This type of ceremonial cremation, though usually in the case of ordinary euthanasia victims not in a "ship" but on a pyramid of logs, was common among Germanic tribesmen such as the Eruli, the "rune masters" whom Scyld Scefing, eponymous ancestor of the Danish Scyldings is said to have intimidated in *Beowulf.*[9] Their own aged or sick family members the Eruli led (or forced) up onto such pyres, repeatedly stabbing them, and setting the logs on fire.[10]

8. Trans. in Jones, *A History of the Vikings,* 428.

9. Jones, *A History of the Vikings,* 29; *Erul,* it is believed, is probably the same word as Old Norse *jarl,* Old English *eorl* — "noble."

10. Turville-Petre, *Myth and Religion,* 253.

The Germanic warrior tribes of northwestern Europe were on several counts not much more attractive in moments of leisurely respite from bloody mayhem than while energetically pursuing their conquest and plunder afield. According to the early chroniclers, they seem to have had the ethics and manners of a motorcycle gang. Tacitus describes them as "lazy louts," lolly-gagging around, drunkenly abusing any who came near, while frightened slaves and women were compelled to do all the menial work.[11] Procupius, the Greek historian, calls those who had ventured further south on raiding forays "faithless, greedy, violent, shameless, beastly and fanatical — the vilest and most inhuman of men."[12] And in other religious practices, as we shall see, from grotesque forms of phallic worship to the ritual sacrifice of human victims,[13] these ancestors of present English-speaking and Germanic peoples were an appalling lot. In our own time it may be salutory to remember that these "people of the swastika" are the same tribes of Teutonic warriors whom Nietzsche (like Hitler after him) idealized as a "herd of blond beasts of prey, a race of conquerors and masters."[14]

Nietzsche, like many other modern neopagans, despised the Christianity which tempered Saxon culture as a religion of "slave morals." For him, the sea change represented by the evangelization and cultural transformation of the Anglo-Saxon peoples was a catastrophe; he was disgusted by the replacement of the rule of strength by the "law of love" and the concomitant New Testament idea that "there is no longer Jew or Greek, there is no longer slave or free, there is no longer male and female; for you are all one in Christ Jesus" (Gal. 3:28). In its upholding of biblical commandments to mutual submission, forgiveness, and mercy, Christianity had, he claimed (correctly), severely compromised the natural will to power of Teutonic manhood.

Instead of unbroken Darwinian development toward the status of an unchallengeable master race, "this splendid ruling stock was corrupted,"

11. Tacitus, *Germaniae*, 15.

12. Cited in Jones, *A History of the Vikings*, 29.

13. Phallic totemism, including ceremonies performed with the amputated member of a horse as part of ritual worship dedicated to the fertility goddesses Freya or Nerthus, indicates how the "deified" phallus (called the Volsi) becomes an embodiment of fertility parallel to Priapus in Mediterranean paganism. See Turville-Petre, *Myth and Religion*, 256-58, for translations.

14. Nietzsche, *Genealogy of Morals;* cf. *Antichrist*, 84.

Nietzsche argues, "first by the Catholic laudation of feminine virtues, secondly by the Puritan and plebean ideals of the Reformation, and thirdly by intermarriage with inferior stock."[15] Nietzsche might have liked the Anglo-Saxon epic poem *Beowulf* almost as much as the pre-Christian continental Saxon *Niebelungenlied,* if only the boasting, drinking, butchery, and slaughter were not in that Saxon poem already visibly softened by such interpositions as Hrothgar's advice to the triumphant Beowulf on the wise ruler's need to temper force of arms and firmness of government with charity. Ironically, his choice among pagan Saxon poems to admire was in fact drastically limited by a single, simple fact. Literacy — the ability to read from and to make a written text — actually came to his Aryan "ruling stock" peoples in the baggage of Christian missionaries.[16]

Roman Missionaries and Saxon Culture

The rich and compendious annals of English literature trace back to fragile, poor, and humble beginnings more than thirteen centuries ago. To be precise, the earliest English texts to be preserved in writing had

15. The formulation is, however, that of Will Durant, *The Story of Philosophy* (New York: Pocket Library, 1956; reprint, 1966), 322. Nietzsche had, of course, other heroes, notably among them the infamous Emperor Fredrick II, whom Nietzsche praised as "that great free spirit." Alasdair MacIntyre observes that what Nietzsche praised in all his heroes "was what he perceived as a ruthless affirmation of the self and its powers," the very same qualities that led Dante, for example, to place the Germanic emperor in the Inferno. Conversely, as MacIntyre notes in *Three Rival Versions of Moral Inquiry: Encyclopedia, Genealogy and Tradition* (Notre Dame: University of Notre Dame Press, 1990), "what Dante and Aquinas saw as achievement of the good, Nietzsche saw as emasculation and impoverishment" (144). For these and related reasons, despite a richer complexity of his thought than his antagonism to Christianity reveals, Nietzsche remains an instructive foil for radical Christian ethics.

16. Runic inscriptions among the Germanic peoples predate the missionaries' alphabet and text by perhaps as much as four centuries. The runic alphabet (or *futhark,* as it is sometimes called from its first letters) was cobbled together from Mediterranean alphabets, principally Roman, but with emphasis upon characters with straight rather than rounded lines. This was because the runes were carved in stone or wood. All archaeological evidence suggests their use for magical purposes; no writing on parchment or vellum, or notion of textuality remotely comparable to that of the missionaries, existed.

their composition in a time scarcely more than a generation following the first tenuous Roman Christian mission to the Angles and Saxons of Kent. There were at that time in Britain small pockets of largely illiterate Christians — residual from the time of the withdrawal of the Romans after Constantine and reinforced here and there by continuing Celtic Christian influence (and syncretism). But little of their practice touched the lives of the conquering and now largely settled Saxon invaders of Britain.

Augustine of Canterbury, after a frightened and Jonah-like effort to evade or postpone fulfilling the apostolic commission to the barbarians of "Angel-lond" conferred upon him by Pope Gregory I, reluctantly landed at Ebbsfleet, Isle of Thanet in 597. The seminal account of this missionary effort to the Germanic peoples is that of the Venerable Bede.[17] Among the things Bede records concerning the early months of the mission is papal correspondence from Pope Gregory I to Augustine ("Austin"). In his letter Gregory wisely instructed him and his forty followers that they were to avoid imposing "the custom of the Roman church in which [they] . . . were brought up" dogmatically on the surviving indigenous Christians. Rather, they were to choose carefully among local practices "those things that are pious, religious and upright, and having, as it were, made them up in one mass, let the minds of the English be accustomed thereto."[18] Gregory had in mind the variant customs of the residual Celtic churches, but it is clear enough that the

---

17. Bede's *Historia Ecclesiasticae Gentis Anglorum (The Ecclesiastical History of the English People)* was completed about A.D. 731, four years before his death in 735. Bede drew on other sources available to him, but his is by far the most complete account of the Christianization of England. Several translations are available, among which that of Thomas Stapleton (London: Burnes, Oates and Washbourne, 1935), prepared in 1565, is perhaps most faithful to the tone as well as the substance of the Latin original. It remains a great classic of the national literature of the English people. The translation by J. E. King for the Loeb Classical Library (Cambridge, Mass.: Harvard University Press, 1930) is based upon it. An important recent assessment of the mission of Augustine of Canterbury ("among the best-evidenced acts of evangelization in the early Middle Ages") is that by Ian Wood, "The Mission of Augustine of Canterbury to the English," *Speculum* 69, no. 1 (1994): 1-17. Wood points out the effort by Gregory to discourage giving too much prominence to the miracles which attended upon the early ministry of Augustine and his followers.

18. Bede, *Ecclesiastical History*, 1.27. See the discussion of J. R. H. Moorman, *A History of the Church in England* (London: Black, 1953; 1958), 14-15.

integration of local custom drew also to some degree upon Angle and Saxon pre-Christian observances. For example, the English name for the Christian passover, *pascha,* was taken from the goddess Eostre. Our days of the week were similarly derived from the old pagan deities: Sun, Moon, Tiw (god of battles), Woden (or Odin, another battle god and founder of the Teutonic race), Thor ("thunder," god of physical strength), Frea (goddess of human fertility), and Saetre (god of agricultural fertility). The animistic names of Anglo-Saxon converts (e.g. Hengst [horse], Horst [mare], Ethelwulf [noble wolf]) were not typically exchanged for biblical or apostolic baptismal names. And with only the slightest of modifications favorite festivals or revelry were often accommodated to Christian sanction; the origin of the English drinking festivals known as the "church Ales" or "Whitsun (Pentecost) Ales," for example, is in distinctly pre-Christian festivities.

Bede leaves us in little doubt that to the apprehensive missionaries the culture gap between late sixth-century Rome (however deracinated and barbarianized) and the altogether brutally pagan world of the British Isles seemed enormous. Yet once both feet were planted firmly upon the ground of his appointed calling, Austin seems to have overcome his fears. Soon he had established good relations with Aethelberht, *bretwalda* ("king" or chieftain) of Kent, baptizing him on June 1, 597. As in other preliterate cultures, group personality far outweighed individual personality; the *societas* thought and acted in substantial and largely unmediated concert. When their king converted, it was for most as if in his confession he spoke for all, and thus many of his people converted with him. As newly consecrated bishop of the "English," within a few months Austin thus had the further satisfaction of baptizing more than ten thousand people in the waters of the Medway river on Christmas Day. He then founded a church and religious house at Canterbury, and in this way prepared the way for a second wave of Roman missionary enterprise in the south under Archbishop Theodore of Tarsus and Abbot Hadrian. Within the first hundred years the church school at Canterbury was training considerable numbers of young men in Latin grammar and rhetoric, in Scripture and its commentary tradition, and in some introductory natural philosophy.[19] Here was educated

19. V. R. Stallbaumer, "The Canterbury School of St. Gregory's Disciples," *American Benedictine Review* 6 (1955-56): 389-407. The great study of the intimate connection

one of the signal authors in early Anglo-Saxon literary tradition, and the earliest native English writer whose works have survived — the man known simply as Aldhelm.

Though none of his Anglo-Saxon writing remains, we have evidence that Aldhelm (ca. 639-709) was a popular vernacular poet, eminent enough that King Alfred the Great later became one of his appreciative readers. Yet Aldhelm illustrates in his surviving Latin writings the ubiquitous and persistent disquiet felt by early Christian writers concerning the question of how to make ordinate use of pagan literature. And for any new Christian educated in the Latin classics, as were all native Saxons formally taught by the missionaries to some degree, the shadow of the Mediterranean gods could seem as threatening to the flickering light of the evangel as that of the northern gods. Aldhelm was himself a skilled master of Latin prose. Latin is the language of his surviving letters, riddles, and theological and spiritual writings. But in a letter to a young Christian named Wihtfrid about to depart for further study in Ireland, where more attention was apparently given to Roman poets like Lucan, Statius, and Ovid than to the expository prose of Cicero, Quintillian, and Seneca, Aldhelm reiterates a familiar Christian warning against any pursuit of pagan poetry for its own sake.

> Rumour has reached me that you are going to study across the sea in Ireland. I pray you, study that you may refute the lies of pagan poetry. How foolish to stray through the tangled and winding bypaths of these legends, to turn from the pure waters of Holy Scripture that you may quench your thirst in muddy pools, swarming with a myriad of black toads, noisy with the guttural bark of frogs! What, think you, does it profit a true believer to inquire busily into the foul love of Proserpina, to peer with curious eyes into things of which it is not even meet to speak — to desire to learn of Hermione and her various betrothals, to write in epic style the ritual of Priapus and the Luperci?[20]

---

between Christian community and the growth of literacy is still Dom Jean Leclercq's *The Love of Learning and the Desire for God: A Study of Monastic Culture,* trans. Catherine Misrahi (New York: Fordham University Press, 1961; reprint 1994); see esp. chaps. 1-5.

20. E. S. Duckett, *Anglo-Saxon Saints and Scholars* (New York: Dutton, 1947), 39-40. Aldhelm wrote a manual, *De Laudibus Virginitate* for the community of nuns at Barking

That this early Saxon apprehension concerning the dangers posed to the gospel by the more enlightened Roman poetry ironically should mirror the fears of literate Roman missionaries about threats to the gospel from the darkness of Saxon paganism is perhaps not surprising, but it is instructive. It is often more difficult to perceive syncretism in one's own experience of Christianity than to spot it in the Christianity of another culture. Later the great Anglo-Saxon scholar Alcuin would admonish the monks of Lindisfarne for much the same thing, except that in Alcuin's case the pagan poetry he specifies is clearly Saxon:

> Let the Word of God be heard at the meals of the brethren. There it is proper to hear a reader, not a harper, the sermons of the Fathers, not the songs of pagans. What has Ingeld to do with Christ?

Alcuin is here quoting Tertullian, and probably St. Jerome.[21] But we may remember that this is only part of what Jerome said on the subject; the austere saint had actually much in common with his great contemporary St. Augustine in this matter. In Augustine's version of Jerome's "beautiful captive" theory, riches from an alien source are welcomed if they can be properly baptized:

> to study [non-Christian] poets and philosophers with a view to making the wit more keen and better suited to penetrate the mys-

---

(where now, near the Tower of London, is the church of All Hallows Barking), in which he urges upon his female readers their pursuit of Bible study, the fathers of the church, history, grammar, rhetoric and allegory (or poetics). See R. Ehwald, ed. *Aldhelmi Opera,* in *Monumenta Germaniae Historia:* Auct. Ant., 15 (1919).

21. This is the famous letter of 797 containing the reproach of Alcuin to Hygebald, Bishop of Lindisfarne, *Quid Hineldus cum Christo?* and directed at the Lindisfarne monk's apparently excessive fondness for listening to Saxon oral epics of the old heroes accompanied by the rhythmic harp. Tertullian had asked: "What has Athens to do with Jerusalem?" (*De Spectaculis,* 18). The passage parallels also St. Jerome in his letter to Eustochium (*Epist.* 22.29-30), quoted in chapter 3 above. Alcuin's letter appears here in the translation of D. W. Robertson, Jr., *The Literature of Medieval England* (New York: McGraw-Hill, 1970), 98. Elsewhere Alcuin (*Epist.* 169) reproves a friend for liking the *Aeneid* too much.

tery of the Divine Word is to despoil the Egyptians of their treasure
in order to gild the tabernacle of God.[22]

Here, as in Aldhelm's letter to Wihtfrid, the study of pagan literature is
justified to the degree that it is propaedeutic to the advanced study of
Scripture. But between the great Latin Fathers and the new Saxon bishops there is a difference. For Augustine and Jerome the pagan poets and
philosophers they had in mind wrote in their own Mediterranean languages — Greek and Latin. For the newly literate Saxon converts the
same Mediterranean poets wrote in a language and expressed a culture
alien even to their own pre-Christian experience. If there was a legitimate sense for Augustine or Jerome in which a Christian appropriation
of pagan literature could be a means of redeeming pre-Christian Mediterranean culture — the "beautiful captive" eventually to be taken
honorably to wife — the more natural candidates for English converts
were almost inevitably going to be found closer to their northern home,
among the blue- and green-eyed goddesses of the Germanic sagas. For
the Anglo-Saxons, the natural impulse toward tribal self-approbation
would eventually express itself in a desire for translation of the Scripture
and its textual tradition from Roman vernacular into the Saxon tongue.
First, however, they sought satisfaction for an already flaming passion,
drawing Scripture into the harp song of vernacular poetry, so that its
beauties too might serve equally "in the tabernacle of God."

Caedmon's Miracle

If not chronologically the very first example of biblical "translation" into
vernacular Anglo-Saxon poetic idiom, Caedmon's Creation Hymn
seemed to Bede in his *Ecclesiastical History* nevertheless the signal example, his own exemplar for the Christianization of a heretofore essentially oral and bardic literary practice. As a metonymic narrative, Bede's
account simultaneously characterizes the birth of English vernacular
literacy. To appreciate the mythographic power of Bede's familiar story,

---

22. See Augustine of Hippo, *On Christian Doctrine,* trans. D. W. Robertson, Jr. (New
York: Bobbs Merrill, 1963), 2.40.60–2.42.63; *Contra Faustum* 22.91.

we need to appreciate the context of early Christian community in which the event occurred.[23]

Caedmon was one of a group of typically illiterate peasants in the early Anglo-Saxon Christian community whose agricultural and domestic labors made possible the study, prayer, and scholarly activity of the more learned Christian monks and nuns. He was a cowherd, tender of the livestock in the abbey farm. The Whitby abbey in which he served under Abbess Hilda (d. 680) was one of several English "double abbeys" (others were to be found at Tepton, Ely, Wimbourne and Barking). At Whitby the double monasteries seem to have begun as a convent for women with a few priests or monks occupying adjoining quarters to facilitate their saying of mass for the sisters. Gradually in such institutions the male community seems to have grown in a fashion parallel to the community of sisters, yet in Whitby as elsewhere, the overall ruler remained the Abbess. These "Mother Superiors" (as was the case of Abbess Hilda at Whitby) sometimes participated in the instruction of the men.[24] In Hilda's case, Bede informs us, her prudence was so great that

> not only indifferent persons but even kings and princes, as occasion presented itself, asked and received her advice; she obliged those who were under direction to attend so much to reading of the Holy Scriptures, and to exercise themselves so much in works of Justice, that many there became fit for the ecclesiastical degree — that is, to serve at the altar.

23. At age thirteen Bede was a novice, and one of two survivors of a plague at Benedict Biscop's monastic community in Wearmouth. He was then transferred to Jarrow, where he remained the rest of his life, writing commentaries, theological works, and his great history of the English Church, in which the story of Caedmon is highlighted.

24. This model for Christian community was not favored by the new archbishop of Canterbury, Theodore of Tarsus (ca. 668), and the resulting loss of official support, together with the Viking raids, caused the double monastery to disappear within a century. See S. L. Carpenter, *The Church in England: 597-1688* (London: Murray, 1954), 27; also John Godfrey, "The Place of the Double Monastery in the Anglo-Saxon Minister System," in *Famulus Christi: Essays in Commemoration of the Thirteenth Century of the Birth of the Venerable Bede,* ed. Gerald Bonner (London: SPCK, 1976), 344-50.

But Hilda also saw to it that her Christian community, including the agricultural workers, had time for shared recreation. As had long been the custom in their pagan culture, listening to the singing of bards, their oral recitation of the poetic memory of the Anglo-Saxon peoples, was perhaps chief among the old recreations. It was enjoyed not only by noblemen and thanes but also permitted to attending servants and persons of minimal rank. Bede's recollection of these traditional Nordic occasions depicts the convivial ale-drinking assembly in what is clearly to him familiar terms. Interspersing courses in the feast, the old (pre-Christian) heroic tales and epic or saga narratives would be sung by the participants in turn, the harp being passed from guest to guest as the recitations progressed and conviviality intensified. Whether songs of past kings or mythic heroes of a bygone age, this poetry was still shared property, commonly held and communally performed. But poor Caedmon was unable to take his place in the common order of song. Bede recounts that

> sometimes at the table, when the company was set to be merry, and agreed for the nonce, that each man should sing in order at his course, he, when he saw the harp to come near him, rose up at midst of supper, and got him out of doors home to his own house.

In such a culture, the cowherd's burden of shame must have been grievous. Yet the occasion Bede recounts was to be a night unlike any other festal night for the broken-hearted Caedmon, a night of miraculous deliverance.[25]

> And as he so did on a certain time, getting him out of the place where they were drinking and making merry together, to the stable among the beasts which he had appointed him to keep and look to that night, and when the hour of sleep came, was gone his way quietly to bed, as he lay, he dreamed that a certain man stood by him, and bade him God speed, and calling him by his name, said to him, *Caedmon,* I pray thee sing me a song. Whereto he made answer and said, I cannot sing. For that is the matter why I came

25. It is an oddly harmonious accident, one assumes, by which Caedmon's name, were it Hebrew, would mean "one of the ancients."

out from the table to this place here, because I could not sing. But yet, quoth he again that spake with him, thou hast somewhat to sing to me. What shall I sing? quoth he. Sing, quoth the other, the beginning of all creatures. At which answer he began by and by to sing in the laud and praise of God the creator, verses which he had never heard before, of which the sense and meaning is this. *Now must we praise the maker of the heavenly kingdom, the power of the creator, his counsel and device, the works and acts of the father of glory. How he being God eternal was the maker and author of all miracles, which first unto the children of men created heaven for the top of their dwelling place, and after the omnipotent keeper of mankind created the earth for the flower thereof.* This is the meaning, but not the order of the words which he sang in his sleep. For verses be they never so well made cannot be turned out of one tongue into another word for word, without losing a great piece of their grace and worthiness. Now when he awoke and rose up, he remembered still by heart all the things that he had sung in his sleep, and did straightway join thereto more words in the same manner and form of metre, and made up a song fit to be sung and applied to God. And on the morrow he came to the farmer or baillie under whom he was, and told him of the gift that he had received and being brought to the Abbess he was commanded in the presence of many learned men to tell his dream, and rehearse the song, that it might by the judgement of them all be examined and tried, what or whence the thing was which he reported. And it seemed to them all that some heavenly grace and gift was granted him of our Lord. For more trial whereof they recited unto him the process of some holy story or example, willing him, if he could, to turn the same into metre and verse. Which he took upon him to do and went his way, and on the morrow after came again and brought the same made in very good metre, which they had willed him to do. Whereupon straightway the Abbess acknowledging and embracing this grace and gift of God in the man, instructed and exhorted him to forsake the world, and the life thereof, and to take the monastical life and profession upon him. Which he did and was thereupon by the commandment of the Abbess placed in the company of the brethren, and by her appointment taught and instructed in the course of holy scripture. But he whatsoever he could hear and learn would afterward think upon the same again by himself, and chewing thereon like a clean beast at his cud, would turn it into very sweet metre, and melodiously singing the same, made his teachers to become his hearers again.[26]

Bede's story is worthy of our continued remembrance on several counts. Chief among these is its simple Christian witness to God's redemption of the lowly and the humble in common life: to begin with, Caedmon is illiterate, neither monk nor nobleman nor even a *scop* (poet); his sudden gift of poetry comes as a moment of unanticipated grace. What comes to life in him is, moreover, immediately recognized by the community for what it is — redemptive grace — and accordingly his new gift is directed not to the poetic tradition of their Saxon forefathers, but to the "tabernacle of God." And, Bede suggests, such a gift, when offered back to the giver, multiplies a hundredfold. Bede sees Caedmon's songs as the wellspring of a baptized oral poetry, inspired no longer by the northern myths but by Holy Scripture itself, and hence flowing out of a source transcending anything Caedmon himself could possibly contain:

> His songs were of the creation of the world, and beginning of mankind, and all the story of Genesis, of the going of Israel out of Egypt, and their entering into the land of promise, and of many other histories of the holy scriptures. Of the incarnation of our Lord, of his passion, resurrection, and ascension into heaven, of the coming of the Holy Ghost, of the doctrine and preaching of the Apostles. Also he was wont to make many songs and metres of the dread of doomsday and judgement to come, of the horrible pains of hell, and of the joys and sweetness of the kingdom of heaven. And many others also of the benefits and judgements of God. In all which, his endeavour was to pull away men from the love of wickedness, and stir them up to the love and readiness of virtue and good life.

Seventeen of the extant manuscripts of Bede's *Ecclesiastical History* include, inserted into the Latin text, a copy of the Anglo-Saxon original of Caedmon's first song. In the original we see how closely in form and

26. Bede, *Ecclesiastical History,* 4.24; Stapleton, 240-42.

meter as well as in language Caedmon follows the Nordic pattern, and yet how systematically he has replaced the expected protagonist, a pagan hero, with the God of the Bible:

Nū sculon herigean   heofonrīces weard,
meotodes meahte   and his mōdge þanc,
weorc wuldorfaeder   swā hē wundra gehwaes,
ēce drihten,   ōr onstealde.
Hē āerest scēop   eorðan bearnum
heofon tō hrōfe,   hālig scyppend;
þā middangeard   monncynnes weard,
ēce drihten,   aefter tēode
firum foldan,   frēa aelmigtig.

It is meet that we worship   the Warden of heaven,
The might of the Maker,   His purpose of mind,
The Glory-Father's work   when of all His wonders
Eternal God   made a beginning.
He earliest established   for earth's children
Heaven for a roof,   the Holy Shaper;
Then mankind's Warden   created the world,
Eternal Monarch,   making for men
Land to live on,   Almighty Lord![27]

As Margaret Deanesley has observed,

Where the scop used royal epithets for his hero, Caedmon used them of God; God is the ruler, the lord, the keeper, and his divinity is shown by the adjectives coupled with the epithet; he is the almighty, the eternal, lord and king: he is the ward or guardian, not of a folk or tribe, but of all men: he is the "heaven-realm's keeper," the "glory-father," the "keeper of mankind." Caedmon sang of the glorious works of God just as the scop celebrated the heroic deeds of his royal patron.[28]

27. Translated by Charles W. Kennedy, in *Early English Christian Poetry* (New York: Oxford University Press, 1952), 13.
28. Margaret Deanesly, *The Pre-Conquest Church in England* (London: Black, 1961),

As with most cultures, there were in Anglo-Saxon culture analogies, correspondences to the biblical view of God, humankind and the world upon which to draw. In one of the happiest of these, the Anglo-Saxon word for supreme leader, or chief of the *comitatus* of warriors, was *hlaford*. This word, a contraction of *hlaf* (bread, or loaf) and *weard* (guardian, distributor, or "warden"), readily adapted itself to denominate the character of divine sovereignty, especially the lordship of Jesus, himself the "bread of life," and lord and giver of life, whose supreme self-offering is received in the bread of the sacrament. And so it is still, for English-speaking Christians, that Jesus is "Lord" — *hlaford* contracted still further in subsequent pronunciation.[29]

English poetry thus begins in praise not of a human but of a divine Lord, not of human destruction but divine creation, and its subject matter from the beginning is biblical. Yet as Deanesley reminds us, this first English poem to become part of our literate culture still echoes unmistakably the longstanding oral tradition into which the gospel had now so freshly come. And the native (pre-missionary) poetic style is no less visible. Four-stress alliterative meter, with no fixed limit upon the number of unstressed syllables, is typical of Germanic oral poetry. The stresses we may imagine to have been heavily marked with a strum on the twelve-stringed harp (and probably also by the sound of drinking cups thumping on the floor or table). Every sentence ends emphatically at the end of a line. This is rhythmically vigorous stuff, as unlike the polished urbane hexameters of Ovid as rough timbered halls would have been unlike Roman chambers of soft-hued marble from Spoleto. The missionaries from faraway Rome must have been startled by such differences, arrested by the sounds of Scripture they knew being chanted

168. C. L. Wrenn observes that "what Caedmon did was — so far as we know, for the first time — to apply the whole technical apparatus of the germanic heroic poetry which the Anglo-Saxons had brought with them from their continental homeland to a specifically Christian version of the story of Creation." *A Study of Old English Literature* (London: Oxford University Press, 1967), 102.

29. Rather, e.g., than *Dominus,* the Latin equivalent. In *dominus* what is emphasized is sovereignty over the *domus,* the "house" of faith; the Latin term suggests God's authority and fatherhood. In the English term "Lord" *(hlaford)* the emphasis is upon the link between physical and spiritual sustenance: the Provider / Creator God is the one whom we thank for our daily bread, yet who is himself also the meal, the Bread of Life.

to this unfamiliar beat, heavy like the feet of marching men, stirring up their apprehension at the cadence, too much like war songs in the mead hall. But there is every reason to believe that they came to welcome what they heard and even to encourage it as a means of making the Scripture more widely known to unlettered English hearers. Caedmon, the "father of English poetry," was only the first of many to use his newly won literacy to make poetry out of biblical narrative. Scripture is the central subject matter for almost all that has come down to us from this era of England's conversion to Christ.

The titles in the early Anglo-Saxon poetic canon are in themselves eloquent testimony to the power exercised by biblical narrative over the imagination of the new converts: here are the "Caedmonian" *Genesis,* concentrating on episodes such as the rebellion and fall of Lucifer and of Adam, and the sacrifice of Isaac; *Exodus,* with its focus on the narrative of deliverance from Egypt and the giving of the Law; and *Daniel,* concentrating in particular on the contest between Nebuchadnezzar's pagan idolatry and the faithfulness of the three young men in the fiery furnace, the pagan emperor's conversion (Dan. 4), and Daniel's wisdom in reading the handwriting on the wall in the hall of Belshazzar's pagan revelries. All these poems are free translations of portions of biblical narratives, in each case having to do with the theme of spiritual conflict and divine deliverance. In such poetry we see the striking appeal of the books of Moses in particular to the Anglo-Saxon Christian: *Exodus* begins by immediately referencing itself to the Law given to humankind at Sinai, and the theme of God's ordering Law pervades the poem:

> Hwaet! We feor and neah   gefrigen habað
> ofer middangeard   Moyses domas,
> wraelico wordriht,   wera cneorissum . . .

> Lo! We from far and near have learned
> throughout the world the laws of Moses,
> wondrous law to the generations of men . . .[30]

30. *Exodus,* 1-3; E. B. Irving, ed., *The Old English Exodus,* Yale Studies in English, 122 (New Haven: Yale University Press, 1953).

The theme of exile transformed into pilgrimage, a progress toward the hallowed order of divine rule, where perfect fulfillment of God's Law characterizes the peace of the blessed — this is the undergirding song of deliverance in the Old English *Exodus*. But the theme is to be found in Anglo-Saxon responses to Old Testament narrative generally, and it typically involves a transformation of their own tragic stories of exile upon the sea into pilgrim songs of joy and expectation. The identification of Israel's pilgrims with the Anglo-Saxon's own experience of the terrors of exiled wandering is strong — at several points in *Exodus* the desert-wandering Israelites are referred to as *flotan*, sailors or sea-going men (e.g., 103-106; 133a; 179b; 223a), while Reuben's sons are *saewicingas*, sea vikings. Clearly it is not important to the freely translating poet that his audience get an accurate sense of Mediterranean culture. Rather, he wants to ensure that the revelation of the giving of God's law to Moses (Exod. 20) is concretely related through Israel's experience of deliverance from exile and journey toward restored community in terms that a sea-faring nordic culture could not misunderstand. *Andreas* and the Old English *Fates of the Apostles* similarly apply themes from Exodus to the missionary outreach of the early church into the Gentile world. Though its subject matter is almost exclusively drawn from the Old Testament, it is nonetheless true, as Bede attests, that the early "Caedmonian" poetry is frankly evangelical.[31]

The earliest New Testament passages which appear in Anglo-Saxon poetic translations are likewise chosen to bridge the gap between the gospel accounts of Jesus and a Nordic culture in which points of Jewish law at issue among Pharisees and Sadducees, and even parables about Samaritans, shepherds, and vineyards would be obscure. What was not obscure to the Anglo-Saxons was the concept of spiritual warfare — a titanic struggle of the vulnerable good against malevolent darkness. That Jesus should triumph over Satan (e.g., in the Cynewulfian poem *Christ and Satan*), defeating sin and death — this was the element most likely to capture the Saxon imagination. But how could they understand that such a titanic victory should be won by means of a shameful death?

---

31. Bede, *Ecclesiastical History,* 4.24; Stapleton, 242. A valuable general discussion of the Caedmonian corpus is afforded by James H. Wilson, *Christian Theology and Old English Poetry* (The Hague: Mouton, 1974), 110-40.

The Way of the Cross

It was an inspired poet, trying to imagine how the scandal of the cross — the ignominious suffering and death of an unresisting innocent *hla-ford* — could be made comprehensible to his countrymen, who penned the hauntingly elegiac "Dream of the Rood." The appeal of this poem to its early eighth-century audience of still largely illiterate norsemen may be gauged in part by its partial inscription in crude runic letters on the famous monumental stone cross at Ruthwell (ca. A.D. 750). But it is the full drama of the 156-line poem from the Vercelli manuscript which reveals to us how, twelve hundred years ago, the Christian gospel was not merely being adapted to Anglo-Saxon culture but was in fact radically transforming that culture.

In this poem the cross itself has a voice. The "dreamer" who narrates his vision of the cross records it as speaking, describing the terrible events of the crucifixion. We must try to keep in mind as we read this beautiful poem how strikingly counterintuitive the tree of Golgotha would be as a symbol or sign of victory for a Germanic culture. A lord's passive acceptance of death in any form, let alone a shameful, ignominious death, was to most pagan societies intrinsically dishonorable and self-contradictory. To the Germanic tribes such a death was anathema. Honor in death was above all to be won by death-dealing valor in armed struggle against the foe: this is the notion of heroism championed by *Beowulf*, by the "Battle of Maldon," and by virtually all the Norse and Icelandic as well as Saxon sagas. The worst shame the author of the *Edda* can imagine, for example, is submission or cowardice in battle: as we have seen, the fate of such a person is execution. Afterwards, in pre-Christian Nordic thought, his doom is to be thrust down into the prison of Hela, death, from whence he then must fall still deeper into Nifhleim, oblivion or extinction, in the bottomless abyss of the ninth world. Bede reminds us how hard it was for Anglo-Saxons to accept as virtuous the Christian commandment of forgiveness: the East Anglian earls, he notes, killed their own converted King Sigebert "because he was too ready to forgive his enemies."[32] How could such a society — justly called by

---

32. It was usual, as in Kent, for kings or chieftains to be converted first, while the conversion of the people took much longer — really centuries — to effect thoroughly. During this time the battle against paganism and syncretism was waged with varying

historians and anthropologists a "heroic culture" — come to terms with the scandal of the cross?

The force of this question is at once intensified if we consider that the northern Germanic tribesmen had their own disturbing but contorted simulacrum of sacrificial death upon a tree. It was part of the ritual cult of Odin which was widely practiced among the western Germanic tribes from the seventh to the ninth century. Odin, or Oðinn (cf. Old Saxon Woðenaz) was variously construed by the tribes as either the son of Woden or perhaps as Woden himself. He was a battle god, inspiring especially the *berserkir*, and perverse in his affections. The "arch-deceiver," he took his chief delight in strife between kinsmen.[33] Like his counterpart Loki, he is sometimes said to be bisexual, or sexually "inverted," and in some locations homosexual rites attached themselves to his observances.[34] In the *Ynglinga* (6ff) he is celebrated as the *skaldskapr*, the inventor of poetry, and as a master of the primitive and totemic runic "alphabet" of the northern Germanic tribes.[35] Poetry is said to be the "waterfall" of Odin, or the mead Odin brewed from "Kvasir blood," and to be carried by him to the rest of the gods while Odin was in the shape of a battle eagle:[36] that is to say, the matter distilled in poetry is understood to be bloodshed and slaughter.

Odin required copious sacrifice and, as H. M. Chadwick notes, in records where it is "distinctly stated that the sacrifice was offered to Odin . . . the victims are always human."[37] Typically the victims for

---

success. Interestingly, the Saxons who remained on the continent were the last Germanic tribes to be converted. See Henry May-Hastings, *The Coming of Christianity to Anglo-Saxon England* (London: SPCK, 1972), 29ff.

33. Todd, *Everyday Life,* 126; Turville-Petre, *Myth and Religion,* 51-53.

34. Despite the fact that homosexuality *(ergi, ragi, stroðinn, sorðinn)* was punishable by death or permanent exile, it was apparently regarded as permissable among these particular gods, and possibly by their priests. A cult, the *Vanir,* associated with homosexual practice *(seiðr),* pursued a type of witchcraft accompanied by gross *ergi.* See Todd, *Everyday Life,* 131-32; Turville-Petre, *Myth and Religion,* 219, 312 for references.

35. Odin used the runes to "wake up" hanged men and make them talk; their origin is associated with pursuit of occult wisdom. See Turville-Petre, *Myth and Religion,* 44-45; also above, n. 16. A *locus classicus* is the text of the *Skaldskaparmal,* chap. 5 in the *Edda Snorra Sturlsonnar,* ed. F. Jonnson (1912-15).

36. Turville-Petre, *Myth and Religion,* 38-40.

37. H. M. Chadwick, *The Heroic Age* (Cambridge: Cambridge University Press,

sacrifice to Odin were not, as was otherwise the case, weaker members of the tribe or common prisoners, but rather captured warlords and princes. In such instances torture and death might be wrought by excision of the "blood eagle" *(bloðan rista)*, in which the rib cage was cut from a living victim's back and the lungs drawn out as an "eagle" offering to Odin. This ritual was performed by Torf-Einar, Jarl of Orkney, when he defeated Halfdan Highleg, son of Harald Fine-hair, and captured him alive. The sons of Ragnar Loðbrok performed it on the captured Northumbrian king Ella (A.D. 867).[38] But the more typical sacrifice to Odin was made by hanging the victims upon a tree, then piercing them with a spear. Sometimes victims met their fate singly, sometimes in larger numbers, as in groups of nine.[39] But the ceremony was said to mirror the hanging of Odin himself upon a windswept tree for nine nights, wounded with a spear, during which he sacrificed "myself to myself / on that tree / of which none know / the roots from which it rises." In the *Havamal* Odin is made to say

> Peering downward
> I grasped the runes,
> screeching I grasped them. . . .
> and I got a drink
> of the precious mead. . . .
> Then I began to be fruitful
> and to be fertile,
> to grow and to prosper;
> one word sought
> another word from me:
> one deed sought
> another deed from me.[40]

1912; repr. 1967), 3. A classic narrative is that of the hero Starkað, found in chap. 7 of the *Gautreks Saga* and translated by Turville-Petre in *Myth and Religion*, 44-45.

38. Turville-Petre, *Myth and Religion*, 254.

39. The classic account of an Odin sacrifice is by Adam of Bremen (ca. 1000) in his chronicle *Gesta Hammaburgensis Ecclesiae Pontificum* (trans. Turville-Petre); more ancient accounts include those of Tacitus, *Germaniae*, 7 and Procopius (sixth century), *Gothic War*, 2.15.

40. *Havamal*, 138-45, trans. in Turville-Petre, *Myth and Religion*, 42ff.

Odin's invitation to response or repetition of such a deed here invokes the ritual sacrifice, and indeed other unpleasant practices.[41] But it is evident that Odin, god of the hanged and grasper of the runes, might provide a contrasting point of reference for the chief focus of Christian redemption. In a symbolic commemoration of Christ's atoning death such as the Ruthwell Cross, on which are inscribed lines from "The Dream of the Rood," and, more amply, in the poem itself, the terrible rite of sacrifice to Odin cannot have been far from the Christian artist's mind and not, one imagines, unproblematically. How might these two notions of sacrifice to the deity be clearly distinguished?

"The Dream of the Rood" provides a striking answer. To begin with, the first-person account of the crucifixion is put in the voice of the cross itself, cast as a loyal thane of his regal Lord. Christ the Savior is pictured as submitting to his death in a gesture not of resigned defeat but of heroic courage, as in battle, yet he refuses the use of his eternal power to engage in a conventional conflict. It is a battle to the death to defeat death itself, his *agon* a struggle which can only be won for his people by the expedient of his own self-sacrifice. Christ is the *frean mancynnes / efstan elne sycle*, "King of all Mankind / in brave mood hasting" to climb up upon the cross, the "young warrior, God the Almighty" *(ʒeonʒ Haeleð, þaet waes ʒod aelmihtiʒ)*, the hero in "lordly mood" who "mounted the Cross to redeem mankind." The personified cross, as a faithful retainer, has had to suppress its natural instinct to fight back, or to refuse its terrible task. In obedience to the Lord of Creation it must stand firm in this supreme test:

> Bifode ic þa me se Beorn ymbclypte; ne dorste ic
>   hwaeðre buʒan to eorðan,
> feallan to foldan sceatum. Ac ie sceolde faeste standan.
> Rod ðaes ic araered; áhof ic ricne Cyninʒ,
> heofona Hlaford; hyldan me ne dorste. (42-45)

41. Tacitus, *Germaniae*, 9; in *Beowulf* (2939) Swedish King Ongenðeow, after slaying Haeðeyn, King of the Geats, threatens his fleeing retainers with what is likely the Odin fate — hanging as raven food. (The events described likely took place mid-sixth century.) The raven is said to be "Odin's bird."

When the Hero clasped me I trembled in terror,
But I dared not bow me nor bend to the earth;
I must needs stand fast. Upraised as the Rood
I held the High King, the Lord of Heaven.
I dared not bow![42]

The poet does not seek to diminish the horror of so terribly para-doxical a construal of duty. Rather, he intensifies it empathetically for the reader by inviting him to imagine what radical self-restraint and abasement of personal honor must be entailed for one who would be faithful to Christ in his suffering and "take up the Cross" in this un-equivocal way. The mute suffering of the cross as obedient instrument is thus mimetic in a fashion that implicates the human reader, but also centers the anguish felt by all Creation:

Feala ic on þam beorʒe ʒebiden hæbbe
þraðra wyrda. ʒeseah ic weruda 3od
þearle þeniam. þystro haefdon
bewriʒen mid wolcnum wealdended hraeþ,
scirne sciman; sceadu forðeode,
wann under wolcnum. weop eal ʒesceaft,
cwiðdon Cyninʒes fyll; Crist waes on rode. (50-56)

Many a bale I bore on that hill-side
seeing the Lord in agony outstretched.
Black darkness covered with clouds God's body,
That radiant splendour. Shadow went forth
Wan under heaven; all creation wept
Bewailing the King's death. Christ was on the Cross.

Crist waes on rode: it is the last stark phrase which, metaphorically, drives home the spear point, to the pagan mind tersely summarizing a hideous contradiction of any imagined human glory, while to the Chris-tian mind declaring the terrible paradox of substitutionary atonement

42. The poem is edited by Bruce Dickins and Alan S. C. Ross (New York: Apple-ton-Century-Crofts, 1966); the translation of these lines is by Kennedy, *Early English Christian Poetry*, 94.

without which eternal glory for fallen humanity could never be conceived at all. Here the poem is not an argument, but rather an exemplum, a sign which at once contradicts or repolarizes a fundamental
sign in the culture to which it has now come. As a "sign of triumph"
for the Christian, Christ on the cross is not in any natural sense a symbol
of mastery or of heroic conquest, but acutely its opposite: the apparent
stigma of utter defeat. But in the poet's deliberate and scripturally apt
characterizing of the atonement, the cross is of course revealed as so
much more than that — the sign of complete obedience and love, of
the Lord's substitutionary self-sacrifice unto death that *others* might not
have to die but instead receive their true source of life. To be sure, this
source of life, unbeknownst to those who are to receive it, has been "in
Him" (Col. 1:17) all along. But by his heroic self-sacrifice on the cross
our *hlaford* has provided for his faithful retainers an everlasting source
of the *hlaf*, their bread of life. Unlike Odin in so many respects, above
all in this, God now requires no further propitiation, no human sacrifice;
Christ himself has been the sacrifice, to put away even animal sacrifice
forever.

The poet accordingly is at pains to prompt — and to counter — the
natural Anglo-Saxon imagination in respect of the scandal of the cross.
In his recollection of the dreamer's vision he will insist that it is "no
cross of shame!" Yet he knows that this sign of supreme glory for the
faithful can never, of course, be fully divorced from shame. Though in
his vision he sees it momentarily as a token of triumph,

> . . . ʒeseah ic wuldres treow
> waedum ʒeweorðod wynnum scinan,
> ʒeʒyred mid ʒolde; ʒimmas haefdon
> bewriʒen weorðlice Wealdendes treoþ. (14-18)

> . . . I saw the wondrous tree, arrayed in glory
> Shining in beauty
> gilded with gold and precious gems
> adorned worthily, the Cross of the Savior.

— still, the splendor of the cross as the sign of redemption is forever
alternating, even as he gazes upon it, with the ghastly reality of Calvary's
dark hour, the tortuous execution of Christ in his supreme sacrifice.

ȝeseah ic þaet fuse beacen
wendan waedum & bleom: hwilum hit waes mid waetan bestemed,
beswyled mid swates ȝanȝe, Hwilum mid since ȝeȝyrwed. (21-23)

. . . I saw the Cross
Swiftly, varying vesture and hue,
Now wet and stained with the Blood outwelling,
Now fairly jewelled with gold and gems.

That which makes of the cross Christianity's dearest, most glorious treasure is here inseparable from that which makes of Calvary the moment of humanity's deepest and most representative ignominy. We ourselves have been among the perpetrators; even so, our *hlaford* has become for us our final redemptive sacrifice.

The centrality of the Christian paradox is revealed in this poem as a radical redefinition of Anglo-Saxon notions of the heroic: the cross declares to the dreamer that what transcends in glory any human notion of the heroic is the divine commitment to mercy and reconciliation. This means that honor must now be reconceived in a fashion which can do no less than turn a tribalistic pagan culture inside out:

. . . But the time is come
That men upon earth and through all creation
Show me honour and bow to this sign.
On me a while God's Son once suffered;
Now I tower under heaven in glory attired
With healing for all that hold me in awe.
Of old I was once the most woeful of tortures,
Most hateful to all men, till I opened for them
The true Way of life. Lo! the Lord of Glory,
The Warden of heaven, above all wood
Has glorified me . . . as Almighty God
Has honoured His Mother, . . . even Mary herself,
Over all womankind in the eyes of men.[43]

43. Trans. Kennedy, 95. John V. Fleming, in " 'The Dream of the Rood' and Anglo-Saxon Monasticism" in *Traditio* (1966), has argued persuasively for the poem's expression of English Benedictinism in the age of Bede.

The gospel proposes a new ideal of womanhood as well as manhood. No more shall women's honor any more than men's be won by violence upon the field of tribal conflict. Brunehild no more than Sigfried is to provide the exemplum for the Christian future. The Way of the Cross is to be the way, the self-effacing life of the word hidden in the heart. The rallying cry to bloodlust and *wergild* is now to be replaced by quiet acquiescence of a prayerful heart: "Thy will be done," and "Be it unto me according to thy Word."

It is of course lamentably true that the old Anglo-Saxon idealization of pagan and militaristic heroic virtues continued to resurface even in the christianized poetic record. The Old English *Judith,* for example, found in the same manuscript as *Beowulf,* is much like other battle poems of the tenth century, a reiteration or rationalization of the old Germanic heroic codes almost as much as a retelling of one of the apocryphal narratives of the Old Testament.[44] Yet this is also the period of the so-called *Genesis B,* the Old English translation of a continental Old Saxon poem which is sometimes thought to have influenced Milton in the writing of his *Paradise Lost.* For in *Genesis B* it is Satan who bears the heroic Saxon manner, and thus Satan who here as well as in Milton most completely models the woeful inadequacy of the old despotic "heroism" for a sin-stricken world.

Kingship and the New Wisdom

Any account of the impact of the gospel upon early Anglo-Saxon culture (even one so attenuated as this) would be lamentably partial if it omitted any mention of the remodeling of Anglo-Saxon notions of kingship as a specific instance of translation of the pagan heroic. Most vividly, it is in the response of the visible "strong men" of Anglo-Saxon Britain to the challenge of Christianity that we may obtain our clearest sense of the transformation of the *witan,* the council of the wise concerning justice and wise governance in their time.

44. Judith becomes, even more than in the apocryphal Old Testament Judith (12:10–15:1), a kind of Brunhild figure; the account of her decapitation of Holofernes is vividly realistic, a battle scene is added to her narrative, and she is praised extensively as a mighty maiden warrior. See the edition by B. J. Timmer, 2nd ed. (London: EETS, 1961).

The practice of tribal Germanic kings was not only to surround themselves with a bodyguard, a *comitatus* of loyal retainers, but also to include among them a group of *ealdermen* (from which we get the modern English civic office of "alderman"), elders, or "counselors," whose specific offices include the application of cultural wisdom to pressing questions of domestic and military policy. In Bede's account of the conversion of Edwin, king of Diera (roughly present Yorkshire and Northumberland), and with him his court and peoples, he provides us with an account of the *witenagemot* or council at which the king sought the advice of his "friends, princes and counsellors" concerning the new faith. The council knew that Edwin's wife was Christian, and that he had already granted permission for his daughter's baptism. Yet his approach to his council is reported by Bede as respectful and tentative. Edwin asks each in turn to give his view. Finally it is the turn of Coifi, chief among his pagan priests. Coifi's view is characterized by a typical pagan pragmatism: to Coifi there seems "no truth and no usefulness in the old religion." After all, "no man had honored the old gods more than he had himself, and what advantage had it been to him? If this new faith now preached among them proved better and stronger medicine, they should receive it." But the clinching argument comes from the next speaker, whose concern is rather for wisdom in a deeper sense. In his speech he casts his counsel in metaphor:

> Such it seems to me, dear Sovereign, that the life of men present here in earth (for the comparison of our uncertain time, and days to live) is as if a sparrow beaten with wind and weather should chance to fly in at one window of the parlour, and flitting there a little about, straightway fly out at another, while your grace is at dinner in the presence of your dukes, Lords, Captains, and high guard. The parlour itself being then pleasant, and warm with a soft fire burning amidst thereof, but all places, and ways abroad troubled with tempest, raging storms, winter winds, hail, and snow. Now your grace considereth, that this sparrow while it was within the house felt no smart of tempestuous wind or rain. But after the short space of this fair weather and warm air the poor bird escapeth your sight, and returneth from winter to winter again. So the life of man appeareth here in earth, and is to be seen for a season: but what may, or shall follow the same, or what hath gone before it,

that surely know we not. Therefore if this new learning can inform us of any better surety, methinks it is worthy to be followed.[45]

Bede records that Coifi, the man of practical measures, upon the agreement of all and further instruction from the missionary Paulinus, asked and obtained permission from the king to ride to the pagan temple which, by casting into it a spear, he straightway profaned, and gave orders that it and all pagan altars should immediately be burned. The king, with large numbers of his people, then prepared for baptism, and all were baptized on the vigil of Easter, A.D. 627.

What has transpired here is a clearly imaged exchange of conventional pagan pragmatism for biblical wisdom. The pagan wisdom had elevated the heroic code of the strong man and anchored itself upon the decorum of subservient *comitatus* fealty. Both mead hall and battlefield demonstrated that these were interrelated and pragmatically effective structures for the ordering of life in a harsh and violent world. But as the unnamed counselor's beautiful simile suggests, the pagan wisdom had little or nothing to say about the possibility of further dimensions to life and, ultimately, about life's spiritual or transcendent meaning. The cosmos for the norsemen expressed a wildly chaotic and darkly malevolent power; one's *wierd* or fate was part of an incomprehensible determinism. Part of the heroic code was the requirement to bluff one's way forward in the face of this incomprehensibility, to spite the chaos and absurdity of the universe, and when one's time of life came inevitably to its sudden end, to "die laughing," as the death hymn of Ragnar Loðbrok has it.[46] That is to say, the typical bearer of pagan Germanic wisdom makes a virtue of cruel necessity, and is logically driven to a rough-handed Darwinian expediency because for practical purposes he believes only the present moment of temporal existence has meaning; no sense of ordered derivation or obligation to a creator, and no sense of providence or future design exists. On this stark view the universe is mere immanence, without plausible transcendence, and hence questions of ultimate meaning are patently meaningless. Might is right.

---

45. Bede, *Ecclesiastical History,* 2.13.
46. Loðbrok, whose ferocity is of legendary proportions, may well be at least in part legendary. The customs he is said to have practiced, unfortunately, are not. See Jones, *A History of the Vikings,* 212, 215, 219, and Chadwick, *passim.*

Pagan wisdom in the Anglo-Saxon world is therefore largely a composite of strategies born of what Nietzsche so much later would call the will to power, or, alternatively, of resignation and despair. And of course, for such a drastically limited sense of human possibility, literacy in any developed sense was also largely an irrelevancy. The sword is not only mightier than the pen, the very notion of their comparison is laughable.

These are among the considerations which help us understand why the Saxons who stayed behind on the continent were the last Germanic tribes to be converted, and often, like some of their Scandinavian cousins, without the benefit of text or argument but simply with a sword at their throat.[47] Yet these are the same factors which make the success of the Christian missionaries four centuries earlier in Britain seem all the more like the miracle of grace Bede took it to be — and a true triumph of biblical over pagan wisdom.

The first hint of an effective Christian challenge to the customary pagan way is apparent already in the missionaries' own first community on the Isle of Thanet where they were tolerated but effectively quarantined by the *bretwalda* of Kent, Aethelberht. Here, Bede says,

> After they were now entered into their lodging, they began to express the very Apostolic order of living of the primitive church, serving God in continual prayer, watching, and fasting, and preaching the word of life to as many as they could, despising the commodities of the world, as things none of their own, taking of them whom they instructed only so much as might serve their necessities, living themselves according to that which they taught others, and being ready to suffer both trouble and death itself in defence of the truth they taught.[48]

Aethelbert and some of his people were at first amazed by this strikingly alternative manner of life, with its code not of heroic power but of self-sacrificing servanthood. Then, one by one, they were drawn to

47. A famous but not isolated example is Olaf Tryggvason (963-1000), who is said by the *Anglo-Saxon Chronicle* to have been offered the option after his unsuccessful attack on London in 994, and who then for political purposes "Christianized" Norway and Iceland by such intimidation. See Jones, *A History of the Vikings*, 132-35.

48. Bede, *Ecclesiastical History*, 1.26.

share in the community of faith. By observation of the missionaries' shared life (we must imagine how much, for the non-Saxon speaking Roman missionaries especially, example was necessarily precedent to word), the Anglo-Saxons seemed to have grasped almost immediately the essence in which Christianity was radically counter to the code by which they had themselves until now been living. This recognition is made immediately transparent in the dramatically un-Saxon way Aethelbert participated in the evangelization process after his own conversion:

> there began more and more [persons] daily to resort unto their sermons and, renouncing the rites of their old worship, to join themselves by the faith to the unity of the holy church of Christ. Of whose faith and conversion though the King much rejoiced, yet he would force none to become Christian, but only shew himself in outward appearance more friendly unto the faithful as companions of one kingdom of heaven with him. For why? he had learned of these his masters that the service of Christ must be voluntary and not forced.[49]

It is only at this point in his history that Bede tells us that the missionaries were directed by Pope Gregory I (in a detailed letter to Austin) both to "follow that course of life which our fathers did in the time of the primitive church"[50] (a custom by now less than common in the Roman church itself) and, as we have seen, not to insist dogmatically on customs of the Roman Church but rather to choose virtuous elements from local observances. This principle of accommodating wisdom clearly encouraged the missionaries' openness to generous use of the Anglo-Saxon tongue so dear to the hearts of the English, and made vernacular translation and hence the development of literacy of much wider cultural impact than it could otherwise have been.[51]

49. Ibid.

50. This letter is preserved by Bede (1.27). Married clergy were to be supported out of the common fund but to live in separate dwellings. The model used by Austin in setting up his episcopal see at Christ Church was thus communal but not strictly monastic.

51. The letter also helps to explain how it was that the astonishingly large number of thirty-two early Anglo-Saxon churches were dedicated to St. Gregory, and that his principal feast was accorded the highest rank in the calendar of the English Church. Gregory's

A Man of the Book

But here too an Anglo-Saxon king was to play a crucial role, and in so doing to reveal, two centuries after Caedmon, how far-reaching had been the transformation of Anglo-Saxon culture by the gospel. Alfred of the West Saxons is alone of all English monarchs accorded the title "the Great." This epithet has, almost singularly among kings and queens of history who bear the adjective, nothing to do with Alfred's potency as a conqueror of other nations, or with vast numbers of his own countrymen put to the sword or brought under his yoke. It has rather to do with his unprecedented regal leadership in providing literate instruction for his people. Alfred was perhaps the least predictable of all things to come from the rough barbarian north, a Christian version of Plato's wished-for philosopher king, a ruler who was first and foremost a "man of the book."

How he came to be that is in itself a remarkable chapter in the annals of European evangelization, of which only a minimal sketch can be given here.[52] The essential elements are these: Alfred ascended to the throne of his father (and, briefly, his brother) in a time of continuous military assaults and harassment by neighboring tribes and maurading vikings. Successful militarily (despite life-long debilitating illnesses), Alfred nonetheless judged that the long-term good of his people could not be served unless above all the Christian literacy of the first missionary period, now fallen into desuetude, were to be revived. Accordingly he dedicated himself to the acquisition and promotion of literacy and Christian wisdom. As a result of his remarkable literary and scholarly accomplishments he not only achieved much of what he set out to by way of cultural and spiritual reformation, but he also left to English cultural memory an arresting new image of great civic leadership — not the warlord, the conquering warrior with heavy double-handed

---

association with miracles is an evident reason for his popularity in Anglo-Saxon Britain. See here William D. McCready, *Signs of Sanctity: Miracles in the Thought of Gregory the Great* (Toronto: Pontifical Institute of Medieval Studies Press, 1989), and especially his *Miracles and the Venerable Bede* (Toronto: Pontifical Institute of Medieval Studies Press, 1994).

52. For a good general discussion see F. M. Stenton, *Anglo-Saxon England* (Oxford: Oxford University Press, 1943; 1971), 248-76; Rosamund McKitterick, ed., *The Uses of Literacy in Early Mediaeval Europe* (Notre Dame: University of Notre Dame Press, 1990).

sword aloft in war-gloat over the slain bodies of his enemies, but the scholar, the dedicated student of Scripture and philosophy, bent over a desk of books in thoughtful musing, holding rather in one hand the mere lightness of a feather pen.

The neglect of Christian learning in England from the time roughly following the death of Bede until Alfred's reclamation had been a function, no doubt, of several deflections of purpose. For one thing, the monasteries themselves, such as Bede's Jarrow and Weremouth, or Hilda's Whitby, were regularly attacked by Vikings and often sacked and destroyed (with all their manuscripts), the resident scholars along with everyone else put to the sword. This meant that not only were the guardians and propagators of literate culture being exterminated much more quickly than time, support, and diligence could replenish their ranks, it meant that many young persons who might well in more peaceful times have become their replacements were required rather to learn the old arts of war so as to help their families attempt to survive.

This was certainly the personal situation of Alfred. His biographer Asser (d. 910), a priest of St. David's (Wales) who had become his friend, writes that it was early evident that Alfred possessed "a love of wisdom above all things; but, with shame be it spoken, by the unworthy neglect of his parents and nurses he remained illiterate even till he was twelve years old or more." As a child he was a great hunter, and as a youth plunged into the rites of almost annual battle against the Danes. However, Asser notes, "he listened with serious attention to the Saxon poems which he often heard recited, and easily retained them in his docile memory."[53] That these Saxon poems were limited to the traditional oral poetry of his ancestors seems most unlikely. We may more plausibly imagine that the repertoire, in a royal household such as this, by now included biblical paraphrases such as those associated with Caedmon and his successors.

In any case, Asser records that when Alfred's mother offered a beautifully illuminated volume of Saxon poetry to whichever of Alfred and his brothers could first memorize it verbatim, Alfred, the youngest, got his tutor to read it aloud to him, memorized it, and won the prize. He seems thereafter to have memorized the prayer book or missal, along

53. *Asser's Life of King Alfred,* trans. D. W. Robertson, in *The Literature of Medieval England,* 107.

with the proper psalms, and to have practiced his reading by keeping a volume containing these texts with him in a shirt pocket everywhere he went. But for more advanced instruction he remained frustrated because, as Asser remembers him to have said, "there were no good readers at that time in all the kingdom of the West Saxons."[54] By "readers" here Alfred would have meant not simply people who could read off the words on a page, but rather those who were literate enough to teach in some richer expository fashion the content of the texts. ("Rede," in Anglo-Saxon and indeed until after Chaucer's time, means also to teach, expound, or give counsel.[55]) Frustration seems finally to have driven him — at first not fully consciously perhaps — to become, for the sake of his people, just the sort of "reader" he himself was looking for.

Asser and all the chroniclers express admiration and amazement at Alfred's dauntless perseverance in learning. All of his scholarly endeavors were necessarily pursued intermittently "during the frequent wars and other trammels of this present life, the invasions of the pagans, his own daily infirmities of body, carrying on of the duties of government,"[56] and while teaching his workers, building houses, and making practical improvements to the instruments and conditions of labor. Nevertheless he learned

> to recite the Saxon books, and especially to learn by heart the Saxon poems, and to make others learn them; and he alone never desisted from studying, most diligently, to the best of his ability; he attended the mass and other daily services of religion; he was frequent in psalm-singing and prayer, at the hours both of the day and the

54. Ibid.

55. Thus, the unfortunately feckless monarch of Chaucer's time, Richard II, is described by a derogatory alliterative poem of the day as "Richard the Redeless": the poet does not mean that he was illiterate (he wasn't) but that he too often acted unwisely, without a balanced counsel, and thus gave poor leadership in a time when it was most wanting. In these respects Richard II is seen by some of his contemporaries as Alfred's complete opposite.

56. During this time Alfred had to contend with a great deal. The Vikings had sacked the monastic communities at Lindisfarne in 793, and Iona three times in the next thirty years. In 834 there were massive invasions of the mainland, especially destructive of monasteries and churches. By 866 the whole of Northumbria had been lost, and York was a Scandinavian city. The battle of Ashdown in 871, in which Alfred played a significant part, was the battle that began to turn the tide.

night. He also went to the churches, as we have already said, in the
nighttime to pray, secretly, and unknown to his courtiers; he be-
stowed alms and largesses on both natives and foreigners of all
countries; he was affable and pleasant to all, and curiously eager
to investigate things unknown. . . . Moreoever the king was in the
habit of hearing the divine scriptures read by his own countrymen,
or, if by any chance it so happened, in company with foreigners,
and he attended to it with sedulity and solicitude.[57]

To this remarkable characterization of the scholar-king is added
the crowning virtue of generosity with his learning. He is said by Asser
to have instructed the sons of his earls, especially in "letters" and
"good morals." He was zealous to obtain coworkers and successors,
and "would avail himself of every opportunity to procure coadjutors
in his good designs, to aid him in his strivings after wisdom." In all
this he seems to his biographer to have imitated the model of wise
and pious kingship found in the younger Solomon, seeking first the
kingdom of God and his righteousness, and then finding that much
was added unto him.

Alfred kept several learned men by him in the court, priests and
scholars noted for being "well versed in divine scripture," and erudite.
The books of the Bible and works of wisdom and commentary available
to these men would have been, of course, still largely in the Latin
language. Yet

night and day, whenever he had leisure, he commanded such men
as these to read books to him; for he never suffered himself to be
without one of them, wherefore he possessed a knowledge of every
book, though of himself he could not yet understand anything of
books, for he had not learned to read any thing.[58]

---

57. *Asser's Life of King Alfred,* 109-10. R. E. Kaske, in *"Sapientia et Fortitudo* as
Controlling Themes in *Beowulf," Studies in Philology* 55 (1958): 423-56, argues for a
synthesis of old Latin and Germanic virtues of kingship in *Beowulf,* with, he acknowledges, a heavily Old Testament coloration of the Christian virtues. Alfred, I think, offers
a more completely New Testament modeling, coupling *sapientia* not merely with *fortitudo* but with *caritas* and *humilitas* — self-effacing love and humility.
58. *Asser's Life of King Alfred,* 110.

Asser means here, we assume, that to begin with Alfred literally could not read the text from the page. The books which he had learned were learned by heart, as with his aural retention of the Saxon poems, or perhaps that such a limited capacity to read letters on the page as he possessed until the middle of his adult life sufficed only for Anglo-Saxon texts he already possessed, having learned them by heart. It is in this sense that we are to understand Bishop Asser's statement that, after much instruction in "literary science" from his teachers, Alfred began, in 887 (when he was thirty-eight years of age), "on one and the same day to read and to interpret" Latin texts — almost certainly what is meant here is "expound and translate." Alfred now devoted himself at every opportunity to exposition and to translation from Latin to Anglo-Saxon, the making of a vernacular "wisdom-hoard."

Asser's account of his own role as counselor in the mead hall of Alfred, being asked to write excerpts of Scripture on blank spaces and fly-leaves of whatever book Alfred had to hand, is itself a worthy illumination of the biographer's art. Asser suggested at last that Alfred commence upon a book, a *florilegium* of such quotations. The king gladly agreed, and "eager at once to read and to interpret in Saxon, and then to tell others," he gathered gems of scriptural and Christian wisdom into his *Enchiridion*, a manual which he "kept at hand day and night" as a source of consolation.

Next came his works of translation and their famous prefaces. These included the universal history of Orosius — a book by a contemporary of St. Augustine designed to show the hand of providence in history, that history has had a beginning, that there is in it evidence of meaning and design, and that it will also come to an end by God's design. To Orosius Alfred adds elements of northern and especially Saxon history, and edits out portions of southern European history he imagines to be less interesting or less useful to Saxon readers.

The next important work he took to hand was a translation of Bede's *Ecclesiastical History of the English People,* a history extending from the landing of Julius Caesar to A.D. 731. Again, it is a free translation, with omissions and abridgments. Another of his translations is of Boethius's *Consolation of Philosophy,* the wisdom book of a Christian Roman senator about to die at barbaric hands. Here he was more careful to follow his text "word by word, or sometimes meaning by meaning," translating it first into Anglo-Saxon prose, then into verse. Yet it is Alfred's translation of the great manual for pastors, Gregory I's *Regula Pastoralis* or *Pastoral Care,* which perhaps best shows how much for Alfred spiritual wisdom and secular wisdom were indivisible, and how much he regarded the king's duty as including accountability for his people's spiritual well-being as well as temporal care.

Alfred's preface to Gregory's *Pastoral Care* is a succinct memorial to his own lifelong dedication to wisdom, a précis of the convictions which underscore his greatness, and a reminder to any age of what is the first business of Christian learning. He begins by lamenting the decay of learning in England since the time of Bede, and exhorts Bishop Werefrith, to whom he dedicates the translation, to get busy about doing his own part to repair the decay.

> Think what punishment shall come upon us on account of this world, when we have not ourselves loved it [literacy; reading] in the least degree, or enabled others so to do. We have had the name alone of Christians, and very few of the virtues. When I then called to mind all this, then I remembered how I saw, ere that all in them was laid waste and burnt up, how the churches throughout all the English race stood filled with treasures and books, and also a great multitude of God's servants; but they knew very little use of those books, for that they could not understand anything of them, because they were not written in their own language, such as they our elders spoke.[59]

Why, he wonders, did the Saxon Christian scholars of the earlier period fail to turn more books into the language of the people? Perhaps, he replies, because they wanted to encourage the learning of Latin. But a remedy must be found, for without vernacular texts Christian learning has fallen into decay. Alfred wants nothing less than that "all the youth that is now among the English race, of freemen . . . may be committed to others for the sake of instruction, so long as they have no power for any other employments, until the time that they may know well how to read English writing. Let men afterwards teach them Latin, those whom they are willing further to teach, and who they wish to advance to a

---

59. *The Life of Alfred the Great,* trans. Thomas Hughes (New York: A. L. Burt, 1902), 302-3.

higher state" (304). He then commands that a copy of this instruction for a plan of education, and with it Gregory's rich book of counsel for effective pastoral ministry, be placed with every bishop in England, each copy to be bound richly and decorated with an *aestel*, a jeweled binding, to the exceedingly great value of "fifty mancuses."[60] Clearly, Alfred wanted to be taken seriously.

Alfred's anthology of excerpts from the writings of St. Augustine, especially the latter's *Soliloquirorum* (internal reflections and musings) has a similarly luminous preface. In it the king describes himself as going to the woods like one of his own earls, thinking to find suitable shafts for spears, bows, and arrows — then setting out rather to build a cottage wherein to settle down to live "merrily and softly," as he himself has been quite unable in actuality to do. But the woods are here a figure for the riches of wisdom in which he hopes others like him may choose to dwell, even if they lack the material counterpart, learning therein to progress toward our heavenly home, even as we have been encouraged, he adds, by the example "of St. Augustine, and St. Gregory, and St. Jerome, and many other holy fathers."

Alfred, "England's herdsman" as the twelfth-century collection of proverbs pseudonymously attributed to his name calls him, "was a king of England that was very strong. He was both king and scholar; he loved well God's word; he was wise and *redeful* in his talk — the wisest man in all of England."[61] The *encomium* pictures for us a Saxon *cyning* (king) who eclipsed in greatness all his predecessors — and as well, we may suggest, all his successors. Yet he was great precisely because his virtues were not those of a warlord, but rather those of the faithful disciple. How difficult it would have been for Nietzsche to accommodate Alfred to his imagined heroic age!

In his later years, if we are to trust an old manuscipt source from Ely, Alfred was working toward a translation of the whole Old and New Testaments. Whether he had actually undertaken the task on his own, or whether he merely had given orders to his bishops to produce one, we shall likely never know. Although none of the translations survive, it is fairly certain that he was engaged in the process of translating the

60. A *mancuse* seems to have had the value of thirty shillings — an enormous sum for the time.
61. *The Proverbs of Alfred,* ed. O. S. A. Arngart (Lund, 1955).

Psalms at the time of his death.[62] In this focus Alfred is appropriately representative, for, with respect to literal or close textual translation of the Scripture, by the end of the ninth century, the Psalter along with the Gospels were the biblical books now most frequently being translated into the Anglo-Saxon language. One cannot help but see in this shift of emphasis from paraphrases of the Pentateuch to Psalter and Gospel an ongoing transformation of consciousness being effected by the continued preaching of the Christian evangel. The model for kingship which appears in these latter biblical texts, the praying and teaching of a servant king, is now the model to which at last the Saxon Christians had come to aspire.

*   *   *

No great figure in Christian history is a solitary hero, or a *lusus naturae.* Behind this virtuous exemplar of the Christianization of England, Alfred, "man of the book," "servant of wisdom," "shepherd of his people," lies the shadow of other "people of the book." Among those at whom we have glanced in this chapter, Bede remains an enduring presence in the annals of English cultural memory. More immensely productive than Alfred as a Christian scholar, Bede too wanted to translate the Scriptures into his native Anglo-Saxon. And the biblical book he felt most needed to be carefully rendered in its textual entirety was the Gospel of John. Among his own great labors of learning he had already edited this, his favorite Gospel, in a Latin text of great accuracy.[63]

At the time of his death Bede was fervently working to complete his Anglo-Saxon translation of John, waking between exhausting bouts of fever to dictate to an amanuensis. Slowly, painfully, he found the words to effect the transformation from *in principium erat verbum* to

---

62. There is some evidence that he probably completed Psalms 1 through 50. In all of his scholarship Bede retained a modest opinion of himself, never laying claim to originality. His favorite saying was that in his work he was simply *patrum vestigia sequens* — following in the footsteps of the Fathers. For a sound general essay on Bede, see Paul Meyvaert, "Bede the Scholar," in *Famulus Christi,* ed. Bonner, 40-69.

63. The oldest surviving book written in England is a copy of the Gospel of John now in the library of Stonyhurst College. The provenance of this manuscript is Northumbrian, and it has been suggested that this may be Bede's own copy of his favorite Gospel.

on fruman waes Word: "In the beginning was the Word." The opening lines of John's Gospel concerning the incarnation in Jesus of the logos of creation might well be understood, at several levels, to be the unifying theme of Bede's historical record of the Christianization of Britain. For from Bede's point of view, the word of God made flesh in Jesus, made lively again in the *evangelion* brought by the missionaries, then made articulate in the words of Holy Scripture through which he and his countrymen had acquired literacy not only in Latin but now in their own language — this word was indeed the beginning of everything that mattered.

On Rogation Wednesday of 735 Bede dictated from his bed his final page of translation. After his amanuensis had copied the last sentence, the boy said, "There, it is finished." "Finished indeed," said the old man. "Now lift my head with your hands, for I would be pleased to recline where I may look upon that place where I have been all these years used to pray, so that resting there I may call upon God my Father." Being so placed on the pavement of his cell he said *Gloria Patri, et Filio et Spiritus Sancto,* and died. But the *consumatum est* of the old saint was far from the end of the great project to which he had given his whole life in faithfulness. Rather, the Word come to England had inaugurated among his countrymen an entirely new life of the mind, and with it a rich spiritual and literary identity.

Chapter Five

The Book Without
and the Book Within

*And who but you, our God, made for us the firmament, that is,
our heavenly shield, the authority of your divine Scriptures? For
we are told that the sky shall be folded up like a scroll [Rev. 6:14]
and that now it is spread out like a canopy of skins above us.*

AUGUSTINE OF HIPPO

*All reality is treasured in the Word, not withstanding the divine
generosity which scatters goodness abroad, for God pours out wisdom upon his works, and upon all flesh, according to his gift.*

THOMAS AQUINAS

B Y THE YEAR 1200 THERE WERE FEW PLACES, EVEN IN THE OUTMOST
islands and deepest hinterlands of Europe, where the Christian
gospel had not found a more or less enduring welcome. Where it had
been longer established — for more than five centuries in most of Western Europe — the characteristic commitment of Christianity to literate
learning had begun to pay fulsome cultural dividends. After the so-called
"twelfth-century renaissance"[1] especially, the breadth and depth of the

1. The great contribution of monastic centers of learning such as those at Jarrow,

139

literary riches of late antiquity and the patristic period were widely
enough disseminated even in northern Europe that an unprecedented
textual sophistication was developing both in monastic centers and in
major cathedral towns such as Paris and Oxford.[2] The abundance of
literary theorizing in this period is, accordingly, much too great to
summarize in a chapter or two. Yet for the purpose of grasping something of the central and shaping influence of biblical tradition upon
literary-theoretical assumptions in the age of Dante and Chaucer, one
can learn much that is useful from a consideration of two questions
that characterize literary reflection in this period. Among those whose
principal Book was still the Bible in Jerome's translation and whose chief
magister of its textual exposition was still, a millennium after his death,
Augustine — which is to say, among virtually all serious Western readers
from the lowliest schoolmaster to Bonaventure and Aquinas — these
two basic questions have both a theological (today we might say "ideological") and an aesthetic register.

The first question we may responsibly formulate in a way which
initially suggests to a contemporary reader the profound opposition
between medieval and contemporary sensibility: "How does authority
lead the intelligence?" In this form the question is sufficient to make
many a postmodern theorist bristle. Yet for our medieval Christian
forbears it invoked a straightforward consideration of epistemology.

The second question can be formulated in a way which might
suggest a more contemporary preoccupation: "How does the reader
resist (or not) the authority of the text?" Yet if the contemporary theorist
is likely to anticipate in this instance a more congenial engagement, he

---

Wearmouth and Whitby in England, and others like them in France and Germany
especially, led to an analogous development for the education of parish clergy. These
"cathedral schools," the most famous of which was that of the cathedral of St. Victor in
Paris, produced a revival of the Latin classics, Roman jurisprudence, translations from
Greek and Arabic, and a true revival of ancient philosophy as well as sophisticated
scriptural commentary. See Charles Homer Haskins, *The Renaissance of the Twelfth
Century* (New York: Meridian, 1957) for a still reliable general introduction.

2. The medieval university, entirely a Christian phenomenon and the foundation
of the modern universities, was in part an outgrowth or expansion of the cathedral
school. The best general source for this subject is still Hastings Rashdall's *The Universities
of Europe in the Middle Ages* (1896), re-edited in 3 vols. by F. M. Powicke and A. B.
Emden (London: Oxford University Press, 1936; 1969).

or she is likely once again to be disappointed. For on the mutually central question of the reader's resistance to the text, the medieval theorist was, in a way unparalleled by his modern counterpart, plunged into a personal examination of conscience. Accordingly, to pursue these questions in their medieval context, we need to regard each as a question with distinct ethical overtones. In this chapter I want to suggest that the question about authority is answered less by proposition than by analogy or trope; in the chapter which follows I want to consider the much more slippery question of the resistant reader.

*   *   *

It goes almost without saying that Christian thought (whether in biblical, medieval, or modern times) is based upon a theory of limited understanding. But in the Middle Ages, two elements govern the application of this presupposition. First, there is the apparently contradictory fact that Christian thought holds also, and always, to confidence in an ultimate fullness of understanding. In the representative words of St. Paul:

> For we know in part . . . but when that which is perfect comes, that which is in part shall be done away. . . . When I was a child, I spoke as a child, I understood as a child, I thought as a child; but, when I became a man, I put away childish things. For now we see through a glass in a dark manner; but then face to face. Now I know in part; but then shall I know even as I am known.
>
> (1 Cor. 13:9-12, Vulg.)[3]

Second, Paul encourages his readers to observe attentively the referential nature of the created world:

---

3. In this period the biblical text referred to by Christian writers is Jerome's Latin translation, the "Vulgate," as it is typically called. In this chapter it is therefore the text translated into English in citations; the English translation which most closely approximates Jerome's Latin version is the Douai-Rheims, followed here unless otherwise noted.

For the invisible things of him from the creation of the world are
clearly seen, being understood by the things that are made.

(Rom. 1:20)

From these reciprocating injunctions derive three of the most important practical aspects of Christian thought in the Middle Ages: (1) an
acceptance of the physical order of nature as spiritually significant; (2) a
tendency to see any element of created order as nevertheless known
only in part and therefore (explicitly or implicitly) to look for and refer
it for understanding to a more perfect model; (3) an emphasis on, and
optimism about, the value for spiritual maturity of the processes of
ordinary learning.

Here, then, is a way in which medieval Christians saw authority as
leading the intelligence. Epistemologically, medieval Christian thought
was limited by its acute awareness of man's place in the middle — of
our limited perspective on the possibility of temporal understanding.
At the same time, it was liberated by its being premised upon a confidence in the comprehensive reality of a larger framework in which all
individual human perspectives are seen to participate, even though its
full reality could not be encompassed by any single human perspective.
This confidence in a self-transcending reality generated a keen desire to
explore the seen world, partly in order that its reflection of unseen truths
might be more richly appreciated.

The Word from the Beginning

In this respect, at least, no very illuminating pursuit of medieval
thought can be undertaken without some appreciation of what is
usually called "the doctrine of creation." Few biblical doctrines of wide
cultural application have suffered more from reductivism; we need to
guard against too swift a sense of satisfaction that we really grasp this
idea in the presuppositional richness and complexity it had for the
writers and readers of pre-Enlightenment European Christian culture.
In particular, the primary importance of the doctrine of creation for
medieval literary theory lies not in its straightforward credal affirma-

tion of the Judaeo-Christian belief in God's once-in-time creation of the universe, *ex nihilo*. Nor, even, does it lie in the fideistic appreciation and acknowledgment of the power and plenitude of the Creator's providence. Rather, the most important effect of "in the beginning God created" on medieval intellectual life is its construal of the human perspective as inextricably middled — and hence muddled. Whereas we tend to view history from the stage or state of present knowledge, usually imagined as a kind of evolutionary mountain top, a person in the Middle Ages saw rather from a point "in between," from middle earth, not just a stage between heaven and hell, but somewhere along a temporal route with defined limits, with an end as well as a beginning obscured from view. Repeated and various expressions of this sense of partial perspective among medieval writers serve to remind us, moreover, that for medieval Christians the universe itself was finite, firmly circumscribed by its Creator.

The resulting biblical model for history had an enormous impact on medieval thinking in all areas. From the break in communion between Adam and Eve and God in the garden, on past the promise in Noah's rainbow to Abraham's covenant and the eschatological promise which descends through David's kingship and lineage to Christ, biblical history looks forward toward a fullness of understanding which is denied to the present moment. From the very beginning it is eschatological — it thinks "from the end." Unlike the basic character of Greek philosophical literature which was so profoundly to influence the Renaissance — a literature more readily given to abstract principles, to rational process, to considerations of concepts such as space and to the study of physics and cosmology — literature in the biblical tradition, with its historical perspective, is much more interested in concrete personal and cultural experience and naturally, therefore, in the meaning of time. And because it insists on there being an end to history "in the fullness of time," it finds it necessary to speak also of the beginning.

That the Scriptures should speak of the beginning has sometimes seemed, as it did to Augustine before his conversion, a provocation. In his *Confessions* (book 11), Augustine reminds us eloquently of the frustration that arises from this affront in the opening words of Genesis. For, logically speaking, we cannot by ourselves adequately deal with "the beginning": existentially, in Bonhoeffer's echoing phrase, "where the beginning begins our thinking stops, it comes to an end."[4] From the middle, and acutely conscious of the passage of time that will not come again, we most urgently seek to know something about the beginning, and yet realize, existentially, empirically, that here is one aspect of reality which remains entirely beyond our ken. While still a Manichean, Augustine had encountered this initial offense, that the Bible insists on rubbing our noses in the most unflattering evidence of our limit as readers — our mere mortality.

The other aspect of the creation story which figures largely in medieval consciousness is the Fall. Once again, however, the modern reader needs to distinguish very carefully between what the Fall means and does not mean in medieval Christian thought. In pre-Reformation commentary upon the pertinent biblical texts, the Fall is thought to imply that human intellect, memory, and will are impaired, in need of education, reformed perception, and ultimately an identification with God's will and a return to the original intention of the Creator. What the Fall does not imply before Luther and his successors is that man's will and intellect are totally corrupt and incapable of response to the originals of divine intention. In a medieval Christian world view an aspiration to understanding is vigorously encouraged — but with a *caveat:* frustration is to be expected, because though our minds are wonderfully adept instruments, our fallen use of mind is perpetually encountering experiences of limit. It is in this context that the biblical "grand narrative," setting our sense of both potential and limit in relation to creation's larger story, from beginning to ending, became so useful to medieval Christian discussions of how it is that we learn, and why.

If, for a moment, we consider the Genesis story in its archetypal aspects, as they are treated, for example, in the twelfth-century Anglo-Norman play, the *Jeu d'Adam,* the pertinent features are immediately apparent. When Eve and Adam enact their will to be separate from God (and, in effect, from each other), the consequence is probably less well translated by the common English term "fall" than by words like "fragmentation" or "alienation." The estrangement from Eden constitutes the opening of a great gap, a breach between now and the beginning, between the Creator and his created beings; inextricably *in medias res,*

---

4. See Dietrich Bonhoeffer, *Creation and Fall* (New York: Macmillan, 1969), 1-14, for an extended modern reflection on Augustine's meditation.

human perspective is from the middle, unable to grasp either beginning or end. In the *Jeu d'Adam* Adam and Eve look backward to Paradise and ahead in vain, Adam saying:

> Jotez en sui par mon pecchie, parvoir del recovrer tot ai perdu l'espoir![5]

Narrative after narrative in Christian literature similarly describes this common realization, this discovery of being lost in the middle, where a personal command of structure, narrative, and progress are beyond the reach of ordinary thinking — even out of the grasp of mere words. So Dante, *nel mezzo del cammin di nostra vita,* in the middle of that road of life which we all share, declares himself poetically (representatively) as one having lost his way, confused, coming to self-consciousness *(mi ritrovai)* in a dark wood as bitter, almost, as death itself.[6] And so Chaucer, distraught, insomniac, fitfully dreaming in "sorwful ymagynacioun" yet without enlightenment as to the meaning of historical experience, wakens in a disappointed skepticism about whether, mortally, we can obtain such meaning.[7] The compensatory tropes of sleepless sleep and frustratingly incomplete dreams beget in turn that most ironic of medieval genres, the "dream vision," in which revelation either remains incomplete or its coherence proves effectively untranslatable back into temporal terms.

Psychologically, the Fall thus represents almost a division of conscious from unconscious states of mind. Even in its biblical name, the tree of the knowledge of good and evil suggests a kind of reflective capacity which can seem to be both the origin and the fruit of the hopeless circularity and subjectivity of fallen thought. Thus, the death which follows Eden is not only the loss of communion, the dissolution of the body and the estrangement of the soul, but, as for St. Augustine in the *Confessions,* loss of the possibility of relationship to the whole story — time's full narrative. "Men perish," said the pre-Socratic philos-

5. *Le Jeu d'Adam,* ed. William Noomen (Paris: Honore Champion, 1971), 1.525-26.
6. Dante Alighieri, *Inferno,* in *The Divine Comedy,* 6 vols., ed. Charles Singleton (Princeton: Princeton University Press, 1970), 1.1-3.
7. *Book of the Duchess; The House of Fame;* see "Sacred and Secular Scripture: Authority and Interpretation in *The House of Fame,*" in *Chaucer and Scriptural Tradition,* ed. D. L. Jeffrey (Ottawa: University of Ottawa Press, 1984), 207-28.

opher Alcaemon of Crotona, "because they cannot join the beginning with the end." We may suppose that this old Greek aphorism could well have been understood by medieval readers as describing also a literary problem, a problem of narrative.[8] But for medieval writers narrative structure was quite transparently a function of world view, a function of all that pertains to theology as well as to what we call variously "history," "science," and "art."[9] In Christian thought down to the Middle Ages it is in fact the problem of "joining" which is seen to be the universal human problem, rife with epistemological as well as spiritual implications; illustratively, the most telling metaphors are often images of narrative, story, and book.

St. Augustine provides a convenient entry point into classic Christian thinking on this subject, not only because he formalizes many of its central paradigms, but because his pre-Christian objections, as recorded in his *Confessions*, tally rather well with perspectives of our own world. For Augustine the convert, natural thinking, the thinking of those who must think from the middle to know anything about the beginning, is embarassingly subjective. "Stuck on ourselves," we think, exist, feel, and will in a circle, and without the possibility of reference to something beyond itself our thinking wants to take this circle for the infinite and original reality and thus orbits obsessively in a narrowing gyre.

For Augustine before his conversion, what makes the opening words of Genesis so objectionable is, then, the text's insistence upon mortal limit as our definitive condition; as a reader he resists being asked to acknowledge his own finitude and subjectivity, or being made accountably conscious of his basic inability to construct the whole of his own narrative, let alone an alternative "grand narrative."[10] It is painfully evident that no one could dare to speak of "the beginning" except One who was in the beginning. No ordinary person in the middle reaches

8. Medieval writers on literary theory held Alcaemon to be, as Hugh of St. Victor puts it in his *Didascalicon: De studio legendi*, "the first inventor of fables" (3.2). The translation of Hugh's *Didascalicon* cited throughout is that of Jerome Taylor, *The Didascalicon of Hugh of St. Victor: A Medieval Guide to the Arts* (New York: Columbia University Press, 1961), 86.

9. For an excellent study of the relationship of medieval "book theory" to modern literary theory see Jesse J. Gellrich, *The Idea of the Book in the Middle Ages: Language Theory, Mythology, and Fiction* (Ithaca: Cornell University Press, 1985).

10. Augustine, *Confessions* 1.6; 11.3-8.

cognitively from *alpha* to *omega,* even for the span of his or her own life. The real question posed by Genesis 1:1 for the reader — and the ultimate question in all forms of Christian thought — is: "In what sense will we let our author be our Author?" Or, what authority will we allow the Author as the story unfolds? To what degree are we willing to be simply a reader, rather than the Writer? For the Christian thinker of the Middle Ages, there is ultimately only one sensible answer: to read the story intelligently one must grant to authorship an appropriate hearing, must be willing to accept, at least *pro tempore,* the author's viewpoint. This disposition is, in the Middle Ages, as appropriate for reading the "book of nature" as for viewing a painting, as apt to books of words as to the book of God's Word.

From Augustine forward, the idea that the book of God's Word essentially accords with the book of his Works is a keystone of Christian thought and particularly of the doctrine of creation. We have already seen how biblical texts such as Psalm 19 become sources for this expectation. Although human perspective is limited, both qualitatively and quantitatively, still one may perceive a larger pattern through correspondence or analogy and may verify it, generally speaking, in an existential way. For medieval Christians such a faith in the indicative value of this correspondence does not threaten, much less seek to annihilate, the personal. Far from it, it gives to personal identity a context, a more intellectable, discoursable place. In the Latin verses of Alanus,

> Omnis mundi creatura
> quasi liber et pictura
> nobis est in speculum:
> nostrae vitae, nostrae mortis,
> nostri status, nostrae sortis
> fidele signaculum.

> All the world's creatures, as a book and a picture, are to us a mirror;
> in it our life, our death, our present condition and our passing on
> are faithfully signified.[11]

---

11. Alanus Insulis (d. 1203), in *Psalterium Profanum,* ed. Joseph Eberle (Zurich: Manesse Verlag, 1962), 126.

This overt correspondence between the Book of God's Works and the little text of the self, between cosmos and consciousness, is rich with implications. To begin with, as metaphor it confirms a provisional disposition to assent to textual *auctoritas* as a productive pedagogical praxis. By our discernment and confirmation of relationships, medieval writers seem to say, we enhance understanding, simultaneously, of both God and the world — which is also to say, of ourselves.

The formulation of Alanus in the twelfth century thus echoes faithfully the Christian world view already worked out in Augustine's *Confessions,* in which the African bishop had written:

> And who but you, our God, made for us the firmament, that is, our heavenly shield, the authority of your divine Scriptures? For we are told that *the sky shall be folded up like a scroll* and that, now, it is spread out like a canopy of skins above us. The authority of your divine Scriptures is all the more sublime because the mortal men through whom you gave them to us have now met the death which is man's lot. You know, O Lord, how you clothed men with skins when by sin they became mortal. In the same way you have spread out the heavens like a canopy of skins, and these heavens are your Book, your words in which no note of discord jars, set over us through the ministry of mortal men.[12]

The analogy between the skins of animals by which God clothed our first parents' fallen mortality and the "skins" of books (the *vellum* upon which medieval books were inscribed) — by which in turn our fallen nature is "shielded" from the searching heat of God's holy judgment (cf. Psalm 19, the text Augustine goes on to quote here) — instaurates a literary "conceit" of telling pervasiveness in late medieval discourse.[13]

---

12. Augustine, *Confessions* 13.15.

13. See, e.g., Pierre Bersuire, quoted in chap. 7, n. 20 below. This type of symbolic language illustrates also the fundamental divergence of post-Enlightenment from pre-Enlightenment thinking. In the former, language itself is typically viewed as an aggregate of symbols; that which is symbolized by language is the world of particular human experience. In texts written from within a sacramental view of the universe, the world itself is "a giant symbol." As Peter Berger has it, "that which it symbolizes in countless broken images is the blazing reality that lurks behind the world — in Christian terms, the face of God." In this apparent inversion of a Fichtean or Feurbachian notion of

In all cases, however, the image not only connects the Scripture whose books were written by human hands to the great book of God's creation and providential "unfolding" [Fig. 6], but it does so in a way which stresses the impermanence of the medium in contrast to the perdurability of the message. As Augustine's seminal meditation goes on to suggest, the book of the cosmos in its perfection leads us to think about the book of Scripture as it might appear in a perfection not mediated through mortal flesh: "There in the heavens, in your Book, we read your unchallengeable decrees, which make the simple learned," he writes, but

> Above this firmament of your Scripture I believe that there are other waters, immortal and kept safe from earthly corruption. They are the peoples of your city, your angels, on high above the firmament. Let them glorify your name and sing your praises, for they have no need to look up to this firmament of ours or read its text to know your word. For ever they gaze upon your face and there, without the aid of syllables inscribed in time, they read what your eternal will decrees. They read your will: they choose it to be theirs: they cherish it. They read it without ceasing and what they read never passes away. For it is your own unchanging purpose that they read, choosing to make it their own and cherishing it for themselves. The book they read shall not be closed. For them the scroll shall not be furled. For you yourself are their book and you for ever are.

For now, the form of that book which is available to us *in vellum* is a text in a sense both opened and closed, "as in a mirror, enigmatically." Yet for all that, what it communicates through the dimness of our mortal limitations is immortal truth:

> The clouds pass, but the heavens remain. Those who preach your word pass on from this life to the next, but your Scripture is outstretched over the peoples of this world to the end of time.

---

symbol and linguistic symbolization (it was they, of course, who inverted the older view), the symbolized turns out to be the symbol. See Berger's *A Far Glory: The Quest for Faith in an Age of Credulity* (New York: Macmillan, 1992), 160; but also chap. 3 above.

Though heaven and earth should pass away, your words will stand.
The scroll shall be folded and the mortal things over which it was
spread shall fade away, as grass withers with all its beauty; *but your
Word stands for ever.* Now we see your Word, not as he is, but dimly,
through the clouds, *like a confused reflection in the mirror* of the
firmament, for though we are the beloved of your Son, *what we
shall be hereafter has not been made known as yet.* Wearing the tissue
of our flesh he turned his eyes to us. He spoke words of love and
inflamed our hearts, and now *we hasten after the fragrance of his
perfumes.* But, *when he comes we shall be like him; we shall see him,
then as he is.* It will be ours to see him as he is. O Lord, but that
time is not yet.

For now, we must make do as best we can with the clouded glass, the
strictures of ink and vellum, the mortal limit.

The literary implications of this dependence for coherent perspective concerning self and the world upon acceptance of divine *auctoritas*
are various and complex — certainly not as simplistic or literalistic as
sometimes they are represented as being. For one thing, among medieval
writers it did not narrowly mean (as it later did to Cusanus) that creation
must be similar to the Creator. Creation for them is his expression or
Word, not his image. The created world is seen as a "voicing," a kind of
narrative — not an imaging of God's "appearance" but rather an expression consistent with other expressions of his divine imagination.
We see here that the original biblical idea (e.g., Ps. 19) persists, as yet
surprisingly resistant to the diverting proximities of Platonism and
Plotinism.[14] Medieval Christian writers do not invite us by the process
of an education in analogies to ascend to a mastery of the realm of pure
ideas. Indeed, such a goal is likely to be characterized by them as the
doomed ambition of Babel. Rather, they see the things of this world as
providing an insight, even as a book provides insight, as a kind of text
informed by the glory of God which in other ways too descends into
our world. Of God's glory the created order is, literally speaking, a lively
"translation," even if never as explicit concerning his glory as other
"historical" manifestations of his Word.

14. See, e.g., Augustine, *Confessions* 7.9-10.

Reading from the Middle

It is possible to construe Christian thought as historicist, and intellectual historians have done so. But once again it is necessary to urge caution against retrospective application of a modern or post-Christian understanding of the term "historicist."[15] Rather than holding a Hegelian view of history, thinkers in the Judaeo-Christian tradition until at least the eighteenth century believed in history that unfolded, like a triptych, or the pages of a book, in a pre-determined narrative, having the balance and the symmeteries of story rather than the forces and counterforces of dialectic. In this story, as in all good stories, meaning is not fully revealed until the ending. The structural prototype, the narrative model for the story of history, is, of course, the Bible. But the implication, epistemologically speaking, of a biblical rather than Hegelian historicist view of history is that historical judgments — just like judgments about personal experience — are not construed in terms of a contest of forces and counterforces moving toward temporal compromise and a new synthesis. Medieval historical judgments are typically interim statements, descriptions of process, construed in terms of contrast between ideal and fallen order, between Eden (or the New Jerusalem) and various Babylons of our own devising. Consistently in medieval historiography, all historical actions constitute to some degree either affirmations or negations of the divine purpose suggested in creation.

In such a view, though there are fundamental and absolute realities — such as good, and God, and creation, as well as evil, and Satan, and destruction — there are no actual earthly bodies which absolutely represent one of these utter polarities, no simple embodiments of black or white. Instead, we live in a world of admixtures, a fallen creation to be sure, but one in which countless transformations and recreations (as well as negations and destructions) are constantly taking place. Chaucer's scandalously humorous Alice of Bath may represent a fairly heterogeneous mix of qualities, but she remains redeemable; his Nun's Priest may express more understanding of love (or love of understand-

---

15. An exemplary rebuttal to conflation of Christian approaches to history with Roman (e.g., Virgilian) historicism is C. S. Lewis's essay, "Historicism," printed in his *Fernseed and Elephants, and other Essays on Christianity* (London: Fontana / Collins, 1975), 44-64.

ing), but, as he himself seems to be aware, he too is capable of falling, and can witness in himself the disintegration of memory, intellect, and will. (Accordingly, he tells his story as one who recognizes his own susceptibility to temptation and miscreance.)[16]

Because there are not, in a fallen world, signal embodiments of any spiritual absolute, there is not, in most Christian narrative, a simplistic opposition between flesh and spirit. Flesh and spirit are different media of human experience, to be sure, and the medium of the flesh may appear to be more susceptible to fallen order, that of the spirit more available to ideal order. But there is much less dualism here than is popularly supposed, and little absolute opposition between flesh and spirit. The two are seen by most medieval writers, in fact, as reciprocal and mutually profitable provisions of creation, both of which are necessary for a full realization of creation's purpose. The more ascetic strain in medieval spirituality that inclines toward dualism represents a minority opinion, popular modernist representations notwithstanding: even Cistercian monastics of the twelfth century argued for respect for the reciprocity and interdependence of body and spirit.[17] And in the next century the Franciscans returned to the referential relationship of creation to Creator and body to spirit to develop the richest application to aesthetics of the idea of the Incarnation that the Middle Ages was to enjoy.[18]

As articulated formally in the aesthetic theory of the thirteenth-century scholastic, St. Bonaventure, the flesh and its experience are indispensably the medium by which we come to understand "the unseen things of God" (Rom. 1:20). Bonaventure's relation of aesthetics to epistemology and the ethical life is succinctly rendered in his *De Reductione Artium ad Theologiam* (usually translated as *Retracing the Arts to Theology*).[19] There, building upon similar paradigms in Hugh of St.

16. See Charles Dahlberg, "Chaucer's Cock and Fox," *Journal of English and Germanic Philology* 53 (1954): 277-90.

17. E.g., William of St. Thierry, *Golden Epistle* (Spencer, Mass.: Cistercian Publications, 1971), 35-37; 52-53.

18. See John V. Fleming, *An Introduction to Franciscan Literature of the Middle Ages* (Chicago: Franciscan Herald Press, 1977), esp. chaps. 4, 6. Also D. L. Jeffrey, *The Early English Lyric and Franciscan Spirituality* (Lincoln: University of Nebraska Press, 1975), chap. 3.

19. See the two-volume edition of the *Works of Saint Bonaventure* by Sister Emma

Victor's *Didascalicon,* he describes what he takes to be the relationship of the "four lights to knowledge" to sacred Scripture: the "external" light, or the light of mechanical skill; the lower light, or the light of sense perception; the inner light, or the light of philosophical reflection; and the higher light, or the light of grace and of sacred Scripture." Of these four, says Bonaventure, "the first light illumines in the consideration of the arts and crafts [in which he includes what Hopkins would later call "all trades, their gear and tackle and trim"]; the second in regard to natural form; the third in regard to intellectual truth; the fourth and ultimate, in regard to saving truth."[20] But Bonaventure's hierarchy of value is not, strictly speaking, temporally identical to that order which his pedagogy recommends. Here, the first "light of knowledge" in the order of time is the light of sense perception, even as the literal sense of Scripture for him is always that sense with which responsible exegesis must begin. (The moral, allegorical, and anagogical senses of medieval fourfold exegesis correspond roughly to the other "lights.")

The familiar medieval strategy for "fourfold" exegesis is itself an outgrowth of the relatively simpler distinction of Paul (e.g., 2 Cor. 3:6) between the "letter" and "spirit" of Scripture, but increasingly nuanced to distinguish between spiritual reading which focuses on the life of the individual and the morality appropriate to it (tropology), the life of the church in the world (allegory), and the condition of the blessed in the world to come (anagogy). The development is anticipated by Gregory the Great (540-604) in his *Moralia* upon Job, when he describes allegory "as a kind of machine to the spirit placed far from God by means of which it may be raised up to God," and elaborated further in Hugh of St. Victor's twelfth-century *Didascalicon,* where he distinguishes between three possible senses of Scripture (6.4; 5.2): history, allegory, and tropology. By the time of Aquinas (1225-1274), the basic distinction of Paul, elaborated in Augustine's *On Christian Doctrine,* has taken on the "fourfold" form suggested by the following:

Thérèse Healy, which provides, in vol. 1, both a translation and a reliable introduction to the *De Reductione Artium ad Theologiam* (St. Bonaventure, New York: Franciscan Institute Press, 1955).

20. Bonaventure, *De Reductione Artium ad Theologiam,* 1; Healy, 20.

God, who is the author of Holy Scripture, possesses the power not only to adapt words to meanings, which we can do, but also to adapt things to meanings. What is peculiar to Holy Scripture is this, the things there signified by words may also in their turn signify other things. The first signification, whereby words signify facts, is called the historical and literal sense; the second signification, whereby the facts signified by the words also signify other facts, is called the spiritual sense. Note that the spiritual sense is based on, and presupposes, the literal sense.[21]

For Bonaventure, it follows by analogy that in sense perception, as in the literal sense, all the other powers of insight are nascent, poised and ready to flower as stimulated, respectively, by the operations of memory, intellect, and will.

In his approach to the primary role of sense perception, as (elsewhere) to the initiating function of the literal sense of Scripture, Bonaventure illustrates how pervasively metaphors of the written Word govern medi-

---

21. Aquinas, *Summa Theologica* 1a1.10. Aquinas instances the system in reference to the sacrament of marriage: "Holy Scripture speaks of four marriages. The first in its historical and literal sense, the bodily union of a man and a woman; the second allegorical, the union of Christ with his Church; the third tropological or moral, the union of God with the soul; the fourth anagogical or eschatological, the union of God with the Church Triumphant" (*Sermons*, 1st Sunday after Epiphany, 20).

For John Wyclif in the fourteenth century, allegory, tropology, and anagogy are aspects of exegesis of the durational rather than temporal syntax of Scripture: "The literal understanding of hooli scripture is the ground of al goostli vnderstondyng therof, that is, of allegorik, of moral, and of anagogik. No goostli vnderstonding is autentik, no but it be groundid in the text opynli, either in opyn resoun, suynge of principlis, ether reulis of feith, seynt Austin witnessith opynli in his pistle to Vincente, Donatiste, and in his book of Soliloquies, and Jerome on Jonas, and Lire on the bigynnynge of Genesis, and in many placis of hooli scripture and Ardmakan in his book of Questiouns of Armenyes. Therfor men moten see the treuthe of the text, and be war of goostli vnderstondyng, ether moral fantasye and ȝyue not ful credence therto, no but it be groundid opynly in the text of hooly writ, in o place or other, ethir in opyn resoun, that may not be auoidid; for eles it wole as likyngli be applied to falsnesse as to treuthe; and it hath dessevued gret men in oure daies, bi ouer greet triste to her fantasies. *Literal ether histor vnderstondyng techith what thing is don;* allegorik techith what we for bileue; moral ether tropologik techith what we owen to do to fle vices, and kep virtues; anagogik techith what we owen to hope of euerlastynge meede in heuen" (Prologue to Isaiah, printed in *The Wycliffite Bible*, ed. J. Forshall and F. Madden, 4 vols. [Oxford, 1850], 3.225).

eval understanding of the ways in which we learn about God, ourselves, and the world. The process of sense perception, says Bonaventure, concerns itself exclusively with the cognition of sensible objects, and occurs in three phases: "cognoscendi *medium,* cognoscendi *exercitium,* cognoscendi *oblectamentum*" (the medium of perception, the exercise of perception, and the delight of perception).[22] Here the consistent triune pattern unfolds again. If we consider the *medium* of perception, he says, we shall see therein the word begotten from all eternity and articulated, made flesh, in time — because of generic, specific, or symbolic likeness to the Creator. Words inhere in the Word: in language and in vision the processes of creativity are analogous to the form of the creator. When the contact between organ or faculty and object is established, there results a new percept, an expressed image by means of which the mind reverts to the object.[23] The *exercise* of sense perception reveals, accordingly, the pattern of human life. But in the *delight,* as we have already observed, is opened the union of the soul with God.

> Indeed, every sense seeks its proper sensible with longing, finds it with delight, and seeks it again without ceasing, because "the eye is not filled with seeing, neither is the ear filled with hearing" [Eccles. 1:8]. In the same way, our spiritual senses must seek longingly, find joyfully, and seek again without ceasing the beautiful, the harmonious, the fragrant, the sweet, or the delightful to the touch. Behold how the Divine Wisdom lies hidden in sense perception and how wonderful is the contemplation of the five spiritual senses in the light of their conformity to the senses of the body.[24]

The potential of sense perception expressed here is remarkable. The spiritual senses not only may but must "seek longingly, find joyfully"

22. Bonaventure, *De Reductione Artium,* 8; Healy, 28.
23. Ibid., 8-9; Healy, 28-30.
24. Ibid., 10: "Omnis enim sensus suum sensibile conveniens quaerit cum desiderio, invenit cum gaudio, repetit sine fastidio, quia *non satiatur oculus visu, nec auris auditu impletur.* — Per hunc etiam modum sensus *cordis* nostri sive pulcrum, sive consonum, sive odoriferum, sive dulce, sive mulcebre debet desideranter quaerere, gaudenter invenire, incessanter repetere. — Ecce, quomodo in cognitione sensitiva continetur occulte divina sapientia, et quam mira est contemplatio quinque sensuum spiritualium secundum conformitatem ad sensus corporales."

the divine wisdom hidden in them. Sense perception begins in delight and ends in transcendent delight, just as language and desire converge in a transfiguration of the body's mortal limit.

Finally, Bonaventure calls upon artisans of music and poetry to illustrate the necessary harmony of the universe, in which the part is subordinate to the whole. In the case of music played upon the harp, for example, he says that the chords should be so proportioned that if any one should be altered so as to give it prominence no harmony at all would remain. In the case of poetry, the words should be so ordered that it would be impossible for the same words to make better sense.[25]

Writing the New Life

These reflections have powerful implications for medieval character- izations of human authorship. Dante Alighieri, a poet educated in the Augustinian and Franciscan tradition, provides a luminous example. Among Dante's formative teachers, the one whose influence most prompted his choice of vernacular language was the Franciscan poet Miro da Colle, a debt he acknowledges magnificently in his *De Vulgaria Eloquentia*. Here, as in his *Convivio,* a formal treatise on hermeneutics, as well as in his greatest poem, the *Commedia,* both as pedagogy and as implicit structure the epistemology and aesthetic employed by Bonaven- ture are richly present. They characterize as well the *Vita Nuova* (The New Life), a briefer work of Dante's that combines lyric poetry with expository prose in such a way as to illustrate the informing power of the trope of the book in medieval poetry.

The *Vita Nuova* notably testifies to a process of education leading to new self-understanding and a conversion from vesting authority in the self or "reader" of the book to acknowledgment of higher authority, the *auctoritas* of the Author. In the book's opening words Dante casts himself as a student searching a book, "the book of my memory." From this book he wishes to take the "words" which he intends to "recollect" in the book he is writing, if not completely then at least "in their

25. Bonaventure, *Commentarium in Sententiarum* 1.44.1.3 (Quaracchi edn., 1.756- 57).

meaning."[26] This very Augustinian notion of the human author as merely a scribe and translator is characteristic of a great number of medieval writers, not only Dante, and the use of the book-scribe metaphor alerts the medieval reader to such a writer's view of himself as a kind of student and of his work as text with a context, with reference for meaning to another and precedent text. That is, the book of memory which Dante studies has as its author God himself, to whose writing in history the poet responds, as a scribe. The analogy with the evangelists taking dictation from Christ, or with patristic writers taking divine dictation in their own fashion from the Holy Spirit, is transparent [Fig. 5a; 5b]. For Dante in the *Inferno* (4.85-102; cf. 15.88-90) the poetic tradition extending from Homer to himself bears a kind of collective witness, as an anthology of scribal translations, to God's continuous narrative presence in the reality of temporal human experience.

That the poet's ostensibly autobiographical witness in the *Vita Nuova* should be thus retrospectively construed, that the story of his love for Beatrice should be recollected as a series of transformations whereby he is led from the limitations of carnal affection through a series of new understandings to a higher love, is completely in accord with the pre-text and con-text to which he refers. From the topical dream vision in which the authority of the God of Love is first mysteriously apparent (Sonnet 1), on through the conventional reactions and responses of love, the poet traces the course of his ardor to the point (Sonnet 7) where his love for Beatrice begins to undergo a transformation. In this transformation he begins to see her in more than her physical aspect: now, with reference to those qualities of her person which "Love himself" admires, she acquires far more profound — and correspondingly more "authoritative" — stature. Gradually his attention moves, in parallel fashion, away from his own frustration and self-pity toward that sort of praise of his Lady which shares her beauty with others, and refers her beauty to God (and to Love, who by this point begins to be identified with God [Canzone 1]). The effect of this sharing and referral is a "humbling," so that "all sins leave his memory": his older memory begins also to be transformed.[27] The purpose of

26. A convenient translation is Dante, *The New Life*, trans. W. Anderson (Baltimore: Penguin, 1964), 37.

27. Anderson, *The New Life*, 65.

Figure 5a. *"Christ Sends his inspired Word to the Apostles."* Sacramentary of St. Denis, ca. 1050. Courtesy: Bibliothèque Nationale de France – Paris.

Canzone 1, Dante now informs us, is itself to initiate reference — to incline all men to Love. Beatrice is seen as the renewed expression of God's creation:

> Dice di lei Amor: cosa mortale
> Com' esser puo si adorna, e si pura?
> Poi la riguarda, e fra se stessa guira,
> Che Dio ne 'ntende di far cosa nova . . .

> Love says of her, "How can a mortal thing
> Have beauty and purity in such wealth?"
> He looks at her, declaring to himself
> "God meant her as a new creation."[28]

The effect of the new creation on Dante is in its turn a cause: his old memory begins to pass away, forcing him in this canzone to seek fresh counsel: "Tell me my way!" he pleads through his poem, as poetry now openly becomes a plea for understanding — and its envoy. Referral becomes more and more explicit, until Beatrice is identified with Christ himself in Sonnet 14, and Love is retrospectively identified with God's Holy Spirit. The apparent restatement of Canzone 1 in Sonnet 16 is thus to be interpreted in a fuller sense than initially is evident in the surface analogy: the words do not entail, as it has seemed to some modern readers, a blasphemous identification:

> Vede perfettamente ogni salute
> Chi la mia donna tra le donne vede:
> Quelle che vanno con lei, son tenute
> Di bella grazia a Dio vender merzede.

> He sees all salvation perfectly
> Who beholds my lady among her companions:
> Whoever walks with her must be constrained
> To thank God for the beautiful grace she is . . .

> (*Opere Poetiche* 1.6)

---

28. Italian text from Dante's *Opere Poetiche*, 1 (Parigi, 1836), 55; trans. from Anderson, *The New Life*.

Figure 5b. *"Christ directs St. John to Write." Miniature in the Bam-
burger Apocalypse, ca. 1000. Courtesy: Staatsbibliothek.*

The liturgical reminders provided by the use of texts from Jeremiah which follow the lines here quoted *(O vos omnes)* are all ones which in their liturgical context invite participants through an identification in Christ's sorrow (as penitents) to a fuller appreciation of his Love, and so to an apprenticeship in the whole story of redemption. It is in connection with this point that Dante carefully explains his repeated use of *nove,* the number nine, which has to do with the time he first met Beatrice as well as with the hour of her death; but the reader is reminded that this is also the hour of Christ's death on the cross. Moreover, Dante adds in chapter 30, speaking of all that Beatrice is, that *nove* means "a new thing, that is a miracle, whose root was solely in the Trinity."[29] Sadly for Dante, it is only after Beatrice's death that he has learned enough both to refer her fully to the Love of God where she resides, and to love first the God of Love who led him through her to Himself. His "memory restored" (Sonnet 18), a new spirit is born within him, and he is enabled now to join those who understand that this chapter of their present life in the world is not their destined country, and who thus become pilgrims in search of a Love known truly, face to face, and not merely as through a glass darkly. These *romei* are the ones to whom he addresses his poem,[30] and what he tells them is that for those of us *in medias res,* the right discernment of analogies requires a referral for understanding to the "grand narrative," in cognizance of which the meaning of our own little pilgrim stories begins to emerge.

The *Vita Nuova* is thus, as poetic autobiography, witness to a conversion, to a transformation of life though Love, and to an identity formed by application of the witness of the Book of God's Word, the Bible, to the Book of Memory. Dante's echo of the pattern in Augustine's *Confessions* is resonant with biblical sense: the plot of history is the redemptive movement from creation through disintegration to a new creation and ultimately to creation reinformed. When the structure of personal experience is made conformable to the design of the Author of history, then Love's new creation may bear fruit in a personal re-

29. Anderson, *The New Life,* 90. The play on number — that three is the square root of nine — is typical of medieval number symbolism in making mathematical properties correspond to spiritual ones. See Russell A. Peck, "Number as Cosmic Language," in *Essays in the Numerical Analysis of Medieval Literature,* ed. Caroline D. Eckhardt (Lewisburg, Pa.: Bucknell University Press, 1979).

30. *Romei* are "pilgrims to Rome" — cf. Romeo.

creation that is here reflected in the re-creation of Dante's poems. Else-where, in the *Paradiso*, Dante will show us that the full blessedness of Beatrice is by him (and us) but partially seen, only to be made fully known when, on the other side of Death's baptism, she welcomes her fellow pilgrim into that place where all faces are turned to gaze "in rapture on the face of Him 'who is *beatrice* (blessed) throughout all ages'."[31] Accordingly, the poem's ultimate reference turns us toward that ultimate ingathering of all chapters in the Book of Memory, those lives and poems whose singular and collective meaning will become clear in the light of our Author's own last chapter, his reading and judgment from that "other text" to which all human poems in time's anthology have been but a murmuring of witnesses — a diverse and temporary glossolalia (*Paradiso* 33.85ff.). Beatrice emerges in the *Commedia*, too, in a new perspective: she herself is not the goal of the pilgrim's quest for happiness, but when rightly "referred" she can help to lead him there.

Closure and Openness

One of the most striking witnesses to the nonmonolothic character of historic Christian thought is in the literary character of its chief text. For the Bible is not an ostensible *summa*, the product of the thought of one human author, but an anthology. The tremendous diversity in temperament and culture of the biblical writers themselves spans a period of something more than a millenium, and subsequent Christian tradition has usually valued the diversity and richness of perspective on the Bible's overall structure which has been thereby obtained. Writ large, this diversity is an illustration of one of the Bible's most common themes, one which pertains much to medieval literature and art. This theme is the integration of creation, that is, of the creation which is still growing toward its final ripeness. Its metaphors in biblical literature are almost always simple creational figures: "I am the vine, you are the branches" (John 15:5), or Paul's extended model for the Christian com-munity (in 1 Cor. 12:12ff.), seen as a human body with diverse but complementary and, when healthy, unified members.

31. The last line of the *Vita Nuova*.

For a medieval writer, the patterns of creation, especially those patterns within the lives of men and women, ideally reflect the mind of the Creator. Happily, this allows one to learn about both God and creation at the same time. For Augustine the universe — that is, all created things which turn toward the One *(unus + versus)* — is like "a great book" to be read and studied.[32] As Bonaventure will explain it again eight centuries later:

> The whole world is a shadow, a way, and a trace; a *book* with writing front and back. Indeed, in every creature there is a refulgence of the divine exemplar, but mixed with darkness; hence it resembles some kind of opacity combined with light. Also, it is a way leading to the exemplar. As you notice a ray of light coming in through a window is coloured according to the shades of different panes, so the divine ray shines differently in each creature and in the various properties. . . . It is a trace of God's wisdom. Wherefore the creature exists only as a kind of imitation of God's wisdom, as certain plastic representations of it. And for all these reasons, it is a kind of book *written . . . without.*[33] [my italics]

Creation, a reflection of God's wisdom, is like a book in which he is pleased to have us exist — the Book of God's Works, so to speak. History (personal or universal) is analogously a book — the book of our fragile memory. Added to this is the scriptural anthology itself — the Book of God's Word. Coming as it does from "without," as revelation — but also from "within" as "ingested word," and by virtue of the Word-made-flesh — for a medieval Christian Scripture is thus (in the radical sense of the word) the definitive or paradigmatic Book. From it all other books, literal and metaphorical, take their intelligible configuration.

Wherever in medieval Christian thought writers write about personal learning, about coming to understanding or to love, these metaphors are usually implicitly or even explicitly present. In book 8 of

32. Sermon on Matt. 11:25, 26, trans. in *Selected Sermons of St. Augustine,* ed. Quincey Howe, Jr. (New York: Holt, Rinehart and Winston, 1966), 224.

33. *Hexameron: Collations on the Six Days,* 12.14, in *The Works of Bonaventure,* trans. José de Vinck (Paterson, N.J.: St. Anthony Guild Press, 1970), 5.179.

Augustine's *Confessions*, the famous conversion chapter, Augustine puts off the old man and takes on the new in a garden, and through the medium of a book understood in reference to the book of creation, affirms his middleness and the authority of creation's Author. Here Augustine combines the advantage of one book "written without" — creation — with another — God's book — to produce his own book, a book more and more fully to be "written within." The model, itself biblical (cf. Isaiah, John, Revelation), came to be foundational to the structure of medieval Christian narratives of discovery — indeed, one may almost say, to all Christian thought about how it is we may hope to learn in a fallen world.

From a postmodern perspective, the limitations of such a dominant trope are not inconsiderable. We may be as irritated by it as the young Augustine — but for precisely the opposite reason. That anyone should suggest that full meaning shall remain hidden until revelation of an ending which is not of our own devising might seem to us the real provocation proposed by the archetypal Book. But the Christian view of history remains a view of history with a definite if unpredictable conclusion. It sees both beginning and ending as beyond our empirical grasp; for their comprehension we are subject to our need for a joining device, something which can knit each middle chapter into the sense of the whole unfolding book.

The ultimate solution to the pre-Socratic apprehension that "men perish because they cannot join the beginning with the end" is concisely figured for the medieval Christian reader in the last book of the Bible. The conjoiner is not just the complete narrative of the great "book that had writing on back and front" (Rev. 5:1), but the word of the One who dares to read it — the Author himself — who in the opening words of St. John the Divine, as at the end of the text, proclaims "I am the Alpha and the Omega . . . who is, who was, and who is to come, the Almighty" (Rev. 1:8) [Fig. 6]. That is, the ending is seen to be really an ingathering of everything, even the original beginning. Its interim appreciation in the structuring of human discourse is expressed in the mediation of analogy — succinctly, the principle of reference for understanding from lesser texts to the Great Book — a principle that makes history and creation alike more readable.

Dante's *Vita Nuova* ends, not untypically, on a tantalizing note, with allusions to a miraculous vision which binds Dante to silence and to a

Figure 6. *"Christ in Judgment." Spanish MS illustration for the Apocalypse, cloister of San Miguel de Escalada, Leon, ca. 926. Courtesy: Francke Verlag.*

life of study leading to translations of such vision as he has been granted. But the full vision itself is withheld. This taciturnity does not, of course, prevent us from seeing in the poem a rewarding integrity. On the one level, while final closure can be anticipated, we accept that it can never be fully "imagined." On the other, the value of the referential epistemology is that even though we see only in part, and not in whole, we may come to see truly. There are few attempts to paint paradise in the right panel of medieval triptychs: that vision remains mysteriously poised beyond the farthest reaches of the imagination, something which may not be discovered but rather is one day to be revealed: "Eye hath not seen, nor ear heard, nor hath it entered into the mind of man all that God has prepared for those who love him" (1 Cor. 2:9). For the medieval Christian thinker, the total or final meaning of history remains evidently inaccessible to our necessarily limited understanding. Yet for Dante, as for Bonaventure and Augustine, the true meaning of history has been already made known, from Creation to New Creation, and it may be studied and responded to with joy, until, as in the words of Isaiah (34:4) and John (Rev. 6:14), "the heavens shall be folded up like a book."

Chapter Six

Authorial Intent and the Willful Reader

Gnostic exegesis of Scripture is always a salutary textual violence, transgressive through and through. I do not believe that Gnosticism is only an extreme version of the reading-process, despite its deliberate esoterism and evasiveness. Rather, Gnosticism as a mode of interpretation helps to make clear why all critical reading aspiring towards strength must be as transgressive as it is aggressive.

HAROLD BLOOM

After thy text, ne after thy rubriche,
I wol nat wirche as muchel as a gnat.

CHAUCER'S WIFE OF BATH

But nathelees, this meditacioun
I putte it ay under correccioun
Of clerkes, for I am not textueel.
I take but the sentence, trusteth well.

CHAUCER'S PARSON

167

A S DANTE FOR MEDIEVAL ITALY, SO CHAUCER FOR ENGLAND WAS THE outstanding poet. Each was a philosophical poet, a wisdom writer, gathering from the rich storehouse of classical, biblical, patristic, and more recent textual learning, and weaving texts of vibrant social criticism and ethical challenge. In the case of Chaucer ("Dante in ynglyssh" Lydgate calls him) this rich acculturation is perhaps most accessibly evident in his great pilgrimage narrative *The Canterbury Tales*, likely "finished" some time after 1396 and shortly before his death.[1] In a sense, the whole of *The Canterbury Tales* is still in the tradition of wisdom literature familiar to readers of Plato or the Proverbs of Solomon: various views are expressed, tested, and countered dialectically; in the most dramatic rhetorical contrasts the "debates" are effectively between wisdom and folly — even Dame Wisdom and Dame Folly — or at least between those whose affections lean to one or the other companion. Chaucer's own inclination to the biblical counsels of Lady Wisdom is perhaps most transparent in the tale he gives his own fictive persona on the pilgrimage, the Tale of Melibee, and in the way he provides closure for the *Tales* as a whole in the Parson's Sermon and his own Retractions; but in fact this central sense of poetic purpose is evident throughout the entire poem.[2]

Wisdom, Counsel, and Authority

Chaucer was a civil servant and court poet; like many medieval Christian writers he seems to have undertaken his craft in a spirit of public duty,

1. The edition cited here is John Fisher, ed., *The Complete Prose and Poetry of Geoffrey Chaucer* (New York: Holt, Rinehart and Winston, 1977), but the line numbers are conventional. It might be better to say "ended," since it is clear that Chaucer provided a framework and closure for *The Canterbury Tales* without actually "finishing" it in every detail.

2. The most comprehensive introduction to Chaucer's intellectual and religious formation is D. W. Robertson, Jr., *A Preface to Chaucer* (Princeton: Princeton University Press, 1962), but important supplements include Lawrence Besserman, *Chaucer and the Bible: A Critical Review of Research, Indexes and Bibliography* (New York: Garland, 1988); Thomas Hill, *Chaucer and Belief* (New Haven: Yale University Press, 1991); and D. L. Jeffrey, ed., *Chaucer and Scriptural Tradition* (Ottawa: University of Ottawa Press, 1984). J. A. Burrow, in *Ricardian Poetry* (London: Routledge & Kegan Paul, 1971), explores the political context of the poetry of Chaucer's age and its role as "counsel" to the court of Richard II, sometimes called "Richard the Redeless."

and offered up the product of his labors as a kind of civic counsel. In this he was in the tradition of the late Roman consul and Christian philosopher Boethius, whose *Consolation of Philosophy* Chaucer not only translated but also drew upon as one of the chief wisdom sources in his poetry. Boethius, whose strategic personification for the Solomonic Lady Wisdom *(Chōkma)* of Proverbs (8–9; 31) is similarly a "Lady Philosophy," writes in the introduction to one of his works that although the "cares of his consular office" prevent him from giving his full attention to study, translation and writing, "yet it seems . . . a sort of public service to instruct my fellow-citizens in the products of reasoned investigation."[3] But this tradition of Christian civic wisdom writing, as we have seen, had already sound English precedent as well. King Alfred, who among his many literary endeavors also translated Boethius's *Consolation of Philosophy*, in his prefaces similarly characterizes as civic duty the wisdom writer's enterprise.

It is a commonplace that until after the seventeenth century the substantial bulk of great English literary texts are actually a retelling of wisdom tales of earlier times: Milton, Bunyan, and Shakespeare in their greatest achievements rework biblical and classical naratives. So too Chaucer, whose every tale in the *Canterbury Tales* (save possibly the Parson's Sermon) has an evident prototype; some of these are translated quite closely, while others are freely reworked. Wisdom in a thoroughly Christian culture is by definition a communal rather than an individual possession; it is typically presented as an inheritance, not the sudden verbal fiat of any one particular genius. And the community that "possesses" such wisdom is not merely synchronic — attuned exclusively to any fleeting political moment. Rather, in Christian thinking, one's fellow citizens are citizens of the City of God, a community against and across time, and every single act of writing (which is to say, accordingly, of reading also) is performed before a great "host of witnesses" (Heb. 12:1): one competes for the laurel crown under the eyes of those who have competed successfully before. A similar sense of diachrony pertains to the community of "noble pagans"; upon following Virgil

3. Boethius translated and commented upon *Porphyry's Introduction to the Categories of Aristotle,* from the preface to which comes this citation, as well as composing works on music, arithmetic, geometry, moral philosophy, and theological tractates. For a general introduction see E. K. Rand, *Founders of the Middle Ages* (Cambridge, Mass.: Harvard University Press, 1941.)

into the company of Horace, Ovid, Lucan, and Homer (*Inferno* 4.79-108), Dante is pleased to recognize that he too is now "one of their company," shepherd and translator of a body of wisdom which is not of course in any post-Romantic sense "original" or "his own." And this is why poets like Dante or Chaucer make no pretense of authoring novelties, but rather present themselves as students or "clerks" ("scribes," as Dante has it) trying to set down accountably the wisdom of the ages and faithfully to pass it on, to translate it (literally or figuratively) for their own fellow citizens. The acknowledgment of their many authorities is not always explicit — especially where the originals are well known (*paroemia* is perhaps the most characteristic of medieval rhetorical devices). But it is pervasive, and there is certainly nothing like embarrassment or "anxiety of influence" about such acknowledgment.

Consider Petrarch, often advertised to twentieth-century readers as one of the most "original" poets of his age, who writes:

> Yes, I use a great many quotations; but they are illustrious and true, and, if I am not mistaken, they convey authority pleasurably. People say that I could use fewer. Of course I could; I might even omit them entirely. I shan't deny that I might even be totally silent; and perhaps that would be the wisest thing. But in view of the world's ills and shames it is hard to keep silent. . . . If anyone asks why I so abound with quotations and seem to dwell on them so lovingly, I can merely reply that I think my reader's taste is like mine. Nothing moves me so much as the quoted maxims of great men. I like to rise above myself, to test my mind to see if it contains anything solid or lofty, or stout and firm against ill-fortune, or to find if my mind has been lying to me about itself. And there is no better way of doing this — except by direct experience, the surest mistress — than by comparing one's mind with those it would most like to resemble. Thus, as I am grateful to my authors who give me the chance of testing my mind against maxims frequently quoted, so I hope my readers will thank me.[4]

"To find if my mind has been lying to me about itself" — this is a key phrase in Petrarch's remarks on the writer's dependence upon authori-

4. Petrarch's letter to Giovanni Colonna di San Vito is dated Sept. 25, 1342.

ties, and it reveals a characteristic skepticism of the faithful Christian about the privatization of interpretation. This skepticism — a fideistic skepticism it should be noted — is fundamental to the dialectical dynamics of *The Canterbury Tales*. In this great orchestration of pilgrim narrators, more or less familiar stories are retold and hence interpreted by their fictive authors in such a way as to showcase both the effects of sin-disposed self-justification upon any of us when we tell our "own" story (so to speak), and the self-correcting qualities of a humble, repentant and dialogic exchange, particularly when that exchange is motivated by a desire for candid encounter with "truth" or, as Chaucer also puts it, with "oure auctor," "oure book."

A principle of medieval Christian appropriation of the wisdom of both past and present is that "authorities" are not validated according to their capacity to confirm self-assessment: a wisdom text is not a mirror for the narcissistic, but a lens, a glass, a *speculum* through which to get an "outside" look at the world — including the little world of the self as it might be seen from another perspective.[5] Nor are authorities tested merely by the concensus gentium of a given moment — the preoccupations of literary fashion. Rather, independently of their placebo effect (cf. Chaucer's Merchant's Tale),[6] the authorities (plural) which are constituted by texts are themselves tested for correspondence to *the* Text, Authority (singular) as it is found foundationally for Christian culture in sacred Scripture. Though the tradition of witnesses to that foundational Text is of the highest authority among postbiblical writings, the canonical Scripture remains the ultimate authority, the one book which is open to all and by which (and figuratively *in* which) all Christian lives are bound.

The good writer or reader is engaged in a continual process of such testing and measuring, a consideration which particularly in respect of

5. The Vulgate translation of 1 Cor. 13:12, "Now we see through a glass darkly . . ." renders Gk ἐσόπτρον as *speculum*, "mirror," through which "now we see ἐναἰνιγματι — enigmatically." This translation from the original is to be preferred to the memorable KJV, but with the caveat that *speculum* would not imply to an ancient or medieval audience a vanity mirror held to the self but rather a refractory or reflecting glass held to both self and the world.

6. In this tale a doting and narcissistic old fool seeks supportive "counsel" to sustain him in pursuit of his carnal folly. While he receives negative counsel from Justinus, another courtier, Placebo, is only too glad to tell him what he wants to hear.

writing involves a winnowing out, in Augustine's sense, of the "fruit from the chaff." Chaucer has his Nun's Priest invoke this phrase to encourage his audience to look beyond the surface fable of the barnyard rooster and wily fox to a deeper spiritual wisdom:

> Lo, swich it is for to be recchelees
> And necligent, and truste on flaterye.
> But ye that holden this tale a folye,
> As of a fox, or of a cok and hen,
> Taketh the moralite, goode men.
> For Seint Paul seith that al that writen is,
> To oure doctrine it is ywrite, ywis.
> Taketh the fruyt and lat the chaf be stille.

(7.3436-43)

It is a measure of Chaucer's success that poets after him regard him as exemplary in the practice of such "tested" wisdom: for Thomas Hoccleve in *The Regimen of Princes* (1412) he is an heir of Aristotle in philosophy, of Vergil in poetry, and a very "mirour of fructuous entendement." For John Lydgate in *The Siege of Thebes* (1420) he is "Chief Registrar of þis pilgrimage" who, carefully mindful of "feyned talis" (fictions) "þing Historial" and "proverbe diverse" alike, sorts and sifts for truth,

> Of eche thyng / keping in substaunce
> The sentence hool / with-oute variance,
> Voyding the Chaf / sothly for to seyn,
> Enlumynyng / þe trewe piked greyn
> Be crafty writinge / of his sawes swete. . . .

The evidence of wisdom in the good Christian poet, in short, is that he seeks a universal truth; Chaucer's exceptional merit, Lydgate's commendation says, is that he has himself become at last one of wisdom's sources: "Rede his making, who list the trouthe fynde."

For a late medieval Christian writer such as Chaucer, wisdom still begins in "the fear of the Lord" (Prov. 1:7) and, accordingly, in considered respect for those who fear the Lord. "Independence," in the casual modern sense, is not a virtue, and not synonymous with integrity. Faithfulness is. Sincere pursuit of the truth — that actuality which is presumed to be universal, accessible, and outside the self — is the activity proper to a virtuous mind.

This does not mean that integrity is not itself a virtue, and certainly not that it has not centrally to do with the self.[7] What it does mean is that the route to authentic selfhood, however counterintuitive it might seem to a modernist perspective, is the way of self-transcendence (the cross) and communion in the mystical body of Christ (the church, the community of believers), not the waywardness of self-seeking, or indulgence of the physical body which results at last in alienation of the self and death (John 12:24-26; cf. Gal. 5:16-26). From Pharaoh to the Pharisees, biblical counsel suggests that self-directed willfulness is inherently not only averse to wisdom, but axiomatically obtuse — blind toward it. Unhappily, this can be especially true when we are pursuing what we imagine to be justice, but when in fact, as Jesus suggests in his numerous rejoinders to the Pharisees (e.g., Luke 18:9-14), we are really seeking only self-justification. Yet this particular loss of integrity — which may take the form of a rejection of wisdom in wisdom's name — is common enough not only in the settling of political scores, but also in the self-justifying stories we habitually tell and the interpretations we make of the stories of others, including distinguished others, or "authorities." Willfull disregard of wisdom — self-justifying instead of truth-seeking intentions in respect of the wisdom which various expressions of *auctoritee* attempt to serve — becomes on these grounds a central subject in *The Canterbury Tales* taken as a whole.

It was not, it must be said, a subject of concern unique to Chaucer in the late fourteenth century. While theoretical reflection in this time was still dominated by the metaphor of the book, the question of authority in interpretation had become increasingly contestable. Indeed, institutional control or sanction of biblical interpretation was challenged regularly by the emergence of notable "strong" readers, intellects of the character suggested by names such as Abelard and Roscellinus. By the age of Chaucer the question about the "reader's resistance" was far from hypothetical. As innovation in interpretation (divergence of

---

7. St. Anselm of Canterbury, for example, observes that "The more earnestly the rational mind devotes itself to learning its own nature, the more effectively does it rise to the knowledge of that Being; and the more carelessly it contemplates itself, the farther does it descend from the contemplation of that Being" (*Monologion*, 66).

opinion) grew to be more pronounced, it acquired a wider intellectual interest, extramural to cathedral school and university. Indeed, as the case of Dante already suggests, poets and artists could become almost as aware as philosophers and theologians of fundamental hermeneutical questions being debated in the universities.

John Wyclif's Faithful Reader

John Wyclif, a professor of divinity at Oxford during the years Geoffrey Chaucer was beginning his own career as court poet, was one of those most deeply disturbed by the trend toward conflict in interpretation.[8] Strongly affected himself by the force of biblical narrative, and finding the clearest definition of Christian identity in Scripture itself, Wyclif undertook to return *ad fontes,* to reinstate the text of Scripture at the heart of a theological curriculum in which it had become increasingly peripheral, having been displaced by current theoretical and method-ological texts and ensuing critical debate upon them. From the point of view of Wyclif's Oxford opponents, a measure of his irritating resistance to academic fashion was his repeated insistence that lesser authorities, stock syllogisms, and canons of subtle distinction based upon other texts (including those of Aristotle) could not substitute for a logic and theory of exegesis intrinsic to the foundational text of Scripture. Like Augustine before him (*Confessions* 3.8; 4.16), for the sake of a sound reading of Scripture he was inclined to find the "ten-stringed harp" of the Com-mandments given to Moses more useful than the "ten categories" of Aristotle.

This obtrusively ethical approach to questions of meaning in biblical narrative seemed to many of Wyclif's peers dismissive of their own enterprise and, moreover, likely to stir up unconventional ideas in others with respect to authority in the interpretation of texts. They were right, of course. But not, perhaps, in the sense that we might, as moderns, expect: Wyclif was not in our sense an advocate for interpretive plural-

8. Part of what follows is drawn from my article "John Wyclif and the Hermeneutics of Reader Response," *Interpretation* 39, no. 3 (1985): 272-87, and appears here, in revised form, by permission.

ism, nor was he in Luther's sense an advocate for the sufficiency of the individual in scriptural interpretation. Wyclif's approach to the issue of authority was, nonetheless, straightforwardly to recognize the problem of competing authorities: for him, these included notably the authority of the text and the enforcing power of institutionalized interpretation. And so he was led in turn to broach a related question: "authority for whom?" Suddenly there appeared to be yet another competing "authority," that of the individual learned reader. This insight, born of the realities of academic experience, led him to consider not only the intellect but, in a fresh way, the *will* of the reader.

With respect to the role of reader intention, an introduction to Wyclif's principles can be found in the inaugural lecture he offered upon proceeding to his D.D. degree in 1372. His theory of interpretation is directed specifically to the text of Scripture, and his traditional assumption is that no one reads Scripture sensibly who does not wish to know what its Author intends us to know.[9] But he also sees that the reader's fallenness must be rather extensively implicated in the partiality or ambiguity in the *actual* motivation one brings to the text. How honest is the reader? How much does he or she really want to know about what the text is saying?

In this context, Wyclif argues that anyone who wishes to read Scripture in pursuit of divine authorial intention would seem to need three prerequisites. The first of these is a sound moral disposition, informing one's guiding affection; the second is experience in studying philosophy (sharpening, presumably, one's powers of concentration); and the third is the actual practice of virtue. In typical late medieval fashion he argues further that these three prerequisites in the faithful reader combat an opposite trio of distracting influences — the world, the flesh, and the devil (cf. 1 John 2:15-17) — whose negative efforts are of course designed to dissuade the soul from acquiring true wisdom and theological truth. Wyclif's "three prerequisites," once realized in the life of the faithful reader, are designed to be spiritually preemptive of the reader's temptation to slight or evade an evident truth in the text. To put it in

9. For more extensive discussion see A. J. Minnis, " 'Authorial Intention' and 'Literal Sense' in the Exegetical Theories of Richard Fitzralph and John Wyclif; an Essay in the Medieval History of Biblical Hermeneutics," *Proceedings of the Irish Academy* 75 (1975): Section C, 1-31.

another way, the threefold preparation makes the reader more teachable, more open to the insight which comes from without: "if matter be fully disposed to receive its form, he who imposes the form cannot fail to inform" the matter (in this case, the intellect of the well-motivated reader).[10] The outline of this fundamentally ethical argument about the role of intention in the reader provides a framework for appreciating Wyclif's general hermeneutical principles.

In his contention that the reader first requires a proper "moral disposition" *(moralis dispositio informans affectum)*, Wyclif suggests that this need is amply proven by reason, authorities, and various practical examples. Tactically, he recognizes that the traditional medieval ordering of faculties places intellect before the will in the order of knowing. Anticipating objections to his somewhat novel inversion, therefore, he sets out the following arguments: (1) A commitment of the will is necessary to every pilgrim throughout this life *(in statu quolibet viatoris)* if one is to work to attain salvation — the more so is this true if one wishes to study that which surpasses human understanding — and this commitment "is given to us only from above" *(ab extra quam studio humano perquiritur)*. (2) It is quite clear, he observes dryly, that heretics, infidels, and persons in mortal sin can all study theology; but they do not, in that state, gain true wisdom by it. (3) The will "is the highest and conclusive power of the soul" *(summa et finalis potentia animi)*, as Augustine and others have always argued. The rectitude of the will, which is equivalent in principle to justice, is generally regarded as the foundation for any virtuous activity. It follows from this that rectitude of the will is needed all the more and from the outset in the study of Scripture, whose author is the Holy Spirit (who, according to Augustine's well-known analogy [*De Trinitate*, 11-12], corresponds in the Trinity to the will in human personality). Wyclif's conclusion on this matter is then blunt: the first condition for the student of Scripture, exceeding any capacity he may have for disputation or logical speculation, is a basic godly morality which will prompt him to seek a just interpretation of the text.

One can see in this argument the influence of the Franciscans upon

10. See Beryl Smalley, "Wyclif's *Postilla* on the Old Testament and his *Principium*," in *Oxford Studies Presented to Daniel Callus, O.P.* (Oxford: Oxford University Press, 1964), 276.

Wyclif: the precedence of the "affective" over the "intellective" faculty in preparing for "contemplation of the divine mysteries" corresponds to Bonaventuran (or pseudo-Bonaventuran) psychology, but is here applied not to meditation or contemplation of the Passion but straightforwardly to a study of the text of Scripture.[11] Philosophy, the discipline of intellect, the second element in his reader's preparation, then naturally follows. Under this heading Wyclif includes "the arts of speech" *(philosophia sermonicalis)* or rhetoric, natural philosophy, and moral philosophy, and his discussion is conventional (cf. Hugh of St. Victor's *Didascalicon*). But here too he returns to consider the role of the will, and thus enters once more upon the subject of ethics.

In the third and last section, on the necessity to sound reading of the reader's practice of virtue, Wyclif argues simply that the right end of interpretation is, like the right end of philosophy, a moral life. One sees here the influence of his reading of Ezekiel: action is the most perfect function of human beings, in which they are most fully "in the image of God." To choose to act according to what has been understood is good. Correspondingly, not to act according to one's insight and talents is sinful. Thus, anyone who has learned to interpret cannot be excused the duty of enlightening (preaching and teaching), perfecting through good counsel, and purging in the cure of souls.

> Let each do his duty, not thrusting himself forward, but modestly, according to the measure meted out to him, in praise of God, the giver. One works in the school, another in the church, one in the world, another in the cloister of virtues, one praying, deep in contemplation, with Mary, another ministering to the people with Martha. Let us all go forward as pilgrims, without discord, seeking not our private advancement, but the unity and perfection of Christ's mystical body, until we ourselves come to perfection, are taught all truth, have full knowledge of Scripture, and read unfailingly in the book of life, in proportion to our meritorious acts and habits.[12]

11. Cf. D. L. Jeffrey, *The Early English Lyric and Franciscan Spirituality* (Lincoln: Nebraska University Press, 1975), chap. 3.

12. *Principium,* quotation as translated by Beryl Smalley, "Wyclif's *Postilla*," 276. See here the helpful article by Michael Treschow, "John Wyclif's Metaphysics of Scriptural Integrity in the *De Veritate Sacrae Scripturae*," *Dionysius* 13 (1989): 153-96.

What this can seem to come to, of course, is a kind of divine catch-22: the reader of Scripture will become, in the largest sense, only as effective an interpreter of its texts as he or she is already a translator of the text in personal life (cf. Augustine, *On Christian Doctrine*, 1.40.44).

Scripture's Own Grammar and Logic

Wyclif undergirded the philosophic formulation of his ethical poetic, however, by means of specific and topical address to two pressing academic debates. The first of these was traditional and ongoing, and involved the overlapping spheres of grammar and logic.

We need to remember that the foundation for all study of the biblical text in the Middle Ages was the *trivium:* grammar, rhetoric, and logic. In his doctoral *Principium,* Wyclif had affirmed the importance of grammar in traditional terms, harkening back for support to Augustine's *On Christian Doctrine.* Careful formal study of grammar is obviously useful, he argues, because it sets our feet on the ground, enabling us first to understand biblical terms according to the literal sense, and subsequently to distinguish figures and tropes according to the mystical sense in whichever of its aspects, allegorical, tropological, or anagogical.

Grammar came, however, to have a larger implication for Wyclif, one which is tied more closely to the disciplines of logic and dialectic. By the time of his major hermeneutical work, *The Truth of Sacred Scripture* (*De Veritate Sacrae Scripturae,* 1376-1377), he had begun to argue that Scripture has its own distinctive grammar as well as logic, and that the principles of its grammar ought to be derived from it, as a Greek and especially Hebrew text, rather than from the typical anthology of Latin authors from which classical grammar was most often taught. As St. Gregory the Great and others (including Jerome, Ambrose, Chrysostom, and Bonaventure) have shown, he says, Scripture exhibits "a new grammar and new logic" (*novum grammaticam ac novam logicam*). These true exegetes expounded Scripture accordingly in terms of a "new sense of the terms in Scripture, whose usage is not to be gotten out of [Latin] grammar texts" (*novas sensus terminorum scripture, qui nusquam originantur ex libris gramatice*). On one level, Wyclif is simply pointing to that characteristic feature of metaphoric language in Scripture which Dante and others called "polysemeity" (many-layeredness), and which is itself the progenitor of the medieval instinct for analogy as a means of enriching our partial understanding. Where, except in the teaching of Scripture, Wyclif asks, is it to be learned that "the world may be hell, a virgin, God in the elements, heavenly life, protoplasm, or global mechanism?" *(terra sit infernus, virgo, deus ac elementum, celica vita, prothoplastum, machina mundi).*[13] While we might choose to understand Scripture according to a childish sense, or simple grammar (of exclusive equivalence), he continues, Scripture has a more mature grammar toward which we should progress. What then, we should ask, is the character of this mature grammar of Scripture, in which something apparently may be that which evidentially it is not, or may be many things at the same time, and how may this equivocality (or polysemeity) assist us toward the understanding to which we aspire?

The first thing that strikes the reader here is the (probably intentionally) awkward character of his example of extended metaphor for normal Aristotelian categories. Wyclif seems to challenge, first of all, the exclusive application of the foundational premise of Aristotelian logic, the law of non-contradiction ("A is not non-A"). In Scripture, he contends, there are crucial exceptions to this normative "either / or." On numerous occasions where we would naturally expect something to be cancelled out by its opposite, Scripture confounds our expectation. Where we are left without possibility, Scripture opens the door: "It *may* be" [*sit*]. Wyclif points out, for example, that the whole character of the gospel as "good news" depends on an optative refutation of the law of noncontradiction — on the word of Jesus, death *may* be life.[14]

To his contemporaries' obsession with apparent grammatical "errors" in the (Latin) text of the Gospels, Wyclif responds with a translator's concern for rendering sense rather than the precise syntax of an

---

13. John Wyclif's *De Veritate Sacrae Scripturae*, 3 vols., ed. R. Buddenseig (London: publ. for The Wyclif Society by Trübner & Co, 1905-1907), 1.42. This edition provides us an unusually reliable Wyclif text; see Williel R. Thomson's definitive MS catalog, *The Latin Writings of John Wyclif* (Toronto: Pontifical Institute for Medieval Studies, 1983), 55-56. Nearly half the manuscript copies of this work were executed by English scribes, a fact which makes it exceptional among the major works of Wyclif.

14. *Sermones*, 4 vols., ed. J. Loserth (London: publ. for The Wyclif Society by Trübner & Co., 1887), 1.209, on John 12:24-26.

unfamiliar grammar. But there is more to it: what conventionally sometimes looks like a grammatical error, he insists, is in fact often authorially
deliberate. For example, as it stands in John's text (14:24), the construction in the statement of Christ, "Mine is not the word which you hear"
(et sermonem quem audistis non est meus) is, on the face of it, a
grammatical incongruity. Why should the accusative for word *(ser-*
monem) appear where every schoolboy should expect the nominative
form *(sermo)?* While his academic contemporaries might reflexively
concur that the rules of grammar and logic are necessarily subordinate
in authority to the dominion of theology, for Wyclif the evidence of
theology's dominion in *this* case is precisely the apparent grammatical
problem. By its very peculiarity of construction the phrase draws our
attention to the fact that Scripture has chosen to express the concept
"word" in the singular *(sermonem)* rather than the plural (*sermones* —
ambiguously nominative or accusative). Though according to conventional rules of grammar this makes for an irregular construct, the
grammatical abnormality actually teaches us subtly the crucial theological point — that all the biblical words are, like the *decalogi,* divine
commandments which, because they are true, are not in the last analysis
formally separable, but are *substantially* the same word spoken in the
totum integrum of Scripture, Christ himself. Therefore these words of
Jesus in the gospel ought to be understood as a reminder to us: "that
which Christ teaches is not realized or served by words alone, but rather
in the context of the Word before all words, the configuration of God's
full discourse with humanity."[15]

The point John's Gospel clarifies here, according to Wyclif, is indeed
everywhere in the book. According to another of his favorite texts, "It
is not possible to fragment the Word which the Father sanctified and
sent into the world," John 10:35-36 *(non potest solvi scriptura quem Pater*
sanctificavit et misit in mundum).[16] What are sometimes thought to be
grammatical and logical "contradictions" may thus be contradictions
only in the eye of the beholder, arising primarily as a result of ignorance
of the whole textual fabric of sacred Scripture and from consequent
attempts to subordinate the text to the narrow conventionalisms of

15. Ibid., 1.210; repeated in *Benedictione Incarnatione,* 115; see also G. B. Benrath,
Wyclifs Bibelkommentar (Berlin: de Gruyter, 1966), 366.
16. Wyclif, *De Veritate,* 1.202.

academic fashion rather than reading it according to its own intrinsic logic.[17] In other words, as Wyclif argues elsewhere in the same work, we need to keep constantly in mind that the ultimate function of the Bible's words is merely instrumental — to lead us within the shell or husk of language *(cortex verborum)* so that we may come in turn to the object of that language — a relationship to the Word as personal knowledge. Language is a means to our desired end, not more, "for Christ and many more saints did not [even] write except in the sense of writing on the tablets of the heart, where alone it [the text] may be perfect" *(quale Christus et multi sancti non scripserant nisi sensum in tabulis cordis, cum hoc sit perfeccius).*[18] This theme is far from limited to the *De Veritate*, but figures largely also in Wyclif's *postillae*, where Wyclif refers again and again to the fourth Gospel (especially chapter 7 and 14:10) to deal with this same issue.[19]

Wyclif's exegesis of John's Gospel in particular allows us to see how the modified realism of this fourteenth-century textual scholar and translator stands against the nominalism in his opponents' hyper-scholastic methods, leading him (in his own somewhat ham-fisted way) repeatedly to quote the pseudo-Dionysius to make his unsubtle point: "It is irrational, irresponsible, and stupid not to pay attention to the virtues of intention, but only to the words; for by words themselves the Divine will is not to be understood — these are only the naked sounds of their utterance."[20]

In Wyclif's treatment of the first conundrum (John 14:24), as in his whole *postilla* on John, he presents a Scripture which, as he says, "cannot be false," simply because on its first and most important level it *is* Christ, the Word from the beginning. He is at pains to point out that the term *scriptura* has in the Bible itself various meanings. Preeminently it signifies the Book of Life described in the Apocalypse, the very person of the Divine Word who alone is fit to read it (Rev. 5:1-5), and secondarily the *decalogi* or expressions of eternal truth which are not really but only

17. Benrath, *Wyclifs Bibelkommentar*, 363.

18. Wyclif, *De Veritate*, 3.44.

19. Wyclif, *Postilla* on Luke 9; see Benrath, *Wyclifs Bibelkommentar*, 362ff. Minnis discusses what he calls "Wyclif's categorical refusal to regard the Bible as a book *per se*" ("'Authorial Intention,'" 14). My emphasis is on Wyclif's seeing it as *liber liberissimus*, the model for all "books," an implicit paradigm for literary theory.

20. Wyclif, *De Veritate*, 3.43.

rationally distinct from it. Only in the light of these "real" first principles may we appreciate the "nominal" sense of the term *scriptura:*

> Scripture is also taken by Wyclif to mean the codices and the words written in them; but these are mere signs of Scripture *par excellence;* they are not Scripture except insofar as they exemplify the latter; they are sacred if they lead us to the knowledge of celestial Scripture, insofar as by faith we see and read in them God's will and ordinance in our regard.[21]

It is this "celestial Scripture" which we ought to identify finally with the Logos, the person of the Divine Word.

Wyclif was of course himself a late medieval scholastic philosopher, as his analogies and his "distinctions" amply illustrate. For him, for example, Scripture provides a five-piece armor to defend its own literal truth: the doctrine of eternal ideas, the existence of universals *(ex parte rei),* the real unity in diversity of creation, the metaphysics of eternity, and the equivocal nature of scriptural language, so essential to its own particular grammar and logic.[22] Only when we appreciate that the discourse itself of Scripture (and not merely the larger narrative devices such as parable) is not a "univocal" or one-dimensional language can we penetrate the surface of that language and apprehend meaning at the level of authorial *intention,* where it will be found to be not merely figuratively but literally true.

Summarily, we can see that for Wyclif each specific act of reading is potentially able to actualize either a conflict of wills, or some form of willed harmony. Wyclif's presupposition is that persons who set out to read the "Word of God" *ought* to be doing so because they hope to come to understand something of what God has to say. Yet he knows from his academic experience, if from nothing else, that this is lamentably enough not always the actual motive — especially when people are reading the text with a view to using it as a basis for argumentation, debate, and career advancement. And this is why he stresses so forcefully that intention is the critical aspect of interpretation from at least two per-

21. M. Hurley, S.J., "Scriptura Sola: Wyclif and his Critics," *Traditio* 16 (1960): 295; see Minnis, " 'Authorial Intention,' " 15; cf. Wyclif, *De Veritate,* 1.107-17.
22. Wyclif, *De Veritate,* 1.167-82.

spectives: that in the text and that in the reader. This, too, is why commitment of heart or rectitude of the will in the reader — placing it in correspondence with the divine will — is of necessity the first requisite of interpretation in any case where the author's intention is the ostensible goal of the interpretation. How clear it is, he says in his *postilla* on Luke, that the interpreter can falsify the text by egocentrism in his own intentions, such as the desire for fame *(laudis humane)* perhaps or, more simply, for self-justification. Then of course one will see in the text just what one wants to see, rather than the vision of its author.[23]

Accordingly, the way to ensure one is expounding the text after its own values and not after a logic imposed on it from somewhere else is via the discipline of the interpreter's self-effacement, letting the form of Scripture govern the form of the exposition. For Wyclif, "a Christian ought to speak the word of Scripture under the authority of Scripture according to the form of Scripture, just as Scripture itself declares" *(Christianus debet loqui sub autoritate scripture verba scripture secundam forman scripturam, quo scriptura ipsa explicat).*[24] The inevitable consequence will be an automatic imitation of biblical rather than of an alien logic, so that a sense of the whole text is naturally and contextually realized, properly prefacing any approach to its several parts. Yet that there can and should be an extension of this principle to language employed by the Christian generally is made explicit at the outset of the *De Veritate.* Holy Scripture, Wyclif says, is "written according to the pattern of our speech" *(forma igitur locucionis scripture est examplar omni alii modo loquendi probabile),*[25] but also, he argues, "it ought to be, in turn, the pattern for all possible Christian discourse" *(ut scriptura, que debet esse exemplar omni humano generi ad loquendum, includat in se omne genus loquendie probabile).*[26] In this, as well as in his subsequent

---

23. Quoted in Benrath, *Wyclifs Bibelkommentar,* 364. There is a caveat: Wyclif wishes to be very clear that the principle of the equivocity of scriptural language must be related to divine intention. Clearly, also, there are a "variety of logical models exhibited by Scripture" *(scriptura sacra habet multas maneries logicarum).* Yet we apply many of these purely interpretively to the text, and to the mysteries of faith — not all of them correspond to the pragmatic logic of daily life.

24. Wyclif, *De Veritate,* 3.52.

25. Ibid., 1.6.

26. Ibid., 1.205.

extensions of *forma* to the larger shape of discourse and dialectic of the text, Wyclif argues, in effect, for dialogical response to an "intrinsic logic" in Scripture as the essential ingredient for any valid theory of biblical interpretation.

Truth and Time

Wyclif had few illusions concerning the historical problems presented by any attempt at retrospective interpretation of a text from the past. He acknowledges, for example, that there are discreet cultural factors to be accounted for, and he acknowledges also that one is always confronted with the exigencies of translation and transmission in approaching such a text.[27] Yet the problem of time in relationship to achieving truthfulness in interpretation is for him the most demanding aspect of the reader's problem.[28] He is not here thinking of the diachronic "then" vs. "now" of contemporary phenomenological hermeneutics, but of the more radical divide between "time" and "eternity." From his *Principium* through the debates with Kenningham to the *De Veritate* and finally in his last work, the *Opus Evangelicum*,[29] he accordingly considers interpretation with respect to two qualitatively different orders of time, *tempus* (Gk. *kronos*) — particular or successive time as apprehended by men — and *duratio* (Gk. *kairos*) — God's time, in which all being is eternally present.

If Wyclif had a distinctly elaborated theory of the imagination, it seems likely that it would be at this juncture that he should have developed it. As his work stands, his "doctrine of possibilities" is richly suggestive of the direction of his mature thinking. When we look at the world of particular existence, Wyclif suggests, we see that all created things are individuated by their occurrence in time, which God creates with the world, by his ordinance. But behind the individuation, of

27. Cf. Roger Bacon and Nicolas of Lyra.

28. See here J. A. Robson, *Wyclif and the Oxford Schools* (Cambridge: The University Press, 1961), 161.

29. For a discussion of the ordering of these works see Beryl Smalley, "The Bible and Eternity: John Wyclif's Dilemma," *Journal of the Warburg and Courtauld Institute* 27 (1964): 84.

course, is the divine idea. Wyclif's modified realism involves him in using the word *ideae* in such a way that it usually means "archetypes in the mind of God," exemplary ideas or patterns *(rationes exemplares)* which are the means by which God knows and brings into being his creatures.[30] We may therefore speak of created things as, in their temporal existence, "intuited" by God, while in their essence they remain before him eternally. By the "doctrine of possibilities," for something to be possible it simply must once have existed, must now exist, or else it must be going to exist at some time in the future, in its own time.

For Wyclif, in whose basically Augustinian view the human mind is (however compromised by sin) after all designed *imago Dei,* from the doctrine of possibilities there arise two primary implications. The first is that if everything possible has to have a real existence in God's mind, then the divine imagination *is* the present and permanent measure of all things, whether they be singular or universal. What seems effectively infinite and without closure to the human mind is actually finite — already "closed" and complete — to God, for whom nothing is infinite either in number, space, or time.[31] Time *(tempus)* is calculated in units of measurement which make sense only within the limits of the created world — weeks and months are after all lunar calculations. Obviously then, the created world marks the furthest extension of that which we can measure. Yet at its ultimate points, the moment of creation and, by implication, the moment of Apocalypse, eternity and the artifice we call time, *duratio* and *tempus,* must meet.

A second implication of the "doctrine of possibilities" focuses not so much on extra-mental (or extraterrestrial) reality as upon the mind and imagination itself. Here "a reality is real by virtue of its existence in God's thought." Intelligibility is synonymous with possibility. In other words, the principles of being and intellection are identical.[32] "What is capable of being thought in a real sense is possible."[33]

---

30. See the summary in S. H. Harrison, "The Philosophical Basis of Wyclif's Theology," *Journal of Religion* 11 (1931): 96. See also Wyclif, *Miscellenae Philosophica* 1.234-35.

31. Wyclif's reference is to Wisdom 11:21; *De Logica* 3.36-37; 87-89.

32. *De Ente,* ed. J. A. F. Thomson (Oxford: Oxford University Press, 1950), 62-63.

33. Cf. Harrison, 111. See Wyclif's *Postilla* on John 1:3: "Every existing thing is in reality God himself, for every creature which can be named *is,* in regard to its 'intelligible' existence, and consequently its chief existence is in reality the Word of God."

This introduces some of the relevant ground for a late medieval Christian aesthetics, and indeed for a characteristically Christian approach to what we now might think of as a "reader-response" hermeneutic. To state this in proximate contemporary terms, Wyclif's argument is simply that in semiotic systems which privilege semantic and cause-logical models, semiotic analysis itself can become a discontinuous and encapsulated process, as opposed to an ongoing, open-ended encounter; the text becomes "an object of reader appropriation rather than an event of involvement in which the reader comes into being."[34] Wyclif's point is not only that for the text to be text-as-discourse it must be rooted in a dynamic relationship in which reader and text are brought together, but, more importantly, that an open disposition toward the author-in-the-text most readily permits the process of reading to create its fullness of possibility. Thought and being are mutual, an incarnation, in that writing / reading which is "on the tablet of the heart" *(in tabulis cordis)*. The projected "world" of the text, when the reader has determined a submission of his or her own subjectivity to the consciousness that generates the work, creates in the reader a *new being* as well as a "new work." In Wyclif, this creation is actualized through a convergence of intentions, much as imagined in more recent theoretical contexts by Georges Poulet, and perhaps more compatibly still by George Steiner's notion of "real presences."[35]

34. The phrase is from a valuable article by Gary Phillips, "This Is a Hard Saying: Who Can Be a Listener to It?" *Semeia* 26 (1983): 25. Cf. Jacques Derrida's critique of the Sausserian view of sign in *Speech and Phenomenon,* trans. David Allison (Evanston: Northwestern University Press, 1973), 140. Derrida's objections bear interesting comparative relationship with the case of Wyclif against his own contemporaries.

35. See George Poulet, "Criticism and the Experience of Interiority," reprinted in *Reader Response Criticism: From Formalism to Post-Structuralism,* ed. Jane P. Tompkins (Baltimore: The Johns Hopkins University Press, 1980). Poulet does not assume that the meaning of literary works is dependent upon the reader but that their "fate" or mode of existence does: "The work lives its own life within me; in a certain sense, it thinks itself, and it even gives itself a meaning within me" (41). Cf. Edmund Husserl, who in describing our inner consciousness with reference to time, says: "Every originally constructive process is inspired by pre-intentions, which construct and collect the seed of what is to come, as such, and bring it to fruition." *Zur Phenomenologie des inneren Zeitbewusstseins, Gesammelte Werke* (The Hague: M. Nijhoff, 1966), 10.52. George Steiner, in his *Real Presences* (Chicago: University of Chicago Press, 1989), argues that fundamental literary creation requires tacit belief in a "rival maker," and that each act

In another dimension of consideration, Wyclif indicates that textual encounter presupposes an interpenetration of times — put in its most radical form, of book-time and reader-time. His idea of the "amplification of time" is, in effect, what governs Wyclif's resolution of some of the "grammatical" problems in Scripture proposed by his colleagues the logicians; it is at the foundation of the "logic of Sacred Scripture." When Wyclif deals with passages such as the first chapter of John's Gospel, he invokes this amplification as a solution to the ostensibly "grammatical" problems seen there. From the perspective of classical grammar there is always a disjunction between the imperative and the indicative, but in the grammar of Scripture there is no comparable tyranny of the *tempus*, of the purely causal. God speaks, and the Word and the event are the same thing.[36] It is not that God's Word *causes* creation; God's Word *is* creation.

Moreover, Wyclif seems to have been aware, if not from an intimate knowledge of Hebrew,[37] at least from familiarity with his favorite *postilla* by Nicholas of Lyra, that the Hebrew verb is tenseless, that it provides no comparable disjunction between the imperative and indicative, and that it encompasses future with present tense.[38] Accordingly, Scripture abounds in qualitative as well as merely quantitative descriptions of time, and provides ample illustrations of situations where the part stands for a much larger or more comprehensive whole. At the grammatical level, the synechdoche complements Wyclif's theory of the mystery of the Incarnation, from which theology much of the preceding passage derives.[39] Yet it also allows him to see apparent particulars such as scriptural numbers as figurative in the same sense; the numbers are not quantitative but qualitative. Moreover, linguistically, this awareness forms a bridge towards understanding a biblical phrase such as "the fullness of time" not merely as a decisive moment in the *tempus* but also as an interpenetration of the *duratio* and the *tempus* in a way that

---

of artistic intention actualizes a wager on the presence of a "sense" of presence — authors or readers — which is at bottom theological.

36. Gotthard Lechler, *Johann von Wyclif und die Vorgeschichte der Reformation* (Leipzig: F. Fleischer, 1873), 2.243.

37. Margaret Deanesly, *The Lollard Bible* (Cambridge: Cambridge University Press, 1920), 167-68.

38. Cf. Smalley, "The Bible and Eternity," 85.

39. Wyclif, *De Benedicta Incarnatione,* 56, 98, 110ff.

reflects that which occurred at the creation (and will occur again at the conclusion) of the world.[40] The Incarnation is preeminently such a moment, in which the person of God whose being is in eternity is made known in time. The "fullness of time" can thus constitute, for those who enter into it by faith, not just a highly significant point in the *tempus* (Gk. *kronos*) but a real apprehension of the *duratio* (Gk. *kairos*) — a time of meaning and ultimate interpretation. Scripture, for Wyclif, is full of a "mystical" sense of this momentous interpretation; consequently, many of its statements can confound a merely progressive or sequential interpretation altogether.

Unsurprisingly then, for Wyclif as for Augustine, the central Christian *symbolum* in this regard is the Incarnation. In considering the Incarnation, the mystical interpenetration of which involves an incorporation of the eternal into the temporal in the understanding as well as in the fact, Wyclif finds this notion of the "amplification of time" to be not merely helpful but essential. It is in this sense that we understand the Incarnation, as the person of Christ, to be an integrative principle, against and across time, redeeming men and women of all ages, before and after the historical "event." Similarly when Christ is understood as Word, he is to be identified with the concept of Wisdom from the Old Testament itself (e.g., Prov. 8:22) — the connection, Wyclif points out, had been made already by Augustine and Jerome. "Thus Ephesians 1:20 [here he must mean Col. 1:19-20] speaks of Christ in whom God purposed to gather together all things in one."[41] Wisdom is the appropriate goal of every attempt at interpretation and in fact is "the whole point of the activity." In the realm of this "form" of interpretation we are absolutely freed from the lockstep of the purely causal syntax of temporal perception and can begin, truly, to apprehend Wisdom as opposed to mere knowledge or, to put it another way, to recognize that Wisdom is not a matter of information but rather of transformation. Thus, in the pursuit of Wisdom, time and space finally collapse as categories.[42] The Wisdom of God the Father, more "moving" than any creature, sums

40. On Isaiah 34:4; also *Postilla* on Luke 9, in Benrath, *Wyclifs Bibelkommentar,* 362-65.

41. Wyclif, *De Benedicta Incarnatione,* 108.

42. Wisdom, or the Word, surpasses everything in its "swiftness," Wyclif concludes, moving through spheres and ages with imperceptible speed, so that it encompasses the world and is virtually everywhere simultaneously.

up all temporalities and thus is universal. It is the metaphysical subject, the Being which *duratio* may begin to apprehend once *tempus* has been surpassed by it. This Wisdom perfectly illustrates the principle that "to God all things are present" (John 12:35) and that Jesus Christ is "the same yesterday, today, and forever" (Heb. 13:8). By it we understand how it is that Abraham can be said "to know" of the Incarnation, and that the faith of the Hebrews is, in essentials, the same as ours.[43]

Yet it is clear, Wyclif argues, that this very concept is operative in all Christian interpretation of Scripture. Unless time, past and future, could be understood as being simultaneously present to God, we would regularly be up against insuperable barriers to interpretation, such as in Psalm 22:16 when David said, speaking "in" this Wisdom: "they pierced my hands and feet." As with many biblical texts, Wyclif finds it impossible to interpret this verse rationally in its own historical context, yet finds that it makes perfect sense in connection with the coming of Christ "in which the boundless eternity of God enjoins all time, past and future" (*in immensa Dei aeternitas coassistit omni tempore preterito et futuro*).[44] We may connect such Old Testament texts to the Christ event typologically, but it would be misleading, from Wyclif's view, either to imagine the relationship simply as repetition or to view the role of the Old Testament texts merely as a kind of mysteriously prophetic harbinger. Rather, it is the Christ event which permeates, from eternity, *all* of God's purposes in lived human history. The end of interpretation is thus not to be reduced to the end of any one historical action, but rather to be referred to the unfolding purpose of the uncreated Wisdom (*sapientia increata*).

When we look again at John 14:24: "The word which you hear is not mine, but the words of the Father who sent me," we see now that the gaining of a right interpretation is more than just a problem of number and case. While the rhetorical figure of synechdoche helps render comprehensible the syntax of individual sentences, the formal principle extends much more profoundly to questions of genre and the larger form, the "divine syntax" in the whole narrative. Christ speaks his historical message under the aegis of the divine scheme of redemption, the intrinsic form of which is the very design and compass of all

43. John 8:56; Wyclif, *De Benedicta Incarnatione*, 111.
44. Ibid., 112.

historical truth. Its meaning and its sense of closure is to be known truly as Word, not simply words, for that which speaks is the integral structure or intrinsic form apprehended in the whole of God's utterance, *Sapientia et Verbum*.[45]

So the form for Scripture is the form for creation: God's creative Word is spoken and the void is shaped, drawn to form. Yet this creative Word, "set up from everlasting, from the beginning, or ever the earth was . . . daily his [God's] delight, at play always before him" (Prov. 8:22-30), is the same Word made flesh in the Incarnation. Thus, by *form* Wyclif clearly intends a metaphysical sense. He cites Philippians 2:6-7: "being in the form of God . . . he emptied himself, taking the form of a servant," and says that clearly this does not mean the physical human shape visible in nature — the literal Jesus — but rather that same Word which he shares with the Father and in which he may truly say: "I and the Father are one."[46] The statement, "My Father is greater than I" is thus not contradictory; it involves simply an equivocity of the historical humanity of Christ in the *tempus* and in his eternal *duratio* as the Word, and it is in this latter sense, after all, that he is the "form" of truth and meaning. This is the form which Jesus "translates" when he speaks. Accordingly, the governing form of our own interpretation should be the eternal Word, the pattern of divine syntax, and not simply the causal or temporal sequence of historical matter, which is the *vocabulary only* of the text we read.[47]

We may summarize Wyclif's thought with respect to the relationship of time to interpretation in this way: in any analysis which attempts to get at truth or larger issues of meaning we soon discover that interpretation transcends an analysis of histories as *tempus*. The question we face looking backward for truth is, in biblical terms, analogous in this respect to the problem we face in looking forward for it. We might ask: "In what sense can anything of the past be a relevant authority for us today?" The hidden question concerning authority, as Hannah Arendt has said of more recent times, is the question of meaning *in* history. What Wyclif says is that this is also a primary question we bring to the text of Scripture. Yet there we find that to direct our quest for meaning

45. Ibid., 113.
46. Ibid., 114.
47. Ibid., 115-18.

only to matter and not to the question of form is to misinform our approach to reading, and so to deny ourselves even historical meaning.

Scripture contains, then, besides its evident vocabulary, two syntaxes of disclosure. One is historical, *tempus,* by which we understand the sequence of statement and event. The other is in the imagination *(ymagionem),* creating or perceiving a spiritual *duratio* by which we gather in the reflections of memory on the one hand and the projections of intention and dream on the other, turning them together toward interpretation and meaning. It is in the realm of this second "syntax" that we apprehend the form of Scripture, which also becomes the form of its present conversation in our experience in the here and now. When we enter into a Galilean conversation, we may well ask, as does Chaucer's dreamer in his *House of Fame,* "Where am I? Is this my country?"[48] These are questions, we now see, about truth and time more than geography. The answer Wyclif gives to them is that Scripture in a unique way meets every person in his or her own country, because its form is more comprehensive than any given time and space can limit.

Authority and the Willful Reader

There remains, however, a sense in which the power of the text to inform and obtain disclosure in the reader remains perpetually limited. For Wyclif, this is obvious whenever we consider the touchy question of motive in the reader. Indeed, almost everything in Wyclif's theoretical oeuvre is written in the shadow of this consideration realized as both ethical and political reality. Chaucer, as court poet and public servant, has no less reason to be sensitive. His *Canterbury Tales,* innovatively theoretical in ways which make it superior to "finished" works (e.g., Gower's *Confessio Amantis*) explicable in terms of the older conventions of reference upon which they mutually depend, acquires much of its superior intellectual attainment from a deliberate centering of the problem of the willful reader. What gives Chaucer's treatment of this late medieval issue particular value is his refusal dogmatically to divide the field simplistically between the sort of "authoritative" reading repre-

48. Geoffrey Chaucer, *House of Fame,* 1.475. Cf. previous chapter, n. 3.

sented by institutions on the one hand and individual heterodoxy or heresy on the other. Rather, as the whole of his longest work makes plain, he represents *all* "readers" as prone to willfullness, to self-justifying interpretation. Accordingly, one of the first questions he invites his actual readers of the *Canterbury Tales* to consider is the character and likely motives of each fictive "reader" in the poem — whether that be Knight, Miller, Reeve, Friar, Summoner, or Wife of Bath.

A chief means of drawing the reader's attention to the question of motive is Chaucer's prominent and repeated use of the word "entente." In *The Canterbury Tales* "entente" typically applies either to the intention (or purpose, or will) of his pilgrim characters in telling their tales or to the diversity and conflict of intentions among the characters within their tales. The Man of Law, for example, announces that he is a narrator whose "entente" or purpose is not to go back on his original promise; he will tell his tale when asked, and make its "text" serve to illustrate the proper accord between behest and personal example:

> "Hooste," quod he, "depardieux, ich assente;
> To breke forward is nat myn entente.
> Biheste is dette, and i wole holde fayn
> Al my biheste; I kan no bettre sayn.
> For swich lawe as a man yeveth another wight,
> He sholde hymselven usen it, by right;
> Thus wole oure text . . .
>
> (2.39-45)

This legal-minded Canterbury pilgrim goes on, however, immediately to complain that finding an "original" tale to tell is difficult, for Chaucer himself has already preemptively told the best ones, albeit executing them poorly (47-48). Further, he disparages also the poetry of Chaucer's friend, the "moral Gower," and that of Ovid, insisting that he will ignore all these "deficient" examples of the craft of poetry and tell his tale in prose. Then, by way of amplifying his preachy prolegomenon, he misrepresents by a radically partial translation the widely known text of Pope Innocent III's *De Contemptu Mundi* (2.99-133), apparently wishing to make the point that all spiritual dangers attach to poverty and not, as might have been thought Innocent's ultimate argument, to riches. As for the Man of Law himself, the reader remembers, he rather likes riches (1.311-20). The obvious and indeed rhetorically overdrawn impression of dissonance between Chaucer and his fictive narrator is so vividly executed that we cannot help but see the actual author and the fictive author here as competing "authorities." Yet we are never in much doubt concerning who finally is in control: Chaucer, reciting this text aloud in a court to which the subversive creativity of legalistic underlings would not have been a novelty, must have obtained knowing laughter for such a lively, multi-strata framing of a tale — all the more knowingly entertaining, one supposes, when Chaucer takes authorial "revenge" on his errant pilgrim by having him tell his tale not in the prose he advertises but in tour-de-force *rhyme royale,* that most demanding verse form in which, let it be said, Chaucer among his contemporaries was without rival.[49]

The explication of "entente" as a subject in *The Canterbury Tales* is to be found everywhere, and everywhere ethically charged. For example, the Summoner in the Friar's Tale abuses his office to obtain bribes from sinners rather than their repentance, an "entente" he is said to share with the devil (3.1369-74; 1447-55; 1477-79), yet he discovers by baleful experience that while the devil's "entente" in this respect is often subverted by God's providential "entente" (3.1493-1500; 1554-68) toward any penitent person, his own hardened "entente," his effectual and obsessive determination upon his own and others' damnation, is acted upon most accommodatingly by God and the devil alike (3.1623-38).[50] Moreover, formally proffered declarations of even pious "entente" can be deceitful, as we see in the comparably transgressive hypocrisy of the Summoner's friar (3.1816-22). This friar, though claiming that his "spirit hath his fostrying in the Bible" (1845), preaches rather from invented private "revelations" and invented "glosses" — and not from the text of Scripture itself (1918-20) — because of course his actual intentions are carnal and self-aggrandizing.

As in his prologue to Melibee, so in his prologue to another of his most explicitly Christian tales of *metanoia,* the Second Nun's Tale of St. Cecilia, Chaucer's explicit subject is the matter of his own authorial

49. See Chauncey Wood, "Chaucer's Man of Law as Interpreter," *Traditio* 23 (1967): 149-90.

50. D. L. Jeffrey, "The Friar's Rent," *Journal of English and Germanic Philology* (1971): 600-607.

intent[51] — a subject he will return to with equal candor in his Retractions. Whatever post-Romantic decorum we may now adopt for begging the question of authorial intention, we are obliged at least to acknowledge that Chaucer seems to have thought he had such a thing. Moreover, he insists that we reflect upon the apparent fact that each and every reader has intentions too.

"Entente" and the Canterbury Progress

Between the General Prologue and Parson's prologue there are twenty-one complete tales, besides fragments such as the interrupted Cook's Tale and Sir Thopas's abortive doggerel, and these appear to be grouped in a characteristically medieval threefold "progress" of seven complete tales each. Each group of seven commences with a wisdom tale of sorts — the philosophical Knight's Tale, the Clerk's Tale, and Chaucer's own pilgrim tale of Melibee. Unfinished a work as *The Canterbury Tales* is said to be, there seems even to be a kind of deliberate experimentation in genres to correspond to this suggestive tripartite development: if the initiating tales in each sequence are wisdom tales, then their immediate successors in each case (the Miller / Reeve diptych, the Merchant's and Shipman's tales respectively) are fabliaux; the next successors are corrupted epic-romance tales (the Wife of Bath's Tale, the Squire-Franklin diptych, the *de causibus* narratives of the Monk and the answering comic relief of the Nun's Priest's mock epic). Then comes in each case a legenda (Man of Law; Physician; Second Nun), and each sequence concludes with a diptych of tales of pseudo-transformation or metamorphosis. At the end of the first sequence, the Friar's Tale is, of course, an anti-*metanoia,* or culminated devil's pact; so also is the Summoner's Tale, with its flatulent parody of transmutation (gold into dung). To the second sequence the Pardoner's Tale is also anti-*metanoia* (a transmutation of gold into death), as is the Prioress's falsely sentimental miracle-cum-revenge-tale. In the third and final sequence, the Canon's Yeoman defects from a life of imposture, of bogus alchemical transmutations of

51. See Russell A. Peck, "The Ideas of *'Entente'* and Translation in Chaucer's *Second Nun's Tale,*" *Annuale Medievale* 8 (1967): 17-37.

base metal to gold, and in his confession himself undergoes a transformation of will and purpose, a true *metanoia*. This hopeful development
is momentarily frustrated by the foreshortened and denied metamorphosis of the Manciple in his tale incompletely borrowed from the *Ovide
Moralisée*.[52] But the reader's frustration here merely underscores or
makes conscious a mature intent that closure at last be realized. The
hightened expectation of final transformation proves, of course, to be
an ideal *introitus,* nearing the very gates of Canterbury, to the Parson's
prologue and sermon — which is a call to repentance or true *metanoia*.

Each of the sequences seems to stress intention at a different level.
In the first, from the palpable mutual hostilities of Palamon and Arcite
or the Miller and Reeve to those of the Friar and Summoner, "entente"
is exposed at the level of reflexive and unacknowledged preconception
— which is to say, prejudice. In the second sequence, from the Clerk's
exploration of the rationalizing "entente" of the cruel Marquis to the
fully self-aware posturing and disingenuous discourse of the Pardoner,
"entente" is a matter of intellectual projection — or presupposition. In
the third sequence, beginning with Dame Prudence and her dialectical
guidance of her obdurate and vengeful spouse Melibee toward complete
transformation of his will, through to the Yeoman's dawning realization
that he can enact an intention or good purpose reversing the charlatanry
commanded by his master, "entente" is engaged at the fully conscious
level of the expression of fundamental desire, a deliberative declaration
of the will — or purpose.

The value of such a schema for our understanding Chaucer as a
Christian poet lies not in the mechanics of the paradigm; variant sche-
matizations are certainly possible, and in any case, in medieval Christian
poetry the staging of the reader's progress or reflection in three levels
is a commonplace.[53] Whether we imagine such a progress as Dante's
Hell, Purgatory, and Paradise; Langland's Dowel, Dobet, and Dobest; or
Augustine's memory, intellect, and will, the central issue for our subject

52. D. L. Jeffrey, "Chaucer's Maunciple's Tale: The Form of Conclusion," *English
Studies in Canada* (1976): 249-63.

53. To employ a musical analogue: we might imagine the General Prologue as
introducing the theme and melodic elements of Chaucer's composition, each of the
three sequences of seven complete tales then forming a "canon" to which the Parson
offers an "eighth" or coda fusing the whole and providing a structure and closure for
which the Retraction then offers a final register.

in *The Canterbury Tales* is substantially unaffected. At least part of Chaucer's "entente," it seems on the evidence, is to lead his reader to think more self-consciously about "entente" itself, whether as prejudice, presupposition, or reconsidered purpose and reformation of the will.

Among the celebrated features of the *Canterbury Tales*, its literary form — a chain of narratives — is not an innovation. That had been anticipated in secular poetry by Boccaccio, even to the framework afforded by a journey in which time is unburdened by the exchanging of stories.[54] But Chaucer's collocation is distinctive in its extended scrutiny of the tales' tellers, the positing of a contest in which the "best" tale is to be determined by Harry Bailey, the Host (an unimpressive reader himself, as becomes increasingly evident). Notably, spiritual portraiture and ethical interrelation between some of the tellers characterizes their chosen "stories" as in various ways self-justifying — in some cases even as predatory assaults upon familiar texts out of some ulterior motive. By contrast, other tellers exhibit a humble submission to text and to the community of fellow readers in the ambience of which both fictive and actual readers are invited to compare notes. This diversity of approaches ensues in a kind of comparative and self-correcting reading of the "larger" text, including ultimately that Book to which the Parson turns in his concluding coda to the pilgrims' narrative-linked journey to Canterbury.

We may focus briefly yet instructively on Chaucer's own excursus into the phenomenon of the willful reader by selecting two of the Canterbury narratives for comparison, the well-known Wife of Bath's prologue and tale, and the less well-known tale Chaucer assigns "himself" as pilgrim narrator, the Tale of Melibee. Though the former is written in verse and the latter in prose, the two tales have much else to sustain useful comparison.

To begin with, the prologues to each tale are explicitly given prominence as a context for the actual reader's interpretation of the tale to follow. Indeed, in the case of the Wife of Bath, whose many pilgrim forays indicate that "she koude muchel of wandrynge by the weye" (General

---

54. Giovanni Boccaccio's narrative is his *Decameron*, written about 1350. The ten-day journey described in this long work is metaphorical; the pilgrims are housed in a place of refuge near the plague-ravaged city of Florence, with ten characters each telling one tale each day.

Prologue 1.467), the prologue to her tale (longest by far in the *Canterbury Tales*) is given far more prominence than the tale itself, suggesting (as does her description in the General Prologue) that character revelation is Chaucer's priority in this instance. Moreover, since the lengthy prologue above all focuses on the Wife's resistance to authority and her (comically) willful and self-justifying misinterpretation of texts, intention in the reader is here made a central subject of her discourse.

To this purpose her resistance to the will of her various husbands provides a most colorful analogue. As she recounts it, they were always seeking to constrain her with proverbial wisdom or with categorical imperatives: "Thou seist . . . thou seist . . . thou seist . . ." Her "thou" here clearly implicates actual as well as fictive (e.g., Friar, Summoner, Pardoner, Parson) hearers of her lecture: both groups may be assured that her resistance to such moral didacticism will be adamant, and that she will counter with an imperative of her own, more accommodating to her purposes:

> Thou sholdest seye, "Wyf, go where thu liste;
> Taak youre disport, I wol nat leve no talys
> I know yow for a trewe wyf, Dame Alys."[55]

> (3.318-20)

Her resistance to the many texts she quotes — biblical, patristic, and classical — must appear (at least to the moderately literate reader) equally and flamboyantly unyielding. It seems only characteristic that she should have taken center stage by usurping the Host's invitation to the "Lollard" Parson (2.1163-1190). What she will offer in place of his sermon, of course, is her own "salutary act of textual violence, transgressive through and through,"[56] in which the scriptural texts to which she and the Parson more than any of the other pilgrims advert will be aggressively subverted. Her triumph concludes in actual physical violence both to clerk Jankyn, her husband the reader, and to his book, from which, symbolically, leaves are torn before it is finally cast in the fire. Yet she herself remains sadly victimized, and not least by the uncorrected misprisions she has wrought upon her many texts.

55. Chaucer, *The Canterbury Tales*, 3.318-20.
56. Harold Bloom, *Deconstruction and Criticism* (New York: Seabury Press, 1979), 6.

The prologue and headlink material to Chaucer's own Tale of Melibee includes the pilgrim Chaucer's throwaway, doggerel rhymed, featherweight romance. When the pilgrim narrator's self-parody is cut short impatiently by the Host as "verray lewednesse" and "drasty speche," the rebuff to wasted words becomes an intensifying frame for the weighty words of the formal prologue. There, both as fictive pilgrim and actual author, Chaucer asks both fictive and actual readers to consider that, at the level of substance, what he is about to say as narrator in the Tale of Melibee corresponds fully with what he is saying as *auctor* in the whole of *The Canterbury Tales.* That is, with respect to interpretation we are to see the Tale of Melibee as a synechdoche for the poem as a whole: in a manner distinctly reminiscent of Wyclif's scriptural hermeneutic, the intrinsic form of this one text is to be imagined by us as declaring the very design and compass of the truth of the larger text:

> "Gladly," quod I, "by Goddes sweet pyne,
> I wol yow telle a litel thyng in prose
> That oghte liken yow, as I suppose,
> Or elles certes ye been to daungerous.
> It is a moral tale vertuous,
> Al be it told somtyme in sondry wyse
> Of sondry folk as I shal yow devyse.
>
> "As thus: ye woot that every Evaungelist
> That telleth us the peyne of Jhesu Crist
> Ne seith nat alle thyng as his felawe dooth,
> But nathelees hir sentence is al sooth,
> And alle acorden as in hire sentence,
> Al be ther in hir tellyng difference.
> For somme of hem seyn moore and somme seyn lesse
> Whan they his pitous passioun expresse —
> I meene of Mark, Mathew, Luc, and John —
> But doutelees hir sentence is al oon.
>
> "Therfore, lordynges alle, I yow biseche,
> If that yow thynke I varie as in my speche,
> As thus, though that I telle somwhat moore
> Of proverbes than ye han herd befoore
> Comprehended in this litel tretys heere,
> To enforce with th'effect of my mateere,

And though I nat the same wordes seye
As ye han herd, yet to yow alle I preye
Blameth me nat, for as in my sentence
Shul ye nowher fynden difference
Fro the sentence of this tretys lyte
After the which this murye tale I write.
And therfore herkneth what that I shal seye
And lat me tellen al my tale I preye."

(7.936-66)

While in terms of formal genre there is certainly no literal parallel between this wisdom text's dialogic assembling of proverbs and the linked narratives (romance-epic, mock-epic, fabliaux, beast fable, saints' lives, homily) of *The Canterbury Tales* in their entirety, with respect to intrinsic *sentence* or meaning, the identity, we are to understand, is complete.

There are evident clues to this identity of intention. One obvious comparison with respect to the question of intention in the reader is that between the Wife as "strong reader" and Dame Prudence in Chaucer's own Tale of Melibee as a "strong reader" of canonically authoritative texts (principally biblical and patristic, but also classical in both cases). It has been noted that Dame Prudence corresponds closely to the personified Dame Wisdom *(chōkma)* of Proverbs.[57] The Wycliffite translation calls the biblical personification "Wys-dam" — she who opposes Dame Folly in contestation for young minds. The allurements of Dame Folly are in the biblical text primarily sensual (Prov. 7), and even in terms of spiritual concerns, represent what Scripture elsewhere metaphorizes as "whoring after alien gods" (Hosea 9:1). Dame Wisdom, by contrast, teaches a higher love, a love of wisdom or *philosophia*, which is the fruit of the wise life personified as the "strong woman" or *mulier fortis* of Proverbs 31. This famous passage, a personification allegory of Wisdom, directly informs the characterization of Dame Prudence in the Tale of Melibee, whose healing instruction to her husband Melibeus draws heavily on Proverbs and other biblical wisdom texts.[58]

---

57. See, e.g., Theresa Coletti, "Biblical Wisdom: Chaucer's Shipman's Tale and the *Mulier Fortis*," in *Chaucer and Scriptural Tradition*, 171-82.

58. Sirach, Wisdom, and Job are quoted, but Proverbs is the book most frequently cited by Chaucer.

But the Wife of Bath's portrait turns out to be the chief ironic counterfoil to this later Canterbury characterization, a parody in which Dame Alice is made to summarize all the arguments — and temptations — of Dame Folly. As a willful "strong reader" the Wife of Bath vigorously resists the authority of every text she reads, whether by foreshortening recollection, inverting the obvious, miscontextualizing, misquoting or by way of direct opposition of her own "experience" and love of "maistrie" to the text's conventionally authoritative interpretation, as in her vitriolic rejection of St. Jerome's arguments in favor of chastity and virginity.[59] That she can seem an attractive teacher of her own "alternative reading" is evident in the press of willing candidates for discipleship around her on the pilgrim ride — the Pardoner (3.163-92), the Summoner, and the Friar (3.829-56). Each of these *afficionados*, as a renegade cleric, has a direct relation to scriptural text; each of them also, in a yet more disturbing fashion, represents the problematic disposition of the willful reader.

On the other hand, the fictive students of Dame Prudence, the orthodox teacher of biblical wisdom, are most obviously Melibee and in due course his "three enemys" (once again, the flesh, the world, and the devil [7.1412-22]). Between these enemies the counsel of Prudence effects peace and a reconciliation of willful antogonisms, rather than permitting a war of retribution (7.1792-1887). Chaucer's pilgrims — also here "fictive" readers — are mostly silent after the conclusion of the Tale of Melibee. Except for the Host's typically self-skewed comments (7.1891-1923) about his own domestic "lessons" at the hands of a carnal *mulier fortis,* "big in armes" (1921), none of the others lines up for registration to study in the academy of Dame Prudence. But the *actual* reader can hardly misconstrue the apparent opportunity, or the point of Chaucer's contrastive models of reading and interpretation of canonical text. The willfulness of the Wife, in her opening gambit that "Experience, though noon auctoritee / Were in this world is right ynogh for me," does not in fact result in a disappearance of authoritative texts: no one, save Dame Prudence, adduces more textual authorities. The Wife simply misquotes or adduces such authorities perversely for her

59. Jerome's *Adversus Jovinianam* is referred to by Dame Alice only late in her prologue (3.674-675), but it is actually being closely parodied for the first 150 lines of her "text."

own cheerfully carnal purposes.[60] Dame Prudence's contrasting motives — spiritual health in others, reconciliation in the community, and a just use of temporal authority, lead her on the other hand to a more thoughtful and self-transcending reading. In Wyclif's terms, her "sound moral disposition" has informed her "guiding affection" for her husband, her "experience in the study of philosophy" has enabled her to martial the resources of wisdom truthfully and cogently to good purpose, and her "actual practice of virtue" has been both her teaching and her insistence on a congruent practice in Melibee — judgment now tempered by mercy toward those who are penitent.

Interestingly, in the Wife's brief tale (about "maistrie," her own ideal woman's achieved domination), a narrative begun in carnal violence (a rape) is in her view "resolved" by effective delusion in the rapist protagonist and by his evasive acquiescence subsequently to a faerie woman's authority. That is, in desiring so fervently to have his cake and eat it too, the Wife's rapist knight abdicates his responsibility to make a moral choice, yielding his will to the "magic" of a witch, and, like Januarius in the Merchant's Tale, having begun in Folly and been tutored without avail by his wife's conventional wisdom, it seems he ends in the Wife of Bath's have-your-cake-and-eat-it world altogether unreconstructed, still Folly's dupe. There is no sign whatsoever that he has actually repented of his original sexual violence, nor is his victim in any way compensated. While his most unchivalrous behavior in the rape is thus conspicuously not answered in the Wife of Bath's "solution," the reader has nonetheless just been given a "noble" ethical standard against which the rapist knight may be measured and found wanting, in the central speech of the old hag-wife in the Wife's tale: the words of this speech are recognizable as an extended series of quotations from Boethius's *Consolation of Philosophy*, dealing with the essentially Christian and spiritual character of noble intent, or gentilesse (cf. Chaucer's short poem on this subject, "Gentilesse," also drawn from Boethius). By contrast with this embedded standard of gentilesse, which has its only validation at the level of the heart's intent

60. See Russell A. Peck, "Biblical Interpretation: St. Paul and *The Canterbury Tales*," in *Chaucer and Scriptural Tradition*, 143-70, esp. 158ff. For further study see also Lawrence Besserman, *Chaucer and the Bible* (New York: Garland, 1988), and his useful article, "Biblical Exegesis, Typology, and the Imagination of Chaucer," in *Typology and English Medieval Literature*, ed. Hugh T. Keenan, Georgia State Literary Studies, no. 7 (New York: AMS Press, 1992), 183-205.

and is not a matter of mere externals, the Wife's own "solution" seeks its validation from the externals of physical gratification, which have been the apparent common bond of intention between Dame Alice and her young knight errant all along.

In Dame Prudence's wise judgment at the close of the Tale of Melibee, by contrast, carnal violence (begun with the assault on Melibee's daughter Sophia) is recompensed by wise and therapeutic tutoring of both offended parties and of the offenders: through the careful reading of ethical texts, all submit in the end to deeper counsel. Prudence's teaching thus obtains repentance of the willful intention to abuse authority on both sides, even as it facilitates Sophia's (i.e., Wisdom's) healing.

Repentance and Metanoia

Repentance and the reconciliation it effects is in fact the advertised principal subject of Chaucer's overall poem.[61] And what is repentance for a Christian? Chaucer's answer is timeless: it is a yielding of the will in acknowledgment of sin, followed by a resolve to turn one's identity from definition by self-justified error toward truthful self-disclosure and a desire to become conformed to the will of God. The normative human occasion — that all have sinned and come short of the glory of God — provides a natural context for Chaucer's treatment of the problem of the willful reader. The outer frame of The Canterbury Tales is, as we have noted, a pilgrimage undertaken during the Easter season.[62] But since pilgrimages in this period were most frequently engaged as an act

61. Though Chaucer's Tale of Melibee, like the Parson's Tale, is often studiously avoided in contemporary university classrooms, the first is notably the synechdoche Chaucer gives himself, the last the conclusion he writes to the whole poem. Melibee is explicit biblical counsel to temper justice with mercy for those who are penitent; the Parson's sermon invites all readers, both fictive and actual, to a personal examination of conscience, followed by repentance and confession.

62. Chauncey Wood, "The April Date as a Structuring Device in The Canterbury Tales," Modern Language Quarterly 25 (1964): 259-71, suggests that not only is the pilgrimage clearly lenten, hence penitential, but typologically at least its beginning is associated with Good Friday.

of penance, and especially so during Lent, we should not be surprised that Chaucer formally concludes his nominally unfinished masterwork with the Parson's sermon on repentance.

The notion of the Christian's life as a penitent's journey between two cities had long been familiar. The city of this world — London in *The Canterbury Tales*, like Augustine's Babylon in *The City of God* — is figuratively a place of easy carnal entrapment. From it the penitent journeys out, like Abraham in the Bible (Augustine quotes Heb. 11:13-16), toward a city prepared by God for the reconciliation and restoration of those penitent and faithful pilgrims to whom his mercy extends. Augustine's celestial Jerusalem, here analogically Canterbury, a representative destination for English pilgrims. Though the overall analogy need only be implied for a medieval audience, Chaucer renders it explicit in the prologue to the Parson's sermon, where he who is chosen to "knytte up wel a greet mateere" (10.28) asks "Jhesu for his grace wit me sende / To shewe yow the way in this viage / Of thilke parfit glorious pilgrymage / That highte Jerusalem celestial" (10.48-51).

Fittingly, the pilgrims have first met at a tavern — The Tabard is an inn in the ambiguously suburban Southwerk — and at a first communal meal they had agreed each to tell his or her own story, so to speak. In their first covenant with the carnally minded landlord of the Tabard, he was to choose among these tales the best, for which the prize was to be another "soper" paid for by the company together, upon their return. But as it happens, of course, in Chaucer's poem they do not return. Their journey in this poem takes them no farther than a pilgrim's destination, not to a tavern but a temple, the sanctuary cathedral of St. Thomas in Canterbury, the house of God.

For Chaucer, as for Wyclif, misreading or misprision — getting it wrong and the entrapment of vision which results — is a function of the distorting power of sin. At the social level, the effects of the Fall (the persistence of sin) have everything to do with the loss of community, of communion, and hence of reliable communication. Repentance is essential in the process of making it right again, overcoming the Babel-like cacophany of contesting misreadings, their antagonism and alienation. How? By a yielding of our willful insistence upon the absolute priority of our own experience to a self-measuring and self-correcting higher Authority. If the pilgrim strategy of Chaucer's General Prologue is the "outer" frame in his *Canterbury Tales*, then its correlative at the level of individual tales is comprised of the head-links, tail-links, and individual prologues, as a sequential ordering of focusing frames. Finally, at the center is each individual tale, so contextualized.

But no individual pilgrim's tale is by itself the means by which a rightly ordered Christian reading can be realized. Rather, we are invited to make our appeal through the tale which is told to a precedent text which indicates the high road — "a full noble wey" as the Parson puts it — to the goal of less partial critical judgment. As much in the tale of a self-confessed and unrepentant villain like the Pardoner as in Dame Prudence's references in the Tale of Melibee, then, that ultimate Text is the final referent and corrective. If a fraudulent preacher like the Pardoner may be exposed for what he is by being read against the text he preaches (radix malorum est cupiditas, "the root of all evil is selfishness" [1 Tim. 6:10]), a faithful teacher — Dame Prudence or the Parson — may be validated by a life ethically consistent with the texts they too "read" and teach to others.[63] For both fictive and actual readers of The Canterbury Tales, the textual destination of the overall poem is thus a careful and faithful submission to the ultimate Text. This submission includes thoughtful analysis of the sins which make misreading the normal human condition, and elaboration of a compensatory discipline of repentance such as can, because of Christ's atoning sacrifice, prove corrective to these many sins both individual and collective, sins of commission and sins of ommission. The good reader in such a world is one who yields up insistent willfulness to accept as a prolegomenon to reading texts a reading of self in the light of the ultimate Text, that form of spiritual inventory which medieval spiritual writers call "an examination of conscience." That is, the good reader of what Chaucer calls "oure Book" agrees to let his author, figurally and literally, be his Author.

Chaucer's "Retraction," the formal conclusion to The Canterbury Tales, is such an examination of conscience, the explicit verbal form of which is called "confession." In its tone as well as its substance it characterizes Chaucer's own desire, as a human author, for submission to the ultimate Text:

63. The Pardoner's text is radix malorum cupiditas est, the Vulgate reading of 1 Tim. 6:10. The KJV and RSV narrow cupiditas (Gk. φιλαργυρία) to "the love of money." Chaucer translates the verse "coveteise is roote of all harmes" (7.1130).

Now preye I to hem alle that herkne this litel tretys or rede, that
if ther by anythyng in it that liketh hem that therof they thanken
oure lord Jhesu Crist, of whom procedeth al wit and al goodnesse.
/ And if ther be anythyng that displese hem, I preye hem also that
they arrette it to the defaute of myn unkonnynge, and nat to my
wyl that wolde ful fayn have seyd bettre if I had konnynge. / For
oure book seith, "Al that is writen is writen for oure doctrine," and
that is myn entente. / Wherfore I biseke yow mekely, for the mercy
of God, that ye preye for me that Crist have mercy on me and
foryeve me my giltes, / and namely of my translacions and en-
ditynges of worldly vanitees, the whiche I revoke in my retrac-
ciouns. . . .

(10.1081-85)

For Chaucer, as for medieval Christian writers generally, the writer is
after all just a reader with an audience — but therefore a reader with
more than singular accountability.

What the problem of the willful reader means for these later
medieval Christian theories of the encounter between reader and text
is self-limiting: we must acknowledge that in a fallen world no one
reader perfectly, or ever, gets it right.[64] Hence, the reader waits in vain
for the Host's announcement revealing which pilgrim has told the tale
"of best sentence and moost solace" and who therefore has won the
free meal, "the soper at our aller cost" (1.798-99). As the pilgrims
wend their way at eventide into Canterbury, and the shadows lengthen
and the moon (Libra, or the sign of Justice) ascends, the focus dis-
solves away from the group of storytellers as a whole and falls, as in
candor for the Christian poet it must, upon Chaucer the narrator

64. In the representative late medieval view of Chaucer and Wyclif, it should be
stressed, this variability or partiality in apprehending the good comes about because of
the variability of sinful willfulness from the perfect will of God; it is not parallel to the
sort of variability in deriving ethical norms or practice ascribed by postmodern prag-
matist ethics to cultural, gendered, or perspectival divergences. In the postmodernist
view such variability is itself a "good," and the ethics to be realized is hence one "without
metaphysics, without otherness, without the law" (Geoffrey G. Harpham, *Getting it
Right: Language, Literature, and Ethics* [Chicago: University of Chicago Press, 1992], 51).
Such a construction would have seemed to the fourteenth-century authors self-
contradictory.

himself.[65] It is a time for personal measurement, examination of conscience before going to the cathedral church of St. Thomas à Becket for confession and, yes, communion. Chaucer does not show his reader this moment of the shared eucharist; the medieval audience knew well enough how to project this personal closure from the clues Chaucer had already given in the Parson's prologue.[66] But suddenly it comes to the Christian reader to realize that it is not after all the pilgrim who in human terms tells the best tale who wins this Last Supper free, nor is it paid for all at "the cost of all." The Eucharist to which all the company goes has been paid for at the cost of One; not an award granted on the basis of any human merit, it is rather a gift of grace, free to the repentant soul: "whosoever will may come." And in this "oure Host" proves quite another Host; the one who bids them come to be "housled" not wordily boisterous Harry, but the Word in humility made flesh for our salvation, that only One who, having read the ultimate Text perfectly, could say softly at the crucial moment: "Not my will but Thine be done."

At the eucharistic moment, the pilgrim understands at last that experience by itself is never "right enough" for anyone, yet that authority, including the authority of texts and even of the Text, has not been quite enough either. What is required for communion is a harmony of intentions, of Author and reader, which comes about because "oure auctor" himself has shown the way, and the "reader" has, in a freedom of obedience, followed him there, to the foot of the cross. But for a penitent Christian this moment of realization is itself, of course, an experience — that *metanoia* by which, symbolically, experience is redeemed — even as it is also that declaration of intent by which the Author's wisdom is confirmed in the believer's own heart. There comes a point when words have served their purpose, and we pass beyond words. At that point we stand in silence before the Word, a silence which is sufficient for those to whom grace reserves the experience.

For Chaucer, as for Wyclif, what can most usefully be established

65. See Russell A. Peck, "Number Symbolism in the Prologue to Chaucer's *Parson's Tale*," *English Studies* 48 (1967): 205-15, still by far the best study of the Parson's prologue.

66. See D. L. Jeffrey, ed., *The Law of Love: English Spirituality in the Age of Wyclif* (Grand Rapids: Eerdmans, 1988), 304ff.

by a self-examining reading is whether, to begin with, the reader really wants to "get it right." For Christian theories of reading, that remains the all-important question — even though persistence in the attempt to answer it is likely to draw us ineluctably toward the *agon* of the Gethsemane prayer.

Chapter Seven

Symbolism of the Reader

The symbol is not added to Scripture, but drawn from Scripture.

THOMAS AQUINAS

As EVERY STUDENT OF EUROPEAN ROMANTIC LITERATURE REMEM-bers, the *Faust* of Goethe opens upon a plausible academic scene: in his narrow and vaulted study sits a jaded and hubristic professor, fidgeting in his armchair at a desk piled high with books.

This simple tableau, as we shall see, would have been for its literate audience a kind of symbol. In Goethe, however, we are to learn that it is a symbol under attack — or, more precisely, that Goethe has calcu-latedly introduced a powerful traditional symbolic configuration princi-pally for the purposes of its dramatic deconstruction. The opening soliloquy of Faust in his study makes apparent that what had once been for this professor of divinity a happy den, a little world full of wisdom and wonder, has now become somehow a prison-house of intellectual despair. Here at his desk, covered with learned volumes and scraps of paper (1.390), he feels "confined with a heap of books" ("Beschränkt mit diesem Bücherhauf"); his study symbolizes for Faust a life of read-ing he can now no more than scorn:

Weh! Steck ich in dem Kerker noch?
Verfluchtes dumpfes Mauerloch,
Wo selbst das liebe Himmelslicht
Trüb durch gemalte Scheiben bricht!
Beschränkt mit diesem Bücherhauf,
Den Würme nagen, Staub bedeckt,
Den bis ans hohe Gewölb hinauf
Ein angeraucht Papier umsteckt;
Mit Gläsern, Büchsen rings umstellt,
Mit Instrumenten vollgepfropft,
Urväter-Hausrat drein gestopft —
Das ist deine Welt! Das heißt eine Welt!

Still this old dungeon, still a mole!
Cursed be this moldy walled-in hole
Where heaven's lovely light must pass,
And lose its luster, through stained glass.
Confined with books, and every tome
Is gnawed by worms, covered with dust,
And on the walls, up to the dome,
A smoky paper, spots of rust;
Enclosed by tubes and jars that breed
More dust, by instruments and soot,
Ancestral furniture to boot —
That is your world! A world indeed![1]

In his present frame of mind "every niche" of his study "holds skulls and skeletons and death" (417), each a *memento mori* now of that arid bookish reflection which theoretically might expound "the holy symbols" ("die heilgen Zeichen" [427]), but which actually frustrates his desire to flee beyond such "symbols" to what he imagines to be unmediated nature.

Yet Faust's projected passport out of this now apparently too microcosmic scholar's confinement is, ironically, another book — in this

---

1. Text and translation from the edition of Walter Kaufmann, *Goethe's Faust* (New York: Doubleday, 1961), 1.402-409. Where I depart from Kaufmann in favor of a less poetic and more exact rendition (my own) the line reference will be asterisked.

case specifically a book of symbols. This illustrated tome, associated by him with Nostradamus, is a kind of emblem book, or *Emblemata*.[2] He opens it to the first chapter, to its symbol of the macrocosm, the universe itself. The text speaks of creation, a predictable feature of the initial "symbol" in Renaissance emblem books. As he gazes upon the image — never described in detail for the reader — and reads its accompanying text, this symbol seems to contradict his ambition to surpass mortal restraint, to become a demi-god and rise above the servility of mere creaturely existence. This, we shall see, is because in any of the emblem books available to him the picture and text upon which he would be gazing insists that the world was in the beginning created by God, and remains sustained by his hand of Providence. That is to say, the first symbol in such books is theological, a *symbolum* (Gk. *symbolon*) in the traditional sense of "credal Christian truth," and implicitly figurative for

2. In his *Symbolic Images: Studies in the Art of the Renaissance* (London: Phaidon, 1972), E. H. Gombrich, discussing *Faust*, says that "whatever symbol Faust turned to remains undecided" (172). Part of the reason for this may have to do with the way Goethe's apparent assignation of Faust's book proves to be a red herring. Nostradamus, although he was in the news in Goethe's time for having been condemned by Pope Pius VI (1781) and was regularly the subject of attacks by Calvinists as well, seems not to have been associated with any symbol-book as such (evocation of his name may have simply been intended to suggest Faust's occult interests). Emblem books and symbol dictionaries were widely popular from the sixteenth to seventeenth centuries, and were consulted by graphic, plastic, and literary artists who used them as dictionaries of images. Those still in use in the eighteenth century range from the unillustrated twelfth-century dictionaries of Rabanus Maurus (Migne, PL 112) and pseudo-Hugh (Migne, PL 176) and the late thirteenth-century *Rationale divinorum officiorum* of Durandus (a liturgically organized compendium of Christian symbolism), through the more extensive fourteenth-century compilations like the *Dictionari seu repertori moralii (Repertorium morale)* of Pierre Bersuire, to widely popular Renaissance works such as the *Iconologia* of Caesar Ripa (1593; first illustrated in 1603) and the two-volume *Mundus Symbolicus* of Filippo Picinelli, first published in Italian in 1669 and addressed specifically to "orators, preachers, academicians, poets." Another major Renaissance encyclopedia of symbolism was that of Piero Veleriano. In France, England, and Germany, emblem books became popular, more widely disseminated examples of this tradition. The monumental *Emblemata: Handbuch zur Sinnbildkunst des 16. und 17. Jahrhunderts* (Stuttgart: Metzler, 1967) collects comparative examples of many of these emblem books, and reflects their typical organization: each starts with a symbol or symbols of the macrocosm, and then moves on to symbols of the Four Elements, the first of which is Earth. A useful study is Mario Praz, *Studies in Seventeenth-Century Imagery*, 2 vols. (Rome: Edizioni di Storia e Letteratura, 1964).

the precedence of divine fiat and revelation over human intellect or imagination as ultimate *auctoritas.* Unsurprisingly then, in gazing at a symbol which sets so obvious a limit to his strident ambition, Faust falls further into despair. In doleful frustration he turns the page to another symbol, next in the book — that of the "earth spirit." Immediately his own spirits are revived — or perhaps we should say, becalmed. It is this seductive, more apparently masterable mundanity with which he feels comfortable, and which then at once he begins to court and conjure: "You, spirit of the earth, seem close to mine: I look and feel my heightened powers" ("meine Kräfte höher" [461-62]). But the emblem of the earth spirit to which he has turned is not, like the previous symbol of the macrocosm sustained by Providence, a Christian symbol. It is nonetheless a potent sign of Goethe's time — emblematic of the self-conception toward which his professor so ardently strives.

In suggesting that the setting or verbal stage upon which we first meet Goethe's Faust can be seen as deliberate to the poet's central purpose because in itself already a powerful "symbol," it will be apparent that I have used the word "symbol" in the older theological sense which Goethe's Faust recognizes if only to reject. I have applied it, however, not to Faust's emblem book, but to the *pictura* which Goethe's careful depiction of the scholar in his room thumbing that book re-creates. When Faust describes his study he itemizes numerous independently recognizable iconic elements — a reader in scholar's garb, a desk, books, tubes, jars, perhaps a skull, stained glass windows, and domed Gothic vaults. Each element he identifies is capable of generating meaning in a diversity of contexts. Brought together in this way, however, the particular combination of these elements sets before the audience a long, well-established association of images, an unambiguous ensemble or *pictura* which makes both audience recognition and reference to a larger, deeper cultural significance of this verbally painted scene quite predictable. It may be that these elements were intended also by Marlowe in his *Tragicall Historie of Doctor Faustus,* as his directions indicating a book-filled study might suggest (2.1.166-71; 177). But beyond doubt Goethe was fully aware of this tradition, since he asked for a late example of it — an etching by Rembrandt [Fig. 7] — to be printed as the frontispiece to his 1790 edition of *Faust.*

As we find them in literary texts composed in the context of Western Christian tradition, words such as "symbol" (and indeed "image" and "icon") have a richly textured history of usage. In applying them to an analysis of texts and graphic art together it is appropriate — particularly if we are to understand theologian Faust's choices — to employ them in a way which accurately reflects that tradition. That our task is instructively obligated by Faust's negation — Goethe's rejection of the first symbol's tradition — affords justification for having commenced upon a general discussion of Christian symbolism of the reader and the book by drawing attention to the opening scene in this German poet's early nineteenth-century *Faust* rather than Marlowe's early seventeenth-century version. Nor is it incidental to our understanding of the later Faust's radical break with Christianity that Goethe was a Mason. He was extremely interested in masonic symbolism, to the lyrical exposition of which he contributed in a number of his so-called "Lodge poems." He was also a devotee of emblem books, both traditional and occult.[3] In having Faust reject one symbol for another, Goethe wrote out of his own study, it seems, in more ways than one. In our own time, as Northrop Frye has observed, the word "symbol" has acquired an almost protean ambiguity.[4] Yet for Goethe this besetting ambiguity had yet to

3. Goethe owned an incomplete copy of Andrea Alciati's *Emblemata* (1531; 1551), and was familiar with many others, including Vaenius, *Emblemata sive Symbola* (1624), and probably *Amoris Divini Emblemata* (1615) by the same author — Otto van Veen. See W. S. Heckscher, "Goethe im Bande der Sinnbilder, Ein Beitrag zur Emblematik," in *Jahrbüch der Hamburger Kunstsammlungen* 7 (1962), who discusses Goethe's interest in (even preoccupation with) symbolism.

Rembrandt's etching, sometimes called "Doctor Faustus" (1652), emphasizes occult symbolism by having such a symbol appear in the place of a radiant *sol iustiae* shining through the stained glass of his study. It is known that Goethe admired Rembrandt's painting and obtained a reproduction of it, illustrating with it his 1790 first edition of *Faust.* The title given to this etching, one of a series showing scholars in their studies, probably derives in turn from Goethe. It is not in any of the early Rembrandt catalogues, although one of them calls it "practiserende alchimist." The light symbol which comes through the window does have significance for Freemasonry, although Rembrandt may have been unaware of how the Masons would later construe it. The cross within the circle was not for Masons a Christian symbol, but a symbol of nature and creative wisdom; the letters INRI within each quarter of the crossed circle might be identified by a Christian with the inscription on the cross, *"Ihesu Nazareth Rex Iudaorum,"* but for Masons this came to signify rather "Igne Natura Renovatur Integra" — suggesting the sacred fire of Masonry that renews humankind naturalistically.

4. "The Symbol as a Medium of Exchange," in *Symbols in Life and Art: Royal Society of Canada Symposium in Memory of George Whalley,* ed. James A. Leith (Montreal: McGill-Queens, 1987), 3-16.

appear: there were Christian symbols and occult symbols, and in drama-
tizing a choice between them he suggests that nothing less than a world
view is at stake.

Symbolism of the Faithful Reader

The *pictura* in Goethe's mind in thus setting the stage for his revisionist
presentation of Faust owes — as does Rembrandt's etching [Fig. 7] —
to a conventional representation of the faithful reader which had been
widely disseminated in art from the thirteenth to the seventeenth centuries. In one of the best known sixteenth-century variations, a 1511
woodcut by Albrecht Dürer of St. Jerome in his study (one of several
such representations by Dürer executed between 1492 and 1521)[5] we
see a pertinent model [Fig. 4]. For the later Middle Ages, Jerome was
in a sense the archetypal scholar and faithful reader, a careful student
of the scriptural text and translator of the texts both of Scripture and
other derivative Christian works (e.g., Eusebius's *History*) for others'
reading. The iconic elements in Dürer's representation are traditional.
The devoted lion, which in legend Jerome's fearless trust in God helped
him heal, represents the watchful eye of divine Providence and, indeed,
the sustaining presence of Christ ("the lion of Judah") himself.[6] Though
here foregrounded, the familiar lion is less immediately pertinent to
Goethe than is the overall study scene, with its Gothic ecclesial vaults,
its bookshelf and scattered books, the tubes and jars of medicinal liquids,
the hour-glass and (though this item, like the lion, is significantly
missing in the study of Goethe's Faust), ever before the scholar as he
annotates or translates his text, a memorial of the atoning sacrifice of
the Suffering Servant, the Word of God made flesh — a crucifix.[7] In all

---

5. There are at least six of these extant, all reproduced in *Dürer: The Complete
Engravings, Etchings and Woodcuts*, ed. Karl-Adolf Knappe (Seacaucas, N.J.: H. Abrams,
n.d.).

6. These associations are conventional in the dictionaries referred to in note 3
above.

7. The skull, visible behind the scholar in Fig. 7, and though not in Dürer's 1511
St. Jerome, prominent in his rendering of 1514 [Fig. 15], is of course a *memento mori*,

remaining respects Goethe's verbal detail, the item by item correspondence of his setting, is too complete to be other than suggestive.

Such iconically rich Renaissance representations of Jerome in his study — a widely popular subject in European art — are as pictorial constructs already themselves in an established tradition of symbolic representations of faithful readers and their formative books. Less frequently we find complementary representations of other notable medieval scholars / readers which (without the lion, or the dog which sometimes substitutes) employ most of the same iconic elements. A Flemish example executed a few decades before Dürer's woodcut depicts Vincent de Beauvais in a decorated manuscript of his *Speculum Historiae,* or *Miroire Historiale.* Here the scholar is surrounded by books, the reading of which has given rise to his writing, and upon his desk stands not a crucifix but a speculum, emblematic of that mirror of history, or glass through which now we view things as puzzling shadows, and of which Vincent's synthesized reading is essayed to afford other readers a deeper glimpse.[8] Though less frequently, St. Augustine was also represented in this general way in the fifteenth and sixteenth centuries, as more rarely were St. Gregory the Great, St. Anthony of Florence, Nicolas of Cusa, and Martin Luther — in each case modeled after earlier representations of St. Jerome.

At the level which I have been calling Christian symbolism of the reader and the book, however, there is resonance to the typical representations of Jerome in his study which had been generated still more profoundly in late medieval and Renaissance representations of an earlier reader, one whose "book" is also unambiguously the sacred page. The Virgin Mary appears regularly in late medieval depictions of the Annunciation as a prototypically faithful reader. In Roger Van der Wey-

---

a reminder of our transient mortality. Numerous paintings and drawings of St. Jerome in his study have him pointing to the skull or resting his left hand upon it, in a fashion similar to the way his own right hand supports his head — an indication, among other things, of his awareness that the thoughts which now form in his own brain, like those which once formed in the skull in his left hand, are going to pass away, whereas the Word of God open before him on his desk will never pass away.

8. Fifteenth-century Flemish MS miniature from Jean de Vignay's translation of Vincent de Beauvais, MS Roy. 14.E.1 (vol. 1), fol. 3r, reprinted in Joan Evans, ed., *The Flowering of the Middle Ages* (London: Thames and Hudson, 1966), 192.

Figure 7. "*Doctor Faustus*" *by Rembrandt, 1652. Courtesy: The Pierpont Morgan Library/Art Resource, NY.*

den's *Three Kings Altarpiece* (ca. 1420, Munich), for example [Fig. 8], Mary is found by the angel Gabriel in the symbolic posture of the prayerful reader of Scripture. The vaulted room, with reminiscences of others we have seen and shall see, is furnished with the white lily, unmistakably a reference to her virginal purity. In Roger's composition, the angelic scepter, symbol of divine potency, is proleptically also the sign of the cross, transversed here by the pneumatic trajectory of the seminal Word, the Logos about to become flesh by virtue of the Spirit's descent (the white dove).[9] The meaning of the Book, that perdurable witness to the Word of God now about to be enfleshed in Mary, is echoed in the painting's center panel (not reproduced). Here are depicted the Magi, whose adoration of the Christ child is metonymic for that respect which the wisdom of this world ought to pay to the "epiphany" or revelation of the supreme Wisdom of God. The right-hand panel of the Munich altarpiece reminds the celebrants at the

9. The conception by Mary in the Incarnation of the Logos is referred to by Christian theologians frequently as the "seminal conception" which becomes the model for the generation in the church of "the fruits of holiness and justice." This motif appears in many places — in allegorical treatments of the Song of Songs of course, but also in discussions of the fruits of the Spirit (Gal. 5:22-23), e.g., in John Colet's *De Sacramentis*, 60. Colet was a father of the English Reformation, yet unsurprisingly his grounding of a thoroughly sacramentalist notion of God's redemption of physical human nature by grace depends for its model — and its tropes — on a traditional doctrine of the Incarnation. In this respect Colet parallels precisely his friend Erasmus, who articulates traditional incarnational symbolism relating the *mysterium* of human wedlock to the *magnum mysterium* of God's redemptive love at work in the church. In Erasmus, Christ the divine husband "daily begets children through his spouse by means of the dispersion of his heavenly semen of the divine Word, as James the apostle writes: 'Of his own will he has begotten us by the word of truth that we might be, as it were, the first-fruits of his creatures (James 1:18)." As Erasmus notes in his *Institutio christiani matrimonii*, this language of "seminal" analogy is found everywhere in the New Testament (e.g., 1 Cor. 4:15; Gal. 4:19; John 1:13), and everywhere rooted in the doctrine of the Incarnation (J. Clericus, ed., *D. Erasmi Opera Omnia* [Leiden, 1704], 5.620-21). For a helpful discussion see Walter M. Gordon, *Humanist Play and Belief: The Seriocomic Art of Desiderius Erasmus* (Toronto: University of Toronto Press, 1990), 249-54. In typical theological development of this analogy the direct tropic connection between the Word made flesh in Jesus and the disseminated word of the *evangelium* — through Scripture and by preaching — is assumed. Annunciation paintings, in their iconography, both reflect and articulate the theological connection as symbol. Individual representations may vary: in Campin's Annunciation [Fig. 11] what passes through the stained glass is not the dove of the Holy Spirit but a cross-bearing homunculus.

Figure 8. *"Annunciation" by Roger Van der Weyden. The Three Kings Altarpiece, Munich, 1420. Courtesy: Foto Marburg/Art Resource, NY.*

eucharist as they stand before it that to have sacramental experience of this incarnate revelation is the consummation of all that the faithful spirit longs for: "Let now thy servant depart in peace," says Simeon the faithful priest, "according to thy Word. . . ." (Luke 2:29 [KJV; Vulg.]).

What makes Mary central to altarpiece representations of the Incarnation is her historic instrumentality; she is chosen to be the medium by which the Logos is enfleshed, and we in turn are enabled to ingest the incarnate Word in part because of her exemplary faithfulness to that Word.[10] This is a ubiquitous emphasis in medieval and Renaissance annunciations. Fra Angelico's Mary in his (1440) Annunciation in San Marco Church, Florence, iconically expresses, with her hands and book folded over her breast, attentive receptivity to the Word: "*Ecce ancilla* . . . Behold the handmaid [NRSV "servant"] of the Lord." So also does the Virgin in the Ghent polyptich of Van Eyck [Fig. 9]. Van der Weyden's Mary holds her hand over the sacred page: in the language of the painter's iconography she is saying, "Be it unto me according to thy Word." In this most practical sense, Mary's humility and receptivity as "reader" is, according to St. Ambrose, the virtue which "commends the Mother of the Lord to those who read the Scriptures, and, as a credible witness, declares her worthy to be chosen to such an office."[11] Thus, whichever aspect of the dialogue and narrative from Luke is reflected in late medieval representations of the Annunciation, one element *not*

10. Mary's faithfulness under the Law is reflected in a diversity of ways. In the tempera Annunciation by Simoni Martini (Uffizi, Florence, ca. 1333) the interrupted reader is depicted as if frightened by the annunciation of her angelic visitor, recoiling from him in the direction of her book ("How shall these things be, since I know not a man?"). In one attributed variously to Hubert Van Eyck and Petrus Christus (Metropolitan, New York, ca. 1435) Mary greets Gabriel formally at the door of a Gothic church, book in hand, already with the poised self-possession of practiced regal decorum. Here she is both the Church as Bride and the expectant Mother of Salvation. But the text of Scripture in her hand is central to both examples.

11. Humility was regarded by medieval philosophers of education as a *sine qua non* for the serious pursuit of truth in reading (e.g., Hugh of St. Victor, *Didascalicon* 3.13). But modesty and humility are those special qualities of *bona fide* virginity, literal and spiritual, which St. Ambrose highlights in his influential discussion of Mary as a model reader of Scripture, and are qualities accordingly to be pursued by all who would read Scripture faithfully (*De officiis* 1.18.68-69). Martini's Mary (n. 10, above) is "reacting" in a way which symbolizes this appropriate modesty.

Figure 9. "Ecce ancilla" *by Hubert and Jan van Eyck. Ghent Altarpiece (detail), 1432. Courtesy: Giraudon/Art Resource, NY.*

found in the scriptural narrative (except of course in the purely symbolic sense) remains central — the open Bible.

Even after the Nativity Mary is often depicted as the ideal reader of the ideal book, and the painters make it clear that this is to be understood by us as intrinsic to her being chosen as incarnational medium of the Logos himself. In some representations, such as Van Eyck's *Ince Hall Madonna*, as in versions by Petrus Christus, Quentin Metsys, and Hans Memlinc, she is shown with the infant Jesus, holding him on her lap while she reads Torah — and so presenting, as it were, the Word made flesh with the Word he has come to fulfill. One of the best of this type is Botticelli's *Madonna of the Book* [Fig. 10].[12] Mary's hand over the text ("Be it unto me according to thy Word") is mirrored by that of the infant Christ. Yet the tenderness of the body language of both mother and child bids us think not only of the fulfillment already realized as the Word made flesh, but also, in the bracelet of rosemary around the Christ-child's arm so suggestive of the crown of thorns to come at Golgotha, to think ahead to a fulfillment less tranquil. Here we see, in fact, symbolic representation which, for practical purposes, defines the essential nature of pre-Enlightenment Christian symbol. In the words of H. Flanders Dunbar, "Jesus had come as the fulfilment of that for which the world had been preparing, and so gave meaning to all symbolism. More than this, in *him* was defined the very function of symbolism itself, in uniting eternally the infinite meaning and its finite expression."[13]

Incontrovertably, the characteristic symbolism of Reader and Book through the Renaissance points us to the centrality of the Incarnation in traditional Christian understanding of cosmos and microcosm, creation and creature, God and the self. Faithful reading is at once the pathway to such understanding and the reality of its possession, an ingathering of perspective which establishes true identity. This is transparent, for example, in the lovely Annunciation attributed to the Master of Flemaille, probably Robert Campin [Fig. 11]. The Virgin's chamber in Campin's rendition is a comfortable reading room: the second book and note script suggest even a study. Campin's Mary is in fact such an

12. Milan, Museo Poldi Pezzoli, ca. 1485.
13. In *Symbolism in Medieval Thought and Its Consummation in the Divine Comedy* (New York: Russell and Russell, 1961), 254.

Figure 10. *"Madonna of the Book" by Botticelli, ca. 1483.*
Courtesy: Alinari/Art Resource, NY.

Figure 11. *"The Annunciation" by Robert Campin. Center panel of the Triptych of the Annunciation, 1428. Courtesy: Metropolitan Museum, New York.*

absorbed and careful reader of the Word (she cradles it in a cloth to protect its binding — a prophetic gesture) that she does not realize that the angel is already present with her in her room, about to announce her imminent conception of the "Word from the beginning." Gabriel's hand is raised — he is poised to speak, but has not yet spoken. Campin's final stroke is breathtaking; with the rush of Gabriel's wings the candle by which Mary reads has just been extinguished. The smoke drifts up and, perhaps subconsciously alerted, her eyes have just begun to turn away from the page toward the presence she has not yet physically "seen." We catch her therefore at a pivotal and charged symbolic moment in Christian history: faithfully intent upon the Law, she is about to be, in the twinkling of an eye, surprised by Grace.[14]

In the bower of the Virgin we may seem to be at some distance from St. Jerome in his study, but in reality we are not very far away at all. Although the topic is beyond the scope of this study, virginity itself as a virtue of singular focus is yet another reason for traditional identification of Mary as exemplary reader, as those familiar with the letters and biographies of St. Jerome will be aware.[15] But for the matter of the faithful reader and the authoritative text — our central subject — we need to locate more adequately the connection between representations of the scholar in his study and the Blessed Virgin in her maiden bower. It turns out that the connection is fundamental: their common rootedness in the most basic features of Christian *symbolum* — or doctrine.

14. See n. 9, above. Campin's St. Barbara (1438) is the right-hand panel of a diptych in the Prado, Madrid. His representation of the sanctity of St. Barbara mimes the Annunciation setting naturalistically. Here too is an absorbed reader of the sacred page. The potted flower near her in her study (an iris rather than lily) helps us confirm the analogy, letting us know that while Barbara is not Mary she is like unto her in faithful attention to the Book of books; in this panel painting the symbolic representation over her fireplace of the "throne of Mercy," God the Father presenting the crucified Jesus, symbolizes the meaning of the text she reads, linking again the written word to the Word made flesh in terms of the ultimate purpose of both.

15. Jerome was celebrated also for his *Contra Helvidius,* a treatise on the perpetual virginity of Mary, and was perhaps the most celebrated champion of virginity as necessary to the perfection of Christian vocation.

Taking the Word to Heart

It will also be apparent that the derivation of the Book / Reader symbol, like many other aspects of Christian identity, is Jewish. By the Renaissance literate Christians had long been aware of this, but were finding new ways to express appreciation of the symbolic derivation. In Cesar Ripa's *Iconologia* for example, "Fede Cattolica" is symbolized by a woman dressed in white wearing the helmet of salvation (Eph. 6:17), and holding in her right hand a candle mounted on a heart, symbolizing "the illumination of a mind reborn through faith dispelling the darkness of ignorance and disobedience," while in her left hand is a book out of which grows "the table of Moses," symbolizing the New and Old Testaments together as the summary of faith and law of Christ [Fig. 12].[16]

The Old Testament figure from whom Christians absorbed most of their typological understanding of what it is to be "a people of the book" was typically not Moses, however, but that most fervent reader of "his" book, David the shepherd king and poet. The first page of countless medieval psalters (the most widely copied of all parts of the medieval Old Testament) displays a portrait of David in an initial capital either for the title (*Carmina* or *Psalterium*), or the "B" of *Beatus vir*, the first words of Psalm 1 [Fig. 13]. In some of these he has to hand both Scripture and a "ten-stringed harp" (Ps. 144:9; cf. Augustine, *Confessions* 3.8); in others, he is presented simply as reading, and in these we see that the book David reads so intently is the Law of Moses, sometimes represented figuratively as the two stone tablets of the Law. What the symbol declares is a certain textual filiation: "that text gives rise to this text." Attentive reading of the Law, and the benefits of *mishpat*, of doing the Law, are of course the subject matter of the first poem in David's "book":

> Blessed is the man that walketh not in the counsel of the ungodly, nor standeth in the way of sinners, nor sitteth in the seat (Vulg. *cathedra*, "chair") of the scornful. But his delight is in the law of the Lord; and in his law doth he meditate day and night. And he shall be like a tree planted by the rivers of water . . . his leaf also shall not wither, and whatsoever he doeth shall prosper.

16. Caesar Ripa, *Iconologia* (Padua, 1611; reprint, New York: Garland, 1976), 163-64.

Figure 12. *"Fede Cattolica," from Caesare Ripa*, Iconologia, *Padua, 1611.*

Figure 13. "Beatus Vir," *in the Albani-Psalter. Courtesy: Dombibliothek Hildesheim.*

The psalmist's invitation to those who will "delight in the Law of the Lord" is not, however, merely commendatory. It is diagnostic. Psalm 1, much like Goethe's opening depiction of the scholar in his study, tacitly contains its value opposite. This has not escaped the notice of generations of Christian readers: the Ordinary Gloss on the Bible observes, as do the Renaissance commentaries of Jesuit Cornelius Lapide and Calvinist Theodore de Beze, that verse 1 implicitly also defines the condition of one who is *not* a *beatus vir,* and accordingly takes no delight in God's book. The "person who is condemned" *(damnatus vir)* is one who in fact does take counsel with the ungodly, who does stand in the way of sinners, and sits not in the *cathedra proprie doctorum,* as the academic language of the Gloss puts it, but in the chair of the scoffer.[17] The blessed effect of David's meditative reading is, by way of radical contrast, a humble incorporation of the Word ("Thy word have I hid in my heart, that I might not sin against Thee"), an ingestion of divine ordinance which subsequently orders in harmony his own thought, speech, and action.[18]

Christians, even nominal ones, could traditionally be expected to recognize Mary's faithful reading of Scripture as one of the primary evidences of her being, like her Son, spiritually of the line of David. To be "next to God's own heart" — for both David and Mary — is, most evocatively, to have already become a dedicated reader of God's word. Tellingly, an harmonious register of Psalm 1 appears in the Spirit-filled greeting of Mary by her cousin Elizabeth. Here, in the place of "Blessed is the man who . . ." is: "Blessed are you among women, and blessed is the child you bear! . . . Blessed is she who has believed that what the Lord has said to her will be accomplished!" (Luke 1:42; 45). *Beatus vir; beatus mulier.* Mary, too, is one who had put herself "under the Law" (Gal. 4:4); the ingested Word, or the Word hid in the psalmist's heart, is found resonant still in the woman who "kept all these words, ponder-

---

17. The KJV translation is somewhat less apt than the Vulgate Latin, which reads: "et in cathedra pestilentiae non sedit" (nor sits in the chair of pestilence). According to Picinelli, *Mundus Symbolicus* (1.2.106), the "water" of verse 3 may be understood as a symbol of that grace which is made available by the "irrigation" of reading sacred doctrine. But for the *Glossa ordinaria* the contrary of the *beatus vir* is already given in the first verse of the psalm (Migne, PL 113.844).

18. See the article "Harp" in D. L. Jeffrey, ed., *A Dictionary of Biblical Tradition in English Literature* (Grand Rapids: Eerdmans, 1992).

ing them in her heart" (Luke 2:19 [Vulg.]). It is on this account fitting, says Aquinas, that she should be chosen to be "mother of the Word of God."[19]

But if David and Mary in Christian tradition become prototypes of the ideal reader, it is because the Book they read is not merely the Torah *ad litteram,* but the Torah which is revealed, *in spiritus vivificat:* for medieval commentators and illustrators alike, in the text of Torah what they really read is Christ. According to Pierre Bersuire's influential four-teenth-century dictionary of symbols:

> Christ is a sort of Book in the skin [vellum] of the virgin. . . . That book was spoken in the disposition of the Father, written in the conception of the mother, expounded in the clarification of the nativity, corrected in the passion . . . illuminated in the outpouring of [Christ's] blood, bound in the resurrection, and reviewed in the ascension.[20]

Even in early medieval Christian art Christ is often presented as the Living Logos: enthroned upon the book, bearing the book, being the Book, the text which the evangelists' texts will "translate" or copy [Fig. 5a; 5b; 6]. The book that medieval Christ figures carry or proclaim is thus not only Torah, but Torah fulfilled. Hence, the open text may be the New Testament, or symbolically, the "Law and the Prophets," the "meaning of the Scriptures" explained to the disciples.[21]

All this is commonplace — for centuries Christians had been famil-iar with this general pictorial convention for conveying the doctrine of the inspiration of Holy Scripture[22] and its mirroring in the notion of the Spirit's guidance for faithful commentators such as the church fathers. But as familiarity with this conventional symbolism of fidelity to the Book of God grew general, it became possible for artists to

19. *Summa contra gentiles* 4.34.

20. *Repertorium morale* (Cologne, 1730), vol. 1.

21. Wolfram von den Steinem, *Homo Caelestis: Das Wort der Kunst im Mittelater,* 2 vols. (Berne and Munich: Franke Verlag, 1965), gives numerous excellent examples from gospel illustrations of the ninth to eleventh centuries. See especially 2.63, 65, 155, 179.

22. Often an evangelist will be shown receiving his "book" from Christ, or via dictation by the Holy Spirit. See *Homo Caelestis* 2.68, 81, 83, 199.

"naturalize" it. Some of the annunciations we have seen offer examples of this. So also do many of the earlier medieval representations of the evangelists: Matthew, Mark, Luke, and especially John [Fig. 14a; 14b] are typically presented in this way in illustrations on the front of decorated copies of their respective Gospels.[23] What we recognize in these scenes is nevertheless symbolic rather than realistic representation, and that which is symbolized may be thought of in terms of the foundational Jewish and Christian appeal to becoming "a people of the book." Here, in the specifically Christian context of medieval representation, that book is then "God's Book" in two conventional senses: Scripture, and the Word made flesh in Christ.

Accordingly we may say of the evangelists as symbolic readers what we say about David or Mary, that their faithful reading is an incarnational activity and part of an incarnational process whereby the Word becomes, for all who will so faithfully read it, an "ingested" or "seminal" word"; once incorporated it generates and gives birth to life, as well as to other words and books. One attractive representation of St. Luke as faithful reader comes from a beautiful thirteenth-century manuscript devotional book and is significantly located in the midst of an anthology of extracts from the Gospels having to do specifically with the Incarnation. The passage above the figure is from John (1:13, 14): "born of God. The Word became flesh and made his dwelling among us. We have seen his glory, as the Only begotten of the Father, full of grace and truth. Thanks be to God."[24] That which follows is from Luke 1 (beginning at verse 26) "In that time the angel Gabriel was sent by God into a Galilean city called Nazareth . . . ," the narrative of the Annunciation.

The Professor as Reader

In Christian art of the Middle Ages (and beyond) the reliable writer or teacher is only that person who is first a faithful reader. The precedents for this standard are luminous. In biblical terms, the authority of a prophet's counsel resides in his having been first and foremost a faithful

23. Ibid., 2.71-73, 82-83, 87, 158.
24. Bodleian Library Oxford, MS Douce 276.

Figure 14a. *"John the Evangelist."* Frontispiece to copy of Gospel of John, Constantinople, ca. 960. *Courtesy: Athens National Library.*

Figure 14b. *"Mark the Evangelist."* Trier, ca. 1010. *Courtesy: Bibliothèque Nationale de France – Paris.*

reader of Torah. In Dürer's representations, Ezekiel and John are shown, on the basis of their respective vocational narratives in Scripture, as virtually ingesting the Book of God before they set pen to parchment: this is particularly vividly depicted in Dürer's 1498 representation of John on Patmos [Fig. 21]. The Epistle of St. James was thought richly to reflect James' understanding of the Word of Jesus as a call to *misphat*, to *doing* the Word as the Law (Torah) of God, so that James, like the prophet Isaiah, can be represented as a careful student of Scripture [Fig. 2] — the relevant iconic clue being his fingers inserted in several pages at once for the sake of textual comparison.[25] Augustine's posture when preaching is said to have been deliberately that of a reader — seated before his hearers with the open Scriptures upon his knees,[26] much in the manner of early representations of David with the tables of Moses upon his knees. Later, in the high Middle Ages, Augustine's foundational value as a faithful reader and transmitter of God's book might be represented symbolically by use of the *lector-in-studium* configuration whose ancestry we have been exploring: in a mid-fourteenth-century representation by Theodoric of Prague the swarthy African bishop appears alone in his study (desk in background) with his beloved book; in one of Botticelli's late fifteenth-century versions the study has become a full repository of the scholar's tools of trade; in this respect the painting resembles Dürer's representations of St. Jerome.[27]

It is well to remind ourselves that in a medieval context the notion of "reading," as John of Salisbury points out in his *Metalogicon*, has a double sense: "It may refer to the activity of teaching and being taught, or to the occupation of studying written things by oneself."[28] This sense of the Latin is preserved analogously in the Middle English of Chaucer's time, where the English verb "to read" also bears two simultaneous senses — to obtain by means of deciphering letters counsel from a book,

25. *Homo Caelestis*, 2.125.

26. See the valuable article by Donald Marshall, "Making Letters Speak: Interpreter as Orator in Augustine's *De Doctrina Christiana*," *Religion and Literature* 24, no. 2 (1992): 1-18.

27. Florence, Ognisanti, ca. 1509, where in fact it hangs opposite Ghirlandao's "St. Jerome in his Study."

28. *Metalogicon* 1.24. On the continuation of this double sense of the verb "to read" through the eighteenth century, see Anne Ferry, *The Art of Naming* (Chicago: University of Chicago Press, 1988).

but also the giving of counsel to others such as is derived from books. When Chaucer's Dame Prudence says, "I rede the" as a preface to some piece of counsel for her dull-spirited husband Melibee, she is actually about to quote from an authoritative text. When medieval political poetry refers to the last king in whose court Chaucer served (Richard II) as "Richard the Redelesse," the poets do not mean that he is, strictly speaking, illiterate, but that he is averse to wise counsel, including notably that of this own prudent consort, Queen Anne.[29] This older sense of the word "reader" is of course the origin of the academic teaching rank still found in British universities, "Reader," and in the analogous derivation (also, in Canadian and Commonwealth universities) of "Lecturer" (from Latin *lector* or "reader"). Similarly, "lesson" derives from Latin *lectione,* a reading. Accordingly, when Jerome is referred to by John of Salisbury, for example, as a "teacher of teachers," it is not to say anything different from those who, like John Wyclif, proclaim him as the "perfected reader of all Scripture as *lex dei, lex Christi.*"[30]

Jerome's fame as an exact and exacting reader of the text of Scripture evidently is the matter which preoccupied Dürer in his 1514 engraving [Fig. 15]. In this rich composition the sleepiness of the pet dog and relaxed pose of the lion contrast with the intense attentiveness to the text of the sanctified scholarly reader. We may contrast this with an earlier (1492) woodcut by Dürer [Fig. 16], in which we see, despite the prominent comparative texts of Scripture in Hebrew, Greek, and *Latina antiqua,* focus turning to the conventional lion, here figurative of Christ's protective watchfulness (much as the dog represents faithfulness [hence, *Fido*] more generally). Other contemporary representations, such as those by Antonio de Fabriano, by Carpaccio, and by Allori, more often emphasize the meditative aspect of Jerome's scholarly reading.[31]

29. See here the excellent discussion of Mary Carruthers, *The Book of Memory: A Study of Memory in Medieval Culture* (Cambridge: Cambridge University Press, 1990), 30, 38, 156-88.

30. *Policraticus,* 7; John Wyclif, *De Veritate Sacrae Scripturae,* 3 vols., ed. R. Buddenseig (London: Wyclif Society; Trübner, 1905-7), 2.

31. Meditation is generally taken to be intrinsic to serious reading. Hugh of St. Victor says: "The start of learning . . . lies in reading, but its consummation lies in meditation . . ." (*Didascalicon* 3.10). The discussion of Hugh of St. Victor in the *Didascalicon* is conventional, representative of what might be found on the subject for another three or four centuries — a version appears even in the writings of John Wesley in the

Still other works stress the ascetic, self-denying discipline of the humble, penitent reader of Scripture, as in a painting of Jerome ascribed to Piero della Francesco (1440), or in yet another of Dürer's engravings, which shows Jerome reading Scripture in a desert cell, recalling his asceticism or abstention from the pleasures of the world for the sake of uncluttered focus on the Word of God.[32] If the Virgin Mary became appropriately a model for devotional readers, as Ambrose suggested, St. Jerome, champion of her virginal singularity, thus became the principal Renaissance model for scholarly readers.

Like Erasmus, for example [Fig. 17]. The great Dutch scholar spent much of his own life as a corrector and editor of the text of Scripture and its tradition of commentary. One of his greatest achievements, by his own estimate, was his great edition of the *Works of St. Jerome,* to which he attached as a preface his own biography, or *Life,* of the saint. Erasmus praises Jerome as the "best scholar, writer and expositor" among the Fathers, as a reader who has acquired a "perfect command of Holy Scripture," a reader of Scripture in the original tongues who then translated it for his countrymen into their own vernacular.[33] All this was possible, says Erasmus, because Jerome was the perfectly equipped and utterly dedicated reader, "equally and completely at home in all literature, both sacred and profane," one who read many volumes, yet whose crowning ornament was that he "had the whole of Scripture by heart . . . drinking it in, digesting it, turning it over and pondering upon it."[34] For Erasmus, Jerome as reader shows us, in both his teaching and writing, the perfect application of "encyclopedic learning."[35] The

eighteenth century. Fabriano (Walters Art Gallery, Baltimore) is reproduced in the *Collected Works of Erasmus,* vol. 61, *The Edition of St. Jerome,* ed. and trans. J. F. Brady and J. C. Olin (Toronto: University of Toronto Press, 1992), xiv.

32. In the case of Alessandro Allori (Princeton University, ca. 1600), as with these other representations of St. Jerome studying in his desert cell, the connection of meditation with penitence and flight from the "muses of the theatre" and pleasures of the flesh is emphasized.

33. Erasmus, *Epist.* 141.2-9; 335.232-47; see also Craig R. Thompson, "Jerome and the Testimony of Erasmus in Disputes over the Vernacular Bible," *Proceedings of the Patristic, Medieval and Renaissance Conference* 6 (Villanova University, 1981), 1-36.

34. Dedicatory Letter, in his *Edition of Jerome, Collected Works of Erasmus,* 61.7.

35. According to Erasmus, Jerome saw his apostolic task as "taking every thought captive for Christ." He made it his business, Erasmus notes, to get "a thorough education

entire *Life of St. Jerome* penned by Erasmus echoes and re-echoes this praise of Jerome as a reader and a teacher of readers (including women readers). And it is this repeated praise of Erasmus for his model which keeps us from being surprised at the evident imitation in subsequent portraiture of Erasmus himself.[36] It has been often suggested that Erasmus seems to have modeled his whole scholarly life on the saint who counselled his correspondents: "Read the divine scriptures constantly; never, indeed, let the sacred volume be out of your hand."[37] Certainly Erasmus in many places echoes the admonition Jerome

---

in profane literature" and in classical philosophers — at least those whose declared purpose in study was to know "that which is good." Further, "he diligently examined all the libraries and met men who were distinguished either for their learning or their moral integrity, and everywhere he appropriated what he thought useful for the Christian life" (*Collected Works*, 61.28). We could do worse than to imitate him, Erasmus suggests, adding thoughtfully: "At length he went into hiding, as it were, in that remote desert," discouraged with the crass and materialist superficiality of much of what passed for Christianity — even in Antioch. There "for four years, far removed from the assembly of men, he commenced only with Christ and with his books." Amidst a routine of prayer and fasting, "he reread his entire library, renewing the memory of his old studies; he [memorized] Holy Scripture word for word. . . . From the Gospels and the apostolic letters as from the purest springs he drew the philosophy of Christ. . . . He read other exegetes with discretion and judgment, overlooking no writer at all from whom he might glean something, pagan or heretic. For he knew, prudent man, how to gather gold from a dung-pit . . . [and to] take from the Egyptians to adorn the temple of the Lord with the riches of the enemy" (33).

36. A classic example is the often reproduced portrait attributed to Quentin Metsijs, 1517, in which one can see that the text he works on is his paraphrase upon St. Paul to the Romans, while the first volume on the shelf above him bears upon its spine the name Hieronymus (Jerome). Holbein's portrait (Radner Collection, Longford Castle) shows Erasmus in his study with his hand upon his own edition of Jerome.

37. Jerome, *Epist.* 52.7. According to Lisa Jardine, in *Erasmus: Man of Letters: the Construction of Charisma in Print* (Princeton: Princeton University Press, 1993), "in graphic and textual representations of himself Erasmus chose to inhabit the familiar figure of St. Jerome, with all the grandeur and intellectual *gravitas* that might thereby accrue to him, [and so] claimed a role in the secular sphere equivalent to Jerome's in the spiritual" (4). She goes on to suggest that ". . . as we watch the strategic recuperation for the charismatic man of letters of the aura which had traditionally surrounded the portrait and the 'life' of the holy man in conventional hagiography, we are, I believe, witnessing the transition from 'sacred' to 'learned' as the grounds for personal salvation" (59). About this judgment I feel less comfortable: Erasmus is not yet Faust, by any stretch of the evidence.

Figure 15. "*St. Jerome in his Study*" *by Albrecht Dürer, 1514. Courtesy: Giraudon/Art Resource, NY.*

Figure 16. *"St. Jerome Curing the Lion" by Albrecht Dürer. From edition of St. Jerome's Letters,* Liber epistolarum Sancti Hieronymi, *Basel, 1492.*

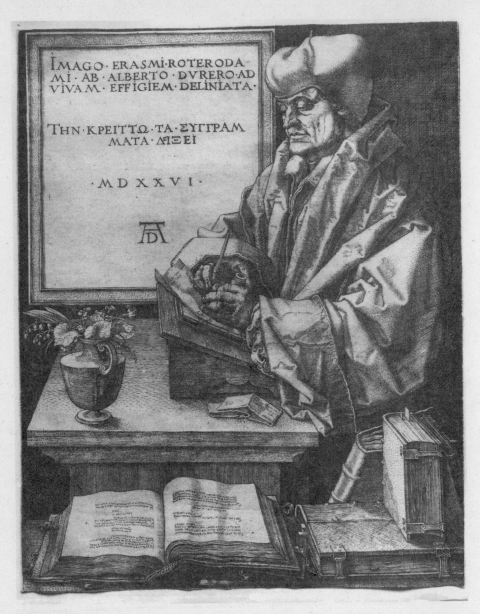

Figure 17. "*Erasmus of Rotterdam*" by Albrecht Dürer, 1526. Courtesy: *Victoria & Albert Museum/Art Resource, NY.*

offered to the Roman matron Laeta on the education of her young daughter: "Let her treasures be not silks or gems but manuscripts of the holy scriptures; and in these, let her think less of gilding, Babylonian parchment, and arabesque ornamentation than of correctness and accurate punctuation" (Jerome, *Epist.* 107.12). For both scholars, though they lived twelve centuries apart, serious reading is characterized by careful study and meditation on the biblical text.

When we reflect on Renaissance iconography of the readerly virtues, as found, for example, in the traditionalist *Iconologia* of Caesar Ripa (1593-1603), we see that two iconic elements have characterized the particular portraiture of St. Jerome in his study as a symbol of serious reading. The first is the symbolism of *Meditatione* [Fig. 18]. Here again the attentive reader is a woman of "mature and modest visage." The book is momentarily closed, but her finger inserted in the volume, like those of St. James [cf. Fig. 2], marks the page upon which she ponders. The "mountain of books," as Ripa calls it, upon which she sits is not the sign of a messy reader, but of a reflective, comparative, and synthetic reader. When, additionally, a pen is present, as in *Studio* [Fig. 19], it signifies not necessarily writing in the literal sense but an intensity of studiousness and exclusivity of focus in *reading:* the attention the scholar here pays to the open book demonstrates, says Ripa, that study is a "fervent application of the soul to the knowledge of things," while the pen in the right hand signifies the intention to abandon preoccupation with the self [cf. Fig. 3, 4, 15, 17, 24]. The rooster *(gallo)* figures the solicitude and vigilance appropriate to genuine study, and plays thus — especially when the subject is a clerical figure (and hence apostolically associated with St. Peter) — a role analogous to Jerome's lion.[38] When *Meditatione* and *Studio* are brought together in the symbolic portraiture of St. Jerome in his study, the configuration produces a symbol of the ideal Christian *lector* — one who reads always, as Hugh of St. Victor says, "as though his mind were fixed upon Christ."

38. Cf. n. 4, above. Ripa, *Iconologia,* 331, 506.

Figure 18. *"Meditatione," from Caesare Ripa,* Iconologia, *Padua, 1611.*

Figure 19. *"Studio," from Caesare Ripa*, Iconologia, *Padua, 1611.*

Symbol, Creed, and Incarnation

As much as for any Christian symbol of the Middle Ages, this portraiture of the ideal reader and his book thus answers to the radical theological meaning of the word *symbol* itself. As Christian theologians were fond of observing, the Greek *symballein* meant "to put together"; the noun *symbolon* meant "token" or "sign," usually of a pledge or covenant.[39] But in Christian theological use "symbol" recollects especially the place of the Incarnation as the central doctrine of Christian faith, making *symbolum* practically synonymous with "creed." Thus Augustine's famous exposition on the Nicene Creed before the African bishops is entitled *De fide et symbolo* — Of Faith and the Creed.[40] This Augustinian text, similar in some ways to his *Enchiridion* (Faith, Hope and Charity), begins by stressing the doctrine of creation as the beginning point for any Christian discussion of the nature of truth and reality, but then proceeds straightway to the doctrine of the Incarnation, the Logos or Word made flesh in Jesus Christ, as the great analogue for our understanding of the very language of faith and understanding.[41] Centuries later Aquinas still uses the word in this way: "The name 'symbol' [*symbolum*] derives from its being a gathering together of authentic teachings [*sententiae*] of the faith."[42] Effectively a symbol in this sense may be verbally expressed as a synthesis of biblical references confessionally spoken as a statement of Christian belief (e.g., "eternally begotten of the Father, God from God, Light from Light, true God from true God, begotten, not made . . ." — Nicene Creed). But axiomatically the doctrine of the Incarnation is first figured forth by the event itself, only secondarily by the words or images which represent it to our imaginations.[43] The incarnate Logos, whom to see is to

---

39. A good introduction to Christian theology of symbol is afforded by Jeorg Splett, "Symbol," in *Concise Sacramentum Mundi,* ed. Karl Rahner (New York: Seabury, 1975).

40. Trans. Charles T. Wilcox, ed. Roy J. Deferrari, *The Fathers of the Church* (New York: Cima, 1955), 27.311-45.

41. This view of the Incarnation parallels, as we have already seen, development of the same view of language in St. Augustine. Cf. chaps. 1, 3.

42. Aquinas, *Summa Theologica* 2a2ae.1.9: "Et ab huismodi sententiarum fidei collectione nomen symboli est acceptum." Thus the title of the great precursor to Karl Rahner's *Sacramentum Mundi,* H. Denzinger's *Enchiridion Symbolorum: Definitionem et Declarationum de Rebus Fidei et Morum* (33rd ed., 1965).

43. Aquinas, *Summa Theologica* 1a1.10; also 7 *Quodlibets* 6.14; ad 1-4; 15c; ad 1; 16c.

see the Father (John 14:6-10), is thus the Symbol which liberates symbol.[44] While all creatures great and small are each in their own way traces of God *(vestigia Dei)*, in the visible manifestation of his invisible nature (Rom. 1:20) in the person of Jesus, as incarnation of God's self-expression, the symbol actually effects what it signifies.[45] Jesus is the *symbol* of all that is contained in the Law and the prophets. All other symbolism in Christian thought and expression is secondary, dependent upon the Word made flesh and, after the invention of type, one might say, secondarily made print in Scripture. Hence, Aquinas notes,

> The truth of faith is contained in sacred Scripture, but diffusely, in divers ways and, sometimes, darkly. The result is that to draw out the truth of faith from Scripture requires a prolonged study and a practice not within the capacities of all those who need to know the truths of faith; many of them, taken up with other cares, cannot find leisure for study. That is why there was a need to draw succinctly together out of the Scriptural teachings some clear statement to be set before all for their belief. The symbol is not added to Scripture, but drawn from Scripture.[46]

The physical book which is Scripture, or a book derivative of the truths of Scripture, is by this token not itself a symbol but a sign,[47]

44. Partly because it liberates the *imago Dei* in humanity. See Splett, 1656-57. This is not in any way to affirm Carlyle's notion of "intrinsic symbol" which can be manifest in "great men," prophets and analogously in Jesus. Frye ("The Symbol as a Medium of Exchange," 6) is right to sense Carlyle's distortion of Christian theology; he is wrong, however, to represent the *symbolum* of the Incarnation as though it were a function of Jesus' human personality. He is more accurate about Christian doctrine when he speaks of the Eucharist as a representative Christian symbol of "exchange" (15-16).

45. Normally we say that a distinction between symbol and the sign is that the symbol, chosen for its aptness or naturalness, is closer to the thing signified, and accordingly less arbitrary than the sign. See Splett, 1655.

46. Aquinas, *Summa Theologica* 2a.2ae.1.9.

47. So Aquinas follows Augustine on the nature of language as it appears in Scripture, finding in it generally two levels of "sign" or mode of signification: "God, who is author of Holy Scripture, possesses the power not only to adapt words to meanings, which we can do, but also to adapt things to meanings. What is peculiar to Holy Scripture is this, the things there signified by words may also in their turn signify other things. The first signification, whereby words signify facts, is called the historical

functioning in respect of the Word analogously to the way written or spoken signs correspond to the word in the mind or the way the literal level of a text corresponds to the spiritual meaning to which it gives legible or visible form. "The spiritual sense of Holy Writ," says Aquinas, "is the planned symbolism of real things in their courses"; or again, "The spiritual sense is restricted to the symbolism of real things and events; it is present when they have been chosen to typify Christ, shadows of his substance."[48] The Bible by itself is thus not a symbol, as is the Incarnation. But authentic relation of a reader to the text of Scripture, a reading intent upon ingestion of the Word, taking it to heart, is a different matter. In its actuality, the "putting together" or "configuration" of faithful reader and sacred text effects a valid symbolic relation.

As the cross at the level of sign represents the Christian faith yet an individual Christian actually living in the Way of the Cross at a far deeper level symbolizes or "bodies forth" the radical transformation (redemption) effected on Golgotha, so likewise the faithful reader with her book of Scripture not only represents the process whereby each person may come to understand what "the Law and the prophets have spoken," but she also symbolizes the radical inner transformation which ensues when, by undivided attunement to it, the Word becomes flesh again in a penitent, obedient heart. The Reader / Book symbol is in this respect the express function of an incarnational aesthetic, and what it symbolizes is the transforming force of the Incarnation for all Christian understanding of self and the world.[49]

---

and literal sense; the second signification, whereby the facts signified by the words also signify other facts, is called the spiritual sense. Note that the spiritual sense is based on, and presupposes, the literal sense" (*Summa Theologica* 1a.1.10). Cf. pp. 153-154 above.

48. Thomas continues: "Then the allegorical sense is superimposed on the historical sense. When, however, Christ is signified by pictures of fancy, this meaning remains part of their literal sense, as when Christ was symbolized by the dream-image of the stone cut out of the mountain without hands [Dan. 2:34]" (7 *Quodlibets* 6.16c).

49. A key difference between Western iconic "vocabulary" and the role and function of Byzantine or Orthodox icon is that the latter is actually said to "participate" in the spiritual reality to the degree that an icon of the Logos can be seen as a kind of theophany. This is not, properly speaking, the case with Western Christian symbol, which is so elaborately verbally based that the given work of art functions much like a text to be read, and so has direct affinities with the book and the act of reading. The Western art object is thus *pictura* in Hugh of St. Victor's sense (*Didascalicon* 3.4) or *figura* in

This is what the Christian viewer of Van Eyck's Munich *Annunciation* and Dürer's *St. Jerome in his Study* sees as *symbolum,* symbolic witness. But in this resonance it does not effect the kind of "self-discovery" (via nature or "earth symbols") spoken of by the German idealists who adapted the symbolic imagination to their purposes: Christian symbol affords a discovery of self and others in relation to the Other; in the common symbol is found a reciprocating, mutual reference, a being-in-common.[50] In this way, Christian symbolism of the ideal reader engaging the ideal book remains analogous to the liturgical (verbal) *symbolum,* the common Christian saying of the *credo* or creed. For fundamental to one's saying the creed is the presence of witnesses — and not only those who say it also in our present company but, as it says in the Apostles' Creed, the whole "communion of saints," including those who have read in their heart and have gone on before (Heb. 12:1). Or, as Aquinas says, "In the creed *(in symbolo)* the profession of faith is witnessed in the person as it were of the whole Church, which is bound together through faith" *(per fidem unitur).*[51]

In Goethe's Faust's first symbol from the emblem book — having to do with Creation and God's providence — the professor's contemplation immediately reveals his recognition of the orthodox character of this "common" Christian symbol. His first words are:

Wie alles sich zum Ganzen webt,
Eins in dem andern wirkt und lebt!

(447-48)

Auerbach's *(Mimesis),* but certainly not, to borrow a colorful phrase of Jacques Ellul's (in Joyce Main Hanks' translation), "the dazzling locus of the *mystery in the form of an image*" (*The Humiliation of the Word* [Grand Rapids: Eerdmans, 1985], 103).

50. In Splett's summary, "the 'self-discovery' in the Christian encounter with the other is not 'one-way' but essentially two-way traffic. Just as the I finds itself in you, so too the You in the I, in the common symbol; and the two not only find themselves and each other, but also their mutual reference, their being-in-common" (1655). In Fichte, or in Schopenhauer's *The World as Will and Representation* (1819), the emphasis is on the striving of self for discovery in the self of the essence of the cosmos. When (as Kaufmann notes in his introduction, 22) Spengler took up the same theme a century later, he saw Faust as the representative of modern Western man, and he called Western civilization "the Faustian culture."

51. Aquinas, *Summa Theologica* 2a.2ae.1.9.

All weaves itself into the whole,
Each living in the other's soul.

But it is precisely this entailment of *common* witness which finally repels
him, because it contradicts his cherished self-perception that he is after
all unique, an exceptional case, an extraordinary man.

Faust's Emblematic Choices

A still largely Christian audience, on the other hand, would normatively
expect that a professor should have something to profess — especially
if, like Faust, he is a professor of divinity. This expectation can only have
been enhanced by Goethe's careful verbal stage-painting of the opening
study scene, which so patently calls up the symbolic configuration expressed in familiar images of the Virgin at the Annunciation, John the
Evangelist in his study, Jerome in his study, or Erasmus so self-
consciously in his. At first blush, Goethe's felonious imitation would
seem to be a reciprocating witness to shared *symbolum* (creed) or *fides*
(faith) in the familiar terms of Jerome's Bible, a common covenant
(foedas). In Dürer's characterizations of St. Jerome, to draw a natural
comparison, the *foedas* or covenant between serious reader and authoritative book exemplifies pointedly the *foedas* or covenant between any
faithful person and that sacred revelation to which the book bears
ongoing witness. If, even in the narrowest literary sense, a symbol still
"suggests something else to the degree that it is almost impossible to
regard the construct without thinking of that for which it has become
the symbol,"[52] then we can see how the composite portraiture of St.
Jerome in his study had by Goethe's time become such a symbol. In it,
as Carlyle says in *Sartor Resartus*, "there is both concealment and revelation," and, as in the phrase of his Teufelsdröckh, in it "a celestial
essence is thereby rendered visible."[53] Carlyle's notion of symbol as "a
meeting point between the finite and the infinite," like Coleridge's, that

---

52. Hibbard and Loomis, *Dictionary of Literary Terms* (New York: Odyssey Press,
1960), 478-80.
53. Thomas Carlyle, *Sartor Resartus*, 3.1.

a symbol "partakes of the reality which it renders intelligible," suggests something of the way in which a nineteenth-century literary understanding still depends (however confusedly) upon traditional Christian concept and vocabulary.

All of this helps us very much to understand what it is that Goethe in the person of Faust is rejecting in part 1 of his great poetic drama, and how he transforms Marlowe's more compressed treatment in the earlier writer's drama, *The Tragicall Historie of Doctor Faustus*. In Marlowe's version the first study scene suffices to declare the analogy and inversion which in Goethe is split into two parts. In Marlowe's opening scene, Faustus reviews his academic options in terms of their potential for power and influence, rejecting in turn logic, medicine, and law, especially canon law ("too servile and illiberal for mee," he says), before a last departing look at his first calling, "Divinitee": "Ieromes Bible, Faustus, view it well" (1.65), he cries. He opens the large pages of the Vulgate to Romans 6:23, reading the Latin of the first half of the verse only: " 'The reward of sinne is death': that's hard." Omitted is the answering phrase, "but the grace of God is life everlasting in Christ Jesus our Lord" (Vulg.). When Faustus turns to 1 John 1:8, "If we say we have no sinne / We deceive ourselues, and there is no truth in us," the perfidy is repeated. Again he stops, omitting the ninth verse: "If we confess our sins, he is faithful and just to forgive us our sins, and to cleanse us from all unrighteousness." Thus in a grotesquely decontextualized misreading, he concludes as if with a penetrating syllogism:

> Why then belike we must sinne,
> And so consequently die,
> Aye, we must die, an everlasting death.
> What doctrine call you this? *Che sera, sera:*
> What will be, shall be; *Divinitie* adieu.

It is then that Marlowe's Doctor Faustus summarily discards "Jerome's Bible" in favor of his books of magical symbols, "Lines, Circles, Letters, Characters . . . ," from the magical mastery of which he hopes to become "a Demi-god."

Let us compare this with Goethe's opening scene. In Goethe's treatment Faust opens the book of symbols first (1.354ff). What repels him, we now realize, is a typically Christian symbol of the macrocosm.

Macrocosm symbols in emblem books of the period cluster around one basic theme, more or less that of Psalm 19:1: "The heavens declare the glory of God, the firmament sheweth forth his handiwork." In German symbol books of Goethe's time such a symbol for the macrocosm would most likely be one of two general types. The first usually shows a globe or spectrum of natural landscape — the created earth — illuminated by an anthropomorphized sun or held up by the hand of divine Providence. The legends which accompany these emphasize the dependency of temporal life upon the Providence of the Creator. The scriptural epigraphs are cryptic — e.g., "In the hand of the Lord are all the ends of the earth"; the poems under such emblems are likely to say that behind the visible things of our universe lies the invisible power of God (Rom. 1:20), or to emphasize the unreasonableness of disbelief in God's omnipotence.[54] While the Sun / Providence symbolism in all such macrocosm symbolism points to the linkage between creation and the Incarnation of the Word, one of the best known German examples synthesizes the connection in a way particularly appropriate to our reflection here [Fig. 20]. The epigraph text is Ezekiel 44:2 (Vulg. "Tamen haut violata recessit"), "And the Lord said to me: this gate shall be shut. It shall not be opened and no man shall pass through it, because the Lord the God of Israel hath entered in by it, and it shall be shut." The pictorial symbol shows a child holding a book upward to the rays of the sun which stream down upon her over the steeple of a nearby church, and through panes of window glass [cf. Fig. 6]. The sunbeam passing through glass without being altered had long been a figure of the Virgin conception of the Word,[55] so unsurprisingly this emblem is appropriated to the Feast of the Annunciation with its prescribed Gospel text from Luke 1:26ff. Here the German poem which follows declares the incarnational theology of Christian symbol, and explicitly directs the reader to understand the poem in relation to typically cited Scripture sources for the central Christian *symbolum* of the Incarnation —

54. For example, "Die gantze Welt war gar bedeckt / Mit Sund vnd Laster gantz befleckt / Kein Mensch jhm selber helffen kund / Christus den Teuffel vberwund: / Wer nun anselben glaubet fest / Dem ist der Glaub das allerbest / Der jhn von Sunden machet rein / Vnd fuhrt jhn in den Himmel nein." *Emblemata*, 44; cf. 10, 13, 47.

55. See D. L. Jeffrey, *Early English Lyric and Franciscan Spirituality* (Lincoln: University of Nebraska Press, 1975), 236.

Figure 20. *"Symbol of the Macrocosm."* 17th-century German from the Sacra Emblemata *of Johann Mannich, Nuremberg, 1580.*

connecting Malachi 4:2, Hebrews 1:3, 2:14, Galatians 4:4, and John 1:14.[56] Other versions depict here the mother of Christ or the *sol iustitiae* (sun of justice) as a munificent Natura, the streams from whose ample breasts flow out to nourish humankind — an allusion to which may be suggested by Faust's reference to streaming breasts (1.454-59).

The second type of macrocosm symbol with which Goethe would have been familiar features a different representative human figure, a mature pilgrim making his way through the world, whose choices as a pilgrim are measured against Gottes Wort, a scriptural text. This text may be, as in one German emblem book, a passage which refers to the Incarnation, from Galatians: "So we also, when we were children, were serving under the elements of the world. But, when the fulness of the time was come, God sent his Son, made of a woman, made under the law, That he might redeem them who were under the law, that we might receive the adoption of sons" (4:4). In this example from the *Emblemata,* the emblem is assigned to the Feast of the Purification of the Virgin Mary, for which the Gospel specified is the passage in Luke 2 which concludes with the benediction of Simeon, "Now lettest thou thy servant depart in peace according to thy Word" (v. 29). Another of this type [Fig. 22] is designated for the second Sunday after Trinity. Here the Gospel is Luke 14:16ff., but the rubric text comes from Romans 2:4: "Would you despise the riches of his goodness, patience and longsuffering, not realizing that the goodness of God leads you toward repentance?" The German poem beneath this macrocosm tells how the Book of Creation is to be understood by means of the Book of Scripture, and how alike it reveals the sustaining providence of God. Its epigraph says, "Blind contempt never finds grace" (Verachtung blind / Gnad nimmer

---

56. *Emblemata,* 30. Here the poem reads: "DIE Sonn die steht am Himmel schon / Bedeutet die ander Person / In der vnzertrennten Gottheit / Der ist der Glantz der Herrligkeit / Der alls ertragt mit seinem Wort / Erfullet alle end vnd ort. / Das Fenster mit der Scheiben fein / Bedeutet die Mariam rein. / Dann wie die Sonn durchscheint das Glaß / Vnd doch nimmer versehret das; / So hat die Sonn der Grechtigkeit / Da nun erfullet ward die zeit / Sich in Maria Leib gethon / Vnd da verricht die Vnion / Daß Gott ein waarer Mensch geborn / Von der Jungfrawen außerkorn. / Das bedeut mit dem Fleisch der Knab / Daß Gottes Wort vom Himmel rab / Genommen an sich Fleisch vnd Blut / Gleich wei die andern Kinder gut: / Daß er so Fleisch durch Fleisch erwurb / Vnd sein Geschopff nicht gar verdurb."

Figure 21. *"St. John Ingests the Little Book" by Albrecht Dürer, ca. 1497-98. Courtesy: Giraudon/Art Resource, NY.*

Figure 22. *"Symbol of the Macrocosm: the Sun and God's Word."* 17th-century German *from the* Sacra Emblemata *of Johann Mannich, Nuremberg, 1580.*

findt).[57] Hence the emblem's circumscribed question: "What? do you come puffed up only to reject it [i.e., God's Word which announces that we are creatures of God — *creaturae Dei*]?"

The pictura in this instance is strikingly familiar, indeed almost precisely converse to one we have already seen — Dürer's depiction of the visionary apostle's acceptance of the Word. In Dürer's woodcut [Fig. 21] St. John kneels before the anthropomorphic *sol iustitiae*, whose hand likewise presents from a mystical cloud the figural book. John on Patmos, of course, not only receives the word, he actually eats the book (Rev. 10). But the apostle's graphic ingestion of the word-as-book is quite precisely reversed by the refusing, radically averted face of the apostate in the *Emblemata*. The *recuso* figure from the German symbol book wants no part of a book which tells him he is a creature of God. Small wonder that one whose sense of intellectual superiority is so overreaching that he asks with apparent seriousness "Bin ich ein Gott?" (Am I a god? [1.439]) should find any of these symbols of the macrocosm repellant.

More attractive to any Faust would be those earth symbols, next in order in typical symbol books and first of the series on the "four elements." The earth symbol Goethe has his offended Faust turn to might emphasize the "worldliness" of the world and its power, *vulgati supra commercia mundi* (*Emblemata* 61), the world's changeableness and instability (73), the alchemist's search to transmute base metal to gold (89-90), or even the resistance of human language to reason (66). All share, however, a common emphasis upon human as distinct from divine power. In the example in Figure 23, the emblem is the "Feuerstein aus dem Funken geschlagen werden," the power of fire being struck as a spark from flintstone by a human hand. Here, however, we have a familiarly constructed context for it: a learned man in a study, with a

---

57. *Emblemata,* 13. Here the poem reads: "IN der Figur ein Sonn man sicht / Wie sie deß morgens fru außbricht: / Die zeigt vns Gottes Gutigkeit / Die er vns in seim Wort anbeut / Sie ist all morgen new behend / Sein Gut hat nimmermehr kein end. / Auß der Wolck geht ein Hand herfur / Die da ein Brieff weist von Papier / Deß HERREN Wort zeigt der Brieff an / Was er von vns will allen han. / Daß wir dasselb mit allen Ehrn / Fleissig solln lesn / vnd gern horn. / Der Mann hie mit vmbkehrten Gesicht / Der Menschen art vns schon bericht / Die jmmerdar exorbitirt / Vnd Gott in seim Wort reformirt: / Nur nach dem zeitlichen stets tracht / Deß ewigen gar wenig acht / Drumb muß er endlich beydes lassn / Wenn er wird fahren seine Strassn."

Figure 23. *"Earth Symbol." From* La Morosophie *of Guillaume de al Perrièrre Tolosain, Lyon, 1553.*

companion beast (a dog) on the floor, but this time without books. Beneath it one reads this legend:

Wie das Feuer aus dem Stein nicht sprüht . . .
As the fire will not spark from the stone
Unless struck with iron by violence
By the same token, without [our] making a great effort
Truth will not make itself evident.[58]

This kind of a symbol Faust can relate to, presumably because it seems to make the might of man rather than the Creator's Providence or written revelation the central factor in obtaining power from truth. Whichever precise emblem from his various *emblemata* Goethe has in mind does not much matter; the point they make is constant. Faust's exclamation on first looking at the symbol of the earth-spirit *(Zeichen des Erdgeistes)* is to say, "How differently this symbol works on me! You, spirit of the earth, are more to my taste; wonderfully, I feel my own powers growing . . . !" (460-63). The attentive reader can already sense that Faust's *credo* will become *nego* soon enough.

Logos and Lector

Goethe's full address to the symbol of reader and book is not, however, completed until the second scene, in which we find Faust again in his vaulted study. Into it this time Goethe's professor enters accompanied by a dog, a poodle (which seems already, as "Fido" might, disturbed about the nighing demonic spirits). This time we have, explicitly, as in Marlowe's first scene, "Jerome's Bible" on the desk, and this time the old familiar image of Jerome in his study is likewise inescapably called up when Faust expresses his perplexity over the text. "Mit redlichem Gefuhl einmal," he muses: "How can the sacred original be translated by me into my beloved German?" (1.1221-23). Every German reader realized, of course, that another divinity professor, Faust's contem-

---

58. *Emblemata*, 80. Other common earth-spirit symbols are a blacksmith's anvil with hand on a hammer, or a hand on bellows at the alchemical forge.

porary, Luther, had long been working on such a translation of the
Bible (figuratively, at least, in the study next door) and that his travails
were frequently depicted by him as distracted by the designs of the
devil [Fig. 24].[59]

We may conclude then, with those words of Faustus which show
most clearly that the greatest medieval symbols of reader and book and,
indeed, the incarnational symbolic structure they expressed, were about
to meet their *recuso*, their rejection *(recuso / recurso)*, in a scholar's study
in Goethe's revisionary University of Wittenberg. Faust "opens a tome
and begins," reading from the first verse of John's Gospel:

> Geschrieben steht: "Im Anfang war das Wort!"
> Hier stock ich schon! Wer hilft mir weiter fort?
> Ich kann das Wort so hoch unmöglich schatzen,
> Ich muß es anders übersetzen,
> Wenn ich vom Geiste recht erleuchtet bin.
> Geschrieben steht: Im Anfang war der Sinn.
> Bedenke wohl die erste Zeile,
> Daß deine Feder sich nicht übereile!
> Ist es der Sinn, der alles wirkt und schafft?
> Es sollte stehn: Im Anfang war die Kraft!
> Doch, auch indem ich dieses niederschreibe,
> Schon warnt mich was, daß ich dabei nicht bleibe.
> Mir hilft der Geist, auf einmal seh' ich Rat
> Und schreibe getrost: Im Anfang war die Tat!
>
> It says: "In the beginning was the *Word*."
> Already I am stopped. It seems absurd.
> The *Word* does not deserve the highest prize,
> I must translate it otherwise

59. It is of some interest that the historic Faust (b. 1480) was a contemporary of
Luther (b. 1483). According to Melancthon, Luther's colleague, Faust studied magic at
the University of Cracow (Poland), claimed to have made a *pactum diaboli*, taught (like
Luther) at Erfurt University, and was forced to flee because caught sexually molesting
the boys entrusted to his care. In his flight (1525) he is reported by Melancthon to have
been accompanied by the devil in the shape of a dog. He died at Staufen in Briesgau in
1540. On Luther's sense of the devil's distractions see Heiko Oberman, *Luther: Man
Between God and the Devil* (New Haven: Yale University Press, 1990), 161-67.

Figure 24. *"The Devil enters Luther's Study"* *(woodcut). Courtesy: Wolfenbüttel Library.*

If I am well inspired and not blind.
It says: In the beginning was the *Mind*.
Ponder that first line, wait and see,
Lest you should write too hastily.
Is mind the all-creating source?
It ought to say: In the beginning there was *Force*.
Yet something warns me as I grasp the pen
That my translation must be changed again.
The spirit helps me. Now it is exact.
I write: In the beginning was the *Act*.

(1224-37)

Faust rejects in this formulation the source of all Christian symbol, "the Law of the Lord," but most specifically the Logos, the doctrine of the incarnate Word. At precisely this moment the little dog begins moaning uncontrollably; then, as Faustus would eject him from the room, the "poodle" *(Pudel)* metamorphoses with smoke and sparks into Mephisto, the devil Mephistophilis, dressed as *ein fahrender Scholastikus,* a travelling scholar or, as we should say nowadays, a "visiting professor." *Fido* has become *Recuso.* To Faustus's curious "Who are you then?" comes the mocking reply which presages already the burning of books and the damning of souls: "Ich bin der Geist, der stets verneint!" says the scholar's particular devil, "I am the spirit that negates" (1338).

In both representations of the narrative of *Faust,* the symbol of the *beatus vir* has from the beginning been turned inside out, so that as readers or viewers we enter briskly into the scornful progress of its negation in the *damnatus vir.* In Goethe's version, however, the result is not to be for Faust himself a tragedy; indeed it becomes the very opposite. The Chorus Mysticus at the end of Goethe's version will declare plainly the symbolic character of the poem and its protagonist's transformation as a movement away from symbolic incarnation of the Word to a visible act of rejection (negation), in which divine Word and human word are eternally to be separated. Goethe is as conscious of the magnitude of his own *recuso / recurso* as his protagonist:

Alles Vergängliche
Ist nur ein Gleichnis;
Das Unzulängliche,

Hier wird's Ereignis;
Das Unbeschreibliche,
Hier ist's getan . . .

All that now concludes
Is but a simile;
That which is beyond imagining
Here came to pass;
That which is unwritable
Here was performed . . .

(2.12104-109)*

That is, Goethe celebrates his arrant professor, and finds in his
monstrous choices no occasion for terror or even, perhaps, for remorse.[60] With Marlowe and his audience it had been otherwise: *The
Tragicall Historie of Doctor Faustus* ends on a note of stark spiritual
horror at the consequences of Faustus's covenant with the devil. Indeed,
it is a reliable index to the great credal gulf which separates the two
works that for Marlowe's stunned audience this horror cannot more
trenchantly be summarized than by having Faustus himself say, in respect of the Law of the Lord, "God forbade it indeed, but *Faustus* hath
done it." Goethe's almost certainly deliberate echo of this line in the
final speech of his Chorus Mysticus just cited is, by contrast, a triumphant assertion of Goethe's own verbal fiat, transforming Faust into a
romantic hero.[61]

60. In this Goethe anticipated his countrymen's response: Faust "was quickly hailed
as the incarnation of the German character and influenced German historiography,
philosophy, and self-interpretation. Millions of young men decided they were like Faust,
and some found the German destiny in boundless, ruthless, Faustian striving" (Kaufmann, *Goethe's Faust*, 22). It is good to bear in mind that the second part of Goethe's
great work, sometimes referred to as *Faust II*, was completed some sixty years after the
initial work was begun, and that significant changes in Goethe's thinking had taken
place in the interval. Optimism about the promise of science, and the theme of evolutionary progress, widely celebrated by the end of Goethe's life, clearly shape the romantic
conclusion to *Faust*. See here John Gearey, *Goethe's Other Faust: The Drama, Part II*
(Toronto: University of Toronto Press, 1992).

61. Goethe read Marlowe's play for the first time in translation only in 1818, before
he had completed the second part of *Faust*, which probably accounts for the echo. In

On Marlowe's stage, after the apocalyptic fireworks and smoke, what "abides" is the enduring Word — now made most painfully "present" to our imaginations by its sudden and spectacular absence from the stage. As we consider the devastated study of the once-great and now damned scholar, we are looking at the ashes of a reader in whom that Word found no faithful reading. The tragic force of Marlowe's scene of terrible desolation thus also depends for its power upon the incarnational symbolism of faithful reader and trustworthy Book which, in that play too, the negating spirit had worked so deliberately to efface.

*   *   *

For effecting an eclipse of the authority of Scripture in the later years of the eighteenth century there were, of course, strategies less dramatic than Goethe's. In their characteristic naturalism, many writers and artists of the waning Enlightenment (subsequently to be associated with Romanticism) nevertheless preferred the "earth spirit" to a cosmic Providence, the light of Nature to the light of Revelation. An engraving of Jean-Jacques Rousseau (1712-1788) depicting the French philosopher and social theorist in his reclusive island retreat at Lac Bienne [Fig. 25] serves modestly but pointedly this general purpose. Here again is the familiar "reader in his study," except that, as in the "earth-symbol" from *La Morosophie* [Fig. 23] which the engraving mimics, Rousseau is not reading. Rather, he is depicted as if he were considering nature, illumined ostensibly by the light of Nature, and perhaps distracted by his dog (who seems to need to go for a walk). Yet the actual subject of Rousseau's reflection as we know from the relevant passage in his *Rêveries*, and the self-proclaimed occasion of his beatitude or felicity, was "nothing exterior to the self, nothing except the self and one's own existence." Nature serves merely to facilitate this self-absorption, the

---

the lyrical last lament of Marlowe's chorus, infused into classical allusion, we may hear something else omitted by Goethe, the tragedy of the *damnatus vir* expressed as utter negation of the felicity of the *beatus vir* — the reader whose blessing is to be "like a tree planted by rivers of living water, whose leaf also shall not wither, who brings forth fruit in his season" (Ps. 1:3). The last stanza of Marlowe's version begins: "Cut is the branch that might have grown full straight, / And burned is *Apollo's* laurel bough, / That some time grew within this learned man . . . (B[1616], 2114-16). The allusion is, of course, classical, but the biblical resonances would, one suspects, have been apparent *inter alia*.

Figure 25. *"Rosseau at Lac Bienne" (engraving; anonymous).*

"feeling" of which Rousseau says: "As long as this state lasts, one is sufficient to oneself, like God."[62] Less overtly, perhaps, but not less certainly than Goethe's Faust, Rousseau here dispenses with external authority mediated by the Book.[63] For each of these pivotal cultural figures, it seemed an impediment to the cult of genius.

The traditional symbol of the faithful reader persisted, but now all the more particularly in contexts where common apostolic virtues rather than the singularity of genius was to be celebrated. One example must suffice: two years after the publication of Rousseau's *Rêveries* (1778), the English painter J. Jackson executed a striking portrait of Rousseau's Swiss compatriot, Jean Guillaume de la Fléchère [Fig. 26]. Fletcher (as he anglicized his name) had become a priest in the Church of England and, of "Methodist" persuasions, was in fact John Wesley's preferred successor. Fletcher quietly refused the honor, certain that his divine vocation was simply to remain priest of Madeley, a rough, working-class parish ten miles out of London. By all contemporary accounts Fletcher (1729-1787) was as saintly a man as Rousseau was not: it is said that when the redoubtable atheist Voltaire was asked who was the most Christ-like person in the modern world, he replied without hesitation, "John Fletcher of Madeley."[64] Jackson's 1780 por-

---

62. Jean-Jacques Rousseau, *Les Rêveries du promeneur solitaire,* in Rousseau, *Oeuvres complètes,* ed. Bernard Gagnebin and Marcel Raymond (Paris: Galimard, 1969), 5.1046-47.

63. This is the specific animus of his own *Confessions,* which are organized as a refutation of the premises and method of Augustine's *Confessions.* See Ann Hartle, *The Modern Self in Rousseau's Confessions: A Reply to St. Augustine* (Notre Dame: Notre Dame University Press, 1983). Interestingly, about this same time paintings of the Virgin Mary gradually ceased to represent her as a reader. Even in the neo-medievalism of the nineteenth century, as for example in the paintings of pre-Raphaelite Dante Gabriel Rossetti, if books appear with the Virgin at all they are closed and function merely as support for ornaments. (See here Linda H. Peterson, "Restoring the Book: The Typological Hermeneutics of Christina Rossetti and the PRB," *Victorian Poetry* 32, no. 3-4 [1995]: 209-32.) One of the consequences of Reformation and Counter-Reformation seems to have been that European Catholic tradition began to prefer "Our Lady Without the Book," even as Protestants were championing "The Book and every man for himself." Something has been lost on both sides.

64. C. J. Abbey and J. H. Overton, *The English Church in the Eighteenth Century* (London: Longmans and Green, 1887), 343. Voltaire, like Rousseau, knew Fletcher. (Fletcher's brother-in-law, M. de Bottens, was an intimate friend of Voltaire.)

Figure 26. *"John Fletcher." Engraving by T. A. Dean from the painting by J. Jackson, R.A., ca. 1780.*

trait captures Fletcher's Christian qualities in a fresh, yet time-honored way; we see a faithful reader, not so much preaching as in beatific reflection, poised between reception of the word on which his left hand rests and transmission of its benediction to some "other." The light (even in the engraving reproduced here) is striking: Fletcher's face, like the face of Moses returning Spirit-filled from the mountain, seems itself to become the source of the portrait's luminescence; it is the reflected light of experienced theophany which here illumines the sacred page. But the gesture of the right hand is unmistakable for anyone familiar with paintings of the first annunciation of the Word made flesh [cf. Fig. 8]: "Be it unto me according to thy Word" continues, even where marginalized, to be the faithful reader's response to the divine Author's invitation.

Chapter Eight

Authentic Narrative

Holy Scripture containeth all things necessary to salvation: so that whatsoever is not read therein, nor may be proved thereby, is not to be required of any man, that it should be believed as an article of the Faith, or be thought requisite or necessary to salvation.

ARTICLE 6, *THE THIRTY-NINE ARTICLES* (1563)

. . . having [the Bible] still with me, I count myself far better furnished than if I had [without it] all the Libraries of the two Universities: Besides, I am for drinking water out of my own Cistern: what GOD makes mine by the evidence of his Word and Spirit, that dare I make bold with.

JOHN BUNYAN (1665)

He that will have no books but his creed and the Bible, may follow that sectary, who, when he had burnt all his other books as human inventions, at last burnt the Bible, when he grew learned enough to understand that the translation of that was human too.

RICHARD BAXTER (1673)

That a story will account for certain facts, that we wish to think
it true, nay, that many formerly thought it true and have grown
faithful, humble, charitable and so on, by thus doing, does not
make the story true if it is not, and cannot prevent men after a
certain time from seeing that it is not.

MATTHEW ARNOLD (1887)

IF ANYONE AMONG CHRISTIANS COULD LAY PERSUASIVE CLAIM TO being a "people of the book," it would surely be the English Puritans. While Anglicans in general subscribed to Article Six of the Thirty-nine Articles of the Established Church (1563; 1571), the Puritans followed John Calvin in believing that the Bible was singularly authoritative not only for matters of doctrine, but also for patterns of acceptable worship and church government — a clear point of division between themselves and other Anglicans as well as Catholics. Friend and foe alike observed that "the speech of the Bible was the Puritans' native tongue."[1] Their "language of Canaan," as the Puritans themselves would come to call it, characterized not only the sermons, spiritual tracts, and theological texts of Puritan divines such as Thomas Hooker, John Owen, and Richard Baxter, and the political speeches of Oliver Cromwell, but flavored as well the diction of Puritan poets as diverse as Edmund Spenser, John Bunyan, and John Milton. If Marlowe, Shakespeare, and Ben Jonson can mock their talk, it is because the imitatively biblical character of that talk was entirely familiar to their audience.[2] Even their name, at first a term of derision, was acquired simply from their being known to read the Bible regularly and then to seek to follow its precepts in daily life; an alternate derogatory term was "gospellers." Richard Baxter recollects

1. This phrase is Hugh Martin's, in *Puritanism and Richard Baxter* (London: SCM Press, 1954), 78.

2. E.g., Christopher Marlowe, *The Tragicall Historie of Doctor Faustus* A.1.2.227-33; William Shakespeare, *Measure for Measure* 1.2.7-40. Isobel Rivers, in her indispensable *Reason, Grace, and Sentiment: A Study of the Language of Religion and Ethics in England, 1660-1780*, vol. 1 (Cambridge: Cambridge University Press, 1991), notes that this Puritan speech involves far more than biblical diction and analagous idiom: "It implies both a particular pattern for the Christian life . . . and a dependence on Scripture for vocabulary, allusion, metaphor, and literary method" (128).

how his father, an adherent of the Established Church, was mocked for being known to read the Scriptures on a Sunday afternoon:

> When I heard them speak scornfully of others as Puritans whom I never knew, I was at first apt to believe all the Lies and Slanders wherewith they loaded them. But when I heard my own Father so reproached and perceived the Drunkards were the forwardest in the reproach, I perceived that it was mere Malice. For my Father never scrupled Common Prayer or Ceremonies, nor spake against Bishops, nor ever so much as prayed but by a Book or Form, being not ever acquainted then with any who did otherwise. But only for reading Scripture when the rest were Dancing on the Lord's Day, and for praying (by a Form out of the end of the Common Prayer Book) in his House, and for reproving Drunkards and Swearers, and for talking sometimes a few words of Scripture and the Life to come, he was reviled commonly by the name of Puritan, Precisian and Hypocrite.[3]

3. Cf. John Bunyan, *The Life and Death of Mr. Badman* (1680), ed. J. F. Forrest and R. Sharrock (Oxford: Clarendon Press, 1988), 144. "The same name in a Bishops mouth," Baxter goes on to say, "signified a Nonconformist, and in an ignorant Drunkard or Swearers mouth, a godly obedient Christian. But the People being the greater number, became among themselves the Masters of the Sense" (*Reliquae Baxterianae* [1696], 1.31-32). Some idea of the vitriolic characterization to which Puritans might be subjected is afforded in the following passage from Thomas Nashe's *The Anatomie of Absurditie* (1589): "A common practise it is now adaies, which breedes our common calamitie, that the cloake of zeale, shoulde be vnto a hypocrite in steed of a coate of Maile; a pretence of puritie, a pentisse for iniquitie; a glose of godlines, a couert for all naughtines. When men shall publiquelie make profession of a more inward calling, and shall waxe cold In the workes of charitie, and feruent in malice, liberall in nothing but in lauishe backbyting, holding hospitalitie for an eschewed heresie, and the performance of good workes for Papistrie, may wee not then haue recourse to that caueat of Christ in the Gospell, *Cauete ab hipocritis.* It is not the writhing of the face, the heauing vppe of the eyes to heauen, that shall keepe these men, from hauing their portion in hell. Might they be saued by their booke, they haue the Bible alwaies in their bosome, and so had the Pharisies the Lawe embroidered in their garments. Might the name of the Church infeaffe them in the kingdom of Christ, they will include it onely in their couenticles, and bounde it euen in Barnes, which many times they make their meeting place, and will shameleslie face men out, that they are the church millitant heere vpon earth, whe as they rather seeme a company of Malecontents vnworthy to breath on the earth. Might the boast of the spirit pind to their sleeues, make them elect before all other, they will make men beleeue, they doe nothing whereto the spirit dooth not

In Baxter's father we see a representative example of what in the early seventeenth century it meant to be a Puritan. After the Restoration of the monarch (1660) and the granting of sole legitimacy to the Established (Anglican) Church, the situation grew ecclesiastically more complex, but this basic characterization of the Puritan by "those without," so to speak, transferred readily in its general terms to others who, like the younger Baxter, at last dissented from the required conformity to Anglican doctrine and liturgical practice. These were often called "nonconformists."[4]

John Bunyan, likewise, more famously represents the degree to which for Puritans the availability of the Bible in print had become the central element in their culture, not merely their religious life. Even before what he describes as his conversion, his knowledge of the Bible was so extensive that he could bring large tracts of it effortlessly to mind. For Bunyan the Bible is the one book needful; all other human learning is beside the point, more likely to discompose or confuse than to clarify the Bible's precepts. To be able to say that he relied upon the Bible alone gave him, he believed, much greater authority: "having that still with me, I count myself far better furnished than if I had [without it] all the Libraries of the two Universities."[5] Among Bunyan's confederates it became particularly clear, as one of Oliver Cromwell's biographers has it, that "the substitution of the book for the church was the essence of the protestant revolt."[6] From the point of view of their Anglican opponents, this seemed to mean that a legalistic biblicism had been sub-

---

perswade them: and what Heretiques were there euer that did not arrogate as much to themselues?" Ed. Ronald B. McKerrow, *The Works of Thomas Nashe* (Oxford: Blackwell, 1957), 1.22.

4. Rivers provides perhaps the best short synopsis of this ecclesiastical complex to have appeared in recent years: see *Reason, Grace, and Sentiment,* 90ff. An important turning point came in 1662, when the revised Book of Common Prayer was restored to mandatory use under the terms of the Act of Uniformity. Approximately two thousand clergy refused to sign to the BCP in its entirety; included in this number were a spectrum ranging from high churchmen on the right (eventually to be identified with the non-jurors of 1688) to sectaries of such as the Quakers and other groups on the left. The majority were, however, Puritans of the Presbyterian and Independent persuasion.

5. John Bunyan, "The Epistle to Four Sorts of Readers," in *The Holy City* (1665), in *The Miscellaneous Works of John Bunyan,* 11 vols., ed. Roger Sharrock (Oxford: Oxford University Press, 1976-), 3.71-72.

6. John Viscount Morley, *Oliver Cromwell* (London: Macmillan, 1923), 53.

stituted for the legalities of (Catholic) canon law which "hitherto [had] governed the outward form of the church."[7]

For their part, the Puritans idealized the apostolic but not the medieval church. The continuity they believed themselves to have forged with this earliest expression of Christian community, bypassing the intervening 1500 years of supposed deviation, depended upon exclusive adherance to a solitary standard for both faith and worship. William Turner's sixteenth-century polemical tract *The Huntyng and Fyndyng Out of the Romish Foxe* is in this respect indicative of the opposition to Catholic practice:

> The word of god which is the law of the chirch lasteth for euer & is not changed so that the chirche of Christ at all tymes hath no other lawe but Christes word.[8]

A century later, the point could be pressed yet more ardently:

> And that the *Bible* should be upon such terms and no other proposed to the belief of the World, seems highly reasonable, when we consider that God intends this book as the great *SHIBBOLETH*, by which he will try the World; that from the believing or not believing of it, shall arise the great *discrimination* between Virtuous and Good Men, and such who free from the prevailing influence of corrupt and sensual Interests pursue the Genuine dictates of right *Reason*, and *improve* those notions of *Divinity* they are born with, and *others* who either choose to be *Sottishly Ignorant*, or else *wilfully* to *oppose* what God has made in it self most suitable and corresponding to the Reason and Conscience of every unprejudiced Man. The truth is, our *Assent*, or *not*, to the *Bible*, is made a matter of *Reward* and *Punishment*.[9]

7. Henning Graf Reventlow, *The Authority of the Bible and the Rise of the Modern World*, trans. John Bowden (London: SCM, 1984), 110.

8. William Turner, *The Huntyng and Fynding Out of the Romish Foxe* (Basle, 1554); cf. *Short Title Catalogue*, ed. A. W. Pollard, G. R. Redgrave, et al. (1926; reprint, London: Bibliographical Society, 1976-86), 24, 353. See also H. C. Porter, *Puritanism in Tudor England* (London: MacMillan, 1970), 28ff.; Reventlow, *Authority of the Bible*, 111.

9. Charles Wolseley, *The Reasonableness of Scripture-Belief* (1672), facsimile reproduction, intro. by R. W. McHenry, Jr. (Delmar, N.Y.: Scholar's Facsimiles and Reprints, 1973), 85.

For Charles Wolseley, in whose voluminous and repetitive book *The Reasonableness of Scripture-Belief* (1672) these words are found, the mainstay of religious security is the verbal inerrancy of the Bible. As he puts it elsewhere, "'Tis this *Book* alone in which there is not a flaw to be found. 'Tis only this Divine Law that is *Perfect*" (195; cf. 199). As law, Scripture is to be regarded not only as necessary, but as the entirely sufficient authority for all matters of faith, conduct, and understanding.

The Great Shibboleth

While among the Puritans excessively literalistic biblicism could in fact vitiate much of the otherwise empowering force of such thorough cultural centering in a common book, the fact is that, in large part because of their influence, the Bible came to be for Protestant England the common text and general standard for rectitude, even in matters of law.[10] The mainstream Anglican William Chillingworth (1602-1644) illustrates this: he began his intellectual career as a Catholic and student of literature with Erasmian persuasions, and wrote an influential work, *The Religion of Protestants A Safe Way to Salvation* (1638), in which he also was prompted to echo the Puritans in saying "The Bible only is the religion of Protestants."[11] Though for him the physical Bible is not itself, as for some Puritans, virtually a sacred object, but merely a vehicle which conveys to us the content of our faith, Chillingworth nevertheless instances an observance in English culture of the seventeenth century generally which owes predominantly to Puritan influence. In the summary of the Victorian historian G. M. Trevelyan,

10. See D. Seaborne Davies, *The Bible in English Law* (London: Jewish Historical Society, 1954). The key texts here are the *Institutes* (1628) of Sir Edward Coke, the English jurist who was at one time Speaker of the House of Commons (1593) and then chief justice of the King's Bench and privy councillor (1613), though he later suffered imprisonment in the Tower (1621-1622).

11. William Chillingworth, *Religion of Protestants* 6.56; for a general discussion of Chillingworth, see Reventlow, *Authority of the Bible*, 147-52.

Family prayer and Bible reading had become national customs among the great majority of religious laymen whether they were Churchmen or Dissenters. The English character had received an impression from Puritanism which it bore for the next two centuries, though it had rejected Puritan coercion and had driven Dissenters out of polite society.[12]

If one thinks of the eighteenth century in terms of Wesley and the Great Revival, and the nineteenth century in terms of that revival's various Victorian legacies, there can be little doubt that Trevelyan's assessment is substantially correct.

On the other hand, there is much to suggest that this radical form of the Calvinist *sola scriptura* was not an unmitigated blessing. When approached in such an obsessive, zealously all-preempting fashion, the Bible could become for some a fetish, almost talismanic. Already in the seventeenth century, moderate Puritans such as Richard Baxter found themselves as troubled by this tendency as anyone. In his *The Life of Faith* Baxter warns his fellow Puritans that it is possible to abuse their freedom of the text by "looking for that in Scripture which God never intended it for," a practice which "doth tempt the unskilful into unbelief." He is especially concerned with the practice of opening the Bible at random, somewhat in the manner of a parlor game, and letting whatever passage the eye falls upon be taken as a divine token for business at hand. This echo of a medieval superstition, divination on the basis of chance openings of Virgil's text *(sortes Virgilianae)*, was, however, but one of several ways of making a superstitious use of Scripture. Too many persons, he opines, think

> that every text of Scripture which cometh into their mind, or every conceit of their own is a special suggestion of the Spirit of God. . . . Though it is certain that every good thought which cometh into our minds is some effect of the working of God's Spirit, as every good word and every good work is, and it is certain that sometimes God's Spirit doth guide and comfort Christians as a remembrance by bringing informing and comforting texts and doctrines to their

12. G. M. Trevelyan, *History of England* (London: Longman, Green and Co., 1929; 1937), 453.

remembrance; yet it is a dangerous thing to think that all such suggestions or thoughts are from some special or extraordinary work of the Spirit, or that every text that cometh into our minds is brought thither by the Spirit of God.[13]

Baxter was not alone in his concern over such practices, several examples of which can be found in the autobiographical or pseudo-auto-biographical accounts of prominent Puritans down into the Restoration times; one thinks of the vestigially religious eccentricities of Samuel Pepys, and especially of the narrator in Daniel Defoe's *Journal of the Plague Year* (1722), whose decision to stay in plague-infested London is made on the basis of an exercise in Bible-roulette.[14] But Baxter is pointedly critical about the way in which such textual abuse opened the way to the vagaries of superstition rather than the spirit of calm assurance that he himself had in mind when he turned to the Bible. Lacking a sound hermeneutical basis, the superstition of the reader who enthusiastically combines a very high view of the Bible with an extremely naive view of the working of language and text, in Baxter's words,

> ... tosseth such mistaken Christians up and down in uncertainties while they think all such thoughts are the suggestions of the Spirit. They meet with the contrary thoughts and so are carryed like the waves of the Sea, sometimes up and sometimes down; and they have sometimes a humbling terrible text and the next day perhaps a comforting text cometh into their minds, and so are between terrours and comforts, distracted by their own fantasies and think it is all done by the Spirit of God.[15]

It would, of course, be wrong to think that the Puritans believed that nothing human came into play when the reader sat before the sacred page. True, unlike Chillingworth and the Anglicans generally, they did not formally insist upon that other authority, "natural reason, the only principle, besides Scripture, which is common to all Christians."[16] In

13. Richard Baxter, *The Life of Faith* (London, 1670), 509.
14. Geoffrey Tillotson, P. Fussell, and M. Waingrow, eds., *Eighteenth-Century Literature* (New York: Harcourt Brace Jovanovich, 1969), 248.
15. Baxter, *The Life of Faith*, 511.
16. Chillingworth, *Religion of Protestants*, 2.3; also 6.55.

practice, however, men like Baxter, Owen, and Thomas Hooker were paragons of the virtue of common sense. And while they rejected the external witness of the Spirit in the tradition and historical witness of the church, what they did allow for formally in their doctrine of "right reading" was the *inward* witness of the Holy Spirit in the heart of the receptive believer. According to the Westminster Confession (1648), "our full persuasion and assurance of the infallible truth and divine authority [of Holy Writ] is from the inward work of the Holy Spirit, bearing witness by and with the word in our hearts."[17]

Yet the practical effect of this emphasis upon authentication from "within" proved to be problematic. Emphasis upon the indwelling Spirit authenticating individualistic interpretation created the greatest difficulties for Puritans in their use of the Bible, essentially because they tended to conflate the Word of Scripture with the "inward word" of the individual's interpretation. In the account of Leopold Damrosch, this came to mean that for many of Baxter's contemporaries,

> the Word that speaks in the heart is indistinguishable from the Word expressed in the Bible, and that in turn is inseparable from the creative Logos that brought the universe into being. For otherwise the ambiguities of Scripture would require the exegesis of experts, on whose interpretation the ordinary believer would have to rely.[18]

As Damrosch points out, this conflation, consciously or unconsciously realized, can readily subtend the argument of a theorist like William

17. Printed in Samuel R. Gardiner, *The Constitutional Documents of the Puritan Revolution 1625-1660* (Oxford: Clarendon Press, 1906); Martin, *Puritanism and Richard Baxter*, 79.

18. Leopold Damrosch, Jr., *God's Plot and Man's Stories: Studies in the Fictional Imagination from Milton to Fielding* (Chicago: University of Chicago Press, 1985), 63. Many among the Puritans regarded it as a sinful interposition or quenching of the Spirit to introduce commentary or exegetical aids into one's study of Scripture. For the Baptist Samuel Howe, while book-learning may "in it selfe . . . be a good thing, and good in its proper place, which is for the repayring of that *decay which came upon man for sin . . .* but bring it once to be a *help to understand the mind of God in the holy Scriptures,* and there it is *detestable filth, drosse, and dung* in that respect, and so good for nothing, but [to] *destroy, and cause men to erre.*" From *The Sufficiencie of the Spirits Teaching Without Humane Learning* (London, 1640), C4ᵛ.

Whitaker that "the scripture is *autopistos*, that is, hath all its authority and credit from itself."[19]

Bunyan, in the passage previously cited from his preface to *The Holy City* (1665), illustrates how readily the Puritan sense that singular authority is vested in Scripture could lead to a feeling of personal authority, justified by the belief that one's ideas are founded upon Scripture alone. After stating his conviction that the Bible by itself is better than access to all the books available at Oxford and Cambridge, he immediately adds a revealing corollary: "Besides, I am for *drinking water out of my own Cistern: what GOD makes mine by the evidence of his Word and Spirit, that I dare make bold with*" (72). This proprietary addendum, buttressed by his confident conflation of Scripture and the "inward witness," translates into an assertion of his own authority; its dialectical opposition in Bunyan's self-representation to the lesser authority of those who rely upon the books of men tends accordingly to confuse authority and authorial originality. Yet the reader is given to understand the force of the corollary for Bunyan's own authorial claims: it is to the degree that his own life and words stand in singular (if not original) relationship to the Bible that they have spiritual authenticity. This is, in fact, also the burden of his autobiography, *Grace Abounding to the Chief of Sinners* (1666).

We should not generalize absolutely on the basis of these examples. On Defoe's accounting, the normative intent of Puritan biblicism may most likely have been to ensure that

> Naked and plain her Sacred Truths appear,
> From pious Frauds and dark Ænigma's clear:
> The meanest Sence may all the Parts discern,
> What Nature teaches all Mankind may learn:
> Even what's reveal'd is no untrodden Path,
> Tis known by Rule, and understood by Faith,
> The Negatives and Positives agree,
> Illustrated by Truth and Honesty.[20]

19. William Whitaker, *A Disputation on Holy Scripture* (1588); see the discussion by John R. Knott, Jr., *The Sword of the Spirit: Puritan Responses to the Bible* (Chicago: University of Chicago Press, 1980), 56ff.

20. Daniel Defoe, *Reformation of Manners*, quoted in Hoxie Neale Fairchild, *Religious Trends in English Poetry*, 6 vols. (New York: Columbia University Press, 1939; reprint, 1977), 1.67.

Nonetheless, the actual practice among Bible-reading Puritans could and did vary as widely and erratically as Defoe's own example suggests. For an Anglican poet like Thomas Traherne, Baxter's cautions seemed more than warranted; in his poem "On the Bible," the reader of Scripture requires humility and reverence above all, not the risks of unexamined and froward self-confidence:

When thou dost take this sacred book into thy hand
Think not that thou the included sense dost understand.

It is a sign thou wantest sound intelligence
If that thou think thyself to understand the sense.

Be not deceived thou then on it in vain mayst gaze;
The way is intricate that leads into a maze.

Here's naught but what's mysterious to an understanding eye;
Where reverence alone stands ope, and sense stands by.[21]

And even if Baxter is to some degree an exception to the general rule of Puritan practice, his repeated encouragement to a proper use of other, albeit Christian, books, pointed the way in which the dissenting tradition as represented by Isaac Watts, Philip Doddridge, and the Wesleys would go.[22] Moreover, Baxter's apprehension that a spiritually counterproductive anti-intellectualism might well result from the sort of position represented by Bunyan at one extreme, proved accurately prophetic. "He that will have no books but his creed and Bible," Baxter warns, "may follow that sectary, who when he had burnt all his other books as human inventions, at last burnt the Bible, when he grew learned enough to understand that the translation of that was human too."[23] Baxter was not being ironic.

21. "On the Bible," *Centuries, Poems and Thanksgivings*, 2 vols., ed. H. M. Margoliouth (Oxford: Clarendon Press, 1958), 2.205.

22. See here J. W. Ashley Smith, *The Birth of Modern Education: The Contribution of the Dissenting Academies 1660-1800* (London: Independent Press, 1954); and my own forthcoming *Learning from Dissent: Education at the Margins of the Enlightenment* (Downers Grove: InterVarsity Press, 1997); also Donald Davie, *Dissentient Voice: Enlightenment and Christian Dissent* (Notre Dame: University of Notre Dame Press, 1982).

23. *The Practical Works of the Late Reverend and Pious Mr. Richard Baxter,* 4 vols. (London, 1707), 2.xiii-xiv.

Rather, well before many of his fellow Puritans he could foresee large and looming difficulties in maintaining a balanced understanding of their central doctrine of Scripture.

The Puritan Self

The doctrine of the indwelling spirit or "light within" was considered by many to have been taken to extremes only among Quakers, Levellers, Ranters, and Muggletonians,[24] but among more conservative Puritans it combined with the obligation for self-examination to bring about a preoccupation with self at least as troubled.

Self-examination was not, of course, a Puritan innovation. As part of the processes of contrition preparatory to repentance and confession, it figured in the recommendations of almost every significant spiritual writer from the early church to the late Middle Ages.[25] But in the Protestant tradition — perhaps especially in Puritan tradition[26] — it plays a distinctive role. Without the assistance of spiritual director, confessor, or even mediating priest or community, the adult Puritan believer was expected to engage in a regular and schematic spiritual inventory. In some cases, as with Matthew Henry's sister, Mrs. Radford, this ensued in "a constant register which she kept of all her approaches to the Lord's Supper"[27] — effectively just a legalistic intensification of

24. See the discussions by Horton Davies, *Worship and Theology in England from Cranmer to Hooker 1534-1603* (Princeton: Princeton University Press, 1970); Charles H. George and Katherine George, *The Protestant Mind of the English Reformers* (Princeton: Princeton University Press, 1961); and especially Christopher Hill, *Puritanism and Revolution* (New York: Schocken Books, 1964), and his *The World Turned Upside Down*.

25. D. L. Jeffrey, *The Law of Love: English Spirituality in the Age of Wyclif* (Grand Rapids: Eerdmans, 1988); *A Burning and A Shining Light: English Spirituality in the Age of Wesley* (Grand Rapids: Eerdmans, 1987; reprint, 1994).

26. William Haller, *The Rise of Puritanism* (New York: Harper, 1938; reprint, 1957); also George and George, *Protestant Mind*, 29ff.; and G. A. Starr, *Defoe and Spiritual Autobiography* (Princeton: Princeton University Press, 1965), 4-10.

27. Starr, *Defoe*, 30; Davies, *Worship and Theology*, 62-64. This was, however, a strong and persistent emphasis from the Puritan tradition on into the spiritual writing of the Evangelical Revival, whose classic manual is Thomas Haweis, *The Communicants' Companion: or, an Evangelical Preparation for the Lord's Supper. With Meditations and*

traditional Christian practice. In other cases it became an all-inclusive and all-preoccupying inventory of one's waking life, a spiritual diary. The purpose of this inventory, however much it might document lapses and ethical calamaties in a private life, was not in fact so much to acknowledge how badly one had been doing, but ultimately to show, despite all, how well one had done. In the autobiography of Oliver Heywood, the stock-taking soul is not necessarily, let alone primarily, a penitent in the older sense. Heywood's purpose is

> to compare my past and present state and obserue my proficiency in christianity, to see whether I be better this year than the last, whether grace be stronger, corruptions weaker, my hart more soft, conscience more tender, wil more bowed, rectifyed, resolved, and my life more reformed.[28]

This characterizing of the spiritual diary or spiritual autobiography as a kind of moral accountancy, with a ledger of debits and credits, has been usefully chronicled by G. A. Starr, who notes that in these Puritan texts "exhortations to self-examination were often expressed in distinctly mercantile terms," and that indeed "this is not surprising in an age which saw nothing ludicrous or profane in the description of a holy man as 'a spiritual Merchant in an heavenly Exchange, driving a rich Trade for the treasurer of the other world'."[29] Starr quotes Thomas Gouge's *Christian Directions, Shewing how to Walk with God All the Day long* (1679) as a representative example:

> As he is the best Tradesman that every day in the Evening taketh an account of his worldly losses and gains; so he is the best Christian that every day in the Evening taketh an account of his spiritual losses and gains, whether he go forward or backward in the ways of Godliness. (11)

Helps for Prayer (1764), published the same year he wrote a "Preface to the Reader" for Newton's *Authentic Narrative*. It had gone through nine printings by 1815.

28. *The Rev. Oliver Heywood, B.A. 1630-1702; His Autobiography, Diaries, Anecdote and Event Books . . .* , ed. J. Horsfall Turner, 3 vols. (Bingley, 1881-1883), 1.133; quoted in Starr, *Defoe*, 5-6.

29. Starr, *Defoe*, 10-11.

Just how representative Gouge is can immediately be grasped by anyone
who has read the annual stock-taking of Pepys in his diaries, of Robinson
Crusoe in Defoe's novel, or even Samuel Johnson's annual (and to his
own mind deficit-ridden) spiritual inventories, in his *Prayers and Meditations.*[30] Indeed, Johnson's often despairing self-analysis is a convenient reminder of the psychological abyss into which an obsessive
practitioner of the spiritual inventory might well descend; one did not
have to be formally a Puritan (or Dissenter) to experience it.

It is difficult even for saints to keep such intensive introspection
from becoming narcissistic and hence spiritually counterproductive.
Lesser mortals might perhaps be excused for failing to keep their ego
entirely in check, especially when the self of notable others in one's
religious tradition has been the object of much approving attention.
While the evident goal of the Puritan spiritual diary was self-instruction,
the answer to the rhetorical "Who am I?" in such texts required positive
as well as negative analysis, and accordingly, as Starr has noted, in them
"self-congratulation is almost as frequent as self-disparagement."[31] In
the case of a genuine egoist like Samuel Pepys, needless to say, the
keeping of a diary might become an almost entirely self-congratulatory
exercise.

Pepys' case, however, is not entirely representative either. For most
of the diarists, it appears, self-instruction of this sort had as its goal a
strengthening of conviction not only concerning one's elect state or
growing material prosperity as an evidence of that election, but also in
respect of lapses from obedience to scriptural law, acknowledgment of
guilt and return to the Lord. Composing such spiritual autobiographies

    30. Samuel Johnson, *Diaries, Prayers, and Annals,* ed. E. L. McAdam, Jr., with
Donald and Mary Hyde (New Haven: Yale University Press, 1958).
    31. Starr, *Defoe,* 31. Damrosch observes that "For the Puritans the self is all-
important not because it *is* one's self but because it represents the sole battleground of
the war between good and evil. 'For what is a man profited if he shall gain the whole
world and lose his own soul?' (Matt. 16:26). But the self is duplicitous and complex,
requiring the most stringent analysis, and its duplicity makes it impossible for direct
introspection like Montaigne's to yield trustworthy results. The truth can only emerge
from a sustained scrutiny of behavior over a period of time, and thus the need for
temporal narrative is born. The narratives that were based on this search for the self
gave it a primacy that the ideal of self-abnegation ought logically to contradict; as their
enemies saw clearly, to study the self so intently, even while accusing it, is in a sense to
glorify it, and so in a sense the Puritans were supreme egotists" (4).

thus became in itself an almost necessary mark of the piety of the elect, and might count in merit for less only than reading the Bible itself and regular prayer. And because, as in the case of Augustine, one's own experience might well serve as instruction to others, however destined to remain unpublished, vast numbers of these neatly written accountings were "kept or revised in presentable form for the sake of families, congregations, fellow-sufferers, or whatever group of readers the manuscript might reach."[32] Excerpts from many diaries were later to be incorporated in funeral orations, biographies, and in sermons of their own pastors, posthumously, and their writers knew this.

A sense of audience can have almost as much effect upon what one commits to posterity as the actualities of life that ostensibly prompt the lifting of pen to paper. Thus ordinary events, and even the ordinariness in remarkable and life-changing events, can in the recounting become somewhat artificially dramatized. Even in the later North American fundamentalist form of Puritan spiritual autobiography and public confession known as the "testimony meeting," narratives tend to have power upon their hearers proportional to the extravagance of the events they purport to retell. There is tremendous pressure upon the narrator to authenticate the narrative by starkness in the contrast of guilt and grace, and even doubly to authenticate the transition from the state of guilt to the state of grace by an array of significant and circumspectly lurid details. The Puritan diarists afford a myriad of precedent examples.

For guilt to be dealt with, it had to be justified — in both senses of the term. It is perhaps too cryptic to say, as Damrosch does, that "whereas psychoanalysis seeks to relieve the sufferer of guilt, Puritanism actually seeks to intensify it, since without guilt there can be no hope at all."[33] But the drive in the Puritan conscience for honesty about the damning effects of sin upon one's spiritual life, and the overbearing influence upon human nature of original depravity, meant that a concern for a full realization of sin's terrors and consequences would be a necessary part of authentic self-examination. A consequence of this drive for an authentic appreciation of the wages of sin seems often to have been an inflationary pressure upon the reporting of it. Puritan self-loathing could eschew the hairshirt

32. Starr, *Defoe*, 33.

33. Damrosch, *God's Plot*, 24; also Haller, *The Rise of Puritanism*, 156-57. Cf. Leland Ryken, *Worldly Saints: The Puritans as They Really Were* (Grand Rapids: Zondervan, 1991).

as a species of mortification best left to the extravagances of a degenerate Catholicism, but psychological equivalents such as spitting at one's reflection in the mirror or verbal self-abnegation were often enough substituted. If the self has its importance as the battleground of the war between good and evil, an authentic Christian self should bear marks of the deadly earnest of that battle. In the words of William Perkins, "there is a fight between the heart and the heart; that is, between the heart and itself."[34] Yet even as this sense of perpetual interior battle (so far from Baxter's goal in *The Saint's Everlasting Rest* [1650]) could drag some down into despondency and terminal despair, in others the sense of conflict, captured allegorically in Bunyan's *Pilgrim's Progress* (1678), *Grace Abounding* (1666), and *Holy War* (1682), could be exhilarating. George Godwin's *Auto-machia* captures the fighting spirit:

> I sing my SELF: my civil wars within,
> The victories I hourly lose and win;
> The daily dual, the continual strife,
> The war that ends not till I end my life.[35]

But so also perhaps in his own way, did that lapsed or antinomian Puritan Walt Whitman, whose formulations in *Song of Myself* are those of an anti-genre, a parody of the Puritan triumph of torment.[36]

And therein lies the rub. Wrought in a conflict of such pressures, the autobiographical impulse can prove an unstable mode of creativity. The basic biblical model — a story of deliverance and pilgrimage grounded upon Exodus as reinterpreted in the light of New Testament

34. *The Estate of Damnation, or . . . Grace,* quoted in Barbara K. Lewalski, *Protestant Poetics and the Seventeenth-Century Religious Lyric* (Princeton: Princeton University Press, 1979), 101; see also Sacvan Bercovitch, *The Puritan Origins of the American Self* (New Haven: Yale University Press, 1975), 19-20. The rituals of self-loathing could be verbal or physical in nature, and could on occasion reach a disturbing intensity. Cotton Mather's *Diary,* in an entry for 16 October 1697, offers a hint: "Inexpressible self-abhorrence, for my abhominable sinfulness before the Holy Lord, was the design and the very spirit of my devotions this day" (ed. Worthington C. Ford [New York: F. Ungar, 1957], 1.237).

35. George Godwin, *Automachia,* trans. Joshua Sylvester, quoted in Owen C. Watkins, *The Puritan Experience: Studies in Spiritual Autobiography* (London: Routledge and Kegan Paul, 1972), 12.

36. *The Oxford Book of American Verse,* ed. F. O. Matthiessen (New York: Oxford University Press, 1950; reprint, 1964), 279-83.

typology — may at some basic level persist, but the uses to which the model is put may well be colorful in a fashion not well calculated to serve the original purpose.[37] Yet this confusion might not necessarily make the resulting confessional narrative any less appealing in the general marketplace, but in fact just the opposite.

Spiritual Autobiography in the Marketplace

No one should imagine that Defoe was such a Puritan as Richard Baxter could approve; he was, nonetheless, a Puritan. His father intended him for the Presbyterian ministry, and sent him to the excellent dissenting academy run by Rev. Charles Morton at Newington Green.[38] Here, as was common among students in such academies, being shut out of the universities by reason of nonconformity proved a distinct educational advantage.[39] Defoe learned languages (he spoke six and read seven), he studied history, civil law, geography, economics, natural sciences, astronomy, and philosophy before leaving the academy, no longer intent upon the ministry, at the age of nineteen. He went into business and financial speculations, made and lost several fortunes, and learned hack writing for both political parties and his own purposes, once he saw where profit lay. He has been credited with more than five hundred works — truly a prodigious output — many of them taking political and ideological positions the opposite of others he had written. Fortunately, it is not necessary to our purposes to ascertain what Defoe actually believed. It is necessary, however, to examine briefly his experimentation with fictionalizing in the fashion of Puritan spiritual autobiography.

Fiction was not, as has sometimes been imagined, automatically

37. A useful reflection on this history is by Michael Walzer, *Exodus and Revolution* (New York: Basic Books, 1985).

38. Defoe attended as an adult Little St. Helen's, Bishopsgate, a church pastored by Samuel Annesley, who had been minister of St. Giles Cripplegate at the time of Defoe's birth. They were close friends, and Defoe wrote a poem *in memoriam* on Annesley's death in 1697. See F. Bastian, *Defoe's Early Life* (Totawa, N.J.: Barnes & Noble, 1981), 15-17.

39. See n. 22 above.

anathema among the Puritans. As long as the texts were allegorical in nature, and referred to the Bible as the evident "absent text" in terms of which the work at hand could be imagined as a kind of expository application (one thinks not only of *The Faerie Queene* here but more particularly of Bunyan's works), there could be little objection. Fiction without such a transparent biblical point of reference was, of course, genuinely problematic, and the theater above all was regarded as notoriously unfit for Christian recreation.[40] But biography, whether ancient, as in the *Lives of Plutarch,* or modern, as in Baxter's *Breviate of the Life of Mrs. Margaret Baxter* (1681), the Puritans might consider very worthwhile, and while few dissenting divines affirmed Samuel Johnson's dictum that after the life of a good man the next most edifying reading would be the life of a bad man,[41] they made some space for such works on their own shelves. As we have seen, they made even more space for autobiography of a religious character.

The issue at stake in all such questions of literary propriety was the relation of the text to truth. In the case of Bunyan's fiction, that relationship was naturally to spiritual truth as grounded in the Bible. In the biography or autobiography of a worthy Christian the same ultimate criterion applied — excepting that in those cases truth to the order of fact and event was obviously more in need of verification than was correspondence to the truth of the Bible. Authenticity demanded sincerity, veracity, and perspicuity of the textual witness: a title such as Defoe's *A True Relation of the Apparition of one Mr. Veal* (1706) — a journalistic reporting of an account of spiritual experience — makes overt the expected point for a reader of Puritan inclinations.

At the same time, criminal biographies, in which such nice scruples were seldom adhered to, constituted a growing form of literary entertainment among the masses generally, and there was money in it. Then, as now, tabloid journalism flourished where responsible journalism wilted upon the vine: accounts of the "true confessions" of condemned prisoners were

40. See here the excellent brief discussion by Martin, *Puritanism and Richard Baxter,* 92-100. On the problematic issue of allegory, see Thomas H. Luxon, *Literal Figures: Puritan Allegory and the Reformation Crisis in Representation* (Chicago: University of Chicago Press, 1995).

41. Samuel Johnson, *Rambler,* no. 60: "I have often thought that there has rarely passed a Life of which a judicious and faithful Narrative would not be useful." In Tillotson, et al., *Eighteenth-Century Literature,* 986.

easy enough to get legitimately; it was easier still to invent whole cloth or at least to embroider. Defoe almost certainly had a hand in this trade, and criminal biography and spiritual autobiography come together vigorously, if not altogether seamlessly, in his novel *The Fortunes and Misfortunes of the Famous Moll Flanders* (1722). The first part of the full title indicates Defoe's appeal to readers of the criminal biography — *Who was Born in Newgate, and during a Life of continu'd Variety for Threescore Years, besides her Childhood, was Twelve Year a Whore, five times a Wife (whereof once to her own Brother), Twelve Year a Thief, Eight Year a Transputed Felon in Virginia.* . . . The last phrases appeal to a Puritan audience with whom Defoe was more intimately familiar — *at last grew Rich, liv'd Honest, and died a Penitent, Written from her own Memorandums.*

Scholars are generally agreed that the religious elements featured in *Moll Flanders* derive from the basic traditions of Puritan spiritual autobiography.[42] Further, it seems evident that Defoe knew he could appeal with this tale to the genre expectations of such readers, as long as he assured them that his text adhered to a familiar pattern of spiritual truth. Defoe's means of effecting his simultaneous appeal to the salaciously and spiritually minded depended in the first instance upon a judicious balance of sensational narrative with an account of moral development toward repentance. For both sorts of readers, he also had to insinuate an order of credibility into his narration; in doing so he permitted his readers to be gratified in either (or both) lewd and circumspect appetites. His "Author's Preface" accomplishes this by a fiction of ingenious convenience in itself; it deserves citation at length:

> It is true that the original of this story is put into new words, and the style of the famous lady we here speak of is a little altered; particularly she is made to tell her own tale in modester words than she told it at first, the copy which came first to hand having been written in language more like one still in Newgate than one grown penitent and humble, as she afterwards pretends to be.
>
> The pen employed in finishing her story, and making it what

---

42. Besides Starr and Damrosch, one should consult here Robert Bell, "Metamorphoses of Spiritual Autobiography," *English Literary History* 44 (1977), and Homer O. Brown, "The Displaced Self in the Novels of Daniel Defoe," *Studies in Eighteenth-Century Culture* 4 (1975): 69-94.

you now see it to be, has had no little difficulty to put it into a dress fit to be seen, and to make it speak language fit to be read. When a woman debauched from her youth, nay, even being the offspring of debauchery and vice, comes to give an account of all her vicious practices and even to descend to the particular occasions and circumstances by which she first became wicked, and of all the progression of crime which she ran through in threescore years, an author must be hard put to it to wrap it up so clean as not to give room, especially for vicious readers, to turn it to his disadvantage.

All possible care, however, has been taken to give no lewd ideas, no immodest turns in the new dressing up of this story; no, not to the worst parts of her expressions. To this purpose some of the vicious part of her life, which could not be modestly told, is quite left out, and several other parts are very much shortened. What is left 'tis hoped will not offend the chastest reader or the modestest hearer; and as the best use is made even of the worst story, the moral 'tis hoped will keep the reader serious, even where the story might incline him to be otherwise. To give the history of a wicked life repented of, necessarily requires that the wicked part should be made as wicked as the real history of it will bear, to illustrate and give a beauty to the penitent part, which is certainly the best and brightest, if related with equal spirit and life.[43]

What all of this rationalization manages to mask almost flawlessly is that the work in question is almost certainly invention from first to last. But to give Defoe his due, there *is* a pattern to the novel which he would have regarded as characteristic of a spiritual truth. That pattern is the normative structure of Puritan spiritual autobiography, which, with the possibility of variation in relative emphasis, is outlined in the autobiographical memoirs of James Fraser of Brae (ca. 1670):

(1) What hath been the Lord's carriage to me before I knew any thing of God, or had so much as the form of religion. (2) Some steps of God's providence while the Lord was drawing me to him-

43. Daniel Defoe, "The Author's Preface," in *The Fortunes and Misfortunes of the Famous Moll Flanders, etc.,* ed. Mark Schorer (New York: Modern Library, 1950), xx.

self; or some preparation-work to my conversion, while my heart was not fully changed, but had only some appearance of godliness. (3) Some things concerning my conversion, the time and manner; and what immediately followed. (4) Of the sad and long decay that happened thereafter. (5) Relate some things touching my recovery out of that decay. (6) Some things that happened immediately after this recovery, for the space of four or five years. (7) Some things relating to my present condition, and some things I have observed in my experience. (8) Some particular mercies I have met with from the Lord at several occasions.[44]

Readers of *Moll Flanders* will be able to confirm the resemblance of Moll's progress to the pattern here suggested, a pattern to some degree marked out by her regular accounting procedures, following crime and liaisons, with assessments of profit and loss.[45] What may seem odd to the uninitiated, however, is how little space is given to the actual conversion itself — in Fraser's case only three out of more than two hundred pages, in Moll's case not much more — and given the extravagant exploits of her preconversion narrative Defoe seems to have wanted to head off possible objections by having Moll recontextualize her repentance:

> I had deeper impressions upon my mind all that night, of the mercy of God in sparing my life, and a greater detestation of my past sins, from a sense of the goodness which I had tasted in this case, than I had in all my sorrow before.
>
> This may be thought inconsistent in itself, and wide from the business of this book; particularly, I reflect that many of those who may be pleased and diverted with the relation of the wild and wicked part of my story may not relish this, which is really the best part of my life, the most advantageous to myself, and the most instructive to others. Such, however, will, I hope, allow me the liberty to make my story complete. It would be a severe satire on such to say they do not relish the repentance as much as they do

44. Quoted by Starr, *Defoe*, 40.
45. Defoe, *Moll Flanders*, e.g. 51, 68, 115, 322.

the crime; and that they had rather the history were a complete tragedy, as it was very likely to have been.[46]

Thus, without the text and within, Defoe finds it necessary to reassure his Puritan reader that this is not in the usual sense a fiction, but rather is authentic narrative — in his own phrase, a "true relation." Whether the voice of Moll is convincing in this respect is another matter.

Common Text, Singular Experience

It might be argued that Christian spiritual autobiography has a very long tradition: the *Confessions* of St. Augustine is commonly regarded as originary, the first autobiography of any kind in our modern sense of the term. It certainly is spiritual autobiography. The claim has been made, moreover, that autobiography is in some sense distinctively a product of Christian rather than classical reflection.[47] Yet what is perhaps odd about this thesis is how few imitators Augustine's *Confessions* acquired in the first millenium and more after it was written. The Middle Ages produced community chronicles, collections of letters containing spiritual advice, and both practical and esoteric manuals on the inner life, but nothing to match Augustine's text. On the other hand, spiritual biography — writing about the life of a saintly person by another admiring narrator — was perhaps the most popular of all medieval genres.[48] To be sure, even in the anthologized collections, such as the famous *Golden Legend* of Jacobus de Voraigne, there is little enough variety and much reduplicative pattern in the lives recorded. From a medieval point of view, the authenticity of such texts as a witness to Christian spiritual virtues was not in any sense dependent on particularity or singularity of event. As Reginald of Canterbury put it, "all things

46. Ibid., 277.

47. See here Roy W. Battenhouse, *A Companion to the Study of St. Augustine* (Oxford, 1955; reprint, Grand Rapids: Baker, 1955); Peter Brown, *Augustine of Hippo: A Biography* (Berkeley: University of California Press, 1967); Pierre Courcelle, *Recherches sur les Confessions de Saint Augustin* (Paris: Gallimard, 1963).

48. Charles W. Jones, introduction to *Saints' Lives and Chronicles in Early England* (Ithaca: Cornell University Press, 1947).

are common in the community of saints."[49] In fact, in this period one spoke of the *life* of saints rather than the lives of saints, since as Gregory of Tours has it, "though there may be some difference in their merits and virtues, yet the life of one body nourished them in all the world."[50]

At the time of the Reformation, in England especially during the years after Henvy VIII, texts of saints' lives and saints' plays were widely destroyed by Reformers as "fables" of idolatrous Romish piety.[51] Puritans like Bunyan found their equivalent to the saints' life in a morbid anthology of Protestant martyrs' gruesome deaths (often with the barest sketch of each life as hasty prolegomena to the ampler detailing of torture and burning at the stake).[52] Avid Puritan readers of *Foxe's Book of Martyrs* (1563) would have been scandalized by any revival of the biographical medieval saint's life. Yet it was they — as Bunyan's example famously illustrates — who more than any others revived the *autobiographical* form pioneered by Augustine. (Not only in matters of the doctrine of grace did the Puritans look back to Augustine's vision of the self before God.) Moreover, the staying power of Puritan spiritual autobiography proved greater in the sphere of religious diary-writing than in the fictional exploitations modeled by Defoe. It seems that some

49. Levi R. Lind, ed., *The Vita Sancti Malchi of Reginald of Canterbury* (Urbana: University of Illinois Press, 1942), 40-41.

50. *Gregorii Eps. Turoniensis Liber Vitae Patrum*, ed. T. Mommsen, et al.; *Monumenta Germaniae Historica*, Scriptores Rerum Merovingicarum, 1.662-663.

51. John Phillips, *The Reformation of Images: Destruction of Art in England, 1535-1660* (Berkeley: University of California Press, 1973), 41-42, 53-61, 96; also D. L. Jeffrey, "English Saints' Plays," in *Medieval Drama*, ed. Neville Denny, Stratford-upon-Avon Studies 16 (London: Edwin Arnold, 1973), 69-89.

52. John Foxe (1516-1587) fled to the continent on the accession of Queen Mary from Oxford, where he was a fellow of Magdalen College (1539-1545). There he associated with other Protestant refugees of Calvinist persuasion, including John Knox, and wrote in Latin his martyrology (published at Strassburg, 1554). An expanded English edition, *Acts and Monuments of Matters Happening in the Church*, appeared in 1563. This is the book commonly known as *Foxe's Book of Martyrs*, and its main purpose is to commemorate, for polemical purposes, the Protestant martyrs of Mary's reign. It went through four editions in his own lifetime, and dozens more afterward; it was especially popular among Puritans and nonconformists of the seventeenth century. Addenda of martyrs after 1585 commonly occur in these later editions, often without due acknowledgment that they are additional accounts, not by Foxe. The standard full edition is still Stephen Reed Cattley's, in 9 vols. (London: R. B. Seeley and W. Burnside, 1837-1841).

among the audience for the "true confession"–styled epistolary novels of Samuel Richardson *(Pamela, Clarissa, Sir Charles Grandisson)* were nurtured on spiritual diaries and Defoe's fictions both, and that many continued to prefer such fictions even after (and despite) the robust rejection of this tradition by Henry Fielding (especially in *Shamela* and *Tom Jones*).[53] But eighteenth-century interest in biography as well as in diary and autobiography of an "improving" or religious character remained strong. Indeed, many important religious and cultural leaders practiced this latter genre in particular. Examples of note include *The Memoir of an Early Life* by the reclusive poet William Cowper (1765; publ. 1816); the *Authentic Narrative* of the slave-trader turned priest, John Newton (1764); *A Brief Account of the Life of Howell Harris,* memoirs of the Welsh evangelist (1791); the *Prayers and Meditations* of Samuel Johnson, the legendary lexicographer, writer, editor, and critic (1785); and the *Memoirs of Charles Simeon,* the sometime professor of chemistry and later eighteenth-century Cambridge divine (1836).

Not all such autobiographical accounts, as these few names suggest, were necessarily by Puritans or Dissenters; it is a measure of their influence that by the late eighteenth century Established Church (Anglican) figures such as Newton and Cowper could still owe something to the spiritual and scriptural practices of the Puritans. The genre itself, however, even as its popularity widened, was, by reason of its record of complicity with more than one kind of fiction, coming under increasing strain. Two examples must suffice to show, respectively, the fragility and the durability of this form of Christian writing.

William Cowper's life was a troubled passage on many accounts. The consensus of historians, literary critics, and biographers alike is that he had a nervous psychological disposition to begin with, that this was aggravated by the death of his mother while he was a small child, and further compounded by abusive treatment at the boarding school to which he was sent.[54] In any event, long before he commenced with any

53. See Damrosch, *God's Plot,* especially chapters 6-7; also Margaret Anne Doody, *A Natural Passion: A Study of the Novels of Samuel Richardson* (Oxford: Oxford University Press, 1974).

54. Lord David Cecil, *The Stricken Deer: or, the Life of Cowper* (London: Constable, 1929), 17-41; Gilbert Thomas, *William Cowper and the Eighteenth Century* (London: Ivor Nicholson and Watson, 1935), 59-82; cf. 199-208; also Charles Ryskamp, *William Cowper of the Inner Temple, Esq.* (Cambridge: Cambridge University Press, 1959).

earnestness upon a spiritual progress, he suffered a complete mental breakdown of spectacular proportions, and repeatedly attempted suicide. By providential mercy, as he later opined, he was sent for treatment to the private clinic of one Dr. Nathaniel Cotton. There, under the patient ministrations of Cotton, and, by his own account, through the discovery and reading of the Bible, he came to a point of repentance and conversion.

Numerous features linking Cowper's *Memoir* with the classic form of the Puritan spiritual autobiography are immediately apparent to the reader. The first of these has to do with the overall structure of the work, the explicit purpose of which is to reveal the providential design in retrospect. Cowper's repeated marks of passage are representatively both laudatory and explanatory:

> "How wonderful are the works of the Lord, and his ways past finding out!" Thus was he preparing me for an event, which I least of all expected, even the reception of his blessed gospel, working by means, which, in all human contemplation, must needs seem directly opposite to that purpose, but which, in his wise and gracious disposal, have, I trust, effectually accomplished it.[55]

Here, too, are reminders that the pattern of half-repentance followed by relapse and despair is evidence that the soul is a battleground upon which Satan makes war with the providential mercy of God. Cowper's stays of guilt and misery are almost always attended by apprehensions of their imminent return:

> Easier, indeed, I was, but far from easy. The wounded spirit within me was less in pain, but by no means healed. What I had experienced was but the beginning of sorrows, and a long train of still greater terrors was at hand. I slept my three hours well, and then awoke with ten times a stronger alienation from God than ever.
>
> Satan plied me closely with horrible visions and more horrible voices. My ears rang with torments, that seemed to await me. Then did the pains of hell get hold on me, and before daybreak, the very

---

55. William Cowper, *Memoir of the Early Life of William Cowper, Esq., Written by Himself* (London: R. Edwards, 1816), 23.

sorrows of death encompassed me. A numbness seized upon the
extremities of my body, and life seemed to retreat before it; a cold
sweat stood upon my forehead; my heart seemed at its every pulse
to beat its last, and my soul clung to my lips, as if on the very brink
of departure. No convicted criminal ever feared death more, or
was more assured of dying. (57-58)

Cowper was a poet, and his emotional malady readily took on the note
of lyric despair expressed in these lines; nevertheless the dramatic sense
of near-Faustian terror pervading his account recalls that repressed by
others among the earlier Puritans, the frequency of which had prompted
the anxious concern of Baxter. Cowper seems actually to have feared he
might have entered into an irrevocable diabolical pact, and that even
his prayers for mercy would thus prove a waste of breath:

Another time I seemed to pronounce to myself, "Evil be thou my
good" [Satan, in Milton's *Paradise Lost*]. I verily thought I had
adopted that hellish sentiment, it seemed to come so directly from
my heart. I rose from bed, to look for my prayer-book, and having
found it, endeavoured to pray; but immediately experienced the
impossibility of drawing nigh to God, unless he first draw nigh to
us. I made many passionate attempts towards prayer, but failed in
all. (52)

Cowper's hyper-Calvinism was in this respect almost as severe as
that so darkly caricatured by James Hogg in his Faustian romance, *The
Private Memoirs and Confessions of a Justified Sinner* (1824). Unlike
Hogg's evil and antinomian protagonist, however, Cowper records a
classic progress from tortured conscience to conversion, the "balm of
Gilead" (54) by which at last he obtained conscious entry into the
community of the elect. The account of his moment of conversion also
conforms to an archetypal pattern, though in this case one much older
than the Puritan examples. A copy of the Scriptures is symbolically as
well as instrumentally present:

Within a few days of my first arrival at St. Alban's, I had thrown aside
the word of God, as a book in which I had no longer any interest or
portion. The only instance in which I can recollect reading a single

chapter, was about two months before my recovery. Having found a Bible on the bench in the garden, I opened upon the 11th [chapter] of St. John, when Lazarus is raised from the dead; and saw so much benevolence, mercy, goodness, and sympathy . . . in our Saviour's conduct, that I almost shed tears even after the relation; little thinking that it was an exact type of the mercy which Jesus was on the point of extending toward myself. (65)

This is followed by his picking up another Bible, and at random opening it to Romans 3:25, the reading of which is immediately followed by his receipt of "the full beams of the Sun of Righteousness" (67). Thus, in June of 1765 Cowper became well enough to leave the asylum. But was Cowper aware, as he wrote these lines, of the closeness of his account to that in book 8 of the *Confessions,* where Augustine too picks up a copy of the Scriptures (in his case the text is Romans 13), and finds in its apt words the decisive invitation to conversion? What seems far less likely is that he could have known the recently published (1764) and already widely read *Authentic Narrative* of the man soon to become his own priest and spiritual advisor, the priest of Olney, John Newton. Yet here too there are many parallels.

Of the two, Newton's is surely the more dramatic and colorful narrative. He, if anyone, had an actual life well suited to the *typoi* of Puritan spiritual autobiography. Although his mother, who was of Dissenting stock, had taught him to read before he was four years old and to know the shorter Catechism and the children's hymns of Isaac Watts before her death when he was just six, his subsequent four years at boarding school gave way to a series of sea-borne adolescent apprenticeships in unsavory company. The results for his own character development were perhaps predictable; even so, he seems to have made the worst of it. After five voyages to the Mediterranean and another to the West Indies, Newton began a pattern of shipboard miscreances and shore-leave licentiousness and truancy that set the course for a rebellious career. Press-ganged into the navy, then favored with early recognition, he overstayed shore-leave again and was arrested as a deserter, publicly flogged, and demoted once more to the rank of a common sailor. He then took up work on a slave-trading vessel bound for Africa, where once landed he became sick, and was severely abused by the African common-law spouse of a broker in the slave trade. An autodidact of superior attainments, while on shore in Africa and later at sea he taught himself Latin, French, Spanish, Hebrew, and Greek. He also read history, mathematics, and books on navigation and natural science. During this time he read the Bible intermittently and began to wrestle with his sinfulness. Still, he kept putting off full repentance, and accordingly underwent renewed hardness of heart. After several near escapes from death by storm and shipwreck, Newton at last converted and married. Preparing to set sail again, at twenty-nine years of age, he had a stroke. Though he soon recovered, the experience brought him to resign his sea-faring altogether, and to seek ordination as a priest in the Church of England. After many refusals he achieved his goal in 1764, the same year he published his *Authentic Narrative.* Newton's first parish was Olney, where Cowper was shortly to move. There in time they would compose hymns together — partly as Newton's idea of therapy for Cowper — and publish them as the famous *Olney Hymns* (1779). Newton's own "Amazing Grace" was to become the best-known hymn in this collection — indeed, perhaps the best-known hymn in the English-speaking world.

Newton's was hardly a run-of-the-mill life: in actual fact his account of his experiences would be a match for *Moll Flanders* or for Defoe's similar tales about Moll's sometime sea-faring gallant, *Colonel Jack* (1722) and the African trader *Captain Singleton* (1760). That very colorfulness, it appears, made of the telling and selling of Newton's *Narrative* a problem. How to distinguish it from the deliberately fictional examples of this genre, not to mention the embroidered and semi-fictional narratives whose form Defoe had exploited? Hence Newton's title, *Authentic Narrative,* is as much a disclaimer of association with the genre it follows as an example of it. In his "Preface to the Reader" of Newton's book (1764), the evangelical preacher Thomas Haweis insists "that the Narrative is quite genuine," and that its form — fourteen letters written at Haweis's own request — is in part a guarantee of that. Haweis has moreoever scrupled on some points to ask for an expansion of the detail: "Some verbal relation of the facts awakened my curiosity to see a more connected account of them, which the author very obligingly consented to, having at that time no intention of its being made public."[56]

56. In *The Works of the Rev. John Newton, Late Rector of the United Parishes of St. Mary Woolnoth and St. Mary Woolchurch Haw, London,* 9 vols. (London: J. Haddon, 1822), 1.A3.

Newton's own "Introductory Observations" which follow suggest that there will be a conformity between his experience and the reader's own, and a conformity of both with the providential pattern revealed in the Bible, sufficient to assure the reader concerning the authenticity of his narrative:

> I say, when we compare and consider these things [the evidence of providential design in personal circumstances] by the light offered us in the holy Scripture, we may collect indisputable proof, from the narrow circle of our own concerns, that the wise and good providence of God watches over his people from the earliest moments of their life. . . . I am persuaded that every believer will, upon due reflection, see enough in his own case to confirm this remark; but not all in the same degree. (7)

Sensible of the likely less extravagant experiences of providential design in the lives of most of his readers, he is cautionary concerning a literalistic application of the pattern:

> The outward circumstances of many have been uniform, they have known but little variety in life; and, with respect to their inward change, it has been effected in a secret way, unnoticed by others and almost unperceived by themselves. The Lord has spoken to them, not in thunder and tempest, but with a still small voice, he has drawn them gradually to himself: so that, though they have a happy assurance of the thing, that they know and love him, and are passed from death unto life; yet of the precise time and manner, they can give little account. Others he seems to select, in order to show the exceeding riches of his grace, and the greatness of his mighty power: he suffers the natural rebellion and wickedness of their hearts to have full scope; while sinners of less note are cut off with little warning, these are spared, though sinning with a high hand, and, as it were, studying their own destruction. At length, when all that knew them are perhaps expecting to hear that they are made signal instances of divine vengeance, the Lord (whose thoughts are high above ours, as the heavens are higher than the earth) is pleased to pluck them as brands out of the fire, and to make them monuments of his mercy, for the encouragement of

others: they are, beyond expectation, convinced, pardoned, and changed. (7-8)

Such, Newton observes, was "the persecuting Saul," and such another display of "efficacious grace in our own times" is "the late Colonel Gardiner." Gardiner, too, is presented as an extravagant case, "habituated to evil," and upon whom "many uncommon, almost miraculous deliverances, made no impression" (9).

Newton allies himself with these apostolic and modern recipients of "uncommon" grace, as one "made willing in the day of God's power," yet whose conversion is not qualitatively different from their own, merely the more apparently amazing for the force of its dramatic reversal. Yet it is this dramatic quality, at last, which justifies publication of his narrative:

> Colonel Gardener likewise was as a city set upon an hill, a burning and a shining light: the manner of his conversion was hardly more singular than the whole course of his conversation from that time to his death. Here, alas! the parallel greatly fails. — It has not been thus with me. — I must take deserved shame to myself, that I have made very unsuitable returns for what I have received. But if the question is only concerning the patience and long suffering of God, the wonderful interposition of his providence in favour of an unworthy sinner, the power of his grace in softening the hardest heart, and the riches of his mercy in pardoning the most enormous and aggravated transgressions; in these respects I know no case more extraordinary than my own. And indeed most persons to whom I have related my story have thought it worthy of being preserved. (9)

While like others before him Newton has thus stressed that there are classic common features in the experience of a life redeemed by grace (and indeed his *Authentic Narrative* has most of these features), he later more strongly repeats his insistence on the singularity of his own account:

> We must not make the experience of others in all respects a rule to ourselves, nor our own a rule to others; yet these are common

mistakes, and productive of many more. As to myself, every part of my case has been extraordinary: I have hardly met a single instance resembling it.[57]

One senses that Newton is torn between two impulses, self-assertion and self-abnegation. Any claim to originality is fraught, he realizes, with the peril of an undue and indeed un-Christian egocentrism — the very fault attributed to so many other examples of the genre by its critics. In protesting his reluctance to come forward on this account, he nonetheless turns a modesty *topos* into something almost its opposite:

> I never gave any succinct account, in writing, of the Lord's dealing with me, till very lately: for I was deterred, on the one hand, by the great difficulty of writing properly when *Self* is concerned; on the other, by the ill use which persons of corrupt and perverse minds are often known to make of such instances. The Psalmist reminds us that a reserve in these things is proper, when he says, "Come and hear, all ye *that fear God*, and I will "declare what he hath done for my soul"; and our Lord cautions us not to "cast pearls before swine." The pearls of a Christian are, perhaps, his choice experiences of the Lord's power and love in the concerns of his soul; and these should not be at all adventures made public, lest we give occasion to earthly and grovelling souls to profane what they cannot understand. These were the chief reasons of my backwardness. (9-10)

He knows his readers: they are practiced in the genre, and in its various promptings of the fiction-making impulse.

Newton's friend and biographer, the Reverend Richard Cecil, makes understandably heavy use of the *Authentic Narrative* in his *Life of Newton* (1809). He, too, feels obliged to make a preemptive apologetic, defending the veracity of Newton's account in terms of the ethical reliability of the author:

> I have heard Mr. N. relate a few additional particulars, but they were of too little interest to be inserted here: they went, however,

---

57. Ibid., 1.35.

like natural incidents, to a further authentication of the above
account, had it needed any other confirmation than the solemn
declaration of the pious relater. Romantic relations, indeed, of
unprincipled travellers, which appear to have no better basis than
a disposition to amuse credulity, to exhibit vanity, or to acquire
gain, may naturally raise suspicion, and produce but a momentary
effect at most on the mind of the reader: but facts, like the present,
manifest such a display of the power, providence, and grace of God;
and, at the same time, such a deep and humbling view of human
depravity, when moved and brought forth by circumstances, as
inexperience can scarcely credit, but which must arrest the eye of
pious contemplation, and open a new world of wonders.[58]

Cecil's defense seems all the more necessary in defending Newton's
narrative method, in which not just the truth of the wondrous facts is
at stake, but a "true relation" of the truths pertinent to faith.[59] Cecil
goes so far as to follow his *Life of Newton* with an appended "Review of
Mr. Newton's Character," pressing again the authentication in identical
terms: "Those who personally knew the man could have no doubt of
the probity with which his 'Narrative' (singular as it may appear) was
written."[60]

The evident tension between probity and the suspicion of fiction,
between singularity and conventional pattern, thus dictates both the
adjective in Newton's title and the anxiety in Haweis's and Cecil's
assurances to the reader. But what is novel about the move toward
resolution in Newton himself is that the defense has subtly moved from
grounds of conformity to the abiding truths of Scripture and the common experience of the faithful in the body of Christ — grounds appealed to from St. Augustine to Dante to Richard Baxter — to authentication on the basis of the perceived reliability of the narrator and the
unique or "singular" nature of his experience. The factuality of a *particular* experience of grace itself is finally what authenticates — or not

58. *The Works of the Rev. John Newton . . . with Memoirs of the Author . . . by the
Rev. Richard Cecil, MA,* 6 vols. (London: Hamilton, Adams and Co., 1820), 1.51.
Hereafter cited as *Works* (1820).

59. *Works* (1820), 1.68.

60. Ibid., 1.91.

— his text. Authenticity, in this shifted sense, involves a personal experience which confirms the author's word in one's own heart, and which is testable both by an answering experience of grace in the reader's experience and by the character witness of reliable interlocutors. This makes one's acceptance of the text of spiritual autobiography analogous with the Puritan test for personally confirming the authority of the Bible:

> To have the witness in ourselves, is to have the truths that are declared in Scripture revealed in our hearts. This brings an experimental conviction, which may be safely depended on, "that we have received the grace of God in truth."[61]

The appeal to personal experience, however, also has the effect of doubling the vulnerability of the Puritan apologetic for the inerrancy and authenticity of Scripture.

To Newton himself the slipperiness of this argument for authentication in respect of Scripture was not apparent. For him, as for the Dissenters with whom he almost joined forces,[62] the Bible was still the all-sufficient authority for matters of faith and practice:

> All that is necessary to make you wise to salvation is there, and there only. In this precious book you may find a direction for every doubt, a solution of every difficulty, a promise suited to every circumstance you can be in.[63]

61. Ibid., 1.183.

62. Newton concludes his *Authentic Narrative* at the point in his life (about 1757) at which he had been repeatedly discouraged in his attempts to obtain ordination, not because he was in point of knowledge unprepared in any way, but rather because he "had not been to either of the universities." At that point, he says, his "first thought was to join the Dissenters" (*Authentic Narrative*, 103). Cecil seems to have persuaded him against this option, and eventually, through the intervention of Lord Dartmouth, he was ordained by Bishop Green of Lincoln. He remained strongly partial to Puritan writers, however, among them John Owen in particular, and in his sermons made filial reference to them frequently: "Such trials have been the lot of our forefathers; when the servants of God, under the names of Gospelers or Puritans, were treated as heretics of the worst sort. We are bound to acknowledge with thankfulness the blessings of religious and civil liberty which we enjoy" (*Works* [1820], 4.371).

63. *Works* (1820), 2.398-99; also 6.417.

But a "Bible Christian," according to Newton, is not, in view of this commitment to the sufficiency of Scripture for knowledge about redemption, entitled to ignore other aids to spiritual reflection. After all, "the Bible is a sealed book, till the heart be awakened";[64] indeed, in his own case the reading of Thomas à Kempis was an important introduction to that opening of the heart which made inward recognition possible. Here also, however, authority rests finally upon experience:

> It is a mercy . . . to be enabled to acknowledge what is excellent in the writings or conduct of others. . . . We should be glad to receive instruction from all, and avoid being led by the *ipse dixit* of any. *Nullius jurare in verbum* is a fit motto for those who have one master, even Christ. We may grow wise apace in opinions, by books and men; but vital experimental knowledge can only be received from the Holy Spirit, the great instructor and comforter of his people.[65]

If "the Word of God affords a history in miniature of the heart of man," Newton implies, it is in the heart of man that the correspondence must be tested and realized.

Despite his own hard-earned linguistic and literary achievement, then, Newton inclines more to Bunyan's than to Baxter's side of the Puritan ledger with respect to "that perfect and infallible system of truth, the Bible." In his ideal "Christian Library" there are few books beside, since "a multiplicity of reading is seldom attended with a good effect . . . by reducing us to live upon a foreign supply, instead of labouring to improve and increase the stock of our own reflections."[66] For him the Bible obviates alternatives:

---

64. Ibid., 1.680.

65. Ibid., 2.100. "Experience" and "experimental" are terms which in both seventeenth- and eighteenth-century spiritual autobiography reflect a continuation of the Puritan's sense that the Holy Spirit provides confirming experience of the presence of grace in a believer's life. For a thorough study, see the landmark book by Geoffrey F. Nuttall, *The Holy Spirit in Puritan Faith and Experience* (Chicago: University of Chicago Press, 1947; 1992).

66. *Works* (1820), 1.238.

The general history of all nations and ages, and the particular experience of each private believer, from the beginning to the end of time, are wonderfully comprised in this single volume; so that whoever reads and improves it aright, may discover his state, his progress, his temptations, his danger, and his duty, as distinctly and minutely marked out, as if the whole had been written for him alone.[67]

Moreover, it surpasses all its competitors aesthetically:

The most laboured efforts of human genius are flat and languid, in comparison of those parts of the Bible which are designed to give us due apprehensions of the god with whom we have to do. Where shall we find such instances of the true sublime, the great, the marvellous, the beautiful, the pathetic, as in the Holy Scriptures?[68]

Speaking metaphorically, he says that the Christian may turn with profit to three analogous books: "the book of Creation," the "book of Providence," and the "book of the Heart." Yet each of these three is to be read as though it were a gloss upon the Bible; in its narratives of the "wise unerring providence of God" are "authentic specimens" by which we learn to "judge the whole" of life.[69] The four books are thus after all one Book, a *biblioteca divina* in one binding, for Newton "a treasure of more worth than all the volumes in the Vatican."[70]

Newton was far from a redneck Bible-thumper; his command of classical texts, effortlessly spliced into his sermons, his year-long cycle of fifty sermons on the libretto of Handel's *Messiah* preached in 1785-86,[71]

67. Ibid., 1.238-39.
68. Ibid., 1.240. Though less flamboyantly expressed, this is precisely the point pressed everywhere by the Puritans a century earlier; see, e.g., Wolseley in his *Reasonableness of Scripture-Belief* (1672): "A man must be horribly hood-winkt in his intellectuals, that does not evidently see 'tis *impar congressus* between the *Bible* and all other *Pretenders*" (164).
69. *Works* (1820), 1.243.
70. Ibid., 1.245.
71. John Newton, *Messiah: Fifty Expository Discourses upon the Series of celebrated Scriptural Passages which form the Subject of the celebrated oratorio of Handel*, 2 vols. (London, 1786), reprinted as vol. 4 of *Works* (1820).

and his own well-tempered English style all bear witness to a much wider cultural appreciation. He saw the Bible, moreover, as the inspirational basis for that appreciation, as well as the Christian's mandate for a generous view of other religious traditions, not just as an antidote to "over-attachment to any system of man's compilation." For Newton authentic Christianity is incompatible with any narrow sectarianism: the "Bible Christian . . . will see much to approve in a variety of forms and parties," and "he sensibly borrows and unites that which is excellent in each."[72] As Cecil observes in the Life, Newton "saw the spirit of Pharasaism working among those who cry the most against it — who exact to a scruple . . . of their own particularities, while they pass over the weightier matters of unity and love — straining at the gnat of a private opinion, and swallowing the camel of deadly discord."[73] His own sense of mission, as bearer of the pastoral office, was in his own often-repeated words, above all "to break a hard heart, and to heal a broken heart." But in his preoccupation with the heart of the individual as the determining judge, finally, of authenticity, he unwittingly helped pave the way for a species of universalism which would have discomfited him deeply.

The Inspired Word

Samuel Taylor Coleridge (1772-1834) was the son of an Anglican clergyman of Chillingworth's persuasion. Having discovered the Neoplatonists, perhaps in the seventeenth-century translations of Thomas Taylor (the Platonist who was to have such an influence upon Blake, Wordsworth, and Shelley as well), he went up to Cambridge in 1791 already disinclined to any very concrete notion of the historicity of the Bible and doubtful of the

---

72. *Works* (1820), 6.417; elsewhere Newton remarks: "The minister who possesses a candour thus enlightened and thus qualified, will neither degrade himself to be the *instrument,* nor aspire to be the *head,* of a party. He will not servilely tread in the paths prescribed him by men, however respectable. He will not multiply contentions, in defence either of the *shibboleths* of others, or of any *nostrum* of his own, under a pretence that he is pleading for the cause of God and truth. His attention will not be restrained to the credit or interest of any detached denomination of Christians, but extended to all who love the Lord Jesus Christ in sincerity" (4.vii).

73. Ibid., 1.125.

factuality of the Incarnation. At Cambridge he lived in the avant-garde fast lane, espoused Unitarianism, and fell into debt so considerable that he was obliged to leave the university two years later without a degree and in some personal confusion. For a time, however, Unitarianism remained central to his sense of his own identity. In his "Religious Musings," the most wide-ranging piece in *Poems on Various Occasions* (1796), he identified with the French Revolution and with former Dissenter Joseph Priestley's Unitarianism in more or less parallel terms: each offered a liberation from restrictive authority. Later that year, partly to support himself, he traveled around England as an itinerant preacher for Unitarian chapels. By this stage of his life he was addicted to opium.

Coleridge's intellectual and spiritual pilgrimage via Lessing and German "higher criticism" toward his return to trinitarian Christianity, a journey far too complex even to digest here,[74] has as one of its landmarks a large treatise compendious of the itinerary: *Christianity, the One True Philosophy* (1814). While the title sufficiently indicates that his concern with Christianity is with its value as an intellectual system, this book marks also his firm turning away from Unitarianism as a credal posture. The Christianity he espouses is still Neoplatonic, and its Logos, at least to that degree, still disembodied; nonetheless its authenticity is defended in terms of the "convictions of the heart," and in this text Coleridge promises to augment his persuasions by forthcoming "fragments of Autobiography."

Among these fragments, which include the *Biographia Literaria* (1817), is a series of seven letters written to himself in a desire to work out, as a poet and as a Christian, an articulate vindication of the Bible's centrality to Christian life and Christian culture. This text was called, by its first editor, according to contemporary perceptions of its relationship to the tradition we have been discussing, *Confessions of an Enquiring Spirit* (1840). Coleridge's own title, "Letters on the Inspiration of the Scriptures,"[75] more aptly describes the contents, although the posthu-

74. See Owen Barfield, *What Coleridge Thought* (Middletown, Conn.: Wesleyan University Press, 1971), 144-57; Anthony John Harding, *Coleridge and the Inspired Word* (Kingston and Montreal: McGill-Queen's University Press, 1985), 78-80, 96ff; and especially Robert J. Barth, S.J., *Coleridge and Christian Doctrine* (Cambridge, Mass.: Harvard University Press, 1969).

75. Harding, *Coleridge and the Inspired Word*, 8; *Confessions of an Enquiring Spirit*, ed. from the 3rd (1853) edition by H. St.-J. Hart (London: Adam and Charles Black, 1956) is cited here.

mous editor, his nephew, Henry Nelson Coleridge, quite accurately if enthusiastically advertised the argument of the text as "a profoundly wise attempt to place the study of the Written Word on its only sure foundation, — a deep sense of God's holiness and truth, and a consequent reverence for that Light — the image of Himself — which He has kindled in every one of his rational creatures."[76] That is to say, on his nephew's account Coleridge's sincere apologetic is based upon a solipsism; what authenticates the Bible is a sense of God's holiness communicated in part by the Bible, and what makes it possible for us to confirm that it is God's holiness we are sensing is the biblical doctrine of the *imago Dei,* whereby we know that our own receptive intelligence (imagination) is constructed to be precisely resonant to the imagination of the Creator. But it is also the case for Coleridge that the human faculty thus takes on, as it does for Goethe, God's own powers in its creativity: the circular logic which ensues might have been thought blasphemous by Augustine, for in Coleridge's view "the primary IMAGINATION [is] a repetition in the finite mind of the eternal act of creation in the infinite I AM."[77]

But to say only this much would be greatly to shortchange Coleridge in respect of his evident determination to champion the Bible. His is a deliberately accommodationist apologetic, frankly personal, yet plainly essayed in an effort to rescue the Bible from what he takes to be the

---

76. Coleridge, *Confessions,* 11.

77. Coleridge, *Biographia Literaria* 1.304; this famous remark of Coleridge might be compared to that of Wordsworth in his Preface to the *Lyrical Ballads* (1802), where the latter parodies St. Paul (Acts 17:28) as he erects "the grand elementary principle of pleasure, by which [mankind] knows and feels, and lives, and moves." See here also M. H. Abrams, *The Mirror and the Lamp* (New York: Oxford University Press, 1953), 278. In the end Coleridge's conflation also accounts for his dismissal of traditional apologetics, such as was represented popularly in his time by William Paley's *Evidences of Christianity* (1795), and his preference for imaginative affirmation in the "intelligent Self" (*Aids to Reflection,* ed. Henry Nelson Coleridge [Port Washington, N.Y.: Kennikat Press, 1971], 92) or personal experience: "I more than fear the prevailing taste for books of Natural Theology, Physico-Theology, Demonstrations of God from Nature, Evidences of Christianity and the like. Evidences of Christianity! I am weary of the word. Make a man feel the want of it; rouse him, if you can, to the self-knowledge of his need of it; and you may safely trust to its own Evidence" (ibid., 272). See also John Spencer Hill, ed., introduction to *Imagination in Coleridge* (London: MacMillan, 1978); Barfield, *What Coleridge Thought,* 69-91.

perilously credulous "bibliolatry" of the descendents of the Puritans on the one hand, and the dismissive skepticism of the Enlightenment on the other.[78] He clearly wants to secure the Bible's continuing preeminence in the life of Christians. But the means by which he attempts to do so represents a slide down the slippery slope from the authentication of the heart so visible already in Newton and more popularly championed by such figures as John Wesley.[79] Coleridge wants the Bible ("the Book," he calls it) to have preeminent authority, but in terms of an authenticity derived from what he takes to be the indisputable confirmations of experience. Yet at the same time he would resist the charge of cultural relativism:

> I will not leave it in the power of unbelievers to say that the Bible is for me only what the Koran is for the deaf Turk, and the Vedas for the feeble and acquiescent Hindoo. No; I will retire *up into the mountain,* and hold secret commune with my Bible above the contagious blastments of prejudice, and the fog-blight of selfish superstition.[80]

That is the burden of his first "Letter." The first lines of the second "Letter" in *Confessions of an Enquiring Spirit* translate what for him this commitment means:

78. See Harding, *Coleridge and the Inspired Word,* 74-94; also Stephen Prickett, *Words and the Word: Language, Poetics and Biblical Interpretation* (Cambridge: Cambridge University Press, 1986), 4-6; and Stephen Prickett, ed., *Reading the Text: Biblical Criticism and Literary Theory* (Oxford: Blackwell, 1991), 202-6. Not all descendents of the evangelicals trod this path. John Henry Newman, from the evangelical wing of the Established Church, held to a conviction of the plenary inspiration of canonical books of the Bible, both as an Anglican and after he became a Catholic, but his way of dealing with the historical character of textual transmission differs strikingly from that of Coleridge. See his *On the Inspiration of Scripture,* ed. J. D. Holmes and Robert Murray, S.J. (London: Geoffrey Chapman, 1967).

79. "The Law of Conscience, and not the Canons of discursive reasoning, must decide" (*Aids to Reflection,* 108). But see here Richard E. Brantley, *Locke, Wesley and the Method of English Romanticism* (Gainesville: University of Florida Press, 1984); also Umphrey Lee, *John Wesley and Modern Religion* (Nashville: Cokesbury Press, 1936); cf. Robert C. Munk, *John Wesley: His Puritan Heritage* (London: Epworth Press, 1966); cf. Fredrick Dreyer, "Faith and Experience in the Thought of John Wesley," *The American Historical Review* 88 (1983): 12-30.

80. Coleridge, *Confessions,* 41-42.

In my last Letter I said that in the Bible there is more that *finds*
me than I have experienced in all other books put together; that
the words of the Bible find me at greater depths of my being; and
that whatever finds me brings with it an irresistible evidence of its
having proceeded from the Holy Spirit. But the doctrine in question requires me to believe, that not only what finds me, but that
all that exists in the sacred volume, and which I am bound to find
therein, was — not alone inspired by, that is, composed by men
under the actuating influence of the Holy Spirit, but likewise —
dictated by an Infallible Intelligence; — that the writers, each and
all, were divinely informed as well as inspired. (43)

There are two points here of central importance. The first is that
Coleridge sees the Bible as a text that discovers ("finds") or reads *him*
(cf. Hebrews 4:12) more than does the totality of other writings. In this
he echoes Bunyan. The second is that this sense of being read *by* a text,
rather than having read or mastered the text in question, is for him
signal evidence of it having been authored by the Holy Spirit, "dictated
by an Infallible Intelligence," "inspired." In this he echoes Newton. So
far, it will be apparent, he has said little that fails to find precedent in
the evangelical tradition.

Moreover, he has no intention "to speculate on the formation of
either Canon" (47), Jewish or Christian — though he clearly recognized
that such questions are at the heart of an increasingly skeptical tradition
in biblical scholarship itself (45-54). For himself, he only desires an
inward assurance: "it concerns both my character and my peace of
mind," he says, rather "to convince myself and others, that the Bible and
Christianity are their own sufficient evidence," and regarding that effort
the "unprejudiced" reader, he feels, will surely be satisfied if Coleridge's
"present convictions should in all other respects to be found consistent
with the faith and feeling of a Christian" (47). The language of the "inner
light" is here unmistakable and, from the point of view of his overall
project, increasingly troubling.

Coleridge, in fact, is not an adherent of the doctrine of verbal inspiration of Scripture. While he allows that something very like it may pertain
to passages recording "the word of the Lord" to prophets such as Samuel
or Isaiah (44), he finds the notion of a plenary and inerrant inspiration,
guaranteed in the texts which have come down to us, to be the source of

"positive harm" to the credibility among his contemporaries of Scripture generally. To the doctrine which asserts "that every sentence was miraculously communicated to the nominal author by God himself" (58) he attributes a legacy of "forced and fantastic interpretations" of two kinds, "the arbitrary allegories and mystic expansion of proper names, to which this indiscriminate Bibliolatry furnished fuel, spark, and wind," and a still more pernicious "literal rendering of Scripture in passages which the number and variety of images employed . . . to express one and the same verity, plainly mark out for figurative" (58-59). Such practices, coupled with the forced conjunction of sentences widely detached from each other in the biblical anthology by the efforts of systematic theology "contrary to the intention of the sacred writer," have produced a *credendum* actually incongruous with the texts so conflated. He associates these untoward practices not only with the Puritans ("Church dignitaries in the reign of Charles I") but through them, on account of their "stultifying, nugifying, effect of a blind and uncritical study of the Fathers," with the early Church as well.[81] Here Coleridge separates himself from the tradition of evangelicals such as Bunyan and Newton as sharply as he had allied himself with them initially.

He returns to his task almost, it seems, by the route foretrodden by Baxter. The Bible is central, he now wants to say, a necessary condition for Christian identity, but not its sufficient condition:

> The Bible is the appointed conservatory, an indispensable criterion, and a continual source and support of true Belief. But that the Bible is the sole source; that it not only contains, but constitutes, the Christian Religion; that it is, in short, a Creed, consisting wholly of articles of Faith; that consequently we need no rule, help, or guide, spiritual or historical, to teach us what parts are and what are not articles of Faith —

this, he concludes, is unacceptable (60). His position at this point might seem even more like a Catholic stance than Baxter's.

> I, who hold that the Bible contains the religion of Christians, but who dare not say that whatever is contained in the Bible is the

81. Coleridge, *Literary Remains,* 3.175, 183; quoted in *Confessions,* 59n.

Christian religion, and who shrink from all questions respecting the comparative worth and efficacy of the written Word as weighed against the preaching of the Gospel, the discipline of the Churches, the continued succession of the Ministry, and the communion of Saints, lest by comparing I should seem to detach them; — I tremble at the processes, which the Grotian divines without scruple carry on in their treatment of the sacred Writers. . . . (61)

The "Grotian divines," in their utter rejection of verbal inspiration, err in the opposite direction from the evangelicals, for whom, "whatever the doctrine of infallible dictation may be in itself, in *their* hands it is to the last degree nugatory, and to be paralleled only by the Romish tenet of [papal] infallibility" (61). That is to say, he holds for tradition as a part of the process by which inspiration becomes understanding, but he will not ascribe to the bearers of the tradition an authority — even a collective authority — surpassing the witness of his own inner light.[82] Here he is not of course "Catholic" at all. Rather, in his romantic confidence in the self as interpreter, declared even as he mounts a vigorous hermeneutic of suspicion concerning the interpretations of others, he is acting in accordance with that least fortunate impulse of the logic of the Reformation by which in the search for authenticity one is likely to find oneself at last in a church of one.

Coleridge, then, is fully a modern in his romantic emphasis on the self and, perhaps more fully than descendents of the Puritans would like to think, he has followed the logic of the evangelical tradition's own defense of Scripture to get there. The best he can say for eminent writers of past Christian tradition is that, like himself, they too have been able to judge the authenticity of the Bible by inner feelings of accord, or conformity to their own personal experience: "In every generation, and wherever the light of Revelation has shone, men of all ranks, conditions, and states of mind have found in this Volume a correspondent for every movement toward the Better felt in their own hearts" (68). Precisely because it proves so confirming of the various heart-felt experiences of men and women, the Bible is irreducible to system, but rather a "many-chambered storehouse" of personal revelation.

It is in respect of this last point that the Bible, for Coleridge, is an

82. Cf. Barfield, *What Coleridge Thought,* 152-53.

indispensable foundation to culture. While its power to command obedience is proscribed by the degree to which it produces resonance in
the heart of its individual reader, its power to induce civilization and
culture is a matter of general record and assent:

> For more than a thousand years the Bible, collectively taken, has
> gone hand in hand with civilisation, science, law, — in short, with
> the moral and intellectual cultivation of the species, always
> supporting, and often leading the way. Its very presence, as a
> believed Book, has rendered the nations emphatically a chosen
> race, and this too in exact proportion as it is more or less generally
> known and studied. (69)

Indeed, it is in the cultural sphere that the foundational value of the
Bible is to be found most unarguable even for the believing Christian:

> This I believe by my own dear experience, — that the more tran-
> quilly an inquirere takes up the Bible as he would any other body
> of ancient writings, the livelier and steadier will be his impressions
> of its superiority to all other books, till at length all other books
> and all other knowledge will be valuable in his eyes in proportion
> as they help him to a better understanding of his Bible. (75)

For Coleridge, comparative study of the Bible has been in fact a route
by which his own assurance of its authority has been increased, or so
he says. But he will no longer accede to what he sees as the corrupting
inanity that (as Chillingworth had it) "the Bible is the Religion of Protestants!"[83] And though he would not "withhold the bible from the
cottager and the Artisan," he feels sure that to read the Bible properly
such a study as that in which he has engaged over a lifetime is required,
and that such study is likely to be reserved for "scholars — for men of

---

83. Coleridge, *Confessions,* 76; in the *Literary Remains* he writes: "The Papacy
elevated the Church to the virtual exclusion or suppression of the Scriptures; the modern
Church of England, since Chillingworth, has so raised up the Scriptures as to annul the
Church: both alike have quenched the Holy Spirit, as the *mesothesis* or indifference of
the two, and substituted an alien compound for the genuine Preacher, which should be
the *synthesis* of the Scriptures and the Church, and the sensible voice of the Holy Spirit"
(3.93).

like education and pursuits as myself" (76). The magisterium to which the romantic poet is content at last to subscribe, it seems, is a magisterium of high culture.

The Poetic Bible

On this issue at least, the distance separating Coleridge and Matthew Arnold (1822-1888) is not so great as one might imagine. The first modern professor of English literature, Arnold was the son of Thomas Arnold, headmaster of Rugby. The senior Arnold was an advocate both of subservience of church to a dominant state and simultaneously of the universal priesthood of the laity. He had read Coleridge's *Confessions,* and Coleridge's convictions concerning the inspiration of the Scriptures influenced his *Sermons Chiefly on the Interpretation of Scripture* (1845) in particular. There the senior Arnold characterizes Bible reading as "participation in an historical process rather than as an act having intrinsic and unconditional spiritual value."[84]

Matthew Arnold's own career path led him, via a term as an inspector of schools, to his appointment as professor of poetry at Oxford (1857), where he was the first of that title to lecture in English. A modernist by every personal disposition, he was at the same time committed to developing an idea of culture strong enough to offset the troublesome individualism of the Protestant middle-class mind. In *Culture and Anarchy* (1869) he decried the "dissidence of dissent" which, if unchecked, in his view could lead only to anarchy. Culture, on the other hand, he argued, opens the mind to "national right reason," the only proper grounding for the state (and thus it takes the place, effectively, of religion in his father's scheme of things).

Arnold believed that in order for culture to function as religion it must, as a kind of latter-day "Hellenism," displace the tradition of English "Hebraism" which, in the wake of Puritan influence, had proved so preoccupied with sin and obsessed with moral conscience that it

---

84. Harding, *Coleridge and the Inspired Word,* 104. For reflection on the influence of Coleridge upon Arnold senior, see Bernard M. G. Reardon, *From Coleridge to Gore: A Century of Religious Thought in Britain* (London: Longman, 1971), 89, 360ff.

effectively denied the possibility of human perfection so indispensable to a modernist credo. Like other social determinisms of the nineteenth century (Freud, Marx), Arnold's system is predicated upon a conviction that individual perfection is not possible without a coercive extension of "culture" to mankind in general. He was, in short, utopian in his ambitions.

Like Coleridge, Arnold had been heavily influenced by German thinkers (though he tried to deny this), principally Lessing and Feuerbach. This is particularly clear in his *Literature and Dogma* (1873). Here, continuing his effort to replace religion with culture, he argues that traditional language about God is "without public cognitive content"[85] and that while such language can perhaps mean something at the purely personal and subjective level, it cannot function as a basis for civic or communal discourse. Biblical language, Arnold asserts, is merely "poetic," a term which here means "mythical" or "legendary," and the result of a kind of primeval naiveté or *Urdummheit,* blameless among more primitive peoples, but not so among modern well-educated Englishmen.[86]

In *God and the Bible* (1875) he presses his case further:

> Now, the old ways of accounting for Christianity, of establishing the ground of its claims upon us, no longer serve as they once did. Men's experience widens, they get to know the world better, to know the mental history of mankind better; they distinguish more clearly between history and legend, they grow more shy of recourse to the preternatural.[87]

Arnold styles himself as the spokesman for heirs of the Enlightenment who can no longer live either with the literal interpretations of the Puritans or with Pascal's recommendation that we should, provisionally, act "as if" the Scripture's account of the character and doings of God were literally reliable (xii). For such persons, he says, modern historical consciousness precludes belief in the miraculous just as modern critical

---

85. Prickett, *Words and the Word,* 63. See David J. Delaura, *Hebrew and Hellene in Victorian England: Newman, Arnold and Pater* (Austin: University of Texas Press, 1969).
86. Matthew Arnold, *Literature and Dogma* (London: Smith, 1895), 80.
87. Matthew Arnold, *God and the Bible* (London: Smith, 1887), x-xi, cf. xxxi.

methods undermine the possibility of belief in an inerrant or even verbally inspired Bible. Accordingly, a momentous point of irrevocable decision regarding the authenticity of biblical narrative has been reached:

> That a story will account for certain facts, that we wish to think it true, nay, that many have formerly thought it true and have grown faithful, humble, charitable, and so on, by thus doing, does not make the story true if it is not, and cannot prevent men after a certain time from seeing that it is not.
>
>   And on such a time we have now entered. (xiii)

That is, the narrative of the Bible will not on his view stand up to our knowledge of historical "fact," to what Arnold feels may be "verified" about God. Concerning just exactly what this process of verification would be he is not very clear; that the Bible should be granted a more or less perspicuous reading in respect of what it attributes to God, on the other hand, he rejects absolutely. He insists that "no one has discovered the nature of God to be personal, or is entitled to assert that God has conscious intelligence" (13). On this basis he concludes:

> We have to renounce impossible attempts to receive the legendary and miraculous matter of Scripture as grave historical and scientific fact. We have to accustom ourselves to regard henceforth all this part as poetry and legend. (235)

Any language which suggests otherwise is itself merely "poetic" or "literary," certainly not "scientific" (6).

Arnold's portentious high seriousness and dogged concern to assert his authenticity led T. S. Eliot to suggest that his protestations betray "a powerful element of Puritan morality," albeit in parodic form.[88] While at one level we may readily take Eliot's point, at another the association misleads; Arnold's own notion of a "scientific" definition of God, such as will reach behind the merely poetic to something which can be regarded as in his sense authentic, is curiously contorted in a way which confounds Puritan directness:

88. T. S. Eliot, "Arnold and Pater," in *Selected Essays* (London: Faber and Faber, 1932; 1972), 434.

"A personal First Cause, that thinks and loves, the moral and intelligent governor of the universe," is the sense which theologians in general assume to be the meaning, properly drawn out and strictly worded, of the term God. We say that by this assumption a great deal which cannot possibly be verified is put into the word "God"; and we propose, for the God of the Bible and of Christianity, a much less pretentious definition, but which has the advantage of containing nothing that cannot be verified. The God of the Bible and of Christianity is, we say: *The Eternal, not ourselves, that makes for righteousness.* (6-7)

His central claim in this work is that he wants to save the Bible for culture, and that to do so he has to rescue it from the ignominy of boorish and irrational middle-class piety: "We want to recommend the Bible and its religion," he repeats, "by showing that they rest on something which can be verified" (7). "Poetry," for this poet and professor of poetry, is most definitely not a basis for such verification. As Prickett has shown, poetry is for Arnold merely "the husk that protects the seed" or kernel of scientific facticity.[89] Yet, paradoxically, the only merits he allows the Bible's own narratives are in the end a matter of cultural values; as George Tyrell, the Catholic modernist, wryly observes, what Arnold seems really "to have hoped for was, roughly speaking, the preservation of the ancient and beautiful husk after the kernel had been withered up and discarded."[90]

God and the Bible was written largely to answer a huge chorus of hostile criticism of *Literature and Dogma.* It came from many quarters within British Christendom, as well as without, and Arnold's preface shows that he was stung by much of this rejection, and angered especially by those he took to be instigating spokesmen for its most sharply defined point of view. Curiously enough, Dwight L. Moody, the American evangelist, and Ira Sankey, his partner in charge of music, are the featured villains of Arnold's initial pages, and they reappear for condemnation in the conclusion of the text proper.

Moody and Sankey had begun an evangelistic tour of Great Britain

89. Prickett, *Words and the Word,* 64.

90. See Nicholas Sagovsky, *Between Two Worlds: George Tyrell's Relationship with the Thought of Matthew Arnold* (Cambridge: Cambridge University Press, 1983), 25.

in 1873,[91] the year that *Literature and Dogma* was published. The tour met with unexpected success and lasted for two full years, until 1875, just about the time Arnold's *apologia* came onto the bookstands. Moody's unflamboyant, commonsensical manner of preaching the gospel appealed to his British audiences, and he was supported by clergy of all denominations. A Congregationalist lay preacher, Moody had begun his working life as a Boston shopman. With his background in the YMCA and in a nineteenth-century version of urban renewal, he was interested in both the redemption of souls and the renewal of society which might follow from that. This, too, seems to have appealed to his British audiences. Unsophisticated as a theologian, Moody was nevertheless a gifted orator, and made powerful use of this gift both straightforwardly to recount biblical narrative and to illustrate its lessons with analagous tales from contemporary life. Hundreds of thousands of people heard him during this time, and there were thousands of converts. As a result, evangelical views of the Bible's authenticity and its authority for faith and life were given renewed and widespread prominence.

Arnold went to hear the American evangelist preach, from what motives we may only guess. His synopsis in *God and the Bible* must be in part caricature, but it is worth reflection:

> I heard Mr. Moody preach to one of his vast audiences on a topic eternally attractive — salvation by Jesus Christ. Mr. Moody's account of that salvation was exactly the old story, to which I have often adverted, of the contract in the council of the Trinity. Justice puts in her claim, said Mr. Moody, for the punishment of guilty mankind; God admits it. Jesus intercedes, undertakes to bear their punishment, and signs an undertaking to that effect. Thousands of years pass; Jesus is on the cross on Calvary. Justice appears, and presents to him his signed undertaking. Jesus accepts it, bows his head, and expires. Christian salvation consists in the undoubting belief in the transaction here described, and in the hearty acceptance of the release offered by it.
>
> Never let us deny to this story power and pathos, or treat with

91. Mark A. Noll, *A History of Christianity in the United States and Canada* (Grand Rapids: Eerdmans, 1992), 288.

hostility ideas which have entered so deep into the life of Christendom. But the story is not true; it never really happened. (xiv)

Arnold's argument against Moody makes him party to a confusion of biblical narrative and illustrative narrative which could not, under examination to see if it might be "verified," be sustained. Speaking of Moody's version of the old medieval allegory of the "Four Daughters of God,"[92] he rejects the veracity of the gospel account of the crucifixion along with that of the illustrative tale: "These personages never did meet together," he seamlessly continues, "and speak, and act, in the manner related. The personages of the Christian Heaven and their conversation are no more matter of fact than the personages of the Greek Olympus and their conversations" (xiv). Nor did Jesus' disciples actually understand him, "if he talked to them at all" (198). To the undeniable fact of Moody's success among his countrymen he replies with class-snobbism, and attack upon the evident lack of Arnold's kind of high-culture among Moody's hearers:

> Mr. Moody's audiences are the last people who will come to perceive all this; they are chiefly made up from the main body of lovers of our popular religion, — the serious and steady middle class, with its bounded horizons. To the more educated class above this, and to the more free class below it, the grave beliefs of the religious middle class in such stories as Mr. Moody's story of the Covenant of Redemption are impossible now; to the religious middle class itself they will be impossible soon. Salvation by Jesus Christ, therefore, if it has any reality, must be placed somewhere else than in a hearty consent to Mr. Moody's story. Something Mr. Moody and his hearers have experienced from Jesus, let us own, which does them good; but of this something they have not yet succeeded in getting the right history. (xv)

Arnold's condescension is transparent, expressing the disdain a self-styled educational elite reserves for the painfully unfashionable and yet-to-be

---

92. Familiar medieval versions are the adaptation of Grosseteste's parable, drawn on Ps. 85:10, in the morality play *Castle of Perseverance* and in the widely popular *Meditations on the Life of Christ*.

elevated underclasses.[93] Such persons are, like Moody and Sankey, hapless unfortunates who require that the authenticity of the Bible be constituted of both factual and spiritual truth together, indivisible as in the body of Christ; they think the authenticity of the text guaranteed by its status as revelation, and refuse to understand that mankind is actually saved by a superior and esoteric knowledge such as Arnold could give them if they would only pay him more respectful attention. "It is the habit of increased intellectual seriousness," Arnold intones,

> bred of a wider experience and of a larger acquaintance with men's mental history, which is now transforming religion in our country. Intelligent people among the educated classes grow more and more sceptical of the miraculous data which supply the basis for our received theology. The habit is a conquest of the advancing human race; it spreads and spreads, and will be on the whole and in the end a boon to us. But many and many an individual it may find unprepared for it, and may act upon him injuriously. Goethe's saying is well known: "All which merely frees our spirit, without giving us the command over ourselves, is deleterious." (xx-xxi)

The unintended effect of Arnold's citation of Goethe in relation to religious high-seriousness and anti-supernaturalism is to underscore the distance that has been traveled in his search for authentic narrative. His announced intent, on the other hand, justifies Eliot's remark that "the effect of Arnold's religious campaign is to divorce Religion from Thought," and, in Eliot's yet more apt summary, suggests how "The total effect of Arnold's philosophy is to set up Culture in the place of Religion, and to leave Religion to be laid waste by the anarchy of feeling."[94] Eliot's criticism of Arnold is naturally formulated from the point of prospect afforded by his own Anglo-Catholicism, and his suspicion of subjectivist claims to be able to verify categorically higher reality on the basis of singular experience is to that degree *partis pri*. But he has surely touched upon that most vulnerable chink in the old Puritan armor — Bunyan's sense that the authority of the

---

93. Some of this tone attaches even to Northrop Frye's *Creation and Recreation* (Toronto: University of Toronto Press, 1980) and *The Great Code: The Bible and Literature* (London: Routledge, 1982).

94. Eliot, *Selected Essays*, 434, 436.

Bible, its claim to universal truth, is sufficiently authenticated by the confirmation of personal experience alone. The "water from one's own cistern" may not in the end prove to be that sort after whose draught one never thirsts again, or to put it more plainly, it may become too easy to confuse the one sort of water with the other. To the degree this is so, the authenticity one peddles may become a small draught indeed. Eliot captures the well-spring of Arnold's confusion in a terse aside in his essay on Bradley, but the application might easily be far wider:

> In *Culture and Anarchy,* which is probably his [Arnold's] greatest book, we hear something said about 'the will of God'; but the 'will of God' seems to become superseded in importance by 'our best self, or right reason to which we want to give authority'; and this best self looks very much like Matthew Arnold slightly disguised.[95]

Who could doubt that Arnold's kind of easy, almost unconscious imposture is a species of the untoward but spiritualized self-preoccupation against which Baxter had tried to make warning?

The petulance of Arnold's *God and the Bible* is almost its overriding quality — rivaling its self-importance and condescension. Yet we cannot, any more than Eliot, afford to dismiss it on these grounds. In making his case for "culture" as the one viable religion, and himself as its current high priest, Arnold has to get the Bible safely out of the way. The way to do that, he reasons, is by reducing the familiar "witness in the heart" to "sentiment," and the prophetic and miraculous content of biblical narrative to "poetry" and the sphere of the merely literary. In this effort he has made of the Bible what in America Emily Dickinson would call an "antique volume," a curiosity and relic of culture, great in its cultural importance but as dated and stale as the tombs of the Pharaohs. Even from the point of view of the Bible as literature Arnold would leave his readers with a text which has authenticity only to the degree that we see its narrative as, strictly speaking, untrue.

Meanwhile, on a ship returning to America, Dwight L. Moody and Ira Sankey were preparing to bring their revivalist gospel to a decadent Puritan culture in some ways yet more curious than that which they had left behind.

95. Eliot, "Francis Herbert Bradley," in *Selected Essays,* 452.

Chapter Nine

The Bible and the American Myth

God has, in this American quarter of the globe, provided for the woman and her seed. . . . He has wrought out a very glorious deliverance for them, and set them free from the cruel rod of tyranny and oppression . . . leading them to the good land of Canaan, which he gave them for an everlasting inheritance.

SAMUEL SHERWOOD (1776)

We Americans are the peculiar, chosen people — the Israel of our time.

HERMAN MELVILLE (1849)

The promised kingdom is America Now.

ELIZABETH CLARE PROPHET (1993)

WHEN THE PILGRIMS FIRST SET FOOT ASHORE AT PLYMOUTH THEIR Bibles arrived with them, not just in the physical sense of many well-worn copies but as a conscious and vividly developed mythography. Partially codified in marginal notes to the Geneva and subsequently King James versions, the volatile and still evolving Puritan understanding of the Bible would become almost at once the charter and provisional blueprint for life in a new "promised land."[1] Back in Europe, with the advent of Christianity more than a millenium past, the stories of the Bible had only gradually displaced pagan mythography. In America, by contrast, the Bible supplied for wave upon wave of seventeenth-century immigrants their foundational cultural text; there was no rival to it. In hindsight it must be admitted that this was far from the unblemished virtue it seemed to many among the Pilgrims. As a foundational text, the Bible was looked to by early Americans as the code of practical justice and hence sometimes tended to be read by them with more attention to matters of law than of love, with more concern for covenant than for charity. The special developments in Calvinism characteristic of the American Puritans lent themselves to a strong focus on national destiny, with sometimes a corresponding weakness in the ability to articulate a redemptive approach to personal morality. Both Puritan and later writers sought to repair this deficit, as we shall see, with varying degrees of success.

From the beginning the Bible was so central to the idiom of American literature that classic American writers of subsequent generations, including even notoriously antinomian ones such as Emily Dickinson, are not quite intelligible without some knowledge of the foundational text. Even Walt Whitman can insist that his immediate preparation for writing his triumphantly egoist *Leaves of Grass* was to "go over thoroughly the Old and New Testaments,"[2] and his poetry shows, how-

---

1. For a concise overview, see Mark A. Noll, *A History of Christianity in the United States and Canada* (Grand Rapids: Eerdmans, 1992), 30-113. A useful general history is Edmund S. Morgan, *Visible Saints: The History of a Puritan Idea* (Ithaca: Cornell University Press, 1963). See also Harry S. Stout, *The New England Soul: Preaching and Religious Culture in Colonial New England* (New York: Oxford University Press, 1986); Patricia U. Buonomi, *Under the Cope of Heaven: Religion, Society and Politics in Colonial America* (New York: Oxford University Press, 1986); George M. Marsden, *Religion and American Culture* (San Diego: Harcourt Brace Jovanovich, 1990); and Martin Marty, *Pilgrims in Their Own Land: Five Hundred Years of Religion* (Boston: Little, Brown, 1984).

2. In "A Backward Glance O'er Traveled Roads"; see Roy Harvey Pearce, *The Continuity of American Poetry* (Princeton: Princeton University Press, 1961), 72. Of Dickinson Thomas H. Johnson writes that the Bible was her "primary source, and no other is of comparable importance." Noting the verbal resonance of the King James Version in particular, he offers the judgment that "the shaping of her thought in terms of biblical incident, events and precept is apparent in almost every poem that she wrote," and that accordingly her poetry requires "on the part of the reader a like familiarity if

ever counterintuitively, that the Bible suggested the form for his own personal American myth. Indeed, so pervasive is the American tendency to engraft personal and national ideas into the biblical history that even a modern scholarly assessment such as Giles Gunn's *The Bible and American Arts and Letters* can have as its opening sentences the following declaration:

> In a manner that finds no exact parallel in any other nation, the Bible has become America's book. The Bible has become America's book not only because Americans like to think that they have read it more assiduously than any other people, but also because Americans like to think that the Bible is the book that they, more than any other people, have been assiduously read by.[3]

The extravagance of this claim is its most representative feature.

Puritans and the Bible in New England

Especially since the canon-forming work of Perry Miller,[4] students of literature have learned to relate the shaping influence of the Bible upon the American imagination to the Puritans. In a fashion not fully anticipated in European literature,[5] the apocalyptic fervor of seventeenth-

---

the full import is to be rendered." See Johnson's *Emily Dickinson: An Interpretive Biography* (Cambridge: Belknap Press, Harvard, 1955), 151, 153. (Roger Lundin is currently preparing a new biographical study, in which this particular judgment of Johnson's is amply confirmed.)

3. Giles Gunn, ed., *The Bible and American Arts and Letters* (Philadelphia: Fortress Press; Chico: Scholars Press, 1983), 1.

4. Perry Miller, *The New England Mind: From Colony to Province* (1953; reprint, Boston: Beacon Press, 1961) and *Errand into the Wilderness* (Cambridge, Mass.: Harvard University Press, 1956) have often been challenged, but are the benchmark studies against which the work of later scholars such as Haller and Bercovitch have been essayed.

5. Thus, though the temporal blessings of the Old Testament might be understood by Christians generally as figuring forth spiritual blessings for those "called according to the New Covenant," the American Puritans felt that in their New Canaan the blessings of the Old Covenant — land, prosperity and national fulfillment — would equally be theirs. For Increase Mather, one could affirm of New England that "Without doubt, the

century Puritan theology readily expressed itself in the New World in simultaneously historicist and yet utopian and millennial terms. The instinct for this is already observable in John Winthrop's sermon "A Model of Christian Charity" preached in 1630 to the crew and Pilgrim passengers aboard the *Arbella* during their mid-Atlantic passage to the New World. For Winthrop, the biblical (and Calvinist) idea of God's covenant with his elect extends in a privileged way to the Pilgrims:

> Thus stands the cause between God and us: we are entered into covenant with Him for this work; we have taken out a commission, the Lord hath given us leave to draw up our own articles.[6]

Cotton Mather, author of the *Magnalia Christi Americana* (1698; publ. 1702 as "The Great Acts of Christ in America"), claimed a special visionary call to his vocation, and in this landmark religio-political magnum opus turned the church history of the colonies into an apocalyptic prophecy. Mather advertises himself as "Herald of the Lord's Kingdome now approaching," but in interpreting the Bible's "Prophetical as well as . . . Historical Calendar," he foretells "The Last Hours of Time" in a way contradictory to every European precedent. He sees this not as the end of all temporal kingdoms but rather as "Good Tidings of Great Joy" of a worldly "New Jerusalem" — none other than the New England which should expand, westering, in a "last conflict with the anti-christ," pushing out its frontiers to "the utmost parts of the earth" to bring about in America the biblical millennium.[7] More Augustinian Puritans like Roger Williams decried this hermeneutic temporizing; others like John Owen denounced the American attempt to "make particular Churches to be a species of the Universal Church," though to little or

---

Lord Jesus hath a peculiar respect unto this place and for this people. This is Immanuels Land. Christ by a wonderful Providence hath dispossessed Satan, who reigned securely in these Ends of the Earth . . . and here the Lord hath caused as it were New Jerusalem to come down from Heaven: he dwells in this place. . . ." See his *The Day of Trouble is Near* (Cambridge, Mass., 1674), 12-14; quoted in Sacvan Bercovitch, *The American Jeremiad* (Madison: University of Wisconsin Press, 1978), 60.

6. Perry Miller, ed., *The American Puritans: Their Prose and Poetry* (New York: Doubleday Anchor, 1956), 82.

7. Cotton Mather, *Magnalia Christi Americana* (1702), ed. Thomas Robbins (Hartford: S. Andrus & Son, 1853-55), 1.44, 46; 2.579.

no avail. In Sacvan Bercovitch's concise analysis, the irresistible appeal of the American Puritan typology was that it granted the opportunity to have one's covenant blessings in two currencies:

> With all other Christians, the New England Puritans believed that what the Old Testament described as material rewards were to be understood as spiritual blessings. They had only one reservation: the case was different in New Canaan. Here, as nowhere else, the wheel of fortune and the wheel of grace revolved in harmony.[8]

In a fashion unprecedented in Christian cultural history American Puritan divines applied biblical promises about the coming millennium to America, as if New England had become a heavenly kingdom in the here and now.

American public rhetoric of the eighteenth century persisted in similar curious adaptations of apocalyptic biblical idiom to every sphere of life. In the advocacy of free trade, for instance, John Murray and Ebenezer Baldwin looked for America to become "Immanuel's Land . . . Seat of that glorious Kingdom, which Christ shall erect upon Earth in the latter days."[9] In educational reform, Charles Turner claimed that "if all the youth were educated in the manner we recommend, *The Kingdom of God would appear.*"[10] "If we maintain our rate of westward expansion," said Rev. John Mellen in his *Sermon . . . before the Governor of Massachussetts* (1797), the conquest will be that triumph "which the scripture prophecies represent as constituting the glory of the latter days."[11] Philip Freneau and H. Henry Brackenridge see America as the place where

> the pure Church, descending from her God
> Shall fix on earth her long and lost abode . . .

And if, as they imagine, America is an Eden without the inconvenience of the "dangerous tree" or "tempting serpent," America ought to prove

---

8. Bercovitch, *American Jeremiad*, 46-47.

9. John Murray, *Nehemiah, or, the Struggle for Liberty* (1779); Ebenezer Baldwin, *The Duty of Rejoicing* (1776).

10. Charles Turner, *Due Glory Given to God* (1783).

11. Page 28, quoted in Bercovitch, *American Jeremiad*, 114.

more than mere earthly paradise, but indeed a celestial Zion.[12] By means of their temporized eschatology, self-referential exegesis, and biblical political rhetoric, the Puritans had by the end of the eighteenth century come to influence the eclectic American identity with a characteristic sense of destiny out of all proportion to their own declining percentage of the population. So effectively did they accomplish their mythic vision that, as Bercovitch is able to observe, the Puritans "provided the scriptural basis for what we have come to regard as the myth of America."[13]

Nor did the authority of this enthusiastic myth of America as proleptic heavenly kingdom entirely disappear in the more utilitarian nineteenth century. Timothy Dwight, president of Yale and signer of the Declaration of Independence, had also represented America as "by heaven design'd" to be the second, flawless "Eden" in his nostalgic epic *Conquest of Canaan* (1775). In 1812 he could still speak of the American continent as "soon to be filled with the praise, and the piety of the millennium; *here,* is the stem of that wonderful tree whose topmost boughs will reach the heavens."[14] James Russell Lowell's Harvard "Oration Ode" (1865) likewise praises America as "the Promised Land / That flows with Freedom's honey and milk."[15]

Some of this hyperbole, to be sure, was just the ingrained habit of acculturated and formal public discourse, which in any culture tends to be "preachy" in the best of times. Part, however, followed from the deep-rootedness of biblical narrative in the American popular imagination. So entrenched is the text that even a spiritual expatriate such as

12. "A Poem on the Rising Glory of America," in *Colonial American Poetry,* ed. Kenneth Silverman (New York: Doubleday Anchor, 1968), 440f.

13. Sacvan Bercovitch, "The Biblical Basis of the American Myth," in *Bible and American . . . Letters,* 219-29, here citing 221. Cf. here Jon Butler, *Awash in a Sea of Faith: Christianizing the American People* (Cambridge, Mass.: Harvard University Press, 1990), who shows that civic religion in the colonies was always more eclectic and syncretistic of pagan, occultist, and masonic elements than retrospective nineteenth-century Calvinist estimates in particular would imagine. And it may be that the selective biblicism of deist Thomas Jefferson (1743-1826), with his scissors-and-paste reduction of the Gospels (sometimes called *The Jefferson Bible*), is the more representative strategy. Jefferson's bowdlerized gospel omits all references to the supernatural and miraculous, the Holy Spirit, and the resurrection, so as to come up with an ethical but not divine Jesus.

14. Quoted in Bercovitch, *American Jeremiad,* 130.

15. William Michael Rossetti, ed., *The Poetical Works of James Russell Lowell* (London and New York, 1889), 298.

Ralph Waldo Emerson, in the midst of his railings at "sulphurous Calvinism" and his exultant, almost Faustian determination upon "Self-
Reliance," can find to his chagrin that "Out from the heart of nature
rolled / The burdens of the Bible old."[16] Yet among many antinomian
American writers of the second half of the nineteenth century, even
where King James biblical phrasing colors their every page, we can
readily detect as well a growing resistance to these now increasingly
archaic and (for them) associatively "Puritan" formulations. It is in this
tension between a flamboyant anti-Puritanism among later nineteenth-
century writers and the mythic consciousness of their more reflexively
biblicist readers that the modern myth of the Bible as "America's book"
was being forged.[17]

Second-Guessing the Blueprint

We may capture the evolution of this tension, for example, in the career
of Herman Melville. In his early and philosophically discursive political
novel *White Jacket: or, the World in a Man-of-War* (1850), Melville

16. Ralph Waldo Emerson, "The Problem" (1839). Emerson, as he often pointed
out, was himself descended from Puritan stock and not entirely out of sympathy with
what he took to be some of their first principles. Interesting insights into Emerson's
views in this respect are afforded in the use he makes of Milton's poetry and especially
his *Christian Doctrine*. See here K. P. Van Anglen, *The New England Milton: Literary
Reception and Cultural Authority in the Early Republic* (University Park, Penn.: Pennsyl-
vania State University Press, 1993), chaps. 3-4. Emerson's affection for Rousseau and
Montaigne could take on a self-conscious Faustian edge: in one of his journal entries,
written in Canterbury, England, on April 18, 1824, he performs a Calvinistic inventory
of professional options which transparently mimes the opening lines of Marlowe's play.
Considering and rejecting law and medicine, he declares, "But in Divinity I hope to
thrive." At the end of this self-adulating reflection he writes: "Spin on, ye of the ad-
amantine spindle, spin on my fragile thread." See *The Journals and Miscellaneous Note-
books of Ralph Waldo Emerson*, 16 vols., ed. W. H. Gilman, A. R. Ferguson, and M. R.
Davis (Cambridge, Mass.: Belknap, Harvard University Press, 1961), 2.237-42, esp. 239.

17. Cf. Gunn, *Bible and American . . . Letters*, 1-9; also Richard A. Grusin, *Tran-
scendentalist Hermeneutics: Institutional Authority and Higher Criticism of the Bible* (Durham: Duke University Press, 1991), a useful revisionist exploration of the hermeneutic
principles shared by Emerson, Thoreau, and Theodore Parker.

includes a traditional Puritan-like passage on national destiny. Offered as a narrative commentary, it includes these stirring words:

> The Future [is] the Bible of the Free. . . . We Americans are driven to a rejection of the maxims of the Past, seeing that, ere long, the van of the nations must, of right, belong to ourselves. . . . Escaped from the house of bondage, Israel of old did not follow after the ways of the Egyptians. To her was given an express dispensation; to her were given new things under the sun. And we Americans are the peculiar, chosen people — the Israel of our time; we bear the ark of the liberties of the world.[18]

There is no more room for doubt, Melville wryly concludes:

> God has given us, for a future inheritance, the broad domains of the political pagan, that shall yet come and lie down under the shade of our ark, without bloody hands being lifted. God has predestinated, mankind expects, great things from our race; and great things we feel in our souls. The rest of the nations must soon be in our rear. We are the pioneers of the world . . . the political Messiah has come. But he has come in us, if we would but give utterance to his promptings. And let us always remember, that with ourselves — almost for the first time in the history of the earth — national selfishness is unbounded philanthropy; for we cannot do a good to America but we give alms to the world. (152-53)

Clearly there is grist enough here for the grinding of many a post-colonial historian's mill. It must be added, however, that Melville's view of these matters grew more complex: by the time of his *Confidence Man* (1857), the "ship of state" is not the triumphant "Man-of-War" (in the full title of *White Jacket*) but the symbolic American ship of faith, the *Fidele*. Yet this is the ship which is boarded by Satan, who then deconstructs the authority of all the old texts and, in effect, demonstrates that their Puritan rhetoric notwithstanding, there are now no virtuous captains left — indeed, not even any real Christians aboard the ship.

18. Herman Melville, *White-Jacket; or, The World in a Man-of-War* (Oxford and New York: Oxford University Press, 1967), 152-53.

Although juxtaposing these two novels compresses somewhat Melville's own ambiguities, the contrast indicates a more general and growing disenchantment among American intellectuals with the predominant Calvinian typology and its attendant political covenantalism.[19] Nathaniel Hawthorne's pivotal novel *The Scarlet Letter* (1850) contains a stirring sermon passage so strikingly "Puritan" as to verge on satire. Dimmesdale's election-day address is described as reflecting all the familiar biblical terms, but coupled with this affected "reportage" is the narrator's critical reflection on the key strategy of the myth itself:

> And as he drew to a close, a spirit as of prophecy had come upon him, constraining him to its purpose as mightily as the old prophets of Israel were constrained; only with this difference, that, whereas the Jewish seers had denounced judgments and ruin on their country, it was his mission to foretell a high and glorious destiny for the newly gathered people of the Lord.[20]

Dimmesdale is a charlatan of that type destined to become stereotype in a revisionary American cynicism (or countermyth). That is, he is a perverter of the text he claims to proclaim, his sermon a contradiction in terms. Hawthorne has already noticed — much as did Melville in *The Confidence Man* and, more painfully, in *Pierre* and *Billy Budd* — that with respect to *meaning* the old American myth so "preached" is not really "biblical" at all. In this respect neither writer was criticizing the Bible itself so much as an eccentric reading of the Bible. Indeed, what Hawthorne and Melville seem to say is that, familiar King James phrases aside, the public and putatively "biblical" myth of America is in many crucial respects *antibiblical,* antigospel.

This observation, however conventional, raises important questions for subsequent history of biblical mythography in America. What Hawthorne notes as incongruously missing from the unenlightened Dimmesdale's sermon is the central biblical question of national accountability for a would-be "chosen" people: their requisite of corre-

19. See here Edwin Cady, " 'As Through a Glass Eye, Darkly': The Bible in the Nineteenth-Century American Novel," in Gunn, *Bible and American . . . Letters,* 33-56.

20. Nathaniel Hawthorne, *The Scarlet Letter,* ed. Harry Levin (Boston: Beacon, 1961), 261.

spondence to divine law, and the inevitability of judgment upon their moral failure should they act inconsistently with that covenant. Or to put it another way, Dimmesdale, too typically of the tradition, is in his self-assurance unwilling to link his triumphalist millennial promises to a prerequisite of national faithfulness.[21] Hawthorne rejects the Calvinist tendency toward presumption of righteousness in the so-called "covenant people" and the easy transference of this presumptuousness to a national myth in which America as a nation has been tacitly designated the one true bearer of the Covenant, the ultimate "New Israel." In the moral analysis of his novel, Hawthorne suggests to us that any credible notion of covenant promise must be conditional to some extent on credible covenant obedience: in this much his critique of the falsely "biblical" myth is thus itself most properly biblical.

In *Billy Budd* (not published until 1924) and *Pierre* (1852) Melville comes at false biblicism in the American myth in another way: a truly biblical identity, Melville suggests, would be rooted in the recognition not merely of sin but of suffering. The pertinent biblical model is thus not the triumphant millennial perfection of the heavenly kingdom, the "glory of Zion," but rather participation in the struggle to redeem a sin-sick world, the imperfections of which make the biblical doctrine not only of charity but also of substitutionary atonement and repentance so unavoidable — and so self-qualifying. Another way of putting this might be to say that Melville seems to wish to move his reader's biblical consciousness forward from a covenant typology drawn from the Old Testament to a more plausibly New Testament sense of temporal purpose and ethical accountability.[22] Melville's tentatively biblical an-

21. Cf. Fredrik Crews, *The Sins of the Fathers: Hawthorne's Psychological Themes* (Berkeley: University of California Press, 1989), 146-49.

22. Melville's poem "The Enthusiast" enacts his need to distance himself from his own Calvinist roots, and describes his sense of Calvinism's oppression in imagery drawn from the book of Job (13:14-18). For Melville, persistence in "trust" was painfully exacting and finally self-destructive, at least for his writing, as his poem "A Spirit Appeared to Me" suggests. See here Nathalia Wright, *Melville's Use of the Bible* (Durham: Duke University Press, 1949; reprint, 1969); N. A. Nelson, "Herman Melville's Use of the Bible in *Billy Budd*," *DAI* 39 (1979): 4987A-88A; cf. Thomas Werge, "Moby Dick and the Calvinist Tradition," *StN* 1 (1969): 484-506; John Timmerman, "Typology and Biblical Consistency in *Billy Budd*," *Religion and Literature* 15, no. 1 (1983): 23-50; Susan Van Zanten Gallagher, "The Sane Madness of Vital Truth: Prophets and Prophecy in the Fiction of Herman Melville," *DAI* 43, no. 10 (1983): 3317A; cf. also C. R. LaBossiere,

tidote is accordingly not a model for "success" but, in temporal terms at least, for its opposite: the life lived "foolishly" *imitatio Christi*. It was an alternative, at least as he haltingly tried to formulate it, which seemed not to be widely understood in Melville's America. Or, perhaps, in any America.

Political Prophet

These nineteenth-century expressions of doubt about the biblical grounding of the myth of America prove accurate harbingers of biblical typology's twentieth-century demise. The questioning has intensified, if for no other reason than that prominent versions of the old Puritan myth persist at the political rather than religious and literary levels.[23]

In American politics of the twentieth century too, the incentive to ground complex agendas in simple myths and symbols has often led to the use of biblical slogans. A highly self-conscious example of this tactic came in the 1980 presidential campaign, during the television debate between Ronald Reagan and then President Jimmy Carter. Reagan was led to use the biblical image of the celestial Zion, the "city set upon a hill," to describe his vision of America. Reagan was quoted as saying: "This land was placed here by some divine plan. It was placed here to be found by a special kind of people, a new breed of humans called an American . . . [destined] to begin the world over again . . . [and to] build a land that will be for all mankind a shining city on a hill."[24] As Reagan's speechwriters knew, and as students of American history and literature are aware, the immediate source of this luminous phrase is John Winthrop's archetypal definition of the New England colony in his famous ship-board sermon on "Charity," preached aboard the *Arbella*. Winthrop's biblical source was Matthew 5, in which the image comes as part of Jesus' comfort — and warning — to those who would

The Victorian Fol Sage (Lewisburg: Bucknell University Press, 1989), 69, 77-85, who argues for Solomonic wisdom texts, with their censorious *vanitas vanitatem*, as Melville's chief qualifier to self-assured covenant typologies.

23. Bercovitch, "Biblical Basis of the American Myth," 224.

24. *The New York Times*, 22 September 1980.

be faithful. Biblically literate readers might also remember, however, that this text follows seamlessly upon the Beatitudes portion of the Sermon on the Mount, which begins "Blessed are the poor in spirit: for *theirs* is the kingdom of heaven" (5:3). The biblical passage is a litany of the ironic or parodoxical blessings which attend upon the meek (v. 5), those who "hunger and thirst after righteousness" (v. 6), the "peacemakers" and, indeed, those who are "persecuted for righteousness' sake" (v. 10). As the substance of the *Arbella* sermon makes evident, Winthrop himself was clear-minded enough to see Jesus' encouragement to rejoice in the face of deprivation and persecution (vv. 11-12) as well as his warning not in such adversity to fail of one's calling (v. 13) as necessary conditions for participation in what most clearly is "a kingdom *not* of this world."[25] In Matthew's Gospel it is this Christ-like identification or participation in deprivation and suffering which makes of the company of believers "the light of the world," visible, as "a city that is set on an hill cannot be hid."

In Reagan's remarks, by contrast, the biblical content is entirely missing. Gone are the original trenchant irony and bitter paradox — Jesus' expectation of suffering as the means to a felicity which is eternal, not temporal. That is because Reagan's "city set on an hill" reflects not Jesus' symbol for a community of conditionally bound suffering servants passing *through* the world but the later and decadent Puritan mythic strategy for having one's heavenly kingdom *in* this world. A much less biblically literate late twentieth-century audience seems not to have noticed the textual violence occasioned by the future president's dislocation of the Matthew text — an "obtuseness to the spirit" upon which his speechwriters could presumably depend. A telling irony in all of this is that part of the point of having Reagan use such an old Puritan biblical borrowing was to appeal to so-called "Bible-belt" Americans, the "religious right" who made up such an important part of Reagan's political constituency.

25. Winthrop's sermon is, after all, on the subject of charity and mutual self-transcendence. There is here no reference yet either to the celestial New Jerusalem or to a terrestrial substitute in America; the call is rather to an imminent "duty of love" by which "we must love brotherly without dissimulation, we must love one another with a pure heart fervently, we must bear one another's burdens, we must not look only on our own things but also on the things of our brethren" (Miller, *American Puritans*, 82). These words did not find their way into the presidential candidate's address.

In respect of the political advantages of this calculated cleavage between mythic biblical language and the actual content of the Bible, it may be that political strategists, verily, have had their reward. By the later 1980s speechwriters were increasingly loathe to turn to Puritan evocations of King James diction to valorize the actual myth of America, the gospel of success, or the heavenly kingdom in the here and now. While there seem to be many reasons for this, one is surely the increasingly visible reappearance of the old nineteenth-century critique of the lack of correspondence between the "biblical" myth of America and the Bible. This had already become a subject among writers after World War II — one thinks of Robert Lowell's trenchant poem "Children of Light," in which the Puritans are cast as the very serpents in the New Eden which they claimed to be serpent-free.[26] As in the cases of Melville and Hawthorne, the critique came largely from without rather than from within the "Bible-belt" community, but, as then, the standards by which the charges of hypocrisy were framed were nonetheless based upon a New Testament ethic. The persona in Howard Nemerov's "Boom," a satire of Washington civic religion, for example, speaks in a way that inescapably recalls the attitude of Jesus toward "certain among the Pharisees." The epigraph comes from an Associated Press newsclip dated June 23, 1957, captioned "Sees Boom in Religion, Too." It reads:

> *Atlantic City. — President Eisenhower's pastor said tonight that Americans are living in a period of "unprecedented religious activity" caused partially by paid vacations, the eight-hour day and modern conveniences.*
>
> *"These fruits of material progress," said the Rev. Edward L. R. Elson of the National Presbyterian Church, Washington, "have provided the leisure, the energy, and the means for a level of human and spiritual values never before reached."*

Nemerov's jaded narrator speaks as an observer at a presidential function.

---

26. Robert Lowell, "Children of the Light," in *The Oxford Book of American Verse*, ed. F. O. Matthiessen (New York: Oxford University Press, 1950; reprint, 1964), 1092-93.

Here at the Vespasian-Carlton, it's just one
religious activity after another; the sky
is constantly being crossed by cruciform
airplanes, in which nobody disbelieves
for a second, and the tide, the tide
of spiritual progress and prosperity
miraculously keeps rising, to a level
never before attained. The churches are full,
the beaches are full, and the filling-stations
are full, God's great ocean is full
of paid vacationers praying an eight-hour day
to the human and spiritual values, the fruits,
the leisure, the energy, and the means, Lord,
the means for the level, the unprecedented level,
and the modern conveniences, which also are full.
Never before, O Lord, have the prayers and praises
from belfry and phonebooth, from ballpark and barbecue
the sacrifices, so endlessly ascended.

Nemerov's observer is clearly neither a speechwriter nor in the employ of an organ for the dissemination of civic enthusiasm. His point of instructive dissent, however wryly formulated, has to do not only with the self-indulgent banalities of the American gospel of success but also with its effortless nonengagement of human suffering which, in other historical precincts, made the original gospel *evangelion,* good news:

It was not thus when Job in Palestine
sat in the dust and cried, cried bitterly;
when Damien kissed the lepers on their wounds
it was not thus; it was not thus
when Francis worked a fourteen-hour day
strictly for the birds; when Dante took
a week's vacation without pay and it rained
part of the time, O Lord, it was not thus.

In the poem's final stanza, Nemerov turns away from the "then" of the Bible and its discomfiting encouragement of exegesis-as-praxis to imagining the mock-worship of a modern Pharisee, making public prayer in an obviously American temple:

> But now the gears mesh and the tires burn
> and the ice chatters in the shaker and the priest
> in the pulpit, and Thy Name, O Lord,
> is kept before the public, while the fruits
> ripen and religion booms and the level rises
> and every modern convenience runneth over,
> that it may never be with us as it hath been
> with Athens and Karnak and Nagasaki,
> nor Thy sun for one instant refrain from shining
> on the rainbow Buick by the breezeway
> or the Chris Craft with the uplift life raft;
> that we may continue to be the just folks we are,
> plain people with ordinary superliners and
> disposable diaperliners, people of the stop'n'shop
> 'n'pray as you go, of hotel, motel, boatel,
> the humble pilgrims of no deposit no return
> and please adjust thy clothing, who will give to Thee,
> if Thee will keep us going, our annual
> Miss Universe, for Thy Name's Sake, Amen.[27]

Exponents of the "success gospel" are notoriously difficult to parody, if for no other reason than that the message they peddle is itself already a parody; in this poem, nonetheless, Nemerov has come close to succeeding.

Postmodern Jeremiad

Less humorously and still more recently this focus upon false biblicism has been sharpened in Margaret Atwood's novel, *The Handmaid's Tale*.[28]

27. *The Collected Poems of Howard Nemerov* (Chicago: University of Chicago Press, 1977), 222-23.
28. Margaret Atwood, *The Handmaid's Tale* (Toronto: McClelland and Stewart, 1985). Citations are from the Seal edition (1986).

Her alarming narrative is set in a New England sick unto death, claiming ironically and disingenuously to be governed, as Harold Pinter's screenplay of the novel compresses it, by the "Old Testament, our sole and only Constitution." In Pinter's screenplay the minister who pronounces this credo to a group of captive child-bearers himself bears striking resemblance to another source of contemporary disaffection from the myth — a host of electronic media descendants of Arthur Dimmesdale, confidence-men of the generally discreditable Elmer Gantry kind. In them, Pinter suggests, the success gospel intrinsic to the old American myth is almost perfectly self-parodied.

We touch here upon a matter of extreme sensitivity and not a little embarrassment for many evangelicals. Almost everyone in North America has seen portions of one or more televangelistic shows; a significant percentage see a great many such broadcasts in whole or in part during the course of a year. The number and variety of such programs, although more or less disproportionate to their quality, are great, and the notoriety of their personalities greater. Clearly, many who watch these television regulars — including, it would seem, presidential speechwriters — do so largely out of a yen for diversionary entertainment. Yet for many others this may be the only means by which an impression of contemporary Christianity — especially self-advertisedly "biblical" Christianity — is formed.

Within America all this has become so commonplace it scarcely deserves comment. Yet it bears repeating that the presentation of ostensibly biblical religion in this transparently self-contradictory fashion is *prima facie* evidence of a foundational confusion of God and Mammon at the heart of American biblicism. As with the corruption of Puritan millennial typology and "New Canaan" in the colonial period, so too with the typical televangelist: his or her *evangelion* is above all a key to health and wealth. On one such Sunday morning showbiz hour a decade ago I observed a preacher who seemed at first a comedian doing a take-off: the star appeared, surrounded by the usual Edenic tropical plants and stage scenery; he was dressed in a white dinner jacket with not one but three red roses in his lapel. With rolling eyes and a wobbly wave of both chubby hands he began: "Mah topic for toda-ay is, *Gawd, ah want it all!*" He then went on to declare that verification of God's blessing upon the faithful (according to his definition) could be had by visiting the parking lot of his church, where there was almost nothing of a lower status than Cadillac, Lincoln, Mercedes, and Jag-u-ar. Eventually he got down to the practical business of exchanging for donations talismanic trinkets: a "prayer-timer" (a conventional egg-timer embossed with a Bible verse) and scraps of "healing cloth" over which he had prayed ("just lay it on the a-ffected mem-ber") were the featured items *du jour*. It was as if Chaucer's Pardoner had returned from the grave.

There is also a female televangelist with a variant sales ploy for the nineties: "Reverence Woman, for she is the Mother of the Universe," she intones, claiming that "ascendant masters" have revealed to her that "The I am that I am is standing right where you are now," and that the "coming revolution in higher consciousness is the revelation of the God within us." Hence, for her as for the decadent Puritans of yesteryear, "The promised kingdom is America now." Indeed, as if to answer Atwood's dystopic feminist critique of the Puritan myth with a feminist utopianism to outdo the Puritans, in a recent broadcast she said: "I proclaim to you in the state of California, the state of Amy Semple MacPherson, the emancipation of women." Meanwhile, her followers are rumored to be bunkering down with machine guns somewhere north of Yellowstone National Park.

Where does all of this lead? For Atwood, it might lead to something at last tyrannical. In her *fin de siècle* America, the "religious right" have seized power in a coup, and while using much of the old Puritan biblical typology to effect a tyranny the most stringent of Puritans could not have imagined, they simultaneously stifle religious liberty. They are not at all Christian in any acceptable biblical sense. Catholics, Southern Baptists, and Quakers alike are "smoked out" and slaughtered; the "Children of Ham" and the "Children of Shem" are forcibly resettled or exterminated (79, 188). The "earliest church" in Cambridge becomes a museum; Harvard's library becomes a center for torture, and Harvard Yard the scene of ritual public executions.[29] Empty icons of a dessicated biblical Christianity abound: like the pillow embroidered "Faith" in the imprisoned narrator's room or the name of the new republic itself — Gilead — they are omnipresent witnesses to the absence of what they once signified. The

29. See the comments on Atwood's institutional criticism by David Staines, *Beyond the Provinces: Literary Canada at Century's End* (Toronto: University of Toronto Press, 1995), 62-63.

make-up-caked former gospel singer whose infertility the narrator is forced to redeem is named Serena Joy, but the name of one of her peers of similar pre-coup background, Bambi Mae, provides a transparent reference to yet another disgraced and tawdry televangelistic personality. Despite angrily claiming biblical authority for their despotism, the Commanders of the new regime and their "Angels of Light" military police keep actual Bibles under lock and key. "Prayvaganzas" are only for group weddings or the celebration of military victories (206). Unsurprisingly, literacy in general is also in a process of being stripped away: only in the inner lairs of the evil despots are there books which have not been transferred to computer disks and shredded. In this wordless world an illicit game of Scrabble is to the nameless narrator a luxurious indulgence in the vanishing possibility for language and meaning.[30]

Unlike the Pinter screenplay, Atwood's novel has no catharsis, or even moment of nemesis, let alone a possibility of hopeful conclusion. Her prophetic stance is Jeremiah-like — a denunciation and a cataloguing of culture-destroying consequences. Her text is also far more subtle than the film script. A feminist, she explores the possibility that a misdirected feminism might unwittingly unleash upon itself undreamt-of realizations of "woman-centered" culture (112-16, 120, 204-9, 290); herself a writer with no claims upon institutional Christianity, she suggests that actual faithfulness to biblical values is what the biblicist republic most wishes to eradicate, and that the most important weapon against the regime's perversions might be the very Bible which the despots alone now possess, heavily edited and controlled to suit their purposes. Watching the Commander lift the Bible from its locked box to read the handmaid narrative from Genesis chapter 30, the narrator, about to be subjected to a grotesque ritual mating procedure, looks from a "hungry darkness" toward the open text and thinks: "He has something we don't have, he has the word. How we squandered it, once" (84).

Apocalyptic Gilead is an America where civic religion requires of its free citizens certain pious gestures. One of these is a certain number of billings for dial-a-prayer, of which there are five prayers available in set repetitions, one each "for health, wealth, a death, a birth, a sin" (157). Out of the depths of her own enslavement and misery Atwood's pitiable narrator offers the only real biblical prayer the reader actually meets

30. Atwood, *Handmaid's Tale*, 121, 129, 145, 156, 172, 289.

with in the novel: an amplification of the Lord's Prayer (from Matt. 6:9-13), it reveals her utter dissociation of the God of the Bible and the biblicist rhetoric of the republic. "I don't believe for an instant that what's going on out there is what you meant," she prays, then poignantly asks for help to forgive her tormentors (182). Atwood's broken-hearted, suffering servant is palpably closer to the Jesus of the New Testament than the pharisaical self-righteousness of the patriarchal oligarchy of the new world order. But the point is lost on the smug academics she shows studying the archaeological remains of a self-destructed America a century later. The last chapter of the novel depicts an academic conference in the year 2095 — but it is transparently intended as a stinging rebuke of academic analysis in her own time. Her imagined surveyors of the ashes of Gilead can be moved no further than to say of the handmaid's anguished tale (to a round of self-congratulatory applause), "Our job is not to censure but to understand" (284). Yet what is apparent to Atwood's reader is that the academics of the new age understand little or nothing of the way in which their own kind of thinking inevitably opens up the slippery slope to human horrors such as Offred has been subjected to in Gilead, or, worse, that they understand well enough but lack the self-transcendence necessary to combat the slippage. Pharisaism is a durable virus, taking many forms.

In the light of Atwood's cultural criticism as well as of American religious and literary history, it is hardly an amusing irony that this should be a time of unprecedented biblical illiteracy in America. Ignorance of the contents of the Bible is pandemic not only among the secular and unchurched but notably among many of those who may well fancy themselves to be the descendents, at least spiritually, of the old Puritans. To be sure, when preaching to such folk, the modern Dimmesdale (who often has a similarly parodic Dickensian name — Falwell, Angely, Prophet, Swaggart) may carry a large Bible iconically aloft as he preaches, his thumb holding open the authoritative page. But week in and week out, it is the same page. The thumb never moves, and the sermon seems impervious to its supposed source, which is seldom directly addressed. The audience, partly as a consequence, evidently grows more and more deaf to the text.

Americans themselves are only gradually becoming aware of the shift of the center of world Christianity from North America to South America, Africa, and Asia. Yet it is increasingly unavoidable knowledge that by far the majority of what one might call "biblical" Christians now live elsewhere. Considered in relation to the political viability of a biblically intoned American myth, this fact seems to be comparably disturbing for some to earlier discoveries that a more plausible relation to biblical narrative might have been made in America itself by African-American culture. Who can doubt that in the hymns and preaching of their struggle for liberty the biblical idiom of black Americans has often rung more true than in the status quo speeches of their mainstream white counterparts? Yet these recognitions should also provide opportunity for fresh analysis.[31] Recently it has been widely recognized among Americans that in the former Soviet Union a formative role in Communism's disintegration was played by a widespread, flourishing underground Christian church. Television viewers have also witnessed illustrations of the insatiable Eastern European appetite for the Bible — to the point that even *Pravda* has begun printing it — probably oblivious to the fact that, almost simultaneously, American public education has been firmly disassociating itself from explicit identification with the American biblical heritage. All of these events and their attendant ironies for prevalent myths have been mutually reinforcing, making biblical idiom, formulation, and myth less and less distinctively "American." They also suggest that the final divorce of American public myth from its pseudobiblical foundation in this generation is almost certainly a good thing. Indeed, it may prove a salutary therapy for biblical religion as well as for the sorting out of American national identity.

Bible-Free Myth

But where do these disconnections leave the American myth? Or, to be more pointed, where do they leave the myth-makers — the presidential speechwriters included? Part of the answer, we may suspect, is already

31. See here especially Elizabeth Fox Genovese, *Within the Plantation Household: Black and White Women of the Old South* (Chapel Hill: University of North Carolina Press, 1988); Linell E. Cady, *Religion, Theology and American Public Life* (Albany, N.Y.: SUNY Press, 1993); and C. Eric Lincoln and Lawrence H. Mamiya, *The Black Church in the African-American Experience* (Durham: Duke University Press, 1990).

blowing in the wind of recent political debate. In his last election campaign President George Bush spoke repeatedly of a "new world order." This too, we readily grasp, is the language of myth. But what myth? *Novus ordo seculorum* is, of course, the motto under "the great seal" on the American dollar bill. Over this obscure back side to the seal, with its (Masonic) occult pyramid capped with a floating "eye of Providence," are the Latin words *Annuit Coeptiis,* usually translated as "It [Providence?] has overseen our undertaking" — a retrospective assurance of the divine stamp of approval for Mammon's enterprise. The point was evidently not lost on Atwood, whose Gilead republicans use this reverse seal for their ubiquitous emblem of authority.[32] It becomes the symbol of the *ad absurdam* myth anticipated in *The Handmaid's Tale* because it invokes pseudobiblical authority for a temporal "heavenly kingdom" which has in actuality been stripped of plausible reference or accountability to anything transcendent. To put it another way, it is a symbol which neatly monetizes transcendence, unsubtly deifying what Washington Irving called "the Almighty Dollar." To the modern American myth the dollar is the proffered golden bough. The Hades it might open is rejected in Edward Arlington Robinson's poem "Cassandra," whose prophet observes, "Your dollar is your only Word, / The wrath of it your only fear," and whose hard questions, directed against the myth, are those not only of third-world readers of the Bible but of secular critics much closer to home:

"What lost eclipse of history,
    What bivouac of the marching stars,
Has given the sign for you to see
    Millenniums and last great wars?

"What unrecorded overthrow
    Of all the world has ever known,
Or ever been, has made itself
    So plain to you, and you alone?

"Your Dollar, Dove and Eagle make
    A Trinity that even you

---

32. Although flags bearing the emblem feature more prominently in Pinter's screenplay than in the novel itself, their textual basis is found there; see pp. 18, 181.

Rate higher than you rate yourselves;
   It pays, it flatters, and it's new.

"And though your very flesh and blood
   Be what your Eagle eats and drinks,
You'll praise him for the best of birds,
   Not knowing what the Eagle thinks.

"The power is yours, but not the sight;
   You see not upon what you tread;
You have the ages for your guide,
   But not the wisdom to be led.

"Think you to tread forever down
   The merciless old verities?
And are you never to have eyes
   To see the world for what it is?

"Are you to pay for what you have
   With all you are?' — No other word
We caught, but with a laughing crowd
   Moved on. None heeded, and few heard."[33]

One problem with the now more or less Bible-free myth of the new world order has been that it is so *nakedly* what it is that it lacks the spiritual authority which typically accrues to myth and hence has scant literary or cultural power. Accordingly, the speechwriters have tried fishing in other texts. At the beginning of the Clinton mandate, for example, comparisons were being made to the Kennedy era, and the language of "Camelot" was dusted off. The move from biblical typos to Arthurian myth (second-guessing Milton, so to speak)[34] had — or so

33. Edwin Arlington Robinson, "Cassandra," in *Oxford Book of American Verse*, ed. Matthiesson, 490-91.

34. Milton considered following Spenser's *Faerie Queene* in using Arthurian myth as the basis for an epic theodicy, but as is well known, rejected the plan in favor of the strategy that became *Paradise Lost*. For a detailed discussion see Nicholas von Maltzahn, *Milton's History of Britain: Republican Historiography in the English Revolution* (Oxford: Clarendon Press, 1991), esp. 91-116.

it first seemed to the speechwriters — a timely appeal. A much hazier sense of the Arthurian "romance" in popular consciousness seems to have commended itself to the presidential speechwriters, who seem to have wanted a secular mythos capable of suggesting some sort of vague but reassuring continuity with the temporized and ersatz biblicism of the old Puritan America. For the modernized Arthurian legend can seem also to provide an apparent answer to the drive for unity in a pluralist world, a resolution of the political problem of the One and the Many, *e pluribus unum*. Yet more obviously another *secular* order, it offers accordingly the bargaining table, not the altar, negotiation rather than communion, as its instruments of reconciliation.

From the perspective of literary history, the expedition to Avalon has nonetheless itself been fraught with complication: no selectively appropriate myth, it seems, is without its own countervail. The resulting ironies, predictably, also tend to be overlooked by speechwriters because of their drive for a myth which is vendible — that is, triumphalist. Some of the limitations and consequences were veiled by the romance in Arthur Schlesinger's original crafting of President J. F. Kennedy's "Camelot." At the level of the popularized musical, the myth of Old England seemed therapeutic. But it did not prove sustaining nourishment for civic life, as sober readers of the medieval Authurian texts could have anticipated. Camelot in the books of Arthur was most notably a tragic failure. The naiveté of Arthur's vision of the Round Table as the solution to a tyranny of minorities collapsed disastrously because of corruption from within (Mordred, Lancelot, Guenevere).[35] So the hope in the original Camelot narrative was in the end a hope wrung out of history's disappointment, a recognition that a heavenly kingdom in the here and now has not, and will not, come about. Hence, the last available hope must be for an answer beyond history: *rex quondam, rex quae futuris* — a "once and future king." Inescapably, it would appear, Camelot circles back to a reluctant reading of the Bible, and ends by looking for another Messiah to appear and clean up the mess. For if (decadent Puritan rhetoric notwithstanding), the promised Messiah has proven *not* to be "us" after all, then what?[36] Will a people possessed of

35. D. L. Jeffrey, "Literature in an Apocalyptic Age," *Dalhousie Review* 61, no. 3 (1981): 426-46.

36. Bercovitch's question at the end of his article, "The Biblical Basis of American

a messianic complex, yet finding the messianic enterprise at last beyond their temporal means, be tempted to invent a series of show-biz messiahs to save the appearances, or some peerless Captain America onto whom the complex may be transferred, as to a sports hero, or great general? The erosion of confidence in public figures and in authority itself would seem to argue for caution concerning the probability of residually democratic solutions to the loss of a viable myth. The most recent dodge of the speechwriters, pale imitators of Mather, Sherwood, and Timothy Dwight that they are, is to return again to familiar New England territory. Clinton's "New Covenant" has for cultural and literary historians an all too old and familiar ring about it.[37]

Eschewing Scripture for the Gospel's Sake

The legacy of decadent New England Puritanism has become sufficiently tarnished in every pertinent sphere — religious, political, and literary — that modern American writers have often sought instead to demonstrate their moral seriousness by pillory of any available surviving traces. One has only to think of the novels of John Cheever, John Updike, and Bernard Malamud, or the poetry of Wallace Stevens, Robert Lowell, and Howard Nemerov to confirm the impression. But there is another strain in contemporary American writing which, Christian to the core, formulates a salutary alternative to the New England legacy. This is because it remains both oblique to the exhausted Puritan conventions and yet

---

Myth," is comparably troubling, but the answer he offers calculatedly anti-apocalyptic: "What happens when history severs the symbol from the nation, the logos from the logocracy? It is a prospect that returns us full circle to the Puritan discovery three centuries ago: *I have been to the Bible and America does not exist.* What happens when history separates 'America', divine plan and all, from the United States? Nothing much. Only relativism . . ." (228).

37. Clinton's State of the Union address was reported in *Time,* 6 February 1995, 42-53. Clinton called for a renewal of (Emersonian) self-reliance, saying "I call it the New Covenant, but it is grounded in a very, very old idea that all Americans have not just a right but a solemn responsibility to rise as far as their God-given talents and determination can take them. And to give something back to their communities and their country in return" (45).

affirmative of their original source. I refer to the work of recent southern writers, among the most eminent of whom are Flannery O'Connor, Walker Percy, and Wendell Berry. Each of these in his or her way has contributed shrewdly to a contemporary but biblically informed critique of false cultural biblicism.

O'Connor's short stories and novels reveal the rural South as biblical culture, but biblical in a completely different way than might be imagined if New England were to be used as a template. Some of the difference so evident in stories such as "Revelation" and "Everything that Rises Must Converge," for example, accrues to the considerable differences in southern cultural and historical experience.[38] African-American, poor white, or decadent plantation denizens are all recognizably marginal to mainstream American culture. Historically, each is a product of defeat, whether by enslavement, by poverty, or by coming out on the losing end of the Civil War. Perhaps because defeat and marginalization do not fit very well into the triumphalist blueprint for America as the Promised Land, the Old Testament millennialist typology of the Puritan and its attendant rhetoric have for these people had less appeal or pertinence. If Yankee literature has long been haunted by the new Israel myth, then, by contrast, in the words of Walker Percy, the South has been a "Jesus-haunted country. Even when the Southern writer was not a believer, he could not escape, would not want to escape this haunting presence."[39]

The fiction of O'Connor, like that of Walker Percy and Wendell Berry, tends to draw for its spiritual authority on simple and basic New

38. Flannery O'Connor, The Complete Stories (New York: Farrar, Straus and Giroux), 488-509; 405-20.

39. Walker Percy, Signposts in a Strange Land, ed. Patrick Samway (New York: Farrar, Straus and Giroux, 1993), 177. "Jesus-haunted" might seem to underestimate the considerable role the Old Testament stories of deliverance, particularly the Exodus narrative, have played in the spirituals and sermons of African-American culture. Actually, however, the use of this material is strikingly different from its employment in New England covenant typology; as examination of the material makes clear, it is not national destiny but deliverance from suffering, and the love of Jesus which identifies with suffering, which govern the biblical materials in African-American popular religion. See Noll, History of Christianity, 544; also Albert J. Raboteau, Slave Religion: The "Invisible Institution" in the Antebellum South (New York: Oxford University Press, 1978), and Mechal Sobel, Trabelin' On: The Slave Journey to an Afro-Baptist Faith (Westport, Conn.: Greenwood, 1979).

Testament themes associated with Jesus, such as repentance, forgiveness of sin, and self-sacrificing love, and to eschew jeremiad, theodicy, and utopian vision.[40] It is undoubtedly of some significance that O'Connor and Percy are Catholics. For O'Connor, the Catholic southern writer especially

> feels no call to take on the duties of God or to create a new universe. He feels perfectly free to look at the one we already have and to show exactly what he sees. He feels no need to apologize for the ways of God to man or to avoid looking at the ways of man to God. For him, to "tidy up reality" is to succumb to the sin of pride.[41]

O'Connor offers in some respects the most striking of contrasts to contemporary non-Christian writers. Every Christian writer, she presumes, will be "distinguished from his colleagues by recognizing sin as sin . . . not as sickness or an accident of environment, but as a responsible choice of offense against God which involves his eternal future."[42] In practice, she discovers repeatedly that even her fellow Christian writers shy away from acknowledgment of sin almost to the degree that they loudly insist on a kind of utopian perfection, whether in the church or in the state. Writing to Cecil Dawkins, a fellow writer from Alabama, O'Connor suggests to her that in her impatience with the church for not having brought about a more ideal society Dawkins suffers from "an incomplete understanding of sin." At the same time, she continues, "what you seem actually to demand is that the Church put the kingdom of heaven on earth right here now, that the Holy Ghost be translated at once into all flesh."[43]

---

40. See here Ralph C. Wood, *The Comedy of Redemption: Christian Faith and Comic Vision in Four American Novelists* (Notre Dame: University of Notre Dame Press, 1991); also Rose Bowen, "Christology in the Works of Flannery O'Connor," *DAI* 45, no. 9 (1984): 2874A; and Linda Adams Barnes, "Faith and Narrative: Flannery O'Connor and the New Testament" (Ph.D. diss., Vanderbilt University, 1989).

41. Flannery O'Connor, *Mystery and Manners: Occasional Prose,* ed. Sally Fitzgerald and Robert Fitzgerald (New York: Faber and Faber, 1972), 178.

42. O'Connor, *Mystery and Manners,* 167.

43. Flannery O'Connor, *The Habit of Being: Letters Edited and with an Introduction,* ed. Sally Fitzgerald (New York: Vintage Books, 1980), 307.

These remarks are reminiscent, in reference to the state rather than the church, of Wendell Berry's resistance to "the politics of kingdom come." Having been nurtured in such a mythos so long, he suggests, Americans are trapped in a New Jerusalem *idée fixe*. Even the palpable evidence that life in America repeatedly strikes pins into the balloon of utopian optimism fails to deter wishful thinking:

> As a result the country is burdened with political or cultural perfectionists of several sorts, demanding that the government or the people create *right now* one or another version of the ideal state. The air is full of dire prophecies, warnings, and threats of what will happen if the Kingdom of Heaven is not precipitately landed at the nearest airport.[44]

How strikingly the language of O'Connor and Berry contrasts with typical language of the old Puritan jeremiad! Correspondingly, the idea of grace which pertains, for example, in O'Connor's Christian vision, differs from that typically proclaimed in the New England Puritan theology. Grace is not posited as a concrete asset, the benefit of one's estate as a member of the elect. The emphasis is instead on the surpriseful experience of grace in the midst of trial, and realized as a transformation of understanding by arduous and self-effacing love. This sense of it likewise takes the emphasis away from the experience of grace as elation, the opposite to which would be fearful depression (something from which the Puritan elect often suffered). Grace is not in O'Connor "something which can be separated from nature and served . . . as raw Instant Uplift," but is rather known in the *via crucis* as an ineluctable identification with Christ's compassion for a sinful world, "the sense of being in travail with and for creation in its subjection to vanity."[45] To make sin central in the analysis of human nature, in the light of such a view of the operations of grace, is thus to make the possibilities of salvation equally central to one's view of others. That is, what one does with this

44. Wendell Berry, *Recollected Essays: 1965-1980* (San Francisco: North Point Press, 1981), 153.

45. O'Connor, *Mystery and Manners*, 165. She adds, "This is a sense which implies a recognition of sin; this is a suffering-with, but one which blunts no edges and makes no excuses. When infused into novels, it is often forbidding. Our age doesn't go for it" (166; cf. 204). Cf. n. 54 below.

gift of grace makes a difference. The South is, by impulse, Arminian country, not Calvinist country; its stress is on free will, not predestination, whether the expression of this impulse be some version of the tent meeting or of confession before mass.

Walker Percy, who admired O'Connor greatly, was not born into a Catholic family like she was, but converted as an adult. He nonetheless fully identified with her struggle to find ways to write faithfully as a Christian in a verbal environment that he also found polluted by a language devalued for the very things a Christian might be expected to hold most dear. Speaking to a graduating class of seminary ordinands, he empathized with their task:

> . . . here, surely, is the most difficult challenge of all: to proclaim the Good News in a world whose values seem increasingly indifferent to the very meaning of the Good News. It is a strange world indeed, a world which is, on the one hand, more eroticized than ancient Rome, and yet a world in which the Good News is proclaimed more loudly and frequently than ever before by TV evangelists and the new fundamentalists. There occurs a kind of devaluation of language, a cheapening of the very vocabulary of salvation, as a consequence of which the ever-fresh, ever-joyful meaning of the Gospel comes across as the dreariest TV commercial. How to proclaim the Good News in a society which never needed it more but in which language itself has been subverted?[46]

Elsewhere he spoke of the misery created for the Christian novelist by the same linguistic devaluation:

> Language is a living organism and as such is subject to certain organic ailments. In this case it is the exhaustion and decrepitude of words themselves, an infirmity which has nothing to do with the truth or falsity of the sentences they form. The words of religion tend to wear out and get stored in the attic. The word *religion* itself has a certain unction about it, to say nothing of *born again, salvation, Jesus,* even though it is begging the question to assume therefore that these words do not have valid referents. And it doesn't

---

46. Percy, *Signposts*, 322.

help that when religious words are used publicly, at least Christian words, they are often expropriated by some of the worst rogues around, the TV preachers.[47]

What this means for the novelist who is a believer, according to Percy, is a profoundly discomfiting dilemma:

> . . . they are proclaiming the same good news he believes in, using the same noble biblical words, speaking of the same treasure buried in a field, but somehow devaluing it. If these are the fellows who have found the treasure buried in a field, then what manner of treasure is it?
>
> I hasten to say that his, the writer's, discomfort has nothing to do with the ancient Catholic-Protestant quarrel. Catholic or Protestant, he is equally unhappy.
>
> He feels like Lancelot in search of the Holy Grail who finds himself at the end of his quest at a Tupperware party.[48]

Nor is it only words like "God," "grace," and "redemption" that have come unhinged. One of the words most difficult to recover meaning for, Percy suggests, is the word we need to name the problem:

> In these peculiar times, the word *sin* has been devalued to mean everything from slightly naughty excess (my sin was loving you) to such serious lapses as "emotional unfulfillment," the stunting of

47. Walker Percy, "Why Are You a Catholic?" in *Living Philosophies: The Reflections of Some Eminent Men and Women of Our Time* (New York: Doubleday, 1990), 167-68.

48. Percy, *Signposts*, 180. These comments are reminiscent of similar observations made by Marshall McLuhan in an essay of 1945 entitled "The Southern Quality." Commenting on the scholastic and Calvinistic dialectical disposition of northern literature and the more patristic Erasmian humanism of the South, McLuhan observes that the divide between humanists and scholastics did not, either among Anglicans in England or among Christians in the Americas, follow expected lines of cleavage: "Both Protestant and Catholic camps were in turn divided. Each had its partisans of patristic and scholastic theology." See *The Interior Landscape: The Literary Criticism of Marshall McLuhan*, ed. Eugene MacNamara (New York and Toronto: McGraw-Hill, 1969), 195. This essay, which appeared in the *Southern Vanguard*, was read with evident appreciation by Flannery O'Connor, who drew it to the attention of Ben Griffith in a letter printed by Sally Fitzgerald in *The Habit of Being*, 69-70.

one's "growth as a person" and the loss of "intersubjective communication." The worst sin of all, according to a book I read about one's growth as a person, is the "failure of creativity."[49]

Percy's affluent, jaded and death-seeking protagonist in *The Second Coming*, Will Barrett, accordingly finds a choice for life possible only when he has discovered beyond cavil that the "wages of sin is death" (Rom. 3:23). The scripture verse itself is never cited. Nor at first is sin named by its devalued biblical name. Rather, it is simply called by what Barrett finally sees as its consequences. The turning point for Barrett comes only when he can name what death is in its various embodiments (many of which come proclaiming, ostensibly, the word of life) and choose firmly against it:

> Death in the guise of Christianity is not going to prevail over me. If Christ brought life, why do the churches smell of death?
>
> Death in the guise of old Christendom in Carolina is not going to prevail over me. The old churches are houses of death.
>
> Death in the form of the new Christendom in Carolina is not going to prevail over me. If the born-again are the twice born, I'm holding out for a third go-round.
>
> Death in the guise of God and America and the happy life of home and family and friends is not going to prevail over me. America is in fact almost as dead as Europe. It might still be possible to live in America, said the nutty American dancing in place in old Carolina.
>
> Death in the guise of belief is not going to prevail over me, for believers now believe anything and everything and do not love the truth, are in fact in despair of the truth, and that is death.
>
> Death in the guise of unbelief is not going to prevail over me, for unbelievers believe nothing, not because truth does not exist but because they have already chosen not to believe, and would not believe, cannot believe, even if the living truth stood before them, and that is death.[50]

49. Percy, "Why Are You a Catholic?" 168.
50. Percy, *The Second Coming* (New York: Simon and Schuster, 1980), 312-13.

But the choices for a novelist who seeks to affirm life are comparably complicated by precisely the same smell of carelessly whited sepulchres that now hangs over even the most basic biblical vocabulary. More aristocratic and neoclassical in his tastes, Percy wrestles with the sobering thought that if Flannery O'Connor were still alive to be fighting the good fight in 1986, on many central issues she would "find herself in some strange company, on the same side as Jerry Falwell and Jimmy Swaggart." He adds quickly, "Of course, just because Jimmy Swaggart believes in God doesn't mean God does not exist. But it doesn't make life any easier for the novelist." And then Percy concludes his thought with a reflection at once distinctly un-Puritan and unmistakably biblical — even though no attention is drawn to it:

> Indeed, it is probably yet another sign of the general derangement
> of the times that a writer these days who happens to be a believer
> is more apt to feel at home with the hardheads, the unbelievers,
> rakes, drunks, skeptics, Darwinians, than with the Moral Majority.
> But here again: just because the Moral Majority comes out for
> morality doesn't mean that one should be immoral.[51]

Percy's notion of grace — the novelist's experience of grace — is here precisely parallel to O'Connor's. And it is likewise, of course, modeled strictly on the choices of Jesus as given in the Gospel accounts — though chapter and verse as well as King James diction are thoughtfully suppressed.

In Percy's novel *The Second Coming,* Will Barrett, the irrational man, is shown to us as one who is in every psychological and spiritual sense experiencing rebirth. When, as Percy himself says, he "falls *out* of the cave [the womb of the earth into which he has crawled looking for death] into Allie's arms, i.e., out of his nutty Gnostic quest into sacramental reality,"[52] it is a decisive moment of spiritual parturition. It has yet to be confirmed in regenerated hope, in love and in language, and so to grow toward full consciousness. But Percy clearly is presenting to his readers a nonbiblicist account of someone being "born again." Nicodemus is not quoted directly, but his questions are asked — and

51. Percy, *Signposts,* 159-60.
52. Ibid., 386.

answered — in the novel. Why eschew the Scripture so pertinent here? we might ask. Yet surely Percy's answer is already transparent. It is for the sake of communicating the gospel in a world conditioned to reject any identification of such language with truth, because, of course, it has so often been coupled with the profitable lie.[53]

If the civil typology for the Old Testament so long engrafted into American consciousness as part of the founding myth has ceased to provide useful material for the American Christian novelist, the work of O'Connor, Percy, and Berry demonstrates effectively that such a writer can still be "of the book" in a profound if hidden way. Infusing their fiction and making much of it tacitly if not explicitly biblical is something very like the evidence of grace each identifies as intrinsic to the Christian writer's task. This concept of grace is not Calvinist;[54] it does not undergird the writer's narrative by providing it with a base plot or mythographic blueprint. Rather, it creates an ethos out of which writing empathetic to the reader's own suffering can grow. Percy sees this ethos as grounded in a pervasive sense of the reality of the Incarnation, not understood simply as an idea, but accepted as a fact in terms of which the whole human world that Christ died for may with compassionate intensity be celebrated and explored:

53. This problem of unfortunate association tends, if anything, to be exacerbated in a time in which mercantilist and consumerist values have been in so many ways called into question, not only by secularist eco-critiques but by thoughtful confessional Christians. Thus, for Wendell Berry, it is a biblical standard that most readily reveals the counterproductivity of such language: "The evident ability of most church leaders to be 'born again in Christ' without in the least discomforting their faith in the industrial economy's bill of goods, however convenient and understandable it may be, is not scriptural." Quoted from Berry's essay, "God and Country," in *What Are People For? Essays by Wendell Berry* (New York: Farrar, Straus and Giroux, 1990), 98.

54. As Cotton Mather's *The Duty of Children* (Boston, 1703) illustrates, among the New England Puritans grace is something received in baptism, and hereditary election — the core of covenant theology — means that, as Mather puts it, one is able to say *"He is my God,* who can say, *He is my Father's God"* (22; see 32, 49). While European Calvinists held to the conviction that "few of any nation were of the elect" (C. J. Sommerville, "Conversion versus the Early Puritan Covenant of Grace," *Journal of the Presbyterian Historical Society* 44 [1966]: 187), in New England the state of grace was understood to be not the exception but the rule: as Increase Mather has it, "the line of Election doth for the most part run through the loyns of godly Parents" (*Pray for the Rising Generation* [Cambridge, Mass., 1678], 14-15).

The Christian ethos sustains the narrative enterprise in ways so familiar to us that they can be overlooked. It underwrites those very properties of the novel without which there is no novel: I am speaking of the mystery of human life, its sense of predicament, of something having gone wrong, of life as a wayfaring and a pilgrimage, of the density and linearity of time and the sacramental reality of things. The intervention of God in history through the Incarnation bestows a weight and value to the individual human narrative which is like money in the bank to the novelist.[55]

O'Connor too, for much the same reasons, thought the Incarnation the central Christian doctrine, especially from the point of view of the fiction writer.[56]

Wendell Berry's way of pursuing Percy's "Christian ethos" offers many examples of richly textured and sensitively nuanced biblical ideas, as a perusal of his essays, poems, and stories illustrates. Berry's concern is most often with ethics, and he addresses himself frequently to contemporary issues in medicine, literacy, technocracy, ecology, and especially the ethics of sustainable community life.[57] In his story "Pray without Ceasing," the focusing subject for the ethics of community life is the unavoidable detritus of human sin and the cleansing operation of grace expressed as forgiveness. The narrator in this tale hears from his grandmother about his deceased grandfather's greatest temptation, and victory over it. The events follow upon the great-grandfather's murder by a drunken neighbor, irritated because he would not lend him a large sum of money without first thinking about it. In the first seconds after the murder, in which the old man is shot down on main street in

55. Percy, *Signposts,* 178.

56. O'Connor, *Mystery and Manners,* 153, 161, 176.

57. See, e.g., his essays "God and Country," "An Argument for Diversity," "Waste," "The Work of Local Culture," "Word and Flesh," and "The Responsibility of the Poet" in *What Are People For?* and "Discipline and Hope" and "The Body and the Earth" in *Recollected Essays.* Berry decries the growing privatization of religion in American life, which he feels has coincided with a gradual erosion of moral reflection in public discussion. In this he agrees with the observation of Linell Cady that many of the strands of American Christianity have tended to "absorb rather than temper the individualizing tendencies of the wider culture," in *Religion, Theology and American Public Life,* 21. Harold Bloom, in *The American Religion* (New York: Simon and Schuster, 1992), accords also with this general observation.

broad daylight while talking to neighbors, his son Mat (the narrator's grandfather) has rushed in rage after Thad Coulter, the drunken assailant, only to be stopped, physically restrained despite a titanic struggle, by an otherwise incidental neighbor. Because of the neighbor's compassionate restraint, swift judgment is tempered by mercy.

> "If it hadn't been for Jack Beechum, Mat *would* have killed him," my grandmother said.
> That was the point. Or it was one of the points — the one, perhaps, that she most wanted me to see. But it was not the beginning of the story. Adam and Eve and then Cain and Abel began it, as my grandmother depended on me to know.[58]

Here is the only direct reference to biblical narrative as such in the story, but there is no allegory or typology intended. Like the narrator hearing his grandmother speak, the reader is expected merely to locate the sorrowful events of their shared family past in a past common to all people: original sin and the cycle of violence which it begets. But the grandmother's point is about mercy, not the violence or its vengeance: her actual "text," we come to see, is an internalized gospel of grace. In this gospel the mystery of the Incarnation is most fully made known in the extent of God's love for us, "while we were yet sinners" — as the narrator forbears saying, because it is better for the modern reader's sense of what that might mean when the grandmother says this:

> "People sometimes talk of God's love as if it's a pleasant thing. But it is terrible, in a way. Think of all it includes. It included Thad Coulter, drunk and mean and foolish, before he killed Mr. Feltner, and it included him afterwards." (49)

The narrator has learned that the murderer was a friend of his great-grandfather, that after his drunken rage he had fled, only to be captured and put in a cell in another village, and that there he had finally found a way to take his own life. Before that, however, he had had a visitor.

---

58. Wendell Berry, "Pray Without Ceasing," in *Fidelity: Five Stories* (New York and San Francisco: Pantheon Books, 1992), 11.

His favorite daughter had walked long miles to see him, and when Thad looked up and saw her face, he covered his own with his hands

> "like a man ashamed," my grandmother said. "But he was like a man, too, who had seen what he couldn't bear."
> She sat without speaking a moment, looking at me, for she had much to ask of me.
> "Maybe Thad saw his guilt full and clear then. But what he saw that he couldn't bear was something else." (49)

In the silence that follows, the narrator, like the reader, is left to think about what that "something else" might be. At last the grandmother reaches out and touches the narrator's hand lightly, and says:

> "That's what Thad saw. He saw his guilt. He had killed his friend. He had done what he couldn't undo; he had destroyed what he couldn't make. But in the same moment he saw his guilt included in love that stood as near him as Martha Elizabeth and at that moment wore her flesh. It was surely weak and wrong of him to kill himself — to sit in judgment that way over himself. But surely God's love includes people who can't bear it." (50)

The history concluded by the narrative features at last the murdered man's son, and his widowed mother, standing before their door dissuading a group of the victim's angry friends from rough frontier justice. The narrator also reveals that after a time the family of the murdered man gave leave for one of their daughters to marry a grandson of the murderer. The narrator himself, we learn, is a product of this marriage:

> I am blood kin to both sides of that moment when Ben Feltner turned to face Thad Coulter in the road and Thad pulled the trigger. The two families, sundered in the ruin of a friendship, were united again first in new friendship and then in marriage. My grandfather made a peace here that has joined many who would otherwise have been divided. I am the child of his forgiveness. (59)

In "Pray without Ceasing" Berry captures again something central to Christian identity, and renders it appreciable almost to the degree that he turns away from any hint of biblicist triumphalism and its kind of civic vision, and reflects instead an incarnational and sacramental sense of the practical operation of grace in the forgiveness of sin and comfort of human suffering. In this vision marriage too is experienced as a sacrament, and thus as a means of grace. But so also, in the incarnational aesthetic of this story, is that art which expresses, in human flesh and words, the meaning of the redemption as sacramental act of faithful love.[59] Fidelity, or faithfulness, as Berry's title might remind us, is far more persuasive than the forensic exactitude of any authoritative proof-text or imagined national covenant.

59. See also his magnificent novel on this theme, *Remembering* (San Francisco: North Point Press, 1988).

Chapter Ten

Literary Theory and the
Broken-Hearted Reader

*No, Rodion Romanovitch. . . . This is a fantastic, gloomy business,
a modern case, an incident of today when the heart of man is
troubled, when the phrase is quoted that blood "renews," [yet]
when comfort is preached as the aim of life. Here we have bookish
dreams, a heart unhinged by theories. . . . He forgot to shut the
door after him, and murdered two people for a theory.*

FYODOR DOSTOEVSKI, *CRIME AND PUNISHMENT*

Only someone with a memory can repent.

LUDWIG WITTGENSTEIN, *ZETTEL*

W E RETURN AT LAST TO THE POINT WITH WHICH WE BEGAN — THE
characterization in much contemporary theoretical discourse of
Christian literary tradition as "logocentrism." Does this term grasp well
the dominant characteristics of Christian literary reflection in the West?
What does it tell us about the cultural force of the great library of texts
which mark out the growth and development of Christian literary tradition? Do contemporary theoretical models, explicitly defined over and
against Christian as well as Jewish tradition, have greater explanatory

power for its hallmark texts than hermeneutical principles developed within the tradition itself? Or have the primary texts themselves effectively become anachronistic, incidental, eclipsed by more fashionable theoretical projects? Let us begin at the bottom, so to speak, taking up the last of these questions first, as a point of entry into the others.

Among scholars and critics of "primary narrative," it is widely recognized that the emergence to prominence of literary theory over "explication de texte," despite certain evident attractions, carries with it a disturbing proclivity to occlude the texts which were once, ostensibly, theory's justification. One may confirm this readily in such theorizing as one now associates with figures as widely various in their focus as Gadamer, Barthes, Derrida, Eagleton, and Lacan. But it is important also to recognize that this general displacement is not unprecedented; it holds much in common with usurpation of authority from the narratives that traditionally bear it in other eras. One thinks here not only of Marxism, as one might recently have first imagined, but more anciently, of Neoplatonist systems of all kinds. Embarrassment with biblical narrative and flight from its "shameful simplicities" (the phrase is Augustine's) is highly visible in Philo Judaeus and Origen, for example, each of whose method of dealing with primary biblical narrative is antirealist, prophylactic, and cultivating of what we may call, in the informal sense, an elite *gnosis*.[1] And it may be, as some would argue,

---

1. Another way of putting this, of course, would simply be to note that allegorists such as Philo and Origen resist reading many parts of the biblical texts literally. Origen exclaims, for example, "Who is so silly as to believe that God, after the manner of a farmer, planted a paradise eastward in Eden and set in it a visible and palpable 'tree of life' of such a sort that anyone who tasted its fruit with his bodily teeth would gain life; and again that one could partake of 'good and evil' by masticating the fruit taken from the tree of that name" (*De principiis*, 4.3.1). The more significant effect of such reading is to be found, however, in the typologizing of NT as well as OT narrative in which the realistic surface of representative narrative is taken to be frivolous. Here, as in Origen's elaborately rationalized allegory of the six waterpots mentioned in the marriage of Cana story (John 2), the "logical and literal meaning" is held to be simply inconsistent with the purpose of divine intellect (*De principiis*, 4.2.5-6; 9) — that is, it is assumed that God would not condescend to the authorization of such trivialities. In biblical narrative, rather, the Spirit will "wrap up and conceal within ordinary language under cover of some historical record or account of visible things . . . secret mysteries" (4.2.8). The unambiguous bias against realism privileges "the more skillfull and inquiring readers, in order that these, by giving themselves to the toil of examining what is written, may gain a sound conviction of the necessity of seeking in such instances a meaning worthy

that the reflex of allegorism in late antiquity and the Middle Ages is but one pulse of an historical dialectic for which we might find analogues in any textual tradition.[2]

The Awkwardness of Realistic Narrative

Among literary critics self-consciousness about gnostic impulses is not a recent phenomenon either. But in recent years, acknowledged or not, these impulses have come aggressively to the forefront of the discipline.[3] Few types of contemporary theorizing about literature and its interpretation, we are obliged to reflect, are innocent of the association. It has been persuasively argued by Hans Jonas, for example, that Heidegger's phenomenology is an elaborate analogue of second-century gnosticism.[4] Harold Bloom, the romanticist and literary theorist whose transgressive impulses have so often stimulated reflection in these pages, is a self-confessed gnostic. As such, he regards literary language as "totally overdetermined" and "magical," an approach he presents as

---

of God" (4.2.9). Origen's gnostic "saving of the appearances" is based upon a view of God which is effectively almost non-Incarnational, and in this respect compares to that of Philo of Alexandria and some other Jewish writers of the tannaitic period.

2. One modern analogue must here suffice: in her essay "Narrative Emotions: Beckett's Genealogy of Love," Martha Nussbaum suggests, for example, that an "unwriting" of narrative and a positing of an alternative account is required in a prophetic critique of society's dominant self-understanding (*Ethics* 98.2 [1988]: 225-54). Though Beckett's "unwriting" is still recognizably narrative, its antirealism and antinomian idiom invites — and still obtains — inculcation into a liturgy of calculated mystification.

3. The pretension of much poststructuralist critical and theoretical writing to be first-order discourse has, of course, occasioned concern among those who believe a central task of critical writing is to rank, value, and preserve the contribution of primary narrative. Frank Kermode, for example, argues in *Forms of Attention* (Chicago: University of Chicago Press, 1985) for the traditional place of interpretative criticism as subordinate, a second-order discourse. "The success of interpretative argument as a means of conferring or endorsing value," he contends, is, accordingly, not to be measured by the survival of the comment but by the survival of its object.

4. Hans Jonas, *The Gnostic Religion*, 2nd ed. (Boston: Beacon Press, 1963), and "Delimitation of the Gnostic Phenomenon — Typological and Historical," in *The Origins of Gnosticism*, ed. V. Bianchi (Leiden: Brill, 1970).

similar to that of the Kabbalists.[5] Bloom thinks of deconstruction —
described by him as "a thoroughgoing linguistic nihilism" which views
language operating in "absolute randomness" and exhibiting a "dearth
of meaning" — as polar to his own gnosticism. But deconstruction is
itself arguably one of the most evidently gnostic varieties of poststructuralist theory. Like its second-century predecessor as much as the antinomian structuralism of Barthes on which it more nearly draws,[6]
deconstruction *ad finem* strives to separate its form of knowledge from
any reference to external nature, experience, or historical process.[7] The
transcendent principle in both ancient gnosticism and modern deconstruction is an absence, not a presence; its mode of operation in either
system is, though said to be constitutive, strictly speaking unde-
monstrable (or incomprehensible). Deconstruction, as its chief proponent Jacques Derrida proclaims, is also anti-theological — yet it
desires transcendence, to be "elsewhere," completely other than in the
mundane and gritty world. Finally, like Valentinian gnosis, in which the
fall of Sophia, the primordial wisdom-emanation, was explicitly conceived as the consequence of her mimetic folly, deconstruction especially
is "dogmatically antimimetic,"[8] resisting absolutely those modes of linguistic representation which might once have been described as "realistic." The least we can conclude from these observations is that no
contemporary theory can make unique claim to a "gnostic" poetic.

We should not be surprised that in such an intellectual climate —
a rivalry of competing gnosticisms, so to speak — certain kinds of realistic narrative come to seem "awkward" and accordingly fall into comparative neglect. In this last chapter I want to elicit only one type — a
persistent and centrally formative group of traditional stories that for
convenience we may call narratives of repentance. This category would

5. See Bloom's "The Breaking of Form," in his edited collection *Deconstruction and Criticism* (New York: Seabury, 1979).

6. D. L. Jeffrey, "*Caveat Lector:* Structuralism, Deconstruction and Ideology," *Christian Scholars Review* 17, no. 4 (1988): 436-48.

7. For an extensive critique see John Ellis, *Against Deconstruction* (Princeton: Princeton University Press, 1989); cf. Cedric Watts, "Bottom's Children: The Fallacies of Structuralist and Deconstructionist Literary Theory," in *Reconstructing Literature,* ed. L. Lerner (Oxford: Blackwell, 1983), 106-22.

8. These points are argued usefully by Michael H. Keefer, "Deconstruction and the Gnostics," *University of Toronto Quarterly* 55, no. 1 (1985): 74-93.

include not only biblical narrative, but classic works of both literary autobiography and representative fiction such as may be conjured by a list which includes texts as diverse as Augustine's *Confessions,* Dostoevski's *Crime and Punishment,* and, though it is outside the scope of this study, Isaac Bashevis Singer's *The Penitent.* I want to suggest that the gradual eclipse of such narratives in theoretically motivated studies of Western literature raises serious questions about the capacity of the occluding discourse to give a balanced or "realistic" account of its ostensible subject, especially when a concern for ethics or virtue is part of that subject.[9]

Even the nonspecialist, of course, can guess what must be one of the leading sources of offense in such an increasingly "marginalized" text as the narrative of repentance: not so much an obtrusive credalism, actually, as its explicit insistence on being read as in some fundamental sense "realistic," psychologically, spiritually, or politically.[10] Moreover, and progenitively, repentance narratives are presented as second-order discourse — a reader's response to some other and primary book. These neglected "responsory" texts, whether narratives of social realism or spiritual odyssey, may remain of interest to Marxists, let us say, or to Sartrian cultural critics, or perhaps to sociologists of religion, but they will make relatively little sense in the repertoire of the poststructuralist theorist whose agenda is preoccupied with the reconstituting of criticism itself as first-order discourse.

To this latter enterprise, in fact, a good deal of the narrative which

9. This tends to be a *lapsus* in Marxist theory as well. An example is the survey of Terry Eagleton in *Literary Theory: An Introduction* (Minneapolis: University of Minnesota, 1983).

10. "Realism" continues to be a bedevilled and unstable term in contemporary theoretical writing. Late nineteenth-century and early twentieth-century proponents of "literary naturalism" and "social realism" defined realism partly in terms of what it was *not:* a documentary, unexpurgated examination of life lived in disarray was "realism"; any comedic plot or romance with a happy ending was not. In biblical criticism, the movement away from "realistic narrative" in interpretation, especially after the nineteenth century, denotes the rejection of any sense of the task of the interpreter in which "realism" would mean something like "naively treating the text as though it described something which really happened" (cf. n. 1). In certain types of contemporary theory, notably deconstruction, rejection of realism entails a conviction that meaning and reality have no evident connection, that any imagination of their stable correlation is purely chimerical.

has been most culturally formative in Western tradition can be seen as irrelevant. More precisely, if allowed to remain present in cultural reflection, such narratives tend to be unsettling to the motives which led to their rejection or downgrading in the first place. Some such works may remain somewhere on the syllabus, but cease to get much attention. Or if they do, the motivation may simply be to expose them as, from the point of view of contemporary theoretical discourse, "problematic."

This "canonical" awkwardness seems to be analogous to the reflex Kierkegaard identified as fashionable more than a century ago. In an extended critical review of the 1840s, Kierkegaard described the efforts of eighteenth- and nineteenth-century biblical criticism to "problematize" the text as an explicit strategy to make the Bible a text with little or no ethical application, a species of betrayal by interpretation — a classic *trahison des clercs*. In Kierkegaard's uncompromising characterization, interestingly, this is to be understood as the subterfuge of a phony revolution:

> A passionate and tumultuous age will overthrow everything, pull everything down; but a revolutionary age, that is at the same time reflective and passionless, transforms that expression of strength into a feat of dialectics: it leaves everything standing but cunningly empties it of significance. Instead of culminating in a rebellion it reduces the inward reality of all relationships to a reflective tension which leaves everything standing but leaves the whole of life ambiguous: so that everything continues to exist factually whilst by a dialectical deceit, *privatissime,* it supplies a *secret interpretation* — that it does not exist.[11]

Kierkegaard was a biblical theist. Consequently, for him any realistic account of the problem of subjectivity in understanding must acknowledge *ab initio* the persistence of sin. "Sin" he defines as a rejection of Truth, of reality — especially of realism about one's own actual mode of being.[12] Its patent device — endless artifices for flight

---

11. Søren Kierkegaard, *The Present Age,* trans. Alexander Drû (New York: Harper, 1962), 42-43, emphasis mine.
12. Indicatively, he says in *The Concept of Irony,* trans. Lee Capel (New York: Harper & Row, 1966), "sin is inconsistency" (64).

from this truth — means that no person "by himself and of himself can explain what sin is, precisely because he is in sin," and explanation, if there is to be one, must come via the instrumentation of an external Revelation, the mediation of a penetratingly knowing Other.[13] But each person knows the *effects* of sin as evasion of truth about the self — that is to say, as despair — manifest in the impulse to create unlikely fictions, implausible narratives, reinventing the world. Hence, for Kierkegaard, "the seriousness of sin is its reality in the individual, whether it be thou or I."[14]

Theoretical discourse, which Kierkegaard calls the "dialectic of speculation," is required by its own mode to "look away from the individual" and so becomes abstraction. It focuses, we might now agree, on language, another abstraction, more than on speech, the concrete manifestation. Which is to say, it tends to eschew "reality in the individual, whether it be thou or I."[15] The question which, with Kierkegaard, we might wish to ask in our parallel situation is, what mode of discourse can deal plausibly with this subjective personal reality, put it into relation with other reality, even that announced by Revelation, so as to treat personhood with the "seriousness" which is its due? Kierkegaard's answer is the "dialectic of sin," which he describes as "directly contrary to that of Speculation." And here is where the shadow of primary narrative slips in again by the back door. Where it is read

13. Søren Kierkegaard, *Sickness Unto Death*, trans. Walter Lowrie (Garden City, N.Y.: Doubleday, 1954), 162-63, 232, 251. In this corollary sense, for Kierkegaard as for the medieval philosopher St. Anselm, a search for realism about one's own actual mode of being entails the search for Being, or God, a search which at once defines the searcher's perpetual corrigibility: "God is near enough, but no one can see God without purity, and sin is impurity, and therefore no one can take cognizance of God without becoming a sinner" (*Thoughts on Critical Situations,* trans. D. F. Swenson [Minneapolis: Augsburg, 1941], 25).

14. Kierkegaard, *Sickness Unto Death,* 239-40.

15. Kierkegaard's point here is not unrelated to the formulations of Buber or Levinas. For a usefully contextualized assessment of the contribution of Levinas in this regard see Susan Handelman, "Facing the Other: Levinas, Perelman, and Rosenzweig," *Religion and Literature* 22-23 (1990): 61-84. If there is a deconstructionist method which makes plausible address to ethics, then it seems to me to be rabbinic, and that the most articulate proponent is Levinas. For a thought-provoking reflection see Jill Robbins, *Prodigal Son / Elder Brother: Interpretation and Alterity in Augustine, Petrarch, Kafka, Levinas* (Chicago: University of Chicago Press, 1991).

accountably, that is, where some mode of relation to a penetratingly knowing Other is available, a narrative attempt at realism may become at least provisionally objectifiable as discourse, in part because it is accountable to that Other. This consciousness of the condition of accountability as the matrix of composition assures us, in Kierkegaard's view, that the resulting narrative will be capable of generating a "dialectic of sin." To put it another way, such a narrative will be all the more candidly human — which is to say, personal. Could this be why stories about repentance, whether first- or third-person narrative, include some of the most intensely "realistic" texts in our literary tradition? Yet these are typically texts of which some contemporary theories can speak only frivolously or not at all.

Biblical Repentance Narratives

The Bible, of course, features repentance narratives centrally. There are two foundational types. In the Hebrew Scriptures, these may be represented respectively in the stories of David and Josiah. There are few more memorable narratives than the prophet Nathan's confrontation with the adulterous and murderous David (2 Sam. 12), his unmasking parable prompting that terribly unwitting response, a self-condemnation which strips away from the poet-king his own self-justifying fictions and exposes him in — and to — the reality of his wrongdoing. As A. S. Herbert remarks, Old Testament parable, *mashal*, "had a clearly recognizable purpose: that of quickening an apprehension of the real as distinct from the wished for,"[16] and this particular narrative makes the point forever memorable. Forced into unwelcome self-understanding, the king is overwhelmed by his transgression, and the subsequent chronicle and corresponding poem (Ps. 51) are a dialectic of sin brought to repentance and atonement.

The second basic type of repentance narrative is that modeled in the chronicle of Josiah (2 Kings 22), concerning a discovery among the detritus of abuse, in a temple long bereft of its original purpose, of a

---

16. A. S. Herbert, "The Parable (Masal) in the Old Testament," *Scottish Journal of Theology* 7 (1954): 180-96.

book, a copy of an unknown scroll. As the king hears the Torah read aloud by one of the few members of his court still literate enough to read it, he rends his clothes and tears his hair in anguished and penitent remorse. There is nothing hypothetical or aesthetic in this response. Immediately Josiah moves to enact a transformed identity: he sets about setting things right again, instituting the Law in every sphere of personal and national life.

The David story, earlier in the annals of the kings of Israel, might seem to instance repentance effected by means of interpretation, as though the king finally understood the parable as an allegory, and perforce as a summons to accountability. But in truth, this notion misconstrues the dialectic of sin precipitated by biblical narrative, and made especially transparent in *mashal*. It is the parable that interprets the sinner, "dividing asunder the thoughts and intentions of the heart," as the New Testament writer to the Hebrews puts it (4:12). Which is as much as to say that, when read accountably, the text is not first and foremost an invitation to an act of criticism. Rather, the story breaks the reader's heart to hear it.

The Josiah narrative offers a parallel calling to accounts, in which discovery of the very existence of Revelation, the impact of Torah itself concerning sin, the integrity of God, and evidence of collective disobedience, breaks the heart of a king over the loss of national purpose incurred through ignorance and neglect of the Law. Though the focus of this narrative is political more than personal, the action in which it ensues is similarly a cognitive and moral revolution, a transforming of personal story in which old things pass away and all things become new. We may note: though the catalyst to David's personal repentance is a plausible fiction, while the catalyst to Josiah's communal repentance is overt revelation discourse, the character and effect of their understood readings are virtually the same.

New Testament writing echoes and amplifies each type of repentance narrative, that projected by parable, or *mashal*, and that summoned by prophetic word.[17] It may at first seem surprising that a celebrated literary study of New Testament parable, Frank Kermode's

17. "Prophetic word" may include, of course, a parable understood (as in the case of the example of Nathan), whether or not it is acted upon in repentance, as it is not in the case of Micaiah's parable to Ahab (1 Kings 22).

The Genesis of Secrecy: On the Interpretation of Narrative (1979), illuminating and challenging as it is in many respects, is strangely inarticulate on the subject of repentance narrative in general and parables concerning repentance in particular. But the lapse is explicable upon reflection. Kermode's central thesis depends upon his view that (cf. Mark 4:10-11; Matt. 13:10ff) Jesus spoke in parables as a means of excluding "outsiders" from the knowledge of a salvation which can be made evident to the understanding of "insiders" alone. On Kermode's reckoning the parables thus become a kind of gnostic encoding, like the conventions of any schooled theory, an instrument for effecting the institutional control of interpretation. While this is conceivably one of the possibilities latent in the cryptic distinction Jesus gives the disciples (in Mark) between themselves and "those without," and has its place in the history of exegesis, it is hardly the only one and certainly not that which the Gospels themselves elsewhere underscore. As the longer version of the account in Matthew confirms, "those *without*" in the case of Jesus' parables are typically those *most* evidently implicated in the institutional control of interpretation. In fact, their heavy investment in institutional (and hence elite) discourse is what Jesus tells them makes of their typical acts of interpretation little more than exercises in self-justification. Given that they claim to be persons for whom Torah is the ultimate authority and "getting it right" their vocation and profession, this complete misplacement of focus renders their "reading" axiomatically meritritious. Or, to put it in typical biblical fashion, it reveals them as readers whose hearts have become hardened to what actually "the law and the prophets have been saying."

One parable from Luke, and a narrative of response following upon it, must here suffice to clarify a central distinction concerning interpretation repeatedly elaborated in biblical narratives — the split between unrepentant and repentant hearers of the Word, or to put it in still more biblical idiom, between the hard-hearted and broken-hearted reader. I refer to the parable Jesus tells, according to Luke, to "some who trusted in themselves that they were righteous and regarded others with contempt":

> Two men went up to the temple to pray, one a Pharisee and the other a tax collector. The Pharisee, standing by himself, was praying thus, "God, I thank you that I am not like other people, thieves,

rogues, adulterers, or even like this tax collector. I fast twice a week; I give a tenth of all my income." But the tax collector, standing far off, would not even look up to heaven, but was beating his breast and saying, "God, be merciful to me, a sinner!" I tell you, this man went down to his home justified rather than the other; for all who exalt themselves will be humbled, but all who humble themselves will be exalted.

(Luke 18:10-14)

The context of this parable in Luke is a series of parables, *mashalim*, told by Jesus to indicate the sort of "interpretation" which is to be expected in the Last Judgment. Here the Pharisee is as much an example of the hard-hearted reader as Pharaoh; the Law is unable to call him to repentance because he is after all Master of the Law, not one mastered by it.

The wretched tax collector, whose predatory crimes make him a universal object of contempt, is beyond any such imagination of mastery. He is to the occupying state which employs him a groveling toady, to his neighbors an oppressive traitor. A man without community, without acceptance, without self-respect, and perhaps even without love — all he can do in his miserable moment in the temple is cry out for mercy. He knows himself a sinner under judgment, and pleads for remission, for pardon. The parable manifestly subverts institutional decorum: the one who "gets it right" is the one who seems heretofore to have gotten nothing right. On the plain interpretation of Jesus, it is the self-confessedly sinful man who is justified in his response to the Torah. Why? Because by candid participation in the dialectic of sin and repentance he has, like Josiah, "read" the Torah story in the way it most obviously cries out to be read. The condescending Pharisee's motive from the beginning is here unmasked as a decorum for self-justification, a confusion of institutional membership with personal right-mindedness so thoroughgoing that he can no longer conceive of a reason for repentance.

A primary function of Jesus' parables seems to be simply to distinguish or "judge" between these two types of readers. Who is broken-hearted? Who is capable of repentance? As a narrative of repentance, the purpose of such a parable is evidently to initiate the possibility of repentance in a reader who is not yet irremediably hard-hearted. The succeeding narrative tells of a rich young ruler who, though even in Jesus' eyes an earnest observer of the Law, could not repent of his self-serving, sell all his goods, "and distribute the money to the poor" (v. 24). As the man unwilling to part with his riches walks sorrowing away, he illustrates another order of broken heart — but not one open to repentance. Having heard Jesus' *mashal*, he edges toward response: surely I have done what is required, he says, I have kept the Law since my youth. In his speaking to Jesus, perhaps he seeks to be assured he has *kapparah,* aquittal from sin, or atonement. But he is not willing to follow through with *taharah,* purification or catharsis, the crucial second step in what Rabbi Joseph Soloveitchik has called the restoration of "spiritual viability."[18] If we may follow Soloveitchik formally: for the narrative of repentance to become efficacious, it must pass beyond the remorse of *kapparah,* which seeks acquittal of sin, to a willed removal of the self from "the path of sin," *taharah.* In the terms of the present discussion, this final move is what might grant such a narrative its closure — a closure which in the case of the rich young ruler is lamentably not forthcoming.

In the account of the conversion of the tax collector Zacchaeus in the next chapter, who sells half of what he possesses to give to the poor and uses what is left to restore fourfold to any he has cheated (19:1-10), repentance is, by contrast, brought to its purpose: *mashal* gives rise to *mishpat,* "right reading" emerges, in performance, participation, ethical action. In this way Zacchaeus acquires again his full ethical status as a Jew under the Law: "he too," Jesus says, is now "a son of Abraham" (19:9). To apply Soloveitchik's phrase, by his *taharah* he has truly "entered into the Covenant of the Lord."[19] Indeed, it is the typical claim

18. As recorded in Pinchas H. Peli, *Soleveitchik on Repentance: The Thought and Oral Discourses of Rabbi Joseph B. Soloveitchik* (New York: Paulist Press, 1984), 49-52. (It should be remembered here that in Judaism of this period, one in a state of evident lapse from obedience to Torah lost his legal status, and could not, for example, in that condition even serve as witness in a judicial hearing.)

19. His fourfold restitution is, of course, precisely what is required of him under the Law (cf. Exod. 22:1). Soloveitchik observes that this covenant restitution made possible by repentance is an effect of *hesed,* God's "covenant love." On this point Soloveitchik concludes: "Through repentance of purification man is reborn and he gains a new heart, a renewed spirit, another outlook on life and different horizons. One man enters the bath of ritual immersion and another emerges from the water. The sinful person emerges as a pure one. And, indeed, our sages have pointed out that changing one's name is especially beneficial for penitents" (59).

of biblical narratives that no reading which is not performative (actualized, or in the strictest sense mimetic) *can* be right — or to use our abstracted word, prove responsibly "ethical" at all.

It is noteworthy in this respect that the parable is no less authoritative in its call to repentance than are the explicit imperatives of the Law. *Mashal*, in Hebrew as in other Semitic languages (Aramaic, Akkadian, Arabic), signified figurative discourse generally, not only the narrative units we call parable, but tropes such as similes or metaphors, enigmatic sayings, and proverbs.[20] But in Hebrew alone among Semitic languages the word has another meaning. Its radical is the verb, spelled and pointed in identical fashion, which means "to rule," to have dominion," "to govern." *Mashal* is employed this way in Proverbs 16:32: "One who is slow to anger is better than the mighty, and he who rules his spirit than he who takes a city," and this is the sense invoked when God speaks to Cain about the consequences of obedience and disobedience in Genesis 4:7. In Psalm 78, the verb signifies the lesson to be learned from Israel's history about God's repeated judgment upon sin and calling to accounts. And it is also, in Psalm 89, a "*Mashal* of Ethan the Ezrahite," used in praise of God's absolute authority over his creation: "You rule the raging of the sea; when its waves rise, you still them" (v. 9). Though it may denominate figurative discourse, *mashal* is thus deeply imprinted with a sense of ultimate authority,[21] the weight of historical truth — even the resonance of divine creative fiat itself.

Realism and the Broken Heart

Much of the most formative narrative in Western tradition is comprised of stories of the broken-hearted, and much of that wrought in repentance, or to speak of repentance. Written after the fact, or in the constructs afforded by third-person voice, such narratives are often inten-

---

20. See Joachim Jeremias, *Parables of Jesus* (London: SPCK, 1963), 22ff.

21. Seen in this context of the Jewish narrative practice which features the *mashal*, the modern critical category of New Testament scholars, "parables of the kingdom," can seem ripe with double-sense.

tionally corrective of critical judgment; they constitute an ostensibly more convincing reading of life evidences. Formal confessional narrative is of the most obvious pertinence. Augustine's *Confessions,* for example, models the characteristic mimesis: a wishful but falsifying fiction is at last owned as being such, then corrected or replaced by more realistic representation of the self, a new story.[22] Such a confessional narrative is written in self-conscious retrospect, and thus forms part of the *taharah* or reconstitutive and cathartic performance consistent with the broken-hearted repentance *(kapparah)* which initiated it. It is usually assumed that confessional narrative may (and intentionally) precipitate repentance in another.[23] But so, of course, may a retelling of biblical narrative, or the writing of a fictional analogue, a *mashal.*

The most important flowerings of vernacular drama in the Middle Ages, whether biblical cycle plays or saints plays (such as the Digby *Mary Magdalen*), are offered (often explicitly) to their readers as occasions for repentance. As is recognized by disparaging and adulatory commentary alike, so are Dante's *Vita Nuova* and *Commedia.* As we have seen, Chaucer's florilegium of pilgrimage narratives, *The Canterbury Tales,* moves toward its closure in a call to repentance following examination of conscience in which the author himself necessarily participates (formally, in his "Retraction"). But the list could be extended almost indefinitely. Medieval writers such as St. Bernard of Clairvaux, St. Bonaventure, and the author of the widely popular *Meditations on the Life of Christ,* all insist that efficacious response to the biblical narrative of redemption cannot occur unless an "intellective" engagement is embedded in a prior "affective" engagement of the story. "Think, *in your heart,* how Christ was [tortured to death] on the Cross," Giovanni de Caulibus writes. "Look at him attentively, then, as He goes along bowed down by the cross and gasping aloud. Feel as much compassion for Him as you can, placed in such anguish and renewed derision." "Place yourself there," is the insistent and repeated invitation of the text: as elsewhere in medieval writing, "contemplation" and "meditation" are explic-

22. Saints' lives, the most popular vernacular genre in Christian Europe before the Reformation, stylize or typologize but do not alter the pattern; the occasion of repentance can be almost as easily prompted by reading a noncanonical repentance narrative as by a direct encounter with divine writ.

23. Augustine says he hopes for such a response from some readers.

itly mimetic activities, identification with Christ in his atoning sacrifice. Or the contemplation may be mediated: "Think of how his Mother felt," and "have compassion for her whom you see thus afflicted." But this applies to the entire life of Christ in the world: commenting on Jesus visiting the disciples after the Resurrection "as if they were friends and not servants," the writer adds, "Reflect on this well, and admire and try to imitate it."[24] Otherwise, he says, you read the text in vain.

Imitatio Christi, as in the radical identification with Christ's Passion championed by Franciscan spirituality and symbolized hagiographically in the *stigmata* of St. Francis, is perhaps the most powerfully mimetic of readings, one which can take the text as far as literal emulation.[25] But *lebensnachfolge* (the term used by later theologians to describe precipitated, enacted reading as the script for a whole Christian life) considerably extends the narrative's mimetic reach. Specifically, it is by means of such a mimetic extension — that is to say, a reading in repentance, or broken-hearted reading — that foundational narrative achieves in the reader its ethical authority.[26]

It is possible, of course, to write a history of Western narrative in which every example so far adduced is edited out of the record as impertinent to the question of "realism" as variously and more narrowly defined since Kant, the positivists, and Zola. One might then present a contrary or at least relativizing historical thesis — for example, that mimetic reading of biblical narrative began after all to disappear from serious intellectual consideration following the emergence of Martin Luther's independent Bible reader, and especially after the post-Enlightenment antirealism of German Romanticism. But one could only hope

24. The entire *Meditations of the Life of Christ*, which has been translated from a fourteenth-century MS by Isa Ragusa and Rosalie B. Green (Princeton: Princeton University Press, 1961), is rife with such invitations. Cited here are passages from Meditations 77 and 85. For a general discussion of affective spirituality in the Franciscan tradition see D. L. Jeffrey, *The Early English Lyric and Franciscan Spirituality* (Lincoln: University of Nebraska Press, 1975), chaps. 2-3.

25. See *Early English Lyric and Franciscan Spirituality*, 48-72. Less extreme examples abound in literature of the Franciscans: Jacopone da Todi's *Stabat mater,* with or without the heart-breaking setting by Pergolesi, may still be one of the most compellingly realistic "readings" of the crucifixion narratives. Its purpose is the prompting of a specific act of contrition.

26. Cf. Alasdair MacIntyre's *After Virtue: A Study in Moral Theory,* 2nd ed. (Notre Dame: University of Notre Dame, 1984), 214-17.

to make the case for impertinence stick, I think, by omitting from such a thesis any serious critical consideration of the persistent textual treatment of the matter of repentance.

Frank Kermode's *Genesis of Secrecy* is written in the shadow of such a thesis incorporated as presupposition. The source he cites is "a subtle and interesting book" by Hans Frei, *The Eclipse of Biblical Narrative,* an invaluable resource for the history of late eighteenth- and nineteenth-century professional biblical interpretation.[27] Frei's contention is that any residual "narrative sense" in the reading of the Bible remained primary after the Enlightenment only in allegory such as imitated in Bunyan's *Pilgrim's Progress* or "directly, as in the Methodists' devout use of the Bible . . . in tracing and treading the path from sin to perfection."[28] Moreoever, on the basis of this paradigm he projects the view that "evangelical piety" is in its own way a rejection of realistic biblical narrative: "though real in his own right, the atoning Redeemer is at the same time a figure or type of the Christian's journey," and so "What is real, and what therefore the Christian lives, is his own pilgrimage."[29] Perhaps if Puritan spiritual autobiographies and their American counterparts were the only expression of "evangelical piety," Frei's might be a tenable theses. His larger claims are compromised, however, by evident dependence upon too narrow a sample of Christian readers, even from within that portion of the tradition which might be imagined as most open to his charge.

Here, in a way that helps to explain how Kermode's derivative argument goes wrong, we can see how Frei's subtlety has proved misleading. For the actual textual record of homiletic and practical biblical exegesis among Christians from the time of the Great Revival of the eighteenth century to the Great Awakening of the nineteenth century is replete with almost innumerable examples of detailed narrative exposition which can only be regarded as reading the Bible "realistically." Notably, in these readings, repentance figures prominently as both subject and motive.

Again, examples abound, yet two or three must suffice. The poet

27. Hans W. Frei, *The Eclipse of Biblical Narrative: A Study in Eighteenth and Nineteenth Century Hermeneutics* (New Haven: Yale University Press, 1974).

28. Ibid., 149ff, esp. 152.

29. Ibid., 154.

William Cowper, converted through the intercession of his Methodist cousin Martin Madan, and, as we have seen, pastored by John Newton, wrote thousands of lines of poetry which manifestly afford a "realistic" reading of biblical narrative. These poems bespeak as indubitable a sense of Scripture's imperative to performative response as do the published sermons of his distinguished parish priest.[30] Cowper's spiritual autobiography (1816), modeled transparently on the *Confessions* of Augustine, also clearly articulates the mimetic relation of biblical and subsequent Christian repentance narrative to his own narrative transformed. This is preeminently the case in the spiritual autobiography of Newton himself, titled *Authentic Narrative* (1764).[31] Though the primary influence in Newton's conversion is a transparent reading of biblical narrative, a mediating book which he says made him able to "view the Bible accountably" was Thomas à Kempis's spiritually mimetic reading, the *Imitation of Christ*. Each in his own fashion, Newton, the hard-headed former slave-trader, and Cowper, the psychologically unstable recluse, offer a classic paradigm of the broken-hearted reader.

But in post-Enlightenment literature, convincing *fictional* repentance narratives also occur; notable nineteenth-century examples include the chapter entitled "Janet's Repentance" in George Eliot's *Scenes from Clerical Life* and, more magisterially, Dostoevski's *Crime and Punishment*. These are, of course, written from the third-person point of view. In Eliot's case the writer's stance involves an ostensibly greater psychological distance from her protagonist, though not at significant loss to psychological realism in the chapter. Dostoevski as writer is more obviously implicated in his protagonist's crisis. But he is correspondingly more transparent about his vulnerability to the self-righteous rejection of mundane reality represented in that protagonist. The student Raskolnikov's monstrous and proleptically Nietzschean inability to read any other text than the agenda for his own will to power can only be broken down by a combination of realistically read biblical narrative (the resurrection of Lazarus)

30. Cowper's use of the Bible has yet to be studied as thoroughly as the subject deserves. An early and exploratory treatment may be found in Mary Seeley, *The Later Evangelical Fathers: John Thornton, John Newton, and William Cowper* (London: SPCK, 1914).

31. See chapter 8, above; also G. A. Starr, *Defoe and Spiritual Autobiography* (Princeton: Princeton University Press, 1965), and Leopold Damrosch, *God's Plot and Man's Stories* (Chicago: University of Chicago Press, 1985).

and Sonya the prostitute's vivid (and mimetic) narrative of personal repentance. The novel's very closure is correspondingly effected through the protagonist's own commencement toward repentance, his giving up of his pretense to verbal fiat, the symbol and symptom of his will to power — which is to say, he gives up his dearest implausible fiction, the conviction that he can save himself by extraordinary command of thought and language, by "uttering a new word."[32]

I do not mean to suggest that only contemporary literary theory, or even hermeneutics since the Enlightenment, finds particularly awkward such narratives of repentance. The paradigm-driven theorist is not the only hard-hearted reader. What I do mean to say is that the marginalization of this tradition of repentance texts, as Kierkegaard's analysis long ago anticipated, is a phenomenon that deserves to be considered at several levels. In one form or another, a split something like that which I have called (in biblical fashion) a divide between the hard-hearted and the broken-hearted reader has troubled thoughtful contemporary commentators and writers alike for some time. George Steiner's seminal "Critic / Reader" essay helps to make evident why the stance of the formal critic entails as axiom a decorum of disengagement, sometimes making the "reader" in the "critic" less accessible. But as Steiner suggests, the polarity artificializes: though it explains, it does not describe an ideal state of affairs.[33]

Italo Calvino's novel *If On a Winter's Night A Traveler*, with its ideological and theory-minded Ludmilla resisting the author's story, unlike her more open-hearted sister who reads to engage, somehow, the man behind the pen, evokes a split between reader and writer to some degree compatible with that between reader and critic described by Steiner. And Walker Percy takes up allied issues, both in his books of essays[34] and in his

---

32. The famous phrase is Nietzschean, but here, two decades earlier, is articulated by Raskolnikov in his article championing "those who possess the gift or talent to say a *new word*. . . ." Fyodor Dostoevski, *Crime and Punishment,* trans. David Magarshak (London: Penguin, 1951; 1966), 277. That in his own mind this theory justifies murder is a central element in the novel's ambiguous problematic.

33. This essay, first published in *New Literary History* (1979), is conveniently available in *George Steiner: A Reader* (New York: Oxford University Press, 1984), 67-98.

34. *The Message in the Bottle: How Queer Man Is, How Queer Language Is, and What One Has to Do with the Other* (New York: Farrar, Strauss and Giroux, 1975) and *Lost in the Cosmos: The Last Self-Help Book* (New York: Farrar, Strauss & Giroux, 1983).

Kierkegaardian novel, *Second Coming*. There, the inscribed reader, an escaped psychiatric patient whose willed deliverance from unsustainable pretension lets her see "thou and I" more realistically, is, however embarrassingly, akin to Dostoevski's Sonya in being crucially proactive, precipitating the kind of dialectic which the narrative of repentance seeks. In all of these cases that dialectic requires a mimetic, realistic reading.

What is it that the greatest Teller of parables prayed? "I thank you Father, Lord of heaven and earth, because You have hidden these things from the wise and the intelligent, and have revealed them to infants . . ." (Matt. 11:25; cf. Luke 18:15-17). Is this not the very sticking point — the stumbling block of critical embarrassment with a certain type of literature, biblical and otherwise, parable or historical narrative — that it makes *lack* of critical distance the indispensable condition of "getting it right"? Jesus is not speaking here anymore than he is two chapters later (13:10-17) of privileging for understanding those with special knowledge, or those who govern institutional interpretation. He is saying precisely the opposite.

François Mauriac's *Le noeud de vipères*[35] is among the most effective twentieth-century works employing psychological realism in a narrative of repentance. It purports to be the diary of a self-consumed, hateful and hate-driven invalid, a miser, recording the strategies whereby he will effect revenge on his alienated wife and vulture-like family, who wait in an anteroom for him to die so they can swoop in on his money. In the process, he is also recollecting his life: his diary is his autobiography, a kind of *Confessions* of a materialist. In the act of recollection, however, something happens. Out of a morass of hate and fear, remembrances of brief encounters with love, however fleeting, have gradually emerged to consciousness — a beloved daughter who died young, an unself-centered nephew, a decent priest. . . . As these recollections begin to weave their way into his narrative, we see that the original purpose of the narrative, and certainly his judgment on those around him, have begun to change. At the end, though the narrative is broken off in mid-sentence by his final heart attack, we realize that his process of repentance has brought him to New Life.

Appended to the diary and last testament of Louis are two letters.

35. François Mauriac, *Le noeud de vipères* (Paris: Bernard Grasset, 1933); trans. Warre B. Wells, *Viper's Tangle* (New York: Image Books, 1957).

The first is from his grossly materialistic, hard-hearted son, who has immediately ransacked his father's papers. "Which of us," he writes to his sister, "is not maliciously treated in these pages?" The diary, he tells his sister, should be immediately destroyed by her after reading it, lest it fall into the wrong hands and prove an embarrassment to the family. Having long anticipated disinheritance or at least diminishment of his "due," and taken shameful steps to try to prevent it, he focuses on a small portion of the early part of his father's text and writes, "I thank God that he has granted that these lines of our father's should justify me" (192). The echo of Luke 18 is unmistakable.

The second letter is from the first reader's daughter, Louis's grand-daughter. After abandonment by her husband, mental breakdown, and subsequent release from the psychiatric hospital, she has come to live with the old invalid. During this time a healing relationship is formed with a man who now seems to her to be an entirely new person. Her "reading" of him is accordingly shockingly contrary to that of the rest of the family: "Grandfather," she writes, "is the only religious man I have ever met." "We were wrong," she continues, "our principles remained separate from our lives. Our thought, our desires, our actions struck no roots in that faith to which we adhered with our lips . . . we were [the ones] devoted to material things . . ." (198-99). She begs to be allowed to read the diary, which her parents who have authority over the estate have denied her, because even though she has yet to see it she believes that it will bear "decisive witness" to her grandfather's transformation.

Here Mauriac has provided us a choice between two diametrically opposed "readings" of the same repentance narrative: we may side with either the hard-hearted or the broken-hearted reader. But as to which disposition is likely to be of most help in helping us to understand the apparent shift of motive, the spiritual transformation in the protagonist, we can be of little doubt. The first reader, we are unsurprised, reads each evidence of changing intention — of transformation — simply as a sign of "confusion" in his father's text.

Is there a kind of text which discriminates between readers, not because it is "closed up" by one sort of institutional encoding, or made to seem confused and unrealistic by another, but rather because against its transparent motives the intentions of the reader with hardened cate-gories are implacable? It would seem so. And yet the recurrent value of such ethically powerful texts is that they are the ones which seem able to generate *new story*, to make old new, and so move to bind up the broken-hearted and heal the crushed in spirit.

How might a hermeneutic be developed to deal more adequately with such texts? Well, perhaps, by taking better account of critical misprision, of the interpreter's strategies for avoiding embarrassment, and of the consequences of such evasion. In short, by engaging seriously in a critical "dialectic of sin" as well as the "dialectic of speculation." From this might even follow a fresh insight into contemporary debate over how to incorporate the category of the "ethical" more coherently in literary theory.

What really is required for a sensitive reading of repentance narrative? Clearly, I want to say, a way of reading which does not construe itself as a means to power, but rather as a recognition of "legitimate dominion" in that other sense of *mashal* — recognition of the authority of the primary text. This way of reading would express a theory which does not so imperiously privilege method, mastery, or membership as acknowledge and respect the intimacy of the encounter between the reader and such a text. Let me put this point interrogatively: should not our periodic examination of critical conscience affirm that we are maintaining an active category for texts for which understanding comes about not because we interpret the text, but because, when read accountably, the text interprets us?

Epilogue

Ubi sapiens? ubi scriba? ubi conquisitor hujus saeculi? Nonne stultam fecit Deus sapientiam hujus mundi?

1 CORINTHIANS 1:20

IT SEEMS BEYOND CAVIL THE CASE, AS EMMANUEL LEVINAS SO MOD-estly imagined, that "the action of literature" has produced a wisdom to which the Jewish "People of the Book" have been both originary and abiding contributors.[1] Among their beneficiaries, particularly among the Gentiles whose religious tradition also begins with Moses, the Book itself has come to have an amplified as well as derivative register of cultural authority. For Christian literary history it is almost certainly true, as T. S. Eliot has it, that "the Bible has had a literary influence . . . not because it has been considered literature, but because it has been considered the report of the Word of God."[2] The force of the text as revelation is what has made it powerful, because as *revelation* it unequivocally calls forth response. At the same time, and at least as im-

---

1. Emmanuel Levinas, *Difficile liberté: Essais sur le judaisme* (Paris: Editions Albin Michel, 1963), 165; cf. Susan Handelman, *Slayers of Moses* (Albany: SUNY Press, 1982), 17.
2. T. S. Eliot, "Religion and Literature" (1935), in *Selected Prose,* ed. John Hayward (Harmondsworth: Penguin, 1953), 33.

portantly, it is as revelation that the Bible has become for generations of Christian readers and writers what Moses said of the Torah, a "witness against us" (Deut. 31:19, 26), persistent in its insistence upon the reader's self-examination. For Christians the Bible thus preeminently becomes, in St. Paul's phrase, "the sword of the Spirit, which is the word of God" (Eph. 6:17). The force of this saying is not merely to characterize the Bible as a weapon to be used in defense against the "wiles of the Devil" without, but in the manner suggested by the writer of the Epistle to the Hebrews, to recognize that "the word of God is quick and powerful, and sharper than any two-edged sword . . . a discerner of the thoughts and intents of the heart" (4:12) — that is, our own hearts. If spiritual realism has been a preoccupation of Christian writing from the beginning, this surely is part of the reason: the "witness against" forces us, however much against our will, to look the often uncomfortable truth of our own reality in the face. Or it should, if we are reading honestly.

As our literary history shows, there have been innumerable and often remarkably creative strategies essayed for the purpose of blunting the edge of the text as "witness against," a sharp prompter to scrutiny of conscience both for individuals and for communities. The most common strategies are well enough figured in the ironic "poeticizing" of the Bible by the first modern professor of English literature, Matthew Arnold. Arnold's characteristic evasiveness of the ethical authority of the Bible is repeated in the linguistic nihilism, skeptical relativism and antirealism of literary critics and theorists whose echoing enterprise is designed to evade the moral authority of any other text — but especially that of texts written in the shadow of the Bible.

Meanwhile, there is little evidence to suggest that writers themselves — poets, dramatists, novelists — are willing to see their own texts as devoid of such authority. Indeed, the commitment to examination of conscience and the "witness against" still thrives in novels, plays, and poems — and unsurprisingly, if often less convincingly, among the texts of literary theorists whose own claim to authority sometimes rests upon their claim to have abolished authority. Nor, despite all the preoccupations of theory, are first-order texts of our own time noticeably less committed to the enactment of spiritual realism: in the words of George Steiner,

> No serious writer, composer, painter has ever doubted, even in moments of strategic aestheticism, that his work bears on good

and evil, on the enhancement or diminution of the sum of humanity in man and the City.[3]

It remains a characteristic of great literature written, perforce, in
the shadow of the Book of books, that it depends for its own authority
on the spiritual capital of a biblical tradition to which it may now no
longer owe any conscious fealty. The "trope of transcendence," as Steiner
calls it, remains in some form discernible long after the *credo* ceases to
be overtly invoked. Indeed, this "trope" (does it make us feel safer to
call it that?) has proven so necessary to the articulation of the Other for
which great art inevitably strives that its spectral dynamism has led more
than one writer, even in a self-styled nihilistic epoch, to return to an
obligated witness to the "real presence" encountered in the text. The
Word has not, after all, been silenced.

Is the Christian tradition in literature then properly defined as logocentric? In terms of its rich history, even as in these pages so scantly traced,
the answer must be qualified, a *sic et non*. Logos as *ratio* or reason alone
surely misses the mark, the actual center of Christian literary practice. True,
Christians repeatedly reflect upon the magisterial richness of that *incipit* to
which, for us, every waking word is indebted: "In the beginning was the
Word." But this seminal Word is neither the sum nor the compass of our
words; the divine Word, though progenitive, scatters on varied and uneven
ground. Moreover, it is *like* seed: though from the beginning it portends
our life, it is not in the end as Word alone that it tells our story. In the end
each Christian must also reckon with the Deed, the Deed, as Christopher
Smart has it in his *Song to David*, "Determined, Dared and Done."

Our hearing — the hearing of each Christian who wishes to be
faithful to the faith which comes by hearing — is bound therefore to
an accountable response to the Word of God, to deeds in some measure,
however distant, halting, and unequal, which are mimetic of that Deed
of the Incarnate Word. Christians understand themselves as a people
called to live not in a web of words but to live *imitatio Christi*. This, we
are to learn from centuries of Christian saints and poets, is the only
pronunciation of that Word which can be regarded as authentic.

3. George Steiner, *Real Presences* (Chicago: University of Chicago Press, 1989), 145.
Cf. Robert W. Jenson, "How the World Lost Its Story," *First Things* 36 (October 1993):
19-24.

It is the tendency of metaphors to outlive at last their usefulness and so become consigned to the fate of the merely instrumental. The borrowed metaphor "People of the Book" may be one of these. Yet for anyone who wishes to understand the perseverance and rich legacy of Christian literary history, it captures something essential which has become obscured in the term "logocentric." Put in simple language it is this: to the Christian poet, words matter, and books matter, because people matter still more. The whole force and tenor of biblical experience is a reminder of this: it is not just that the *davar* of God calls forth the *davarim* of his chosen, those wrought in his image. Rather, it is that from the beginning the word and the world together shape, as shaped syllables in the mouth, a poem to the beloved, an invitation to unbroken communion with the Other. It is this final centrality of the Person which, in a world of imperfect speech and imperfect deeds, makes *metanoia* rather than *gnosis* the redemptive goal of poetry as a human instrument. Neither knowledge nor the words by which it is meted out are themselves salvific; only by participatory acquiescence in the Deed performed on Golgotha does the liberty of full communion come.

Though they have made use of many species of writing, and many theories of literature along the way, a common thread among all the examples here gathered is a central concern for something like what Aristotle called *synesis,* a habitual disposition toward understanding of the Other. In Augustinian terms this is *caritas,* reading charitably, and it involves a recognition that such a disposition must exact from each of us a certain effacement of the self. The "handmaiden of the Lord" in Christian tradition thus finds her fellow readers among oddly dissonant bearers of intentions with respect to the written word. Whether calculated allegorically, as in Augustine's belabored but intentionally charitable hermeneutic, or pseudo-objectively, as in the textual piety of the New Critics, or dialectically in a still more belabored consciousness of the infinite regress in fallen human perception and expression both, as among many of the shades of poststructuralist theory, the commitment to love with words one's neighbor as oneself can remain lively only so long as the greater Love which precedes it has not been lost.

We are therefore obliged to remind ourselves, for the truth's sake, that Christians themselves have too often grotesquely perverted this high order of value — and abused both texts and persons as a consequence — when they have lost sight of that Other most holy. It thus continues to be necessary for Christians respectfully to remind each other of the Word from the beginning, to whose holiness every truthful practice must be merely ancillary, *ancilla*, handmaiden. No less than anyone else — as writers from Dante to Dostoevski and Chaucer to Walker Percy declare — our egos are susceptible to the *terrorisme obscurantiste* of rationalized self-fashioning. The corpus of our literature is severely imperfect; our ranks, too, are littered with the corpses of the fallen. Our literary history affords ample evidence of the miscreance and materialism by which instrumentality is subverted either with malice aforethought, as when the critical intelligence of the gifted reader is elevated to the status of the to-be-worshiped, or when the instrument itself is degraded by an evident confusion and failure to distinguish in our own words and deeds between the will to truth and the will to power. The Christian writer or critic has accordingly to recognize such misprision as the effect of sin, and to understand the personal obligation of repentance.

There are glorious evidences of compensatory understanding. When preceded by attentiveness to the Word, self-scrutiny sharpens attentiveness to the world. Who can gainsay the sanctified acuity of Donne, Herbert, Hopkins, or Eliot? Or, in their own way, of Wendell Berry, Flannery O'Connor, and François Mauriac? When faithful to its own tradition, Christian perspective is able to see into human abuses and corruptions of nature to which otherwise it would be blind. From intimate and learned experience the Christian critic is able to observe, for example, that attempts to suppress the Other and attempts to suppress the Word have usually been correspondent. A Faust or a Nietzsche is the expression of a universal impulse to efface both the word and the person of the Other, or to supplant them with the "I am not that I am" and the "new word" of the self-actualized and self-appointed. The vigorous and contestative articulation of this impulse among literary theorists and cultural historians in the academy has, alas, its sordid echo among banana republic tyrants, tribal chieftains, and balkanizing warlords. Yet this fact ought not to call forth mere critique.

In all of these spheres the tactics of suppression can readily betray in the most subtle apologetic or theory a kind of terminal despair. And because repressive theory is thus in despair of itself, the suppressed returns, again and again. Despite myriad attempts to negate God, where human intelligence does not cease to function, "questions linger," as

Mark C. Taylor puts it, "calling us to linger with the question."[4] In a tortured and self-reflexive essay, Taylor depicts the deepest impasse, perhaps, of contemporary critical thinking. In an era so confident of Nietzsche's dictum that "God is dead," a time in its own view not only "post-God" but wishfully striving to go beyond the traces of God even in its language, there remains a trace too deep to be expunged:

> To God we are unaccustomed. Of God we are unaccustomed to speak, even to think, especially to write. If we slip and find ourselves thinking, speaking, even writing of God, it seems embarrassing, horribly embarrassing — even when our inquiry is critical. All of this was supposed to have been over a long time ago. If we venture a word otherwise, the page seems to become a confessional without walls where our most intimate thoughts and unthoughts stand revealed for all to see and hear. Faced with the prospect of such exposure, we grow modest and withdraw. Devising strategies of avoidance in an effort not to think and not to say what nonetheless we cannot not think and cannot not say, we turn to history, politics, economics, literature, art. If it is no longer professionally and socially acceptable to speak of God, perhaps we can continue to think about what really matters by examining other forms of cultural expression. Thus critics repeat — often without realizing or wanting to realize what they are doing — the nineteenth-century gesture of translating theology into philosophy and art. But why? Why do we still search, still probe, still question? What calls us to respond? What disrupts the present? What dislocates our present? Unless our work is *academic* in the worst sense of the word something else haunts the search that is our research. What is this "something else" and why will it give us no rest?[5]

St. Augustine began his *Confessions* with an admission of human intellectual limit, in effect an answer for Taylor's question, and I intend it as no unkindness to recall it here.

> Man is one of your creatures, Lord, and his instinct is to praise you. He bears about him the mark of death, the sign of his own

---

4. Mark C. Taylor, "De-negating God," *Critical Inquiry* 20, no. 4 (1994): 592-610, 594.
5. Ibid., 594.

sin, to remind him that you thwart the proud. But still, since he is a part of your creation, he wishes to praise you. The thought of you stirs him so deeply that he cannot be content unless he praises you, because you made us for yourself and our hearts find no peace until they rest in you.[6]

The condition Augustine calls "rest" or "peace," the "peace that passes all understanding" (Phil. 4:7), painfully eludes any theory of literature or culture which preoccupies itself with strategies of past or present for aggrandizement of the self, for "empowerment" and hence for suppression of the Other. The swordplay of words has wounded us everywhere, everywhere divides us asunder, even from those most properly intimate. In Christian literary tradition, wherever it is found faithful to the revelation to which it is witness, the word of healing is infinitely to be preferred to its more clamorous alternative. Despite all the painful dissonance of disobedience and unfaithfulness which, within and without, recurs to taint the record, Christian literary tradition bears gratefully this confession to those "without": the pen is mightier than the sword, not because, as many have thought while mouthing the maxim, in the end it cuts more deeply (which it can), but because in the long run it has been used best by men and women of faithfulness and loving probity as an instrument of healing (which it still can be). For any theory — or practice — which would remain faithful to this witness, a preference for healing over wounding is the reliable sign of authentic delegation.

The purpose of the Word itself has always been transparent: to minister peace by revealing as much of the necesary truth as we are able to bear. But this Word itself has everywhere acknowledged that the office of binding up the broken-hearted and proclaiming liberty to captives (Isa. 61:1; Luke 4:18) is not finally a matter of words, but is an embodying deed in the Person who by so faithful a reading "becomes" the Word. If there is to be a "balm in Gilead" for those who open the Book and with an expectant heart look for truth, it is therefore likely to reveal itself at last bodily, in precisely that sort of practical mimesis which can only begin to occur after one has closed the book and set it down.

6. St. Augustine, *Confessions* 1.1, trans. R. S. Pine-Coffin (Harmondsworth: Penguin, 1961; 1973), 21.

Index of Names and Subjects

Index of Scripture References